Shapes of Ireland

Maps and Their Makers 1564-1839

J. H. Andrews

Published in Ireland by
Geography Publications,
Templeogue, Dublin 6W

© J.H. Andrews 1997

ISBN 0-906602-95-5

Cover design by Christy Nolan
Typesetting by Phototype-Set Ltd.
Printed by Betaprint, Dublin

Contents

Preface

When map enthusiasts feel the urge to read, their first choice of reading matter will presumably be a map. Even their second choice is less likely to be a work of literature than a list of authors, dates and other standard particulars for a large number of maps – in short, a catalogue. But for every subject of human endeavour, however unbookish in itself, there is a minority of students who wish to read discursively and at length, more or less as they might go through a novel or newspaper article. The present work, on maps of Ireland before *c.*1840, is addressed to this less rigorously minded public.

Five main considerations have been in the author's mind. One is to urge that collectors and librarians should look harder and with more discrimination at the maps in their care and in particular recognise that much of their stock, though interesting in itself, owes at least some of its importance to a small number of more or less original 'key' maps. (The 'methodology' of the key-map concept is discussed in the second part of Chapter 11.) Next it is hoped to show how in Ireland the practice of mapmaking arose from particular circumstances of government, politics and society as described in standard works of historical literature. A third and more general aim is to illustrate the opportunities and pitfalls presented by small-scale national maps in the study of landscapes and spatial distributions that no longer exist. Fourthly, and on the same level of generality, students and practitioners of modern cartography are invited to consider what can be learned from the way maps were made in the past. Finally, and independently of any other motive, non-Irish equally with Irish readers are offered a modest contribution to map history, a scholarly discipline that still needs all the contributions it can get.

While seeking a measure of consistency in both style and structure, this book is based not on any one dissertation or research-project, but on independent ventures into several areas of Irish map-history conducted over a long period. This means that some parts of it are summaries of work already brought to completion (as far as such work is ever complete) and published in a number of scattered outlets, mainly specialist journals. Other parts embody research which in different circumstances might have been carried to the same kind of conclusion but which the author is aware of having left unfinished. Others again can do no more than report the state of general map-historical knowledge at the time of writing. In all three cases, however, particular attention has been paid – more than in many previous studies – to what is actually visible on the face of the map.

The notes following each chapter give primary sources for quotations, dates and other important facts about the maps and cartographers under review, more general information being attributed wherever possible to secondary works. To avoid excessive documentation the course of Irish political, social and economic history has been left unfootnoted, a policy made acceptable, it is hoped, by the comparatively recent completion of the Oxford *New history of Ireland* for the period covered by this book. The secondary literature of maphistory has been cited more extensively, in keeping with the last of the five objectives mentioned above. Sources are fully described at their first citation within each chapter and subsequently identified by short titles. Except when a map is being directly quoted, placenames are given in their Ordnance Survey spelling wherever this exists.

My acknowledgments are numerous. Thanks are due to the following friends, former colleagues, librarians and archivists who have answered queries or otherwise rendered assistance: Peter Barber, Jonathan Bell, Peter Clarke, Richard Clarke, Gerry Daly, Gordon Herries Davies, Mary Davies, Gordon Dickinson, David Drew, the late C.C. Ellison, Kenneth Ferguson, Suzanne Fisher, Richard Hawkins, Francis Herbert, Donald Hodson, Leonard Hynes, Paul Kerrigan, Rolf Loeber, Father Benedictus Millet, Breandán Ó Cíobháin, Patrick O'Flanagan, Richard Oliver, Mary Pedley, Mary Pollard, David Quinn, the late William Ravenhill, the Earl of Shelburne and the Trustees of the Bowood Manuscripts, Anngret Simms, Brian T. Thynne, Patrick Wayman and Anthony Wilson. For permission to reproduce material in their custody thanks are due to the governing bodies of the British Library; the National Library of Ireland; the Ordnance Survey of Ireland; the Public Record Office, London; Trinity College, Dublin; and the West Sussex Record Office.

Other debts are wider and deeper. At Trinity College, Dublin, Professor Russell King and Professor Desmond Gillmor have successively welcomed me back to the department of geography on many occasions during the past six years. Former colleagues to whom I am especially grateful are Eileen Russell for secretarial help, Terence Dunne for supplying photographs, and Richard Haworth for collecting illustrations and, as always, displaying every kind of bibliographical knowledge whenever called upon. All my line drawings were expertly prepared by Sheila McMorrow of the same department. I am particularly indebted to the college map librarian, Paul Ferguson, for help in choosing, collecting and processing illustrations, and indeed for virtually acting as unofficial picture-editor for the whole book. Brendan Dempsey, Photographic Centre, Trinity College Dublin, produced photographs of many of the map extracts with particular care and attention to detail. Among other benefactors, special thanks must go to Brian Adams for valuable advice on map projections and what was once called 'the use of the globes'. In a more recently developed area of mathematical competence, I regret not being able say more about the positional accuracy of the maps under study, but until cartometric analysis comes within the scope of low-priced personal computers few private individuals can hope to make much progress in this field. I am therefore all the more grateful to Waldo Tobler for kindly giving access to his programme on bi-dimensional regression. I also owe a considerable debt to Matthew Stout who ended my two-year search for expert computational help by adapting a similar technique to Professor Tobler's, describing it in an appendix to this book, and supervising its application to data from a number of maps. In the cartobibliographical field my greatest debt is to Andrew Bonar Law for sharing his extensive knowledge of states, editions and kindred matters and for allowing me to read his book, *The printed maps of Ireland, 1612-1850*, in advance of its publication. He has also generously allowed me to reproduce a number of maps from his collection. In the general area of cartographic history my deepest obligation is to a long-time fellow-student of Irish maps, Arnold Horner, for answering queries and offering suggestions, and especially for the tireless vigilance with which he has read every page of my proofs.

Finally this book could not have been started without the encouragement of Kevin Whelan, and could not have been finished without the patience, sympathy and support of its publisher, William Nolan.

March 1996   J.H.A.

List of Illustrations

Chapter 1

Ireland off the map

Islands have always held a fascination for the mapmaker. In the pre-
scientific era of cartography he would exaggerate their size and colour
them more brightly than anything else. He would also make a special
point of discovering their names or if necessary of christening them
himself. If there were no islands in his study-area an irresponsible
cartographer might even invent some, or at least half-invent them by
snipping peninsulas off the mainland. The roots of this strange psycho-
cartographic predilection may lie in some kind of biological analogy:
complete within its enclosure, the island can be likened to a self-
sufficient organism capable of developing its own personality, whereas
a peninsula can never be more than a dependent limb. But the
character of an island must also be influenced by its position and its
size. Ireland for example suffers some loss of 'perceived' insularity by
being easily visible from Britain. This is especially true of the north-east
where, before the reign of James I, Scottish reinforcements could be
summoned to help their fellow-countrymen by fires lit on coastal hill-
tops. The nineteenth-century cartographic equivalent of the Scotsmen's
signals is the observation by the Ordnance Survey of beacons in
Ireland from Britain, or vice versa, through the telescope of a
theodolite. One technical consequence of this cross-channel
intervisibility is a kind of geodetic imperialism whereby the most
difficult stages in mapping one country could be performed in the
other and 'exported' across the sea.[1] A more obvious consequence for
the general reader is that most rectangular maps of Britain show a small
part of Ireland and vice versa.

The smaller the island, the stronger its aura of insularity. Even after
an accurate survey the smallness of Ireland remains hard to express in
quantitative terms, mainly because internal and external water surfaces
are so difficult to distinguish. The Ordnance Survey, it has sometimes
seemed, will give a different acreage each time it is asked, but for
present purposes we shall probably not go far wrong with 20,810,400
statute acres or 32,516 square miles.[2] This makes Ireland the second
largest island in Europe, a status already known to the sixteenth-

century cartographer Abraham Ortelius, and large enough (as Ortelius also acknowledged) to deserve a page to itself in a world atlas. However, its size is psychologically diminished by the nearby presence of an island long thought to be twice as large as itself and actually about 2.75 times as large. The difference in area between Ireland and Britain, together with Britain's closer proximity to the continent, explains if it does not justify the expression 'British Isles', which Ortelius tells us had been unanimously applied by ancient writers to the two countries taken together.[3] Unfortunately the term 'British' also carries political implications. Ireland was invaded and feudalised by Anglo-Norman magnates in the middle ages, conquered by English armies in the sixteenth and seventeenth centuries, and then governed by British civil servants until the twentieth century. Most of its mapmakers have also been British, and its cartographic personality is an amalgam of objective facts and anglocentric judgements.

*   *   *   *   *   *   *   *   *

Area expressed in standard units is a more or less objective property, but for the cartographer it is less important than the length and breadth of the smallest regular quadrilateral that just encloses the subject of his map. There are mathematical advantages in choosing as long axis of a map any line, whatever its direction, that makes this quadrilateral as narrow as possible. But in Ireland hardly anything is lost by using the most widely known of all geographical reference systems, latitude and longitude, to determine the long and short axes respectively. Since parallels of latitude run from west to east and meridians of longitude from north to south, this means that the long edges of a 'portrait'-shaped sheet should run parallel to a meridian. Latitude is measured in degrees, minutes and seconds from nought degrees at the equator to ninety at the poles, a second of latitude being represented on the ground by a horizontal distance of about one hundred feet. Longitude is reckoned in the same units from nought to 180 degrees either eastwards or westwards (whichever is nearer) from an arbitrarily chosen prime meridian. Until the seventeenth century the prime meridian of most European maps was in the Atlantic, usually passing through Tenerife or the Azores. Subsequently most British maps took their longitudes from London, defined (if it was defined at all) first as some point within the city boundaries, often St Paul's Cathedral, and later as Greenwich Observatory.[4] Even the most fervent Irish nationalists have never proposed the longitude of Dublin as a prime meridian.

It is appropriate in considering maps of Ireland to define the cartographer's subject as a part of the earth's surface enclosed by two parallels and two meridians (Fig. 1.1).[5] No portrayal of such a surface on a flat sheet can hope to be totally accurate, and the extent of its inaccuracy depends on the scale of the map and the size of the area represented. The character and magnitude of the resulting errors are hard to quantify because they depend on how the cartographer decides to distribute them, or in technical language on his choice of projection.[6] In the interests of arithmetical simplicity Ireland may be assumed to lie between latitudes 51° 25′ and 55° 25′ north and between longitudes 5° 25′ and 10° 35′ west. We may also follow the Ordnance Survey and many other cartographers in adopting the meridian of eight degrees west of Greenwich as a central axis. Now suppose Ireland's southernmost parallel of latitude to be drawn as a straight horizontal line, straight because its alignment by definition is constant from west to east. Since latitude and longitude intersect at right angles on the globe, the map's extreme meridians may reasonably appear as vertical lines, also drawn straight because they represent the shortest earth-surface distances between the points they connect. The same scale is now chosen for meridians as for parallels and the quadrilateral can be completed by a horizontal upper boundary. At which point the problem arises that although the northern edge of the map has been made the same length as the southern edge, the distance it represents on the globe is shorter. This leaves east-west distance errors, each equivalent to about ten miles, at the north-west and north-east corners of the map. On the scale of ten miles to an inch appropriate for a single-sheet map of Ireland the error on the paper is one inch. These errors could be approximately halved by building the map not upwards from its lower margin, as in the foregoing scenario, but partly upwards and partly downwards from the parallel of 53° 25′ passing through its centre. Both these projections are of the type known as 'cylindrical'.

One remedy for the problems inherent in a cylindrical projection is to give each of the two enclosing parallels its correct length. All lines of latitude now remain straight, but the top margin of the map becomes shorter than the bottom; the side-margins, also remaining straight, now converge towards the north. One disadvantage of the resulting 'trapezoidal' projection is that meridians and parallels no longer intersect at right angles as they do on the globe. The next step is to restore this element of rectangularity by drawing the parallels as curves and thus creating the kind of projection described as 'conical'. Since the seventeenth century most separate maps of Ireland have had converging meridians and curved parallels. In the simplest projection of this form, the 'conic with one standard parallel', errors are still greatest at the corners of the map, but they are now very much reduced. If on

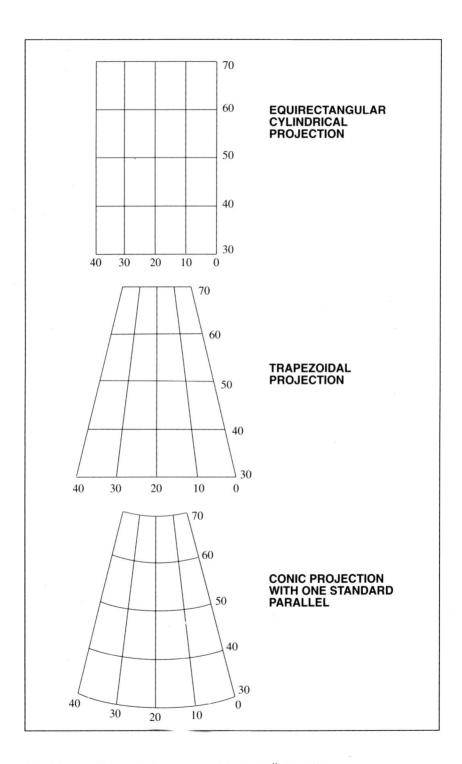

Fig. 1.1   Map projections appropriate to small countries.

our postulated single-sheet map of Ireland the parallel of 53° 25′ is again made true to scale, the errors at the corners in a conical projection are only 0.006 inches, equivalent to about one fifteenth of a mile on the ground. Before the advent of the Ordnance Survey such errors were smaller than those arising from a variety of other causes such as inaccurate surveying, faulty copying or engraving, and the expansion or contraction of the material embodying the map-image. Which means that throughout the period covered by this book there was little point in choosing any more elaborate projection for Ireland than a simple conic.[7]

Early mapmakers did not necessarily think in the foregoing terms. Like mankind in general, most of them doubtless preferred not to think about projections at all if they could avoid it. At any rate they hardly ever divulged what projections they used on their own maps. Admittedly the surveyor of a large territory would be forced to consider the subject when his lines, however carefully measured, proved impossible to plot self-consistently on a flat surface, but in a country as small as Ireland quite accurate surveys can be made at quite large scales without this problem becoming perceptible. What made projections seem interesting even where they had no practical importance was simply the force of professional example, and in particular the habit of furnishing printed maps of large countries not only with marginal scales of degrees and minutes but with selected lines of longitude and latitude forming a network or 'graticule' across the whole sheet.

In post-medieval European cartography, graticules first became important when both sides of the Atlantic had to be put on the same map. Later the idea was applied to successively smaller areas mapped at successively larger scales. Its progress was clearly a function of improved surveying techniques. Graticules articulate a map's claim to accuracy: the larger the scale, the bolder and more disputable the claim. The practical consequence of this rule was that while a sixteenth-century cartographer might show meridians and parallels on a map of Europe or even of the British Isles, on an English county map both he and his more enlightened readers would reject them as too speculative to be worth including.[8] By the eighteenth century, county surveyors were more confident and rightly so. But to some extent the spread of graticule-construction from small scales to large was dictated by fashion, and the lines were often drawn more to give an impression of completeness than because anyone really knew where to put them. This cynical judgement certainly seems applicable to many separate maps of Ireland, where the 'graticule threshold', as we might call it, was crossed towards the end of the seventeenth century.

The problem of projection would be inescapable if a cartographer's raw material was supplied by field observers as a list of latitudes and longitudes. In theory this might happen anywhere: a surveyor could use astronomical techniques to fix so many points that the results when plotted would form a complete map. In practice such methods are impossibly cumbersome as well as inaccurate, and astronomical observations would be made only as an occasional check on other survey procedures, with the number of stations required depending on the size of the area under survey, though even if there were only two latitudes and two longitudes it would still be necessary to choose a projection. In a very small country only one pair of geographical coordinates (with one azimuth or north-south direction) would be needed as a peg fixing the map to the globe and the rest of the survey could proceed by terrestrial measurement. In this context Ireland counts as small or, in the words of a nineteenth-century expert, as 'too limited in extent to allow of its geodetic measurements being advantageously compared with the results of astronomical observations'.[9]

Given one latitude and one longitude, a north point, a choice of projection, and a network of terrestrial measurements, a graticule can be drawn by translating ground distances into degrees. On a spheroid, as distinct from a sphere, the north-south length of a degree increases slightly with latitude. In the far south of Ireland it is 69.13 statute miles, in the far north 69.18 miles.[10] East-west mileages can be reduced to angular measure in the same way, but in this direction the length of a degree is much more variable. At the equator it is virtually the same as a degree of latitude, at the poles it is nothing; in Ireland it ranges from 43.19 miles in the south to 39.39 miles in the north. The conversion of miles to degrees was normal practice in early mapmaking, but to base a whole graticule on such calculations must in retrospect be seen as dangerously misleading. This is because mileages are known to have been more often estimated than measured, with necessarily approximate or inaccurate results, whereas any distance expressed in degrees is likely to suggest that precise observations have been made to fix the positions of the sun and stars.

Latitude may be found by measuring the height of the celestial pole (the point around which the heavens appear to revolve) in degrees above the horizon. Until the early nineteenth century the accuracy of such measurements seemed to be limited only by the precision of the apparatus available, and much was hoped from a large and elaborate instrument known as a zenith sector brought into service at that time. Unfortunately it was then discovered in England that latitude errors of up to two seconds could arise from local gravitational anomalies affecting the alignment of the observer's vertical and horizontal planes. This problem would have ruled out astronomical surveys as a method of mapping small areas even if they had been economically feasible.

Longitude measurements depend on the phenomenon of local time as defined by the positions of the sun and stars in relation to a terrestrial observer. At any moment each meridian has its own time in this sense, and the difference between two such times in chronometric hours, minutes and seconds can readily be converted into angular degrees, minutes and seconds of longitude. In the twentieth century, times could be compared by exchanging radio signals; in the nineteenth century, by transporting chronometers across the required distance. Before that, observers had to time an event remote enough to be seen from two widely separated places, such as an eclipse or (more practicably, and since the sixteenth century more commonly) the angular distance from the moon to a fixed star. The weakness of this 'lunar distance' method is that a small error of celestial distance generates a large error in terrestrial longitude. As a result, cartographers' longitudes were generally less accurate than their latitudes throughout the period covered by this book. This means that Ireland is fortunate in stretching further from north to south than from west to east.

The advantage of astronomy in determining terrestrial distances lies in being unaffected by the magnitude of those distances, whereas geodetic and other non-astronomical measurements become less reliable in proportion to the ground covered. The smaller the survey area, then, the narrower the superiority of astronomical to other techniques. This clarifies the passage quoted above about the effects of Ireland's 'limited extent' and explains why the country has been mapped from landmarks rather than skymarks.

*   *   *   *   *   *   *   *   *

Until well into the twentieth century the only way to observe a country's landmarks was to go and look at them. Something must therefore next be said about Ireland as an environment for travellers. Emphasis will be placed on the early history of intensive mapping in the sixteenth and seventeenth centuries as it was then that the average visitor found Irish conditions most significantly different from those of his own country. The differences were usually for the worse. A surveyor of 1567, for example (admittedly in the month of November), bemoaned the 'short days, dark and foul weather, and the boggy mountains as well full of mire and water, the seasons also more opportune there for the Irish outleaps, stealths and spoils, secretly always suborned and winked at even by those that bear the civillest faces, than for the travel of such company as should have guided and safe-conducted him from place to place.'[11] These and other hazards of the Irish scene will now be considered in turn.

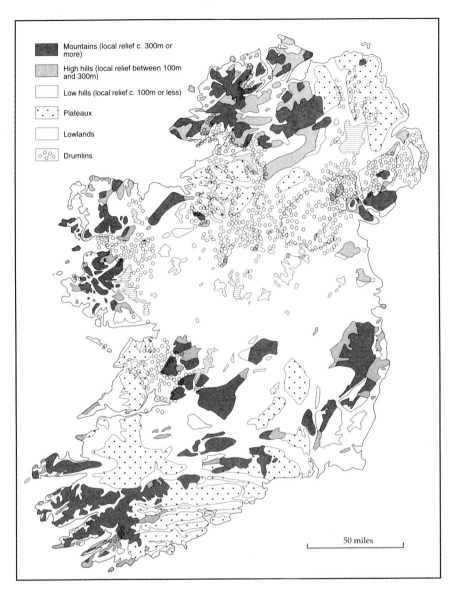

50 miles

Fig. 1.2   Ireland: landforms (from G.L. Herries Davies in Royal Irish Academy,
            Atlas of Ireland (Dublin, 1979), Map 20). Drumlins are shown
            diagrammatically.

Dark and foul weather may be taken to include uncomfortably low
winter temperatures throughout the island, at least in December,
January and February. In a normal year rain could be expected on
every second day even in the well-favoured south-east, and among the
western uplands on two days out of three.[12] And once the traveller is

wet, the dampness of a cool atmosphere can make it difficult to get dry again even after the rain has stopped. Good visibility can never be relied upon, and the wind in exposed situations is often uncomfortably strong: the difficulties of land travel are therefore unlikely to be avoided by taking to the water. Ireland's mountains, in the words of an eighteenth-century observer, stand 'in unconnected groups or masses, of different magnitudes, which are so dispersed through the island, that there are few parts of it in which the prospect is not somewhere terminated by this species of majestic scenery, forming a background seldom more remote than twenty miles.'[13] Collectively the hills have made a strong impression on the national consciousness, despite a certain vagueness about the exact names of individual summits and massifs. No other language, it has been said, can match the Gaelic vocabulary for different kinds of hill-feature[14] and 'mountainy men' have long been a familiar character-type in Irish reminiscence and fiction. The scattered disposition of the mountains has usually allowed the ordinary traveller to wend his way around them; for the geographer it strengthens their claim to attention (Fig. 1.2). Steep gradients and rocks underfoot are fatiguing enough for those unable to escape them, but the worst feature of mountain travel is the weather. In maritime as opposed to continental climates temperature falls sharply with altitude, and in Ireland the increased unpleasantness of cold, rain, cloud and wind becomes noticeable throughout the country at 500 or 600 feet – in exposed situations even lower.

Ireland's hills have been bare of sheltering forest since prehistoric times, much of their surface being 'blanket bog' underlain by sodden peat (Fig. 1.3). Other peat deposits covered much of the central Irish lowland, many of them at about 200 feet above sea level; though slightly convex in shape, these 'raised bogs' appear from above as dark frozen lakes with numerous bays, peninsulas and islands, some of these, like the Island of Allen, actually bearing insular names. Few roads penetrated the bogs until after 1700, and in their natural state they were wet underfoot for much of the year, to be negotiated, according to a modern writer, only by keeping one's weight on 'the foot in the air'.[15] Altogether, blanket and raised bogs covered about one eighth of Ireland until the era of mechanised peat cutting.

Most bogs occupied the sites of former forests, and some were still girdled by aureoles of scrub and woodland when the first of Ireland's regional cartographers visited them in the mid-sixteenth century. The cutting of 'passes' through the woods was a recurrent preoccupation of military tacticians at this period. Well-grown timber appears in nearly all John Derricke's views of Elizabethan Ireland,[16] and one modern estimate makes the woods of c.1600 about as extensive as the bogs,

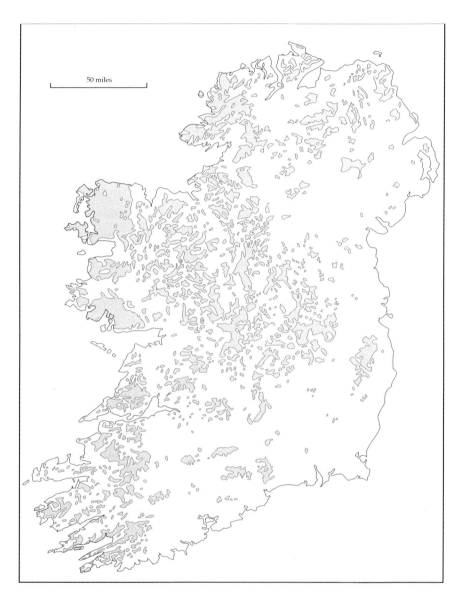

50 miles

Fig. 1.3   Ireland: peat bogs (simplified from R.F. Hammond in Royal Irish
Academy, *Atlas of Ireland* (Dublin, 1979), Map 27).

occupying approximately another eighth of the country's total area.[17]
This may well be an overstatement, and is in any case a small enough
proportion by the standards of northern Europe in general. It is not by
medieval or early post-medieval criteria that the forests of Tudor
Ireland must be judged, but rather in comparison with the denudation
of the eighteenth and nineteenth centuries.

The most impenetrable parts of Ireland are where bog and mountain coexist in four peninsular blocks along the Atlantic coast. Considered from an English standpoint, these outposts – comprising the western parts of Donegal, Connacht, Clare, and Kerry plus Cork – are psychologically as well as physically handicapped. Ireland's conquerors have naturally viewed the island from the capital city that they themselves established half way along the east coast at a point easily accessible from most of the country's larger bog-free lowlands. By the later middle ages much of Dublin's immediate hinterland, though less English than the term 'English Pale' might suggest, was relatively well furnished with roads, bridges, castles and walled towns. Its most frequented routeway led south-westwards through generally peaceful country to the port of Waterford, and it was this distance of about eighty miles from one maritime city to another that gave the late-medieval Dubliner a national sense of scale. Whatever his conscious opinion about the size and shape of Ireland as a whole, he set most store by the area within the Dublin-Waterford radius and would seldom have remembered that some places in the west were more than twice as far away. To find large tracts of inhospitable terrain more remote than Limerick, Galway and Sligo must have come as an unpleasant surprise. This attitude is epitomised by a map of Ireland from the reign of Henry VIII where a small area of English influence in the east and south-east is exaggerated to fill almost the whole island (Fig. 1.4).[18]

Compounding these natural disadvantages was the threat of 'outleaps, stealths and spoils'. These words belong to an account of the Carrickfergus region in the 1560s but they were equally applicable to most areas outside the main zone of anglicisation in Leinster and east Munster. One cause of trouble among Ireland's inhabitants was the language barrier between Saxon and Celt. Another, after Henry VIII's reformation, was the division between 'new English' Protestants and a majority that remained steadfastly Roman Catholic. It is hard to say how an ordinary English traveller would have been received in the remoter districts beyond the Pale because the only travellers on record at this period were government servants. Private tourism was discouraged not just by overt physical danger but by a lack of what contemporaries called 'civility' and particularly by the absence of urban centres throughout most of the north and west. Unlike Shakespeare's Illyria, Gaelic Ireland was no place for feeding one's knowledge of the town.

Apart from periodic rebellions, the last stages in the conquest of Ireland were effectively accomplished in 1603. From now on, travel became easier, population and trade increased, there was a new influx of English and lowland Scottish settlers, especially to Ulster, and a network of towns was gradually brought to completion. The English

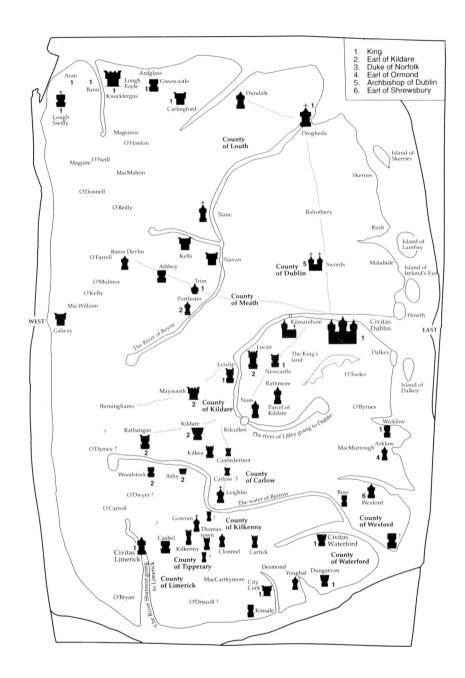

Aran 1 1
Bann Lough Foyle Ardglass
Knockfergus Greencastle
Lough Swilly 1
Carlingford 1
Dundalk 1
Magennis County of Louth Drogheda
O'Hanlon Island of Skerries
Maguire O'Neill MacMahon Skerries
O'Donnell
O'Reilly Slane Balrothery Rush
Island of Lambay
Baron Devlin Kells Navan County of Dublin 5 Swords Malahide Island of Ireland's Eye
O'Farrell Athboy
O'Mulmoy Trim 1
O'Kelly Portlester County of Meath
MacWilliam 2
WEST Galway The River of Boyne Kilmainham Civitas Dublin Howth
Civitas Dublin 1 EAST
Lucan The King's land Dalkey
Leixlip Newcastle 2 1
1 Rathmore O'Tooles Island of Dalkey
Maynooth Naas
Birminghams 2 County of Kildare Parcel of Kildare O'Byrnes
Kildare 2 Kilcullen The river of Liffey going to Dublin Wicklow 1
Rathangan 2 Arklow
O'Dymey ? Kilkea MacMurrough 4
Woodstock 2 Athy 2 Castledermot
O'Dwyer ? Carlow 3 County of Carlow Ross 6
Leighlin The water of Barrow Wexford
O'Carroll Gowran ? County of Kilkenny County of Wexford
? Thomas-town ?
Cashel Kilkenny Clonmel Carrick Civitas Waterford 1 ?
Civitas Limerick 1 County of Tipperary County of Waterford
Desmond Youghal Dungarvan
County of Limerick MacCarthymore City Cork 1 1
O'Bryan O'Driscoll ? Kinsale

Fig. 1.4 Ireland in the reign of Henry VIII, redrawn and edited from British Library, Cotton MS Augustus I, ii, 21. Spelling modernised. Doubtful or illegible inscriptions indicated by question-marks.

language spread rapidly, communications were improved, and agriculture was more widely extended. By the end of the eighteenth century the country ranked in wealth and development with most other parts of western Europe. It had no excuse for being badly mapped and in fact it was quite well mapped.

The foregoing comments apply to every kind of travel, but the itinerant mapmaker was faced with circumstances peculiar to his own profession. Not all of these were unfavourable. In 1824 Ireland was described as the easiest country in the world to survey,[19] another dictum that requires a short technical digression. A comparison has already been made in general terms between astronomical and terrestrial techniques of position-fixing. The most effective terrestrial method of surveying large areas in modern times has been triangulation. This procedure, described by a Dutch writer as early as the sixteenth century, was recommended for Ireland in 1709 by Dr William King[20] and achieved there on a national scale by the Ordnance Survey in 1826-52. Its principles are easily understood. To measure one's way across a region in an accumulation of short and independent local operations has the disadvantage of propagating and magnifying the observer's inevitable errors. The good surveyor minimises this difficulty by proceeding instead from whole to part, fixing a number of widely separated points that can serve as a check on shorter measurements within the intervening spaces.

The 'control' points of an extensive survey should form a network of equilateral or nearly equilateral triangles with intervisible corners and with sides (according to twentieth-century practice) about thirty miles long. The angles of each triangle are measured by a theodolite or similar instrument using sight-vanes or a telescope which can rotate above a graduated circle. Such instruments may be of various sizes with differing degrees of accuracy, but all are considerably less cumbersome than the zenith sector used for determining latitude. One side of one triangle – known as the base line – is measured by repeatedly laying down chains or bars of known length. From the angles and the base, every other distance in the network can be determined by trigonometrical calculation. Unlike astronomical observations, a triangulation is self-checking, because the angles of each triangle must amount to two right angles, and a round of angles at each point to four right angles.[21] If necessary, every side in the network can be verified by measuring a second base and performing a second set of calculations.

Not every triangulation programme meets the highest planimetric standards. The triangles may be small and awkwardly shaped, the instruments primitive and inexact, the bases estimated rather than measured, the other distances found graphically by protracting the angles rather than by mathematical calculation. But the principles – and the name – remain the same. Triangulation may even dispense with numerical readings altogether: instead, intersecting lines of vision can be directly plotted in the field on a plane table using a ruler fitted with sights. Such rudimentary methods were common in the sixteenth and seventeenth centuries. Christopher Saxton is thought to have used them in surveying the counties of England.[22]

A scatter of points is not how most people conceive a map, but large triangles can be subdivided, and these subdivided again, until the network of lines and angles is close enough to be connected with the relevant geographical detail by short and easy measurements on the ground. At this local level, linear and angular observations can be combined in different ratios. In a traverse survey along a road, river or boundary, each of a series of connected lines is measured independently, and so are the angles between each line and the next. In a chain survey, the sides of every triangle are lineally measured – a process now known as trilateration – and the reading of angles becomes unnecessary. Least accurate of all is the sketch survey in which the observer imagines himself directly above the landscape and draws what he thinks he would see below him.

It can now be appreciated that Ireland's alleged suitability for surveying lay in the number of its viewpoints and the distances that they commanded. Poles erected on hill tops provide a good network of theodolite triangles, mist and cloud permitting. One witness in 1824 judged visibility worse in Ireland than in England; another could see well enough in dry weather but agreed that the weather was often wet.[23] It was to illuminate the country's trigonometrical stations that Thomas Drummond invented the limelight for the use of the Ordnance Survey in 1825; as it turned out, the surveyors used his invention only once.[24]

At lower altitudes and for more localised operations, good viewpoints were equally common, thanks partly to the lack of extensive woodlands and luxuriant hedges throughout the period under review. Admittedly there were few places from which twenty churches could be seen in a single panorama (a common experience in Elizabethan Northamptonshire, if we can believe the English surveyor John Norden),[25] for in rural Ireland the addition of high towers to parish churches did not become common until the nineteenth century.[26] Various other landmarks were available, though these were irregularly distributed and not always associated with important places. They included prehistoric ring forts or raths, at least some of which were in commanding locations; the round towers of early Christian monasteries;

Anglo-Norman motes; and the belfrys of late medieval monastic churches. In local surveys even single trees and bushes (superstitiously respected by the inhabitants, according to one nineteenth-century cartographer)[27] could function as triangulation marks.

*   *   *   *   *   *   *   *

A map consists of lines as well as points and in early cartography the most important of those lines were coasts and rivers. At the scales considered in this book the coast of Ireland appears exceptionally indented and fragmented, and it is significant that the same Anglo-Irish word, 'lough', can mean either an arm of the sea or an inland lake.[28] The country's numerous offshore islands have the same fascination for Irishmen that the whole of Ireland has for foreigners, but to the land-based cartographer islands have always been a nuisance. Even the Ordnance Survey gave them less attention than the mainland. The best way to map a highly articulated and interrupted coastline is by combined operations (a strategist's expression adopted by a government committee on the surveying of Ireland in 1824) between map and chart makers,[29] but in practice coordination between these two groups has always been difficult. Ireland also has a long inland coastline, especially in the north and midlands, its freshwater lakes occupying about three per cent of the whole country.

Rivers like lakes have never been much used for commercial navigation in Ireland, but cartographic custom accords them great importance nonetheless. The rivers of a small island might be expected to radiate from a central mountain mass. This was assumed to happen in Ireland by the Welsh-Norman topographer Giraldus Cambrensis[30] and his opinion may have influenced the seventeenth-century belief that Ireland's highest altitudes are in its most central hill mass, the Slieve Bloom.[31] In fact, as so many modern text books point out, the country is shaped (very roughly speaking) like a saucer. Its rivers are discordantly related to relief, cutting through the hill-blocks instead of running round them, descending from one level to another by unnavigable rapids, unexpectedly changing course in right-angled bends, and often following steep-sided valleys hard to observe from any road. To interpolate an unseen stretch of river between two observations was in these circumstances particularly hazardous, but few early cartographers were deterred from trying. A common result, acceptable in a country famous for perversities of nature, was the creation of composite fictitious river systems with two or more widely separated mouths – though such errors may also arise from a copyist's confusion of a river with a territorial boundary. The Boyne and the

Barrow were often linked in this way; so were Lough Foyle and Lough Swilly. Cartographers were not helped by the variability of Irish river names. As a seventeenth-century writer pointed out, 'brooks and rivulets receive their names from the denominations they pass through', and since many of the denominations in question were very small a stream might have a bewildering variety of aliases.[32]

Most of these difficulties are common nearly everywhere in Ireland, but three kinds of region need further attention. Raised bogs posed special problems to the surveyors who first assumed responsibility for mapping their complicated outlines in the seventeenth century. Many bogs separated administrative or political divisions, but since they had none of the summit ridges normally identifiable in upland areas it was usual for exact territorial boundaries to be left undefined in bogland until pressure of population finally made it necessary to map them. By the eighteenth century it was observable that 'bogs of a very large extent have often two outlets for discharging their waters if our maps may be depended on.'[33] The maps were right, but much effort had been needed to make them right. Other areas of difficulty were the limestones of Cos Clare, Galway and Fermanagh, where rivers vanish into swallow holes and lake beds change with the seasons from wet to dry. Even in a scientific age this kind of 'karst' landscape can create confusion, as the ordnance map of Co. Clare showed by putting the wrong colour in a ring contour because its British compilers could not recognise anything as exotic as an enclosed depression so near home. Limestone relief-forms were also hard to depict by traditional methods: the Elizabethan cartographer Robert Lythe used a distinctive pattern of densely-packed profile lines to show that the Burren of Co. Clare was different from other hill areas, but this experiment was not repeated.

In fact Lythe's Burren symbol would have been better suited to the 'drumlins' ('small hills') that occupy a large area of southern Ulster and smaller areas at the head of Clew Bay and in east Co. Clare. Drumlin country was likened by one eighteenth-century writer to a basket of eggs. Its short views and complex drainage systems have made it a difficult subject for mapping at every historical period, not least where the drumlins create swarms of islands and peninsulas as in Clew Bay and to a lesser extent in Strangford Lough. The worst of these archipelagic nightmares were in and around Upper Lough Erne, the last part of Ireland to be mapped correctly.

*   *   *   *   *   *   *   *

Much of Ireland's Gaelic character was still intact when the country first emerged into cartographic daylight under the Tudors. At this time there were about a hundred semi-independent lordships and chieftainries and it was not surprising that one early specification for maps of the kingdom should ask for 'possessions' as well as counties.[34] Some 'countries' had genuine territorial names like Tyrone and Tyrconnel; other names, such as Fermanagh, had denoted peoples rather than places before acquiring a geographical sense. Many were just called so-and-so's country, and these were often shown on maps simply by personal names like Maguire or O'Rourke, indicating the dominant local family. Tribal nomenclature was common enough on early maps of Africa, America and the Holy Land, but in a west-European context it was sometimes a source of confusion, though in manuscript maps the importance of this political dimension could be signalled by writing personal, family and group names in red instead of black. Away from the bogs Irish territorial boundaries were well known and jealously preserved. Early cartographers were not encouraged to name a territory without delimiting it, but for an ordinary political map the boundaries were not thought to need a separate measured survey. They could be threaded by eye between point-symbols indicating places of known territorial affiliation. Whether these places were worth recording in their own right was another question.

Two kinds of central focus could be distinguished in Gaelic Ireland. First there were residences of kings or chiefs and places of periodic secular assembly, identified in several early maps by spelt-out phrases like 'Dungannon: Tyrone his chief house' or 'Kilmacrenan where O'Donnell is made'. Such places were widely scattered and had few permanent buildings. After the Tudor conquest many of them fell into obscurity. Secondly there were early Christian monasteries. Many of these had been deliberately sited in remote areas which had never attracted non-ecclesiastical settlement. Others had become the nearest thing to towns in Gaelic society, though most of them were in decline by the sixteenth century. It was a temptation for the first foreign cartographers to treat these village-like house-clusters as if they were cities in the Roman sense of the word.

The Normans made a considerable effort to bring Ireland's settlement pattern into harmony with other parts of western Europe. By encouraging the Augustinians, Cistercians and other continental monastic orders they helped to increase the country's stock of landmarks in the form of massive new churches. Unfortunately the monasteries were closed down just before map history was due to catch up with them. Some late medieval foundations, like their Celtic predecessors, had attracted local village settlement, for example at Baltinglass, Boyle and Tralee, but after the reformation many soon became functionally insignificant. Otherwise Norman policy was to

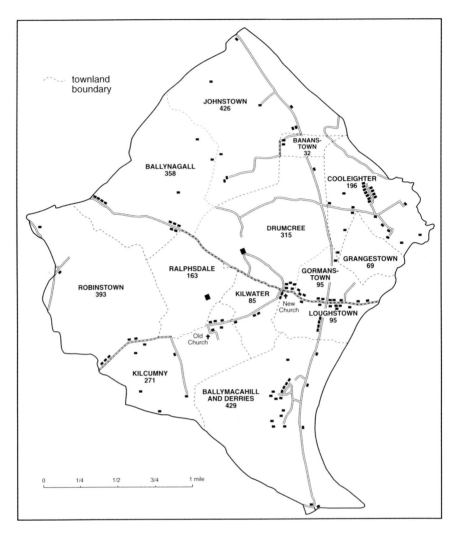

Fig. 1.5 Territoriality and landscape in the central Irish lowland: the parish of
Kilcumny from Ordnance Survey, six-inch map of Co. Westmeath, first
edition, sheets 8 and 13 (1837). Numbers show townland areas in
statute acres.

establish a two-tier pattern of secular settlement comprising chartered
boroughs and manorial villages together with a territorial hierarchy of
counties, baronies and parishes. Baronies were comparable in extent
with the hundreds or wapentakes of Anglo-Saxon geography, and like
the latter they often took their names from places that never attracted
many inhabitants. Administratively and psychologically they were more
important than their cross-channel counterparts, and it was appropriate
that such units should be more common on single-sheet national maps

of Ireland than of England. All these Anglo-Norman or 'old English' innovations were renewed and extended as part of the Tudor and Stuart reconquest in the seventeenth century.

Much medieval and post-medieval Anglo-Irish settlement occupied riverside locations away from the hill-tops so often chosen by the native Irish. This change of focus left the island with an unusually close mesh of roads and trackways, a convenient framework in due course for the organisation of traverse surveys and the making of large- or medium-scale maps. Where English settlement policy failed in Ireland was by not creating enough large nucleated villages with economic, religious and proprietorial functions. Whatever may have been temporarily achieved by the Normans without the benefit of cartography, in the sixteenth century such villages were mainly confined to the immediate neighbourhood of Dublin. One problem for the 'new English' was that their ecclesiastical reforms made little impact on the existing population: a village lost much of its gravitational pull when only a handful of the local people worshipped in the village church. Many Protestant churches were left standing almost alone, and for a topographical surveyor this raised the question of whether Irish parish centres as such were really worth mapping. Catholics, their faith unrecognised and even penalised by government authority, were obliged to celebrate the mass in out-of-the-way places until the nineteenth century. They had no cause to publicise their chapels by putting them on maps, and for a government cartographer to notice them might have been misunderstood as a gesture of legitimisation.

Another obstacle to village life in Ireland was the character of Irish farming, with its simple crop rotations, its small ploughs and plough-teams, and its heavy emphasis on livestock and pasturage. Whether the country's early native farmers lived in single farms or farm-clusters or a mixture of the two is a matter for historical debate, but their settlements were certainly too small for each of them to support a parish church or any of the other institutions of European village life. The dispersal of population produced a network of characteristically Irish territorial units, each smaller than a parish but larger than a normal family farm. These 'denominations' were differently described in different parts of the country – 'ploughland' and 'ballibo' were among the commonest terms – but eventually it became usual to class them all as 'townlands'. Their individual names and boundaries are well known and they still form centres of local awareness and even sentiment. The townland must have originated as some kind of socio-economic entity. Later it became a convenient unit of estate management and local taxation, and in due course a standard form of postal address.

It was the mapping of townland boundaries that first brought the

Ordnance Survey to Ireland in 1824, and the Survey's six-inch-to-the-mile maps, though rich in many other kinds of landscape detail, were often referred to as 'the townland survey'. The number of townlands delimited at this time was approximately 67,000. This meant that, in a large wall map of Ireland's townlands at a scale of four miles to an inch, a square the size of a postage stamp would on average have to accommodate as many as twenty names. Grading all the townlands by relative importance before selecting or rejecting them was simply too difficult to be practicable; at any rate no cartographer seems ever to have managed or perhaps attempted to do it. The result was that two equally good small-scale maps of any part of Ireland might differ almost completely in their choice of names. Here then was a major problem for the country's mapmakers: too few villages, too many townlands (Fig. 1.5).

* * * * * * * *

Placenames occupy a strange position in the philosophy of mapmaking. In theory they can be changed without physical effort by a simple act of will, whereas no one would expect a cartographer to move a town whose location he found inconvenient. Yet toponymy in long-inhabited countries can prove more resistant to change than any material structure, and most cartographers are happy enough to survey names with the same 'non-judgmental' objectivity that they would bring to any other topic. At the same time they can hardly avoid encountering more than one occurrence of the same name, and this often necessitates a choice between incompatible authorities.

Most of the world's placenames have originated within some particular natural language as common nouns, adjectives or other parts of speech that carry an independent meaning. In this sense some ninety per cent of Ireland's names are Gaelic, and although that language has changed considerably since the first Celtic settlement most of them are words with identifiable dictionary meanings, so that a name never previously committed to writing can be correctly spelt by any scribe familiar with the Irish language. Unfortunately, few literate people have been in this position until the twentieth century, and so far as is known none of them was a professional cartographer. Most Irish placenames have been transmitted through the English language before gaining entry to any map.

Finding Ireland's original placenames difficult to speak or write, Englishmen and non-Irish-speaking Irishmen have followed three courses. One possibility was to ignore the existing names and christen or rechristen each locality in English. These importations were usually themselves descriptive in origin, and given Ireland's experience of conquest and colonisation it was natural for most of them to express some form of ownership as in 'Johnstown' or 'Hillsborough'. A second method was to translate Irish into English, as when the 'Ruddery' in Castle Ruddery became the 'Knight's' in Knight's Castle. Synonymous versions like 'Shoemaker's Castle' and 'Cobbler's Castle' (Co. Leix) are presumably evidence of this practice. Finally the foreigner could simply grit his teeth (metaphorically speaking) and 'murder' the Irish forms.[35] Here the difference in linguistic experience between England and Ireland must have played its part, for no visitor from 'London', 'Bristol', 'Coventry' or 'Norwich' would balk at applying an apparently random concatenation of syllables to any Irish town.[36] He would probably first approximate not very closely to the local pronunciation, and then transcribe what he had said either phonetically or according to the English orthographic conventions of the time, in any case deviating radically from the Irish form. The two languages are so different that this operation might well give different results each time it was performed, but in many instances one spelling would gradually and perhaps for no very obvious reason establish itself as 'correct'. The more often a name was written, the sooner it would become standardised. It was a process that continued throughout the eighteenth and early nineteenth centuries, apparently without public comment. Accidental death seems a better term for it than murder.

Outside Ireland linguistic diversity was an accepted fact of life among renaissance cartographers, especially those working near the Teutonic-Romance borderland. Ortelius for instance listed various alternative French, German and Latin names with no hint of disapproval except to note that they were liable to cause confusion among foreigners. Other mapmakers however have willingly or otherwise become involved in placename reform. The most instructive comparison for Irish readers is with Wales, where the mapping of native forms attracted attention from the sixteenth century onwards, and where experts wishing to reverse the process of anglicisation were ranged against those who acquiesced in it. The alignment of opinion on this point was not always predictable. In the 1690s the eminent Celtic scholar Edward Lhuyd, commenting on a draft map of Wales, recommended a policy of laisser faire, 'for if you would have the names of places written in true Welsh they must *all* be corrected ... and be no acceptable piece of service to the English buyer neither'.[37] To write of buyers rather than readers was a salutary lesson in placename economics.

In Ireland a linguistic approach to toponymy was slow to develop, no doubt because Ireland was harder to pacify than Wales and its language therefore more of a threat than a curiosity. The earliest proposed reform was frankly anglocentric, being a recommendation in 1665 that the barbarous and uncouth names then current should be replaced by others 'more suitable to the English tongue'.[38] Pro-Celtic reformism appears only in the late eighteenth century with the cultivation of Irish literature and antiquities by enthusiastic amateurs like Charles O'Conor, Edward Ledwich and Charles Vallancey, and much of this interest was expressed in thematic rather than in mainstream cartography. It was only after the advent of the Ordnance Survey that placename policy was discussed in any detail by Irish cartographers, and for all its commitment to the subject the Survey's directorate did little to repair the damage done by centuries of anglicisation.[39]

*   *   *   *   *   *   *   *

As placenames remind us, where maps are made by foreigners the attitudes of the native population do much to shape the cartographic environment. An interest in mapmaking can overleap the widest of cultural and ethnic chasms, as is evident from native influence on early European representations of North America. In Ireland there was no such meeting of cartographic minds. Its people are famous for a sense of place expressed in ancient topographical writings and in a wealth of local names, not just for territorial units but for innumerable minor physical features. Much of this material deals with non-geographical analogies and associations, among them the pin-pointing of historical events and the comparison of topographical features with various kinds of animate object. But spatial consciousness also appears in many names and beliefs relating to number, size, distance, position and direction.[40] On the national scale, for example, the Hill of Uisneach in Co. Westmeath was long regarded as the centre of Ireland. In a local context the cardinal points have been surprisingly real to many Irish people, including the Kerryman who was heard by an eighteenth-century traveller asking for a ladder to be moved 'a little to the east'.[41]

There is also an interesting category of Irish distance names like 'Eightmile Church' or 'Twomile Borris', many of them earlier than the earliest milestones and signposts.[42] But there are no ancient Irish maps, and only two or three extremely simple quasi-architectural plans; the Irish language seems to have been unusually late in acquiring its own word for 'map'. In a literate people this deficiency needs explaining, but the only theory with any immediate appeal is that Ireland was small enough for Irishmen to keep an adequate knowledge of it in their heads. They might capture an English map and hand it over to the

Spaniards but they had no need to copy it as they copied English defensive architecture and military tactics. Better than capturing maps was to prevent them from being made in the first place. When the people of Donegal beheaded a visiting cartographer in 1602 or 1603 it was not because he was an Englishman or a soldier but simply because 'they would not have their country discovered'.[43]

After the conquest all this was to change. The Irish lost much of their heritage under English rule, but they mastered all the arts that their ancestors had been accused of neglecting. Eventually they were making, publishing and selling as many maps per head of population as any other European nation, setting new high standards in the survey of farms and estates and planning rebellions on the same maps that the government used to suppress them. They had assimilated a cartographic culture and made it their own. But this was a culture with nothing particularly Irish about it. In that sense even an Irishman's map of Ireland represents a view from the outside – in most cases a view from England. Nine of these views are discussed in the following chapters.

References

1.   W.A. Seymour (ed.), *A history of the Ordnance Survey* (Folkestone, 1980), plate 11.
2.   National Archives, Dublin, Ordnance Survey letters, OSL 3673 (1872), 4781 (1886), 1451 (1893).
3.   Abraham Ortelius, *Theatrum orbis terrarum* (London, 1606), p. 10.
4.   The Lizard Point in Cornwall was an alternative to London. One of the earliest cartographic uses of the Greenwich meridian was in Samuel Fearon and John Eyes's *A description of the sea coast of England and Wales* in 1738, but it was not until after the regular publication of the *Nautical almanac* from 1767 that Greenwich finally established itself (Helen M. Wallis and Arthur H. Robinson, *Cartographic innovations: an international handbook of mapping terms to 1900* (Tring, 1987), pp 200-1).
5.   In other contexts this definition would sometimes be unsuitable, especially among maps that do not have north at the top.
6.   The best historical account of map projections is John P. Snyder, *Flattening the earth: two thousand years of map projections* (Chicago, 1993).
7.   According to one recent authority, it is generally impossible to identify from internal evidence the exact projection used in the kind of map considered in this book (Brian Adams, in Roger Hellyer, *The ten-mile maps of the Ordnance Surveys* (London, 1992), appendix 1, pp 179, 182).
8.   According to John Norden, in *Nordens preparative to his Speculum Britanniae* (London, 1596), pp 2, 12, the insertion of latitudes and longitudes in a county map was regarded by one school of thought as 'frivolous'.
9.   William Yolland, *An account of the measurement of the Lough Foyle base in Ireland* (Southampton, 1847), p. 30, n. 'Geodetic' measurements are those accurate enough not just to facilitate mapmaking but to help show how far the earth's shape differs from a perfect sphere.

10. An early, perhaps the earliest, Irish example of a cartographer claiming to recognise this difference, is Emanuel Bowen's *An accurate map of Ireland, on a spheroidical projection*, engraved for the *General Magazine of Arts and Sciences*, 1762, a map first noticed by Andrew Bonar Law.

11. John Chaloner to William Cecil, 12 November 1567, Public Record Office, London, SP 63/22/22.

12. P.K. Rohan, *The climate of Ireland* (2nd ed., Dublin, 1986), pp 46, 56.

13. D.A. Beaufort, *Memoir of a map of Ireland* (Dublin, 1792), p. 10. For anyone literal-minded enough to test this statement it should be pointed out that Beaufort was almost certainly reckoning in Irish miles of 2240 yards. In the present work miles unless otherwise stated are English statute miles of 1760 yards.

14. 'The Irish language has been more happy in distinguishing the size of mountains than perhaps any other' (William Guthrie, *A new geographical, historical and commercial grammar* (London, 1771), p. 459).

15. Frank Mitchell, *The way that I followed* (Dublin, 1990), p. 234.

16. John Derricke, *The image of Ireland with a discoverie of wood karne* (London, 1581). Derricke's illustrations are reproduced in D.B. Quinn, *The Elizabethans and the Irish* (New York, 1966), plates 10-18.

17. Eileen McCracken, *The Irish woods since Tudor times* (Newton Abbot, 1971), ch. 2.

18. British Library, Cotton MS Augustus I, ii, 21. The reverse of this map is endorsed 'some part of Ireland' in an early seventeenth-century hand – a natural mistake, despite the prior existence of an endorsement reading simply 'Ireland'.

19. *Report from the select committee on the survey and valuation of Ireland*, House of commons sessional papers, H.C. 1824, viii (445), p. 19.

20. J.H. Andrews, 'Science and cartography in the Ireland of William and Samuel Molyneux', *Proceedings of the Royal Irish Academy*, lxxx C (1980), p. 250.

21. In an accurate triangulation allowance must be made for the curvature of the earth's surface, on which the angles of spherical (strictly, spheroidal) triangles amount to more than 180 degrees.

22. William Ravenhill, 'Christopher Saxton's surveying: an enigma' in Sarah Tyacke (ed.), *English map-making 1500-1650* (London, 1983), pp 112-19.

23. *Report on survey and valuation*, p. 42 (evidence of Richard Griffith), p. 106 (evidence of William Edgeworth).

24. Seymour, *History of the Ordnance Survey*, p. 140.

25. John Norden, Description of Northamptonshire, Bibliothèque Nationale, Paris, MS 706, p. 8.

26. In 1824 Ireland could still be described as a country with few church steeples (*Report on survey and valuation*, p. 89).

27. *Report on survey and valuation*, p. 106 (evidence of William Edgeworth).

28. Ireland offers a favourable basis on which to argue that according to the theory of 'fractals' every coastline is of infinite length (Tim Robinson, 'A Connemara fractal', *Technology Ireland*, xxiii (1991), pp 32-7, reprinted with some differences in Timothy Collins (ed.), *Decoding the landscape* (Galway, 1994), pp 12-29).

29. *Report on survey and valuation*, p. 8.

30. 'On the whole the land is low-lying on all sides and along the coast; but towards the centre it rises up very high to many hills and even high mountains' (J.T. O'Meara (ed.), *The first version of the 'Topography' of Ireland by Giraldus Cambrensis* (Dundalk, 1951), p. 14).

31. National Library of Ireland, Reeves Down Survey maps, Upper Ossory, Queen's

County, MS 720.

32. Ibid., King's County, MS 716.

33. *A letter to the public concerning bogs* (Dublin, 1757), p. 21.

34. British Library, Cotton MS Titus B.xii, f. 523.

35. This metaphor for the misrepresentation of Celtic names appears to have originated with the mid-eighteenth-century Welsh cartographer Lewis Morris (Gwyn Walters, 'The Morrises and the map of Anglesey', *Welsh History Review*, v (1970), p. 170).

36. One English cartographer to take an interest in his country's 'true and ancient' placenames was John Norden (*Preparative*, pp 21-31) but in deference to the common reader he ended by recommending the 'vulgar' forms.

37. Quoted by J.B. Harley in *The county maps from William Camden's 'Britannia' 1695 by Robert Morden* (Newton Abbot, 1972), p. x.

38. Irish statutes, 17 & 18 Charles II , c. 2, sec. 234.

39. J.H. Andrews, 'The cartography of Celtic placenames', *Ulster Local Studies*, xiv (1992), pp 7-21.

40. P.W. Joyce, *The origin and history of Irish names of places*, two volumes (1875, 1912, reprinted Wakefield, 1972-3), *passim.*

41. D.A. Beaufort, travel journal, August 1788, Trinity College, Dublin, MS 4030, p. 49. For the special significance of the western compass-point in Irish folklore see C.M. Arensberg, *The Irish countryman* (London, 1937), pp 23-7.

42. Six examples refer to rivers, churches and a bridge within a radius of about fifteen miles from Newry in Richard Bartlett's map of south-east Ulster, *c.*1602 (Public Record Office, London, MPF 36). One of these, 8 Mile Church, had already appeared in a version of Francis Jobson's map of Ulster made in 1590 (British Library, Cotton MS Augustus I, ii, 19). See below, chapter 4.

43. *Calendar of State Papers, Ireland, 1608-10*, p. 280.

Chapter 2

Friends in high places:
Gerard Mercator, 1564

The most famous cartographer of all time is Claudius Ptolemy of Alexandria, who mapped the whole world as known to the Greeks and Romans in the second century after Christ. The next most famous must surely be Gerard Mercator, who was born in Flanders in 1512 and spent most of his career at Duisburg in Germany. Mercator was a renaissance man among cartographers, equally distinguished as surveyor, map-compiler, engraver, calligrapher, globe-maker, cosmographer and publisher. Apart from a huge output of maps, his legacy includes two of the most familiar words in the modern cartographer's vocabulary: his own name, as applied to a well-known rectangular map projection, and the term 'atlas' introduced on the title page of his principal work and later extended to all subsequent collections of maps in book form. He is also the first and perhaps the last continental scholar since Ptolemy known to have published a completely original contribution to the map of Ireland.

Besides exploiting his flair for innovation, Mercator was happy at times to do as his predecessors had done, and his output included two maps of Ireland which experts of his own generation would or should have regarded as obsolete. The earlier of these appeared in his edition of Ptolemy's *Geography*. Ptolemy had given the latitudes and longitudes of some fifty Irish capes, estuaries, nations and 'cities', the cities probably being iron-age hill forts rather than urban communities in the Mediterranean sense (Fig. 2.1).[1] These compared with a maximum of eight Irish names (and no geographical coordinates) on the world maps or *mappaemundi* that took the place of Ptolemy in medieval Europe. To that extent it was right that Ptolemy should be revived by scholars like Mercator and that the *mappaemundi* should be forgotten. Unfortunately all Ireland's Ptolemaic names had fallen into oblivion among non-cartographers long before the sixteenth century. Indeed many of them were of pre-Celtic origin and may have already dropped out of everyday use by Ptolemy's own time, which makes it unlikely that his map has ever been of any interest to anyone except historians. Apart from lacking practical value it offered no recognisable framework

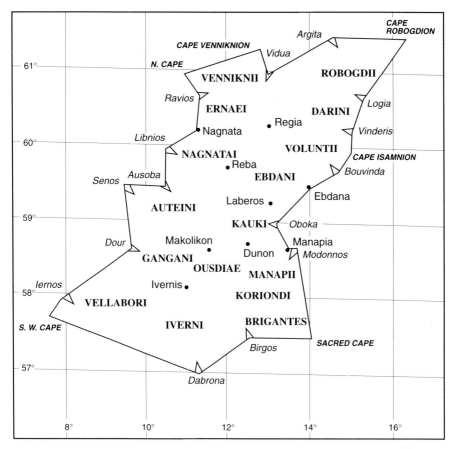

Fig. 2.1   Reconstruction of Ptolemy's map of Ireland by F.J. Byrne (T.W. Moody,
F.X. Martin, F.J. Byrne (eds), *A new history of Ireland*, ix (Oxford, 1984),
Fig. 13). Longitudes reckoned from the Canary Islands, assumed to lie
2.5 degrees west of Cape St Vincent.

for modern revision, though some sixteenth-century editors aware of
Ireland's geographical reputation felt that they could hardly go wrong
by inserting a few extra mountains and rivers more or less at random.
To reprint maps from the *Geography* was an act of homage that
Mercator might have chosen to perform at any stage of his career.
Certainly by the time he did so in 1578 he had long since ceased to
depend on Ptolemy's Irish data in any of his own non-historical
compilations. While most of his contemporaries took the same view,
some of them showed both erudition and courage by equating at least
a few of Ptolemy's names with their supposed modern equivalents, the
most common of these identifications being of the second-century
'Notium' with the sixteenth-century Mizen Head in west Cork.[2]

27

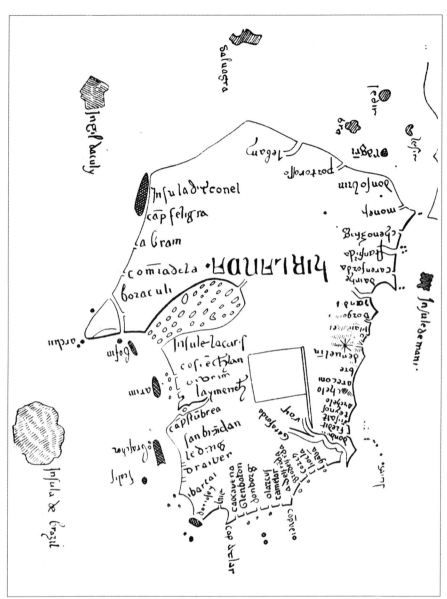

Fig. 2.2 Ireland from the portolan chart of Angelino Dulcert, 1339, as reproduced by T.J. Westropp, 'Early Italian maps of Ireland from 1300 to 1600, with notes on foreign settlers and trade', *Proceedings of the Royal Irish Academy*, xxxi C (1913), plate 42, from original in Bibliothèque Nationale, Paris. A representation of Ireland common on portolan charts from the early fourteenth to the mid fifteenth century and the earliest of six types of portolan outline recognised in Michael C. Andrews, 'The map of Ireland, A.D. 1300-1700', *Proceedings of the Belfast Natural History and Philosophical Society*, 1922 3, pp 16-23.

Otherwise the main importance of the Ptolemaic maps was to frame Britain and Ireland within the same sheet lines and so lend geographical respectability to the notion of the British Isles.

A more recent tradition inherited by Mercator had taken shape in the numerous 'portolan' charts of European coastlines drawn by Italian and Catalan navigators during the later middle ages (Fig. 2.2). Altogether this new generation of cartographers is known to have mapped about 150 Irish names, all of them places accessible to sea-going ships and many with little relevance to the non-mariner. These names were much garbled, seemingly by both oral and scribal transmission, but at least the majority of them are more easily identified than Ptolemy's.[3] Although the portolan coastlines are usually thought to have been based on compass surveys, in Britain and Ireland they are too inaccurate to make this suggestion very plausible. All the same, when Mercator was learning his craft these were the best maps of Ireland available to a foreigner, and their influence is clear in several of his major works, including a world map of 1538 and a globe of 1541 (Fig. 2.3).

* * * * * * * * *

An interest in maps, it has been somewhat gnomically said, may at times reflect a state of historical uncertainty.[4] In Ireland many uncertainties must have been created by the Tudor 'revolution in government' and the associated attempt by English kings and queens to rule the country more effectively. Our first references to post-medieval maps of the interior belong to the period of Mercator's childhood in the 1520s and come from correspondence between King Henry VIII and his cross-channel officials.[5] By the best European standards this may seem an unexpectedly late start, but its lateness would have come as no surprise to any Irish or Anglo-Irish observer of the contemporary scene. Ireland was too poor, wild and dangerous to have inspired a Hibernian equivalent of Edward III's Gough map of England and Wales,[6] or of the regional maps produced a century later in Italy, Germany and Switzerland.

When they finally materialised, the English government's new maps showed a closer knowledge of Ireland than had been achieved by any earlier cartographer, but until the reign of Elizabeth none of them appears to have been based on a regular survey. At this point a digression is required. Historical judgements about the absence of regular surveys at some particular period are a commonplace of cartographic scholarship the world over. How can such judgements be validated? The inclusion or omission of numerical scales and

Fig. 2.3　Ireland, from Mercator's globe of 1541, reproduced in *Sphère terrestre et sphère celeste de Gerard Mercator, de Rupelmonde, editées à Louvain en 1541 et 1551* (Brussels, 1875). Mercator's key to the numbers is: 1 Unflor (Olderfleet?), 2 Solli (Swilly?), 3 Dondal, 4 Dubelyn, 5 Wacfort, 6 Lamerich, 7 Galvei. Apparently based on a late style of portolan chart with some affinity to Michael Andrews's type 3 as exemplified by the sixteenth-century Genoese cartographer Battista Agnese. Ireland's main differentiating feature in the later types of portolan, compared with contemporary land maps, is the narrowness of the country from west to east. Rheba is derived from Ptolemy.

coordinates can tell us little about a cartographer's methods: such marginalia are often the last features to be put on a map, perhaps by an editor or publisher rather than the true author, and sometimes with no safer foundation than the roughest of estimates or guesses. An alternative test is whether a cartographer's positional errors are too gross and too widespread to have been made in the course of systematic field observation. Since no map is likely to be perfect, the distinction between survey and non-survey requires a line to be drawn between degrees of erroneousness on what must surely be a mathematical continuum. To avoid an arbitrary decision on this point, we must somehow identify characteristics incompatible with any normal survey method. One give-away is an excessively simple geometrical shape. The most obvious example is a rectangle, drawn to express the kind of verbal and numerical estimate of a country's length and breadth that has been common throughout history among non-surveyors and non-cartographers. If straight lines are considered too unrealistic, a more sophisticated draughtsman can round the rectangle into an ellipse, and it may have been this process that caused one rather naive sixteenth-century map-reader to conclude that Ireland was shaped like an egg.[7]

A sense of realism will also encourage the avoidance of regular shapes – curves with simple equations, as well as straight lines – in depicting coasts, rivers and boundaries not directly known to the author, even though in this case 'reality' may actually be the product of invention. If an angle in one of these lines can be identified on the ground, however badly distorted, then presumably (if we dismiss the possibility of chance coincidence) someone at some time must have seen that angle for himself. Conversely, if the angle has no terrestrial counterpart it must come from some source other than direct observation. Early cartographers extrapolated from their data in different ways, just as today's students produce different results when given a verbal description of an imaginary island and asked to draw a map of it. Some versions will be rounded, others angular, some simple, some complex, depending on the artist's aesthetic preferences, his theories of physical geography, and his experience of the world, whether at first hand or mediated through other people's maps. At some risk of misunderstanding, the subjective element in a cartographer's linework may be called his 'personal curvature'.

The early mapmaker's sources could lie anywhere between the extremes of true survey and pure fiction. A traveller might draw a freehand sketch of his journeys, either on the road or from memory, in the manner of a modern child asked to map his route from home to school, though one can hardly expect to find such activities explicitly

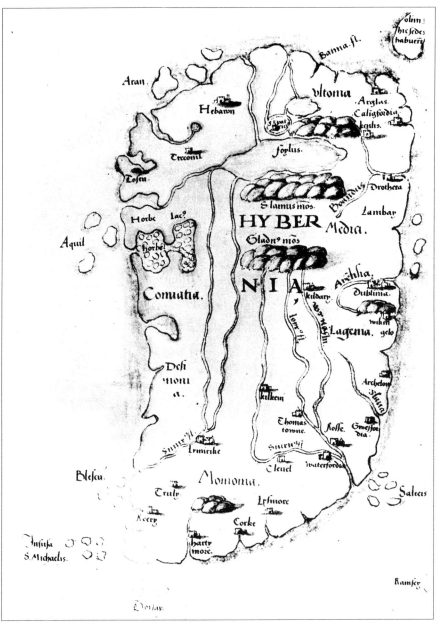

Fig. 2.4   Ireland, from 'Angliae figura', c.1534, British Library, Cotton MS
Augustus I, i, 9. Apart from some echoes of the Cambro-Norman
topographer Giraldus Cambrensis, the Irish sources of this map are
unknown. Its portrayal of England and Wales resembles that of the
fourteenth-century Gough map. The dominance of the English 'Pale'
(see Fig. 1.4) survives in the long distance from Dublin to Drogheda.
Note the misinterpretation of non-towns as towns, e.g. harty more and
Keery. 'lovr' is a miscopying for Nore.

recorded either in ancillary documents or on the finished drawing, especially as roads were nearly always omitted from pre-seventeenth-century maps. Then there were lists of harbours in order of occurrence around a coastline, which could be translated into graphic form on the kind of topological principle made famous by the modern London underground railway map.[8] The sequence of towns along a road or river could also be recorded in a list and later converted into a map, as could the junctions of tributary rivers on a main stream, though again there seem to be no surviving Irish examples. The result of such operations would be a blend of topological accuracy and planimetric error, though where the real-world features are closely and more or less evenly spaced a topological reconstruction can make surprisingly good planimetric sense.[9] On roads the approximate distances between successive towns were likely to be common knowledge among the travelling public, and with such data a map could be plotted by scale and compasses as if from a trilateration, even when no deliberate survey had ever taken place. The accuracy of the distance estimates would depend on how well the roads were frequented by travellers whose knowledge could be tapped by the cartographer.

*   *   *   *   *   *   *   *   *

It is against this background that the somewhat meagre achievements of early Tudor cartography must be judged. Until William Cecil (later Lord Burghley) joined the English government's administrative staff around the middle of the sixteenth century there was no satisfactory official cartographic archive in either London or Dublin. This may explain why nobody troubled to attach dates or authors' names to pre-Elizabethan maps of Ireland, and why only two or three specimens of this period survive from what may well have been a much larger number. Two of these were later acquired by a famous collector, Sir Robert Cotton. One is the Pale-dominated sketch mentioned in the previous chapter and perhaps assignable to the 1520s.[10] The other, more professionally executed but not much more knowledgeable, is a map of the British Isles thought to have probably been drawn in the 1530s (Fig. 2.4).[11]

A third and slightly better map, now in the Public Record Office, London, has been dated to the first year of Elizabeth's reign, but only because it was preserved and annotated by Cecil, presumably in his role as minister of the crown (Fig. 2.5): in fact there was no reason why Cecil should not have acquired an older map and in any case he was already a secretary of state in 1550.[12] All three maps betray their origin by their use of the English language, and all reveal a genuine

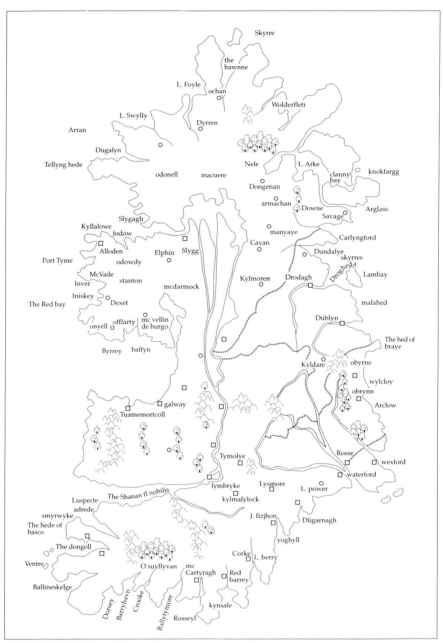

Skyrre

the bawnne

L. Foyle

ochan

Wolderfleti

L. Swylly

Dyrren

Arran

Dugalyn

Nele

L. Arke

clanny bay

knokfargg

Tellyng hede

odonell

macuere

Dongenan

armachan

Downe

Savage

Arglass

Slygagh

Kyllalowe

fodow

manyaye

Carlyngford

Alloden

Elphin

Slygg

Cavan

Dundalye

skyrres

Port Tyme

odowdy

Kylmoren

Drodagh

Drogheda

Lambay

McVade

Inver

stanton

mcdarmock

Iniskey

Dexet

malahed

The Red bay

onyell

offlarty

mc vellin de burgo

Dublyn

The hed of braye

Byrrey

baffyn

Kyldare

obyrne

wylcloy

obrynn

Arclow

galway

Tuamemortcoll

Tymolye

Rosse

wexford

waterford

lymbryke

Lysmore

L. power

The Shanan fl nobilis

kylmalylock

Luspecte adrede

smyrwyke

J. fizjhon

Dügarnagh

The hede of basco

yoghyll

The dongoll

Ventre

O suyllyvan

mc Cartyragh

Red barrey

Corke

L. berry

Ballineskelge

Dorsey

Barryhavn

Crooke

Ballytymore

kynsale

Rosseyl

Fig. 2.5   Ireland, mid sixteenth century, redrawn and edited from Public Record
Office, London, MPF 72. The original has west at the top. Source, date
and authorship unknown. The broken line and associated rivers and
mountains may be an interpretation of the English Pale, with Leix but
not Offaly on the English side of the line and with an outlier in south
Wexford. 'Wolderfleti' is in the handwriting of William Cecil, replacing
the original name 'Waldfryth[?]'.

34

Fig. 2.6   *Hibernia sive Irlanda*, attributed to Ferrando Bertelli, Venice, *c.* 1560, and evidently based on George Lily's *Britanniae insulae quae nunc Angliae et Scotiae regna continet cum Hibernia adiacente nova descriptio* (Rome, 1546). Often described as the earliest separate printed non-portolan map of Ireland, this is inferior in many respects to both the portolan charts and the earliest surviving English maps.

knowledge of their subject. In particular – and this is a long-standing feature of Ireland as shown on English maps – none of their names looks like a complete invention. They are also small, diagrammatic, and well endowed with personal curvature. None seems to have been copied from either of the others, or from any continental source. Such genetic self-sufficiency was another English characteristic, reflecting perhaps simple ignorance (though these authors must have learnt their cartography somewhere), perhaps a rejection of earlier materials as incorrect or irrelevant, perhaps a deliberate avoidance of second-hand information regardless of origin, or perhaps a simple English mistrust of foreigners.

But the foreigners were soon updating their own view of Ireland. None of them seem to have surveyed the interior of the island as the portolan chart-makers surveyed the coast. No doubt particular places were visited on particular errands, most commonly perhaps by pilgrims: one famous centre of religious attraction, St Patrick's Purgatory in Donegal (in the form 'Fegefeuer'), is among the handful of Irish names recorded on Martin Behaim's Nuremberg globe of 1492. But in the unruly conditions of the early Tudor period no stranger would have systematically traversed the length and breadth of Ireland unless some government was paying him to do so and if anyone had accomplished this feat it would surely have been noticed by the Irish annalists or in official English despatches, if not publicised by the successful traveller himself. (This 'argument from silence' will recur in the following pages whenever the possibility of expensive field operations has to be considered.) On the other hand a foreign spy might well have assembled a rough map from hasty and incomplete observations without making himself too conspicuous. Alternatively, stay-at-home cartographers in Europe might have been briefed by Irish or Anglo-Irish travellers either graphically or by interview. The end-products are bad enough to support any of these interpretations.

Apart from the portolans, pre-Elizabethan continental maps of Ireland fall into two groups, and it is in discriminating between these that Mercator first showed his mettle as a maker of Irish map history. One outline was introduced in 1546 by George Lily – whose domicile in Italy can qualify him for present purposes as un-English – in a map of the British Isles published at Rome (Fig. 2.6).[13] Lily's Ireland had many imitators, but its quality was very poor. Besides the four provinces it mentions three rivers and sixteen towns, and without these names (or those of them that are now identifiable) no modern reader could hope to guess what country its pear-shaped form was intended to represent.

The second outline is more complex and probably represents a

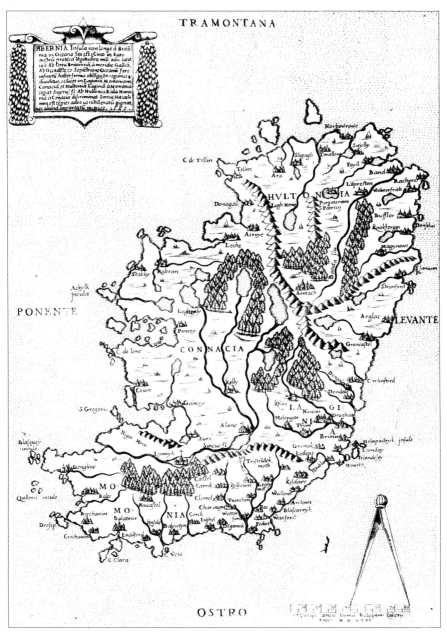

Fig. 2.7   *Hibernia* by Bolognino Zalterius, 1566. This map was anticipated in
Gerard Mercator's *Europa* (Duisburg, 1554). Zalterius omits two of
Mercator's names, Mallaghyd (Malahide) and Brey pr (Bray Head), while
Mercator omits Zalterius's marsh shading and the name Sineus fl.

conflation of several sources, at least one of them a portolan chart. It introduces serious positional and combinatorial errors such as putting Sligo in north Donegal and Olderfleet at the mouth of the Foyle, and unlike Henry VIII's maps it belittles the English achievement by making the south-east of Ireland much too small. But it does clearly distinguish Galway Bay, Clew Bay, Donegal Bay and the bend of the Shannon near Limerick, and with a total of 94 names it is greatly superior to Lily. Yet it was not influential enough to qualify for a full-length essay in this book. Even in Europe's chief map-making country it was largely ignored until a Vatican wall-artist adopted it in the 1560s,[14] and after that it was quickly superseded. The more credit to Mercator, then, for having incorporated the same outline into his map of Europe as early as 1554 (Fig. 2.7). Previous versions of it may conceivably come to light even now, but Mercator would still deserve praise for displaying it on so wide a canvas. He had also given posterity a useful lesson in map-historical method. It is easy to forget that each country's image appears not just in maps devoted exclusively to itself but also in those of all the larger regions that contain it, though admittedly maps of large countries are usually less original than those of small regions. Mercator illustrated this last rule by recycling the 1554 outline of Ireland fifteen years later in his map of the world, in spite of having himself by this time produced something better. The something better was the first post-medieval representation of Ireland to make a lasting impression on the map-using public. It bore the title *Angliae Scotiae et Hiberniae nova descriptio* and it was published from Duisburg in 1564 (Fig. 2.8).

* * * * * * * * *

There is no evidence that Mercator visited either Britain or Ireland while preparing the *Nova descriptio*. On the contrary, according to his biographer he was sent the map by a friend with a request that he engrave it.[15] The implication is that for once Mercator took no other part in the production process. However that may be, the friend's request deserves attention. In the study of cartographic fallibility, the engraver often figures as an anonymous scapegoat, but in this case engraver, publisher and nominal author were the same person, and all bear the same responsibility for what can only be described as a tissue of gross spelling errors, with 'Ballymore' rendered as 'Palermone' and 'Bective' as 'Rechee'. Even if the mis-spellings did not originate with Mercator, they show that he knew very little about Ireland. In this respect he resembled the authors of all other printed maps for the next hundred years.

In the rest of this chapter the word 'Mercator' will mean 'Mercator or

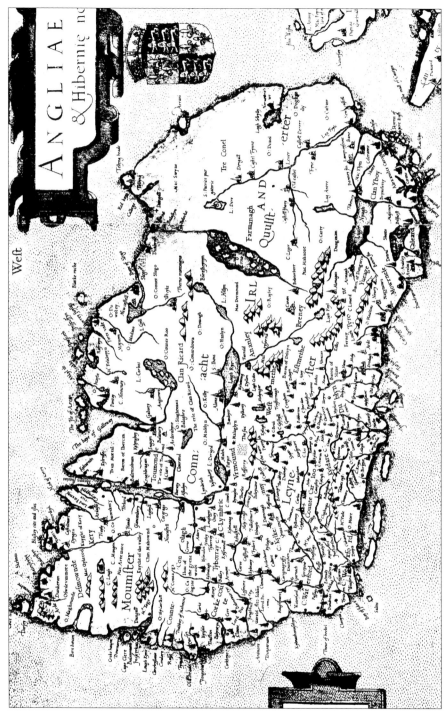

Fig. 2.8   Gerard Mercator, *Angliae Scotiae et Hiberniae nova descriptio* (Duisburg, 1564).

his friend in England'. The friend's identity has been the subject of much speculation. If, as we are told by a contemporary biographer, he was 'distinguished', modern scholars might reasonably hope to have met him in some other connection. But the person who sent the map was not necessarily himself the author of it, and in some discussions of this problem the two roles have become confused.[16] At least eight candidates have been proposed – George Buchanan, John Dee, John Elder, George Lily, Humphrey Lluyd, Laurence Nowell, John Rudd and Christopher Saxton. Of these only Laurence Nowell is known to have visited Ireland (his stay lasted for no more than two months)[17] but he is also the only one against whom there is strong negative evidence in the shape of his own authenticated near-contemporary maps, which as we shall see are not very much like Mercator's. In any case the friend need not have been either English, Scottish or Welsh, and the map has several features, including its orientation, that point towards continental sources unfamiliar to most British cartographers of this period.[18] On this line of reasoning the most plausible contender is George Lily, who may well have picked up a few foreign habits during his long exile and whose Catholicism would not have excluded him from official English archives during the reign of Queen Mary. But Lily's map of Ireland in 1546 was so bad that it is hard to credit him with the ability to produce anything better. The final judgement must be impersonal: in content the *Nova descriptio* looks like a mixture of elements, marking a transition from continental to insular dominance in the map of Ireland, though the transition had gone far enough for Mercator to rank in an Irish cartographic context as an honorary Anglo-Saxon.

The scale of the *Nova descriptio* is one inch to about thirteen English miles, a reasonable choice of units in a map of the British Isles even if the exact length of an English mile remained uncertain.[19] There are no latitudes or longitudes: this omission was against all Mercator's principles and may explain why he made a point of attributing the map to somebody else. The outline shows some traces of 'length and breadth' construction, squarish at the south-west and south-east corners but rounded off in Ulster. That it began as something little better than an oval or rectangle is made more probable by the artificiality with which the author has, so to speak, hollowed out the coastline in various places and dropped islands into the resulting embayments, for instance at Bearehaven, North Arran, Tellyng Head, Achill, the island south of Rafrayn, Balenshyn and Ireland's Eye.

Mercator's interior detail may have come from first-hand knowledge, written documents, or from other maps, and in any mixture of sources the ratio of cartographic to non-cartographic information may have varied from one part of the country to another. The most one can say

Fig. 2.9   Laurence Nowell, Ireland, c.1564, redrawn and simplified from British Library, Cotton MS Domitian, xviii, ff. 101, 102. Spelling modernised. The original also shows woods, hills, major territorial boundaries, latitudes and longitudes at intervals of 15 minutes, and a large number of additional names.

in general terms on this point is that the *Nova descriptio* shows little resemblance to any pre-Elizabethan map. It does however have some features in common with two manuscript maps of Ireland from the same period as itself: one, undated, by the English antiquary Laurence Nowell (Fig. 2.9);[20] the other, of 1567, by an otherwise unknown cartographer named John Goghe (Fig. 2.10).[21] Both maps in their way are better than the *Nova descriptio*. Nowell gives information that Mercator had room for but did not use, which makes him unlikely to have been among Mercator's sources even if this turned out to be chronologically possible. Goghe, though too sparing with detail to help demonstrate genetic relationships, shows better judgement in relating content to scale. Unlike Mercator's, neither of these maps is known to have been followed in its entirety by any later copyist. Their main value at the moment is to point backwards in the direction of some common Mercator-Nowell-Goghe archetype for which there is no other record.

This archetype evidently contained far more information than any of the maps we have yet considered. The most detailed of those earlier maps includes 94 placenames. Mercator has 388 names, Nowell 530, Goghe 235. Among the identifiable rivers appearing for the first time in the 1560s are the Munster Blackwater, Ulster Blackwater, Inny, Brosna, Feale, Finn and Fergus. New lakes include Ree, Leane, Ennell, Derravaragh and Iron. There are also a number of new errors. Mercator, Nowell and Goghe all ignore upper Lough Erne and draw the lower lake long and narrow as in reality, but excessively large and aligned from west to east instead of from north-west to south-east. They all make Lough Neagh too long from north to south and give Lough Ree the shape of a lemon. In all three maps the River Bann bifurcates below Lough Neagh and the Shannon's change of direction near Limerick is too abrupt. On a more localised scale, they all twist the long axis of Dursey Island into a north-south alignment. But if these maps share a common ancestry at least two of them must have had good reasons for diverging from it. One reason may have been that the ancestor was too small to satisfy a later generation and needed filling out with additional data, each author using different supplementary sources for this purpose.

So far the comparison has been restricted to physical features. Nowell and Mercator also have many cultural details in common (Goghe adds nothing to the argument from this point), including the names of settlements that probably boasted little more than one castle or one church. Many such places stood aside from major routeways, had played no part in recent Irish wars or other newsworthy events, and in general had nothing to distinguish them from hundreds of

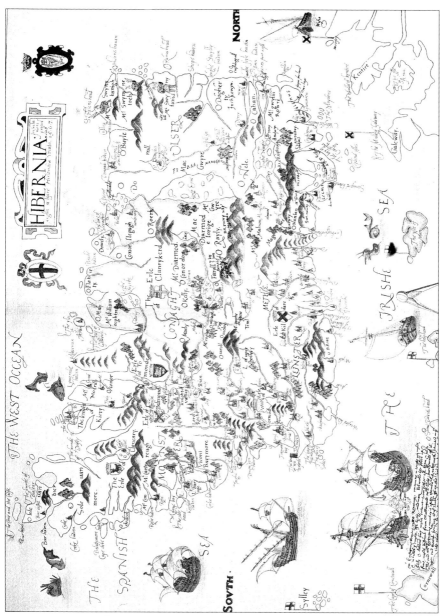

Fig. 2.10   John Goghe, 'Hibernia, insula non procul ab Anglia vulgare Hirlandia vocata', 1567, Public Record Office, London, MPF 68. With many annotations by other hands, one of them that of Sir William Cecil.

43

similar settlements ignored by every sixteenth-century map. Examples are Fulkescourt in Tipperary, Rosegarland in Wexford, Castlemartin in Kildare, and Raharney in Westmeath. Another common feature unlikely to be accidental is the duplication of a well-known Co. Limerick name as 'Kilmallock' and 'Kilmalogh', perhaps a combinatorial error suggesting either an attempted synthesis of two maps further back along the Nowell-Mercator family tree or a compiler's misunderstanding of non-cartographic information.

While neither of these two maps can have been copied exclusively from the other, it remains conceivable that Nowell drew on Mercator as an additional source of names. This possibility may have chronological implications, not just for Nowell's map but for the activities of Mercator's friend in England. The problem here is that Nowell spells better than his hypothetical source. Could he have corrected some names on his own authority, with Mercator simply triggering his memory of places already known to him? This raises the delicate question of just how many Irish names an educated Englishman can reasonably be expected to have heard of. Nowell might well have altered Mercator's 'Trymmo' to 'Trim' but he is unlikely to have decided without prompting that 'Kylensh' in Co. Kildare would look better as 'Kilrusshe'. It seems more probable that somewhere behind both Nowell and Mercator is a lost archetype which included a comparatively large number of minor placenames, more than appear on any surviving earlier map. To judge from the duplication of Kilmallock this archetype is likely to have been a composite product. If so, one of its ingredients may have been a separate map of south-east Ireland, a region which both Nowell and Mercator show in considerably more detail than the rest of the country. There may even have been subsidiary local maps within this region: why otherwise should Mercator map six tributaries of the River Slaney and none of the Barrow? Such speculations lead nowhere except towards a moral for which there was ample evidence to come: more sixteenth-century maps of Ireland have been lost than have survived.

*   *   *   *   *   *   *   *   *

However many maps contributed to the Nowell-Mercator archetype for the interior of Ireland, they must surely have been of English origin. Apart from the antecedent probabilities already reviewed, this statement is supported by Nowell's spelling of Irish placenames, which, unlike that of the portolan charts for example, is free from the kind of language-determined error that no foreigner could hope to avoid. But the elements common to Nowell and Mercator cannot be precisely dated. In England Nowell was a pioneer of historical cartography,[22] and by omitting all the Irish counties he gives the impression of deliberately emphasising the Gaelic and Norman periods, perhaps to the extent of editing-out more recent information. (He did include the earldoms of Clanrickard and Thomond but may not have known that they dated only from 1543.) Mercator by contrast felt the non-specialist cartographer's normal desire for up-to-dateness – within reason. He included the county of Westmeath which was contemporary with the new earldoms and in Offaly he showed Fort Governor, established in 1547. (He also mistakenly applied the name 'Governor' to the twin fort of Protector in Leix, built in the following year, a duplicative error from which no firm chronological conclusions seem deducible.) On the other hand he omitted the important names Philipstown, Maryborough, King's County and Queen's County, which date from 1556. On the face of it this fixes his source for the midlands within a bracket of ten years, an achievement not to be despised in sixteenth-century Irish map historiography.[23]

Given the close connection between cartography and war at this period, the two most likely instigators of a new map of Ireland around the middle of the century were the two royal deputies with the most military experience, Sir Edward Bellingham (1548-9) and Sir James Croft (1551-2), who both followed a more aggressive policy than was generally in vogue among their contemporaries. In default of positive information, Croft must be the favourite: he is known to have made or commissioned plans of certain coastal defence points, and on at least one occasion advised the authorities in London to consult 'the platt of Ireland'.[24]

The kind of English governmental map postulated here cannot have been Mercator's only inspiration. Some of his coastal names are more likely to have come from a maritime source. Most of them are islands which despite their exaggeratedly large scale had no special military, political or scholarly significance, and most of them fall within the area known from the portolan charts to have been frequented by foreign shipping. Examples are the Cow and Calf off Dursey Island, the Skellig rocks, and the Blasket Islands. Most revealing are those coasts whose hinterlands were still largely unmapped: here Mercator's coverage included Achill Island, Inishark, Inishbofin, Burrishoole and Blackrock. Some of these features, like Inishbofin, are set down in the wrong order, as if somebody who knew little of Ireland (like Mercator himself) had taken his names from one map and his outline from another. But whatever Mercator's coastal source it had little resemblance to any known portolan chart, except of course in showing major ports and harbours likely to appear on any map of Ireland.[25]

Fiction is a third and happily small element in Mercator's map, comprising not more than three or four features. Its origin was probably not deliberate falsehood, but the misunderstanding or mishandling of veridical source materials to an extent that rendered their original meaning unrecognisable. Thus a detail may have been moved from the margin to the body of a map; an eye-slip may have transferred a town from one region to another, perhaps even from one land-mass to another; or two references to the same place may have been understood to denote different places, as in the case of Kilmallock already adduced. Most errors of this kind were probably copied from previous maps. Thus Sebastian Munster had anticipated Mercator in showing 'Lampreston' on the lower Bann (conceivably a much misplaced conflation of Lancaster and Preston) at least as early as 1540.[26] Pontoy on Galway Bay also occurs in Bolognino Zalterius's map of 1566, which is typologically older than Mercator and shows no other sign of being indebted to him.[27]

None of these fictions appears on any sixteenth-century English map, either because in England maps were drawn or checked by people who would recognise such names as delusory, or simply because no Englishman had ever heard of them. This makes one wonder whether Mercator's 'friend in England' may have been a visiting foreigner. Another possibility is that Mercator himself, while allowing readers to assume that he adopted the *Descriptio* ready-made, could not resist the temptation to add his own continental touch. This seems to have been a common ploy among eminent cartographers engaged in the production of otherwise derivative maps, including Mercator himself in later years. (It is a counterpart of the deliberate errors introduced by publishers of mathematical tables: in one case the motive is to prevent plagiarism, in the other to deny it.) So perhaps it was with tongue in cheek that Mercator praised an earlier mapmaker for refusing to embellish his sources.[28]

* * * * * * * * *

Of the three elements distinguished in the foregoing paragraphs, the first, embracing the interior of the country, is the most substantial. Mercator's is essentially an English view of Ireland's place in the British Isles, and his title sets the scene by displaying heraldic devices for England and Scotland but not for Ireland and by printing 'Hiberniae' in smaller script than 'Angliae' and 'Scotiae'. But he is also telling us how a professional cartographer of 1564 thought a map should look – and how a deeply religious cartographer thought the world should look. One strain running through sixteenth-century geography was a kind of global optimism, founded on Judaeo-Christian theology and stressing the more beneficent aspects of the region described. Mercator's Ireland was physically well organised. It had no forests and no bogs or waste places ('Morseymore', perhaps originally meant as a bog, is treated as a town) except perhaps for one small patch of unexplained stipple in north Tipperary which suggests that his sources may have included some information about bogs. The implication is that the whole country was cultivated apart from the mountains, and mountains here are less emphasised – and less often named – than on many other sixteenth-century maps. They do not divide province from province or otherwise impede the unification of the country, and their relation to the drainage pattern is more harmonious than in reality, especially where mountains form a watershed for the rivers Inny, Erne, and two of the Blackwaters. This area in fact is not very hilly, but then Mercator's mountain symbols are not very hilly either: he might have justified putting them almost anywhere on the basis that few lowlands are totally flat. Since water is more obviously useful to mankind than mountains it was appropriate that extensive coverage should be given to Ireland's wealth of rivers and lakes, including some acknowledgement of the theory (mentioned by Giraldus Cambrensis) that rivers normally originate in lakes. At the same time water names like hill names are surprisingly inadequate.

In human as in physical geography Mercator gives an impression of peace, order and uniformity. Settlement is hierarchical. Towns as opposed to villages are shown by towers and spires with one or more additional buildings to indicate the more important centres. The contemporary preoccupation with security appears in Mercator's liking for the word 'castle' even at places traditionally associated with the church such as 'Castell Derrey' and 'C.Loger' (a mistake for Clogher). Castles signal a countryside under control, presumably by legitimate forces as in central Europe. Settlements of all kinds are as evenly distributed as Mercator can manage, though in the case of towns this requires some bending of the facts. Twomey on the north shore of Lough Neagh has a more prominent symbol than Armagh, Cavan is made larger than Limerick, and there is a major settlement at Wreyke east of Sligo that should probably not be a settlement at all but simply the family name 'O'Rourke'.

Mercator follows English geographical tradition in giving prominence to the four provinces of Ireland. Unlike Nowell, he also acknowledges the English conquest by mentioning nearly all the counties that existed in his time and usually adding 'C.' or 'Counte' to their names. Early cartographers cannot necessarily be credited with as much political awareness as modern historians, and Mercator is unlikely to have omitted county and provincial boundaries in the interests of national unity. This might nevertheless have been his informants' motive for ignoring the English Pale, which had appeared on one sixteenth-century map[29] but which the government hoped was now obsolete. Mercator also takes every opportunity to notice earls, barons, knights and lords. Religious authority is invoked by single and double cross symbols representing bishops' and archbishops' sees respectively. These may have been a later addition to a secular map by a half-knowledgeable compiler, perhaps by Mercator himself. They incorporate several bad errors, such as the omission of a cross at Ferns and the transfer of another from Emly to Kilmallock. (Other errors and anachronisms appear in the more comprehensive list of British and Irish dioceses printed in the upper left-hand corner of the *Descriptio*.) A different kind of error, later common enough almost to deserve a name of its own – the episcopal fallacy, perhaps – is to portray all diocesan centres in post-reformation Ireland as major settlements in their own right. The same desire to integrate secular and religious themes appears in the spires which confer importance on certain places without even a parish church, such as Corgrig, Co. Limerick, and Dunamase in Co. Leix.

Despite Mercator's authoritarian prejudice, the reassuring surface of his map is repeatedly broken by hints of alienation and recalcitrance. He admits several Irish territories that had not yet been adopted as counties, and numerous family names unlegitimised by English titles. Some of these belonged to immigrant groups outside the framework of authority, like the Scottish Alexander Carogh (other unidentified 'Scots' make two appearances in Ulster) and the Norman Dillon in Westmeath, but most of them carry the Gaelic prefixes 'O' and 'Mac'. Family names were an unusual subject for published maps of this period, even in areas that might seem comparable with Ireland, such as the Scottish Highlands.[30] This made them a source of misunderstanding to foreign cartographers, who showed their own bias towards 'civility' by mistaking families for towns, though as time went by with Ireland still unconquered the Os and Macs grew more familiar.

Another area of conflict between English government and Irish people was the institution of monasticism. Many Irish religious houses continued to function in Mercator's time. Officially, however, they had all been closed in the late 1530s as part of Henry VIII's Protestant reformation. Mercator retains the word 'abbey' for two of these sites and gives names for many other places with monastic associations, among them Athassel, Baltinglass, Gracedieu, Holycross, Moyne, Multifarnham, Rafrayne, Tintern, Tracton and Tristernagh. Some of these, even when ruined, could claim inclusion on purely topographical grounds as the only landmarks within miles, for the abbeys and friaries built between the twelfth and fifteenth centuries were generally more massive than the typical parish church of the Irish countryside. Other monastic locations had no more significance in the new Ireland than the secular rural communities surrounding them. To show such sites on a national map – even on the tacit understanding that they were only historical relics – did no credit to a government that had failed to equip the landscape with alternative focal points.

* * * * * * * *

Perhaps the most interesting feature of the *Nova descriptio* is its verdict on Ireland's regional geography. Three zones are distinguishable and may be called the Pale, the Marches and the Irishry, without prejudice to other uses of these terms and certainly without suggesting that Mercator would have employed them himself. The Pale included Louth, Meath, Westmeath, Dublin, Kildare, Carlow, Kilkenny, Wexford, Waterford, south Tipperary and the eastern parts of Cork and Limerick but excluded the hill country which was later to become Co. Wicklow and which was at least as much Irishry as March. These counties approximately matched the area taken over by Henry II at the treaty of Windsor in the twelfth century, with Leix and Offaly as a recent addition. They were the most tranquil parts of mid-sixteenth-century Ireland and the only parts with a settled system of shire government. Mercator's spelling in the Pale is as bad as anywhere else, but the geographical content of his map is relatively complete. The coastline is no better than elsewhere, perhaps because foreign navigators were showing little interest in eastern and south-eastern Ireland at this period. The drainage system is good but the mountains are understated, as befits potential nurseries of rebellion in what was meant to be a land of peace. The relation of settlements to rivers is especially interesting. This is the only part of Ireland where Mercator locates his towns and villages at any distance from the waterways. In fact he exaggerates the number of dry-point sites by placing some riverside and seaside towns too far back from the water's edge (e.g. Ardmore, Athy, Carlingford, Clane and Inistiogue) and some ports too far upstream, partly because their estuaries are made too narrow. It is as if the map was reluctant to show how precariously the English were still clinging to their escape routes, though it must be admitted that the same characteristic appears in Mercator's treatment of the home country.

The Marches were the area across which medieval English settlement had fluctuated, in the later middle ages retreating rather than advancing. They comprised parts of south Co. Cork, north Kerry and west Limerick, Clare and a discontinuous strip along the west bank of the Shannon. In the north midlands there was no march but a sharp divide, perhaps recognised in the emphasis Mercator gives to the River Inny. In this second zone his physical geography is more drastically simplified, while settlements are fewer and generally at watersides, one town or village per river being a common pattern. Most of these settlements chose themselves and there are few serious omissions.

It was in the Irishry of northern and far-western Ireland that cartography lagged furthest behind contemporary written sources. This was also the scene of Mercator's worst physiographic blunders, including the diagnostic errors that link him with Nowell and Goghe. Among his omissions are Fair Head and Erris Head, two of the most notable turning-points of the entire Irish coastline. Virtually the whole of Connemara is also ignored, as are Sheep Haven, Mulroy Bay, Donegal Bay, Lough Conn and Lough Mask. The distinction between the Sheep's Head and Three Castles Peninsulas is lost, and there is no sign of such later cartographic favourites as the Glens, the Route, and Inishowen. The absentees include a number of settlements often mentioned in contemporary documents such as Baltimore, Dunboy, Roscommon, Enniskillen and Dungiven. Omission and invention went hand in hand. Pontoy and Lampreston were in the north and west. So was the non-existent 'Lo[u]g[h] Antre', which might have owed its name to Antrim but in that case was on the wrong side of Lough Neagh. These fabrications were not wholly inexcusable. All cartographers dislike empty space, and quite rightly: wherever a map-user finds himself, he should be able to summon help from within a reasonable distance, on paper if not in reality. The most striking quality of Mercator's *Nova descriptio* was his failure to achieve this aim, especially in Ulster and north Connacht. It was a failure not just of cartographic knowledge but of colonisation and settlement.

*   *   *   *   *   *   *   *

If Mercator had any Irish customers their names went unrecorded, but at least twelve copies of the *Nova descriptio* are known to have been sent to England.[31] None of these can now be traced and some of them may not have lasted very long. The only reliable safeguard for maps against loss or destruction is a pair of book-covers, and what gave long-term currency to Mercator's masterpiece was its appearance on a reduced scale in a major world atlas, the *Theatrum orbis terrarum* of 1570 published in Antwerp by his friend Abraham Ortelius. Both Ptolemaic and non-Ptolemaic maps had been issued in book form before that time, but Ortelius's was the first modern atlas to maintain a uniform content. Every copy contained a map of the British Isles and it was always the same map, entitled *Angliae, Scotiae, et Hiberniae, sive Britannicarum insularum descriptio*. With a frankness habitual to him (but not to other cartographers) Ortelius made no secret of copying from the colleague he called 'the Ptolemy of our time'.[32]

Two years after the first publication of the *Theatrum* Ortelius was advised by his cousin, the English diplomatic envoy Daniel Rogers, that Ireland ought really to have a page of its own. Rogers offered to supply a new description of the country, unfortunately without saying whether this would be map or text or both.[33] Mercator is known to have had the same idea, perhaps earlier, perhaps later,[34] but not for the first time it was Ortelius who acted more promptly. In 1573, as part of an *Additamentum* to his *Theatre*, he adopted Rogers's suggestion (Fig. 2.11). His title was if anything even more imperialistic than Mercator's – *Hiberniae Britannicae insulae nova descriptio* – and now that Britain was omitted the placing of east at the bottom of the map looked like the expression of an explicitly English view. However, Ortelius did grant Ireland a measure of cultural independence by quoting the native version of its name (*Eryn*) as well as his own Flemish form of *Irlandt*.

Like so many mapmakers Ortelius was flexible in his interpretation of the word 'new'. In essence he was still copying from Mercator, with so few additions of his own that they can be listed individually. He gave names to the principal rivers, added Latin aliases for the four provinces[35] and latinised the words 'lough' and 'river' as well as inserting 'Metrop' after 'Armagh'. He made Ireland seem less attractive by adding many patches of forest, apparently from a source close to Nowell, and he replaced Mercator's placid-looking sea-stipple with the most turbulent waves to be seen anywhere in the *Theatrum*. Of his four new non-cartographic inscriptions, only one was of post-medieval origin, and that referred to a recent colonial venture by Sir Thomas Smith in the Ards peninsula. It was not the first or last time that a cartographer relied on verbal differences to make his map look new. But Ortelius also introduced a number of physical changes. Some of them lay within the permissible limits of sixteenth-century personal curvature; others were more radical, like the re-arrangement of islands in Lough Erne, the scattering of new islands across Lough Neagh, and the flattening of all Mercator's hills in Westmeath. The only genuine corrections were to widen Belfast Lough, to break Mercator's erroneous water connection between this estuary and Lough Neagh, and to improve the shape of Strangford Lough. These changes were probably taken from a map recently published in Smith's account of the Ards,

Fig. 2.11   Part of Abraham Ortelius, *Eryn: Hiberniae Britannicae insulae, nova descriptio: Irlandt,* 1573, with numerous contemporary manuscript additions and corrections.

with Ortelius following the important but seldom-stated principle that of any two maps showing the same area, the map with the more limited territorial coverage is likely to be the more accurate.[36] All the same it was not much of a revision, and on balance no great injustice will be done to Ortelius by attributing the essence of *Eryn* to Mercator. The injustice to Mercator's anonymous friend remains.

In its new guise the map partook in Ortelius's great success with practical men and scholars alike. No less than 5975 impressions of it are thought to have been printed in successive issues of the *Theatrum*.[37] Of the copies containing it, one belonged to William Cecil (who also had the edition of 1570 with its Mercator-based map of the British Isles), and two to William Camden, author of the monumental topographical treatise *Britannia*. Other owners were John Dee and Richard Hakluyt.[38] How often these celebrities turned to *Eryn* is of course unknown. But the map was certainly taken seriously in some quarters for at least ten years. It illustrated an essay on Ireland written by Sir John Perrot in 1581,[39] and in 1583 Christopher Saxton included a narrow strip of it in his wall map of England and Wales. All the same Ortelius was bound to lose authority as Englishmen learned more about Ireland. A copy of *Eryn* annotated in English, apparently at some time after the defeat of the Spanish Armada, included a number of anonymous manuscript corrections,[40] but at least the annotator chose to improve on the original rather than simply discarding it. Ortelius kept the same map in later versions of the *Theatrum* and so did his posthumous editors. Others who remained faithful were Gerard de Jode, Janus Bussemacher and William Camden in his capacity as author. Even the occasional chart-maker adopted the Mercator-Ortelius model, its coastline suitably embellished with portolan-style capes and bays.[41] The map's original publisher was less complacent. In his old age Mercator dropped the map of Ireland that lesser cartographers were still copying from him. He had found a better one.

References
1. G.H. Orpen, 'Ptolemy's map of Ireland', *Journal of the Royal Society of Antiquaries of Ireland*, xxiv (1894), pp 115-28; Eoin MacNeill, 'Ireland according to Ptolemy and other non-Irish authorities', *New Ireland Review*, xxvi (1906), pp 6-15. The latest reconstruction of Ptolemy's map *de novo* from the original coordinates is by F.J. Byrne in T.W. Moody, F.X. Martin and F.J. Byrne (eds), *A new history of Ireland*, ix (Oxford, 1984), p. 16.
2. Examples range from Petrus Plancius's map of the British Isles (1592) and John Speed's map of the invasions of Britain and Ireland (1601) to the eighteenth-century maps of Thomas Jefferys and Thomas Kitchin (see below, chapter 7). The most interesting early use of Ptolemaic names on a modern base is in Richard Bartlett's map of Ulster, *c.*1602 (Public Record Office, London, MPF 35).

3. Examples, as interpreted by T.J. Westropp, are Dorrosey, Drocata, Drorox (Dorsey); Dandul, Dondri, Dondazo (Dundalk); Laymerich, Lamerecht, Lanera (Limerick); Slagoi, Singai, Slago (Sligo). See Westropp's 'Early Italian maps of Ireland from 1300 to 1600, with notes on foreign settlers and trade', *Proceedings of the Royal Irish Academy*, xxx C (1913), pp 361-428; and M.C. Andrews, 'The map of Ireland, A.D. 1300-1700', *Proceedings of the Belfast Natural History and Philosophical Society*, 1922-3, pp 16-23. Andrews's large collection of photographs of representations of Ireland in the portolan charts is among the archives of the Royal Geographical Society, London (*Geographical Journal*, lxxxv (1935), pp 105-6; W.A. McComish, 'Early maps of Ireland in the Andrews collection of the Royal Geographical Society', *Geographical Journal*, cxxxiv (1968), pp 306-8). Ireland like other islands is omitted from Tony Campbell's analysis of portolan placenames in J.B. Harley and David Woodward (eds), *The history of cartography*, i (Chicago, 1987), p. 461. Early printed portolan-like representations of Ireland include those of Guillaume Broucson (*c*.1520, a conjectural attribution) and Benedetto Bordone (in *Libro . . . de tutte l'isole del mondo* (Venice, 1528, reprinted Amsterdam, 1966)), both brought to the author's attention by Andrew Bonar Law. The former appears to be the earliest separate printed map of Ireland. It is illustrated, and its names transcribed, in I.G. Philip, 'Early maps', *Antiquity*, xi (1937), pp 486-9.

4. Hugh Brody, 'Maps and journeys' in Finlay MacLeod (ed.), *Togail tir; marking time; the map of the Western Isles* (Stornoway, 1989), p. 135.

5. *Letters and papers, foreign and domestic, Henry VIII*, v (part 2), p. 1077.

6. E.J.S. Parsons, *The map of Great Britain circa A.D. 1360 known as the Gough map* (Oxford, 1958).

7. Edmund Campion, *A historie of Ireland written in the year 1571* (Dublin, 1809), p. 1. For the antiquity of the tradition of characterising countries by their length and breadth see O.A.W. Dilke, 'Cartography in the ancient world: a conclusion' in Harley and Woodward (eds), *History of cartography*, i , p. 276.

8. Examples are *State Papers Henry VIII*, iii, pp 446-7; British Library, Cotton MS Domitian A.18; British Library, Cotton MS Titus B xii, ff. 437, 482 (Munster only); *Calendar of State Papers, Ireland, 1586-9*, p. 232 and *1601-3*, addenda, pp 676-8; Lambeth Palace, Carew MS 621, no. 87.

9. D.G. Kendall, 'Construction of maps from "odd bits of information"', *Nature*, ccxxxi (1971), pp 158-9.

10. British Library, Cotton MS Augustus I, ii, 21.

11. 'Angliae figura', British Library, Cotton MS Augustus I, i, 9. G.R. Crone, *Early maps of the British Isles, A.D. 1000-A.D. 1579* (London, 1961), pp 8, 22-3.

12. Public Record Office, London, MPF 72. Peter Barber points out in a private communication that Burghley's annotations appear on non-Irish maps known to date from the time of Henry VIII.

13. George Lily, *Britanniae insulae*, discussed in Edward Lynam, *The map of the British Isles of 1546* (Jenkintown, 1934).

14. R. Almagia, *Monumenta cartographica Vaticana* (Biblioteca Apostolica Vaticana, 1945), iv, pl. 1. Reproduction in British Library, 188.i.2(5), with note by R.A. Skelton. The Vatican wall maps were made by Antonio Danti from designs by his brother Egnazio Danti (John Marino, 'Administrative mapping in the Italian states' in David Buisseret (ed.), *Monarchs, ministers and maps: the emergence of cartography as a tool of government in early modern Europe* (Chicago, 1992), p. 23). See also Arthur Dürst, 'Die Europa-Karten von Gerard Mercator, 1554-1595', *Cartographica Helvetica*, x (1994), p. 16.

15. Walter Ghim's life of Mercator, English translation in A.S. Osley, *Mercator* (London, 1969), p. 187. Mercator himself makes a similar statement in the 'address to the reader' included with the *Nova descriptio*.

16. Walter Reinhard, *Zur Entwicklung des Kartenbildes der Britischen Inseln bis auf Merkators Karte vom Jahre 1564* (Zschopau, 1909), p. 103; M. van Durme, *Correspondance mercatorienne* (Antwerp, 1959), p. 36; E.G.R. Taylor, *Tudor geography, 1485-1583* (London, 1930), pp 85-6; R.A. Skelton, 'Mercator and English geography in the 16th century', *Duisburger Forschungen*, vi (1962), p. 167; G.R. Crone, *Geographical Journal*, cxxviii (1962), pp 406-10; Sarah Tyacke and John Huddy, *Christopher Saxton and Tudor map-making* (London, 1980), p. 9.

17. Peter Barber, 'England II' in Buisseret, *Monarchs, ministers and maps*, pp 63-4, and p. 88, n. 44.

18. In 1595 Mercator (quoted in Catherine Delano Smith, 'Cartographic signs on European maps and their explanation before 1700', *Imago Mundi*, xxxvii (1985), p. 26) regarded it as normal for west to be at the top of any map whose long axis ran from north to south, presumably because in atlases this conformed better with a double-page opening, but there is no evidence that English cartographers followed this practice in mapping areas other than Ireland.

19. According to Charles Close (*The map of England* (London, 1932), p. 6) Mercator's English miles each contained about nine and a half furlongs.

20. Peter Barber, 'A Tudor mystery: Laurence Nowell's map of England and Ireland', *The Map Collector*, xxii (1983), pp 16-21. In fact there are three manuscript maps of Ireland by Nowell: a miniature version in black ink (British Library, Cotton MS Domitian A.18, f. 97), a map in two sheets, northern and southern, with personal, family and group names in red and all other detail in black (British Library, Cotton MS Domitian A.18, ff. 101-3); and a map of the British Isles, also in red and black with woods in green (British Library, Add. MS 62,540). All apparently derive from a single prototype, though there are differences of detail. The accompanying written description of Ireland gives no help in dating these maps, because (apart from some seventeenth-century additions) it seems to belong to an earlier period. A few Irish names also appear in Nowell's map of Scotland (British Library, Cotton MS Domitian A.18, ff. 98-9).

21. Public Record Office, London, MPF 68.

22. Crone, *Early maps*, p. 27.

23. This conclusion fits well with Peter Barber's suggestion of a Marian date for Mercator's representation of England (private communication, June 1992).

24. Croft to privy council, 10 March 1552, Public Record Office, London, SP 61/4/21. Croft had also been associated with the surveying and mapping of Cork, Kinsale and Baltimore by John Rogers (L.R. Shelby, *John Rogers: Tudor military engineer* (Oxford, 1967), pp 116-17).

25. In 1576 John Dee (quoted by G. de Boer and R.A. Skelton, 'The earliest English chart with soundings', *Imago Mundi*, xxiii (1969), p. 9) reported that Dutch fishermen, 'making perfect charts of all our coasts, round about England, and Ireland, are become (almost) perfecter in them, than the most part of our masters, loadmen, or pilots are'. It is not known what results of these surveys, if any, would have been available to Mercator twelve years earlier.

26. *Anglia II Nova tabula* (Basle, 1540), reproduced in R.W. Shirley, *Early printed maps of the British Isles, 1477-1650* (London, 1973), pl. 10.

27. Pontoy appears in Mercator's maps of Europe (1554) and the world (1569), and in the Vatican map of *c*.1565 (see note 14 above). It may be derived from

'Ponente', used to mean west on early Italian maps of Ireland, or from one of a number of genuine west-coast names incorporating the prefix 'port'. The '1558' map (see above, note 12) shows 'Port Tyme' somewhere off the Mayo coast. In Mercator's world map of 1569 Lampreston appears in England. Another name that Mercator may have obtained from earlier continental maps and which appears in Zalterius is 'Norbowre' (Northburgh), but this castle, though little known, was not fictitious: see James Lydon in Art Cosgrove (ed.), *A new history of Ireland*: ii, *Medieval Ireland* (Oxford, 1987), pp 288, 289.

28.   Mercator to Abraham Ortelius, 22 November 1570, quoted in *The Map Collector*, xxxvii (1986), p. 53.

29.   Public Record Office, London, MPF 72. See above note 12.

30.   Laurence Nowell's map of Scotland (*c*.1565) includes family names but they are omitted from the maps of Abraham Ortelius (1573), John Leslie (1578), Nicholas de Nicolay (*c*.1580, 1583), Gerard Mercator (1595) and John Speed (1610).

31.   Skelton, 'Mercator and English geography', p. 160.

32.   Robert W. Karrow Jnr, *Mapmakers of the sixteenth century and their maps: biobibliographies of the cartographers of Abraham Ortelius, 1570* (Chicago, 1993), pp 387-8.

33.   Rogers to Ortelius, 20 October 1572, J.H. Hessels, *Abrahami Ortelii epistulae* (Cambridge, 1887), p. 100.

34.   Peter Scott and John Goss, 'Important Mercator "discovery" under the hammer', *The Map Collector*, vi (1979), pp 27-35; Sarah Tyacke, 'The atlas of Europe attributed to Gerard Mercator', *Imago Mundi*, xxxi (1979), p. 65.

35.   Connacia, Hultonia, Langinia, Mononia.

36.   The only known copy of this map is British Library, Harleian MS 5938, no. 129.

37.   M.P.R. van den Broeck, 'Facts and speculations on production and survival of Ortelius' *Theatrum orbis terrarum* and its maps', *The Map Collector*, xxxvi (1986), pp 2-12.

38.   R.A. Skelton, 'Bibliographical note' in Abraham Ortelius, *The theatre of the whole world, London 1606* (Amsterdam, 1968), p. v. Dee's small representation of Ireland in 1580 (British Library, Cotton MS Augustus I, i, 1) is strongly reminiscent of Ortelius.

39.   British Library, Sloane MS 2200.

40.   National Library of Ireland, 16.B.11 (3).

41.   Map of Ireland by Joan Martines, 1587, Madrid, Biblioteca Nationale, MS V.3.5, copy in Royal Geographical Society, Andrews collection, box 39a. Among the last of Ortelius's copyists was an unknown nineteenth-century Irish forger taken seriously in 'Ancient map of Ireland, printed from the original copper discovered in Armagh, engraved in 1572', *Notes and Queries*, 2nd series, iv (1857), pp 250-51, 377. A printed flier arguing the authenticity of this 'Armagh' version is in the library of the Royal Society of Antiquaries of Ireland in Dublin.

Chapter 3

'Baptiste's Isle':
Baptista Boazio, 1599

In England the reign of Queen Elizabeth I is always seen as a golden age. In Ireland it was a time of frustration and waste, and for the most part a time of war. English commanders and administrators came and went. Castles and forts were garrisoned and evacuated. Expeditions were mounted, rebels harassed, loyalists conciliated, estates seized, settlers planted, and reputations won or lost – usually lost. Almost every possible cure for the country's troubles was considered, and almost all the cures that did not cost too much were tried. The main result was a huge mass of official writings, many of them surprisingly ambitious and optimistic. Browsing in this rich archive, one can easily forget that until the dawn of the next century the queen failed in almost all her Irish enterprises. (Cartography was one of her few successes.) The worst of all her setbacks came in 1598 during a nationwide rebellion led by Hugh O'Neill, earl of Tyrone, in which a whole English army was routed on the borders of O'Neill's territory in Ulster. At last the truth had to be faced. There was no substitute for men and money in Ireland, and no prospect of success without huge quantities of both. Even then victory was not necessarily guaranteed. In April 1599 the queen's favourite, Robert Devereux, earl of Essex, arrived in Dublin with the largest military force ever yet sent out of England. His twenty-one weeks as lord lieutenant of Ireland were so disastrous that, a year later, the reconquest had to start all over again. In cartography, however, the Essex fiasco had one consequence that deserves attention.

The course of Irish mapmaking at the turn of the century mirrored political events, with Baptista Boazio as Essex's cartographic representative. At first sight Boazio might be mistaken for one of the Italian civil and military engineers whose duties in Tudor England often included surveying, though usually of particular sites rather than large territories. In fact he was an artist who happened to specialise in regional cartography. He is credited with about a dozen assignments in this capacity, most of them opportunistically set in areas that were making military news.[1] His only known appearance in Ireland before the Essex expedition had been in Dublin fifteen years earlier, colouring another author's map of Co. Mayo.[2] He may have seen something of the country on that occasion, but there had subsequently been no trace of him in Ireland's ample documentary record, and Boazio was not a man to take creditable action without leaving traces. His *Irelande* (Figs 3.1, 3.2) was thus a new departure and a major publishing event: the first map of the kingdom to need two copper plates; the first separate map of any country to bear the name of an English bookseller; and the first map to be issued by John Sudbury, who later won fame with England's most successful county atlas.[3] On publication day in September 1599 *Irelande* must have looked impressive enough to those customers who had been eagerly awaiting it: richly coloured (hand colouring was anticipated in the engraver's explanatory text),[4] elaborately decorated, and replete with interesting marginal information.[5] In retrospect it must be ranked with Essex's Irish enterprise as a costly failure, and the relation between the two episodes may have been closer than mere similarity. One of Boazio's earlier maps had shown an attack on Cadiz in which Essex had led the land forces; another depicted the Azores, where Essex had been prominent as a field officer. Both maps had included flattering references to the earl.

This link, if genuine, may help to define the gestation period of Boazio's map. In theory he could have turned his attention to Ireland at any time, especially after Tyrone's rebellion had begun to attract publicity in about 1595. But if Boazio was in some sense a protegé of Essex, he may not have started work until the earl became lord lieutenant in April 1599, or at the earliest when this appointment began to seem highly probable near the end of the previous year. That would have left precious little time for field work.[6] Here is another long-standing problem of map history: how much 'ad-man's licence' can a nicely brought-up student attribute to a famous cartographer? *Irelande* was claimed by its author to have been 'diligently collected and partly surveyed'. In interpreting this carefully worded self-recommendation we must note that of all Boazio's other extant maps only one (of Falmouth Harbour) describes him as its surveyor, while several, including all his other Irish maps, are acknowledged or unacknowledged copies rather than original productions.

'Collecting' therefore seems a more likely role for Boazio than surveying. Indeed one critic has dismissed the words 'partly surveyed' as a euphemism for 'partly invented'.[7] The inventiveness is most obvious in two imaginary features off the north coast, 'Baptiste's Rock' (named after Boazio) and 'Elstrake's Isle' (named after his engraver, Renold Elstrack), though the fact that islands are by definition bigger

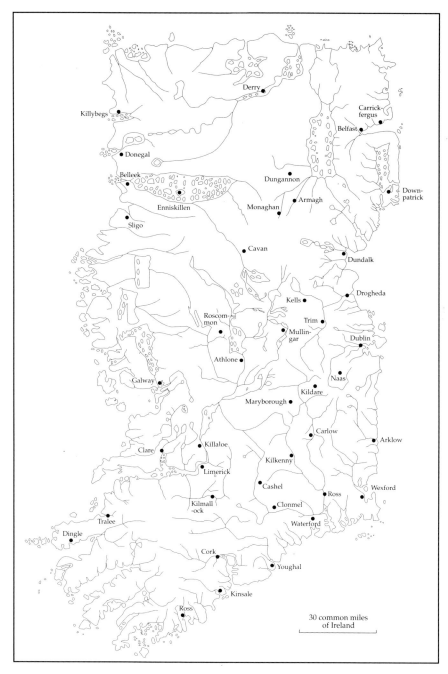

Fig. 3.1   Coasts, rivers and lakes from Baptista Boazio's *Irelande* (London, 1599),
            showing the outline that dominated provincial and national maps from
            the 1580s to the 1600s. The original has west at the top. The towns
            shown here are among those appearing on the map but their names
            have been modernised.

Fig. 3.2   From Baptista Boazio, *Irelande* (London, 1599). Derived, probably at several removes, from Robert Lythe's survey of *c.*1569. Traces from this earlier period include the reference to Sir Peter Carew, who died in 1575. The misplacements of Old Leighlin and Baltinglass are not Lythe's errors, nor is the the use of the River Nore as a provincial boundary.

than rocks may make Elstrack the more probable culprit: a perquisite for map-engravers, as for letterpress printers, is the advantage of having the last word. It may seem humourless to rebuke these follies, which will always be mentioned in fairly indulgent terms by writers on Boazio. Yet anyone who can joke about the perennially sensitive subject of Irish placenames can also joke about being a surveyor rather than a copyist. What finally settles the question of Boazio's originality is that we know whose map he copied. For all its late-Elizabethan embellishments, *Irelande* took its readers back nearly thirty years, almost all the way to Nowell, Goghe and a not-yet-elderly Mercator. Boazio's unnamed source was Robert Lythe, an English military engineer who served in Ireland from 1567 to 1571.[8] Lythe is the real hero of this chapter. To analyse his achievement is to say almost all that needs saying about Boazio. Which makes Boazio not worth looking at unless one is prepared to study Lythe.

* * * * * * * *

Lythe's early career had included a survey of the English pale at Calais. In Ireland he ranged far beyond the Pale. His initial posting to Carrickfergus in September 1567 was a comment on the flaws in existing cartographic coverage of Ulster as revealed for instance in the pattern of annotations written by contemporary users on John Goghe's map of Ireland. It was therefore predictable that Lythe's first Irish assignment should be to map 'the north', where an uncomfortable power vacuum had been left by the recent death of Shane O'Neill, rebellious uncle to the future earl of Tyrone. Such was the wildness of this region, physical and human, that field work proved impossible except in one small area round Carrickfergus and another, the following year, in south-east Co. Down. Thereafter Lythe was directed to more peaceful parts of Ireland. This may now seem an obvious way of ensuring that his journey from England would not be wasted. In fact it was a decision with no recorded sixteenth-century parallel. The usual parsimonious habit of the London government was to map only those parts of Ireland – seldom larger than a province and often much smaller – that happened to be causing trouble at the moment. Successive lord deputies in Dublin did nothing to widen their employers' spatial attention-span; indeed hardly any of them seem to have felt any spontaneous interest in cartography at all. The outstanding exception was the deputy at the time of Lythe's visit, Sir Henry Sidney.[9] Without Sidney the more anglicised parts of Ireland might not have been mapped in detail for another eighty years.

Beginning in 1569 Lythe spent two hard seasons surveying the middle and southern parts of Ireland, wearing out several horses in the process and returning to Dublin lame and almost blind. In the winter of 1570-71 and throughout the following summer he remained under the lord deputy's orders working up his results until illness forced him back to England, apparently for good. His expense account, submitted in December 1571, included the hire of guides through most of the territories and lordships south of a line from Killary Harbour to Strangford Lough.[10] The rest of the country, he had implied in an earlier report, was not yet in a state of 'order and quietness'.[11] Lythe's personal frontier, especially east of the Shannon, lay close to one of Ireland's sharpest and most persistent physical and historical boundaries. To the north of it there were numerous small and closely-spaced lakes, bogs and hills, but not many towns, castles or other conspicuous marks of settlement. Where the drumlin belt began, surveying had stopped.

Large maps have always been physically more vulnerable than small ones and it was inevitable that Lythe's principal work, a 'plat' of Ireland eight and a half feet long and five and a half feet wide, should disappear before any historian had a chance to see it. Of the drafts in his hand that do survive, three cover a large enough area to make them likely ingredients of a general map of Ireland. All are unsigned and undated. One, the 'Petworth' map, is confined to the area of Lythe's own survey (Fig. 3.3).[12] Though certainly in Lythe's style, this includes such gross scribal errors that it may have to be re-interpreted as a copyist's imitation (unless we put the blame on Lythe's impaired eyesight), but at least it is free from the kind of creative editing practised by Boazio and others. Topographical rather than political in emphasis, the Petworth map delimits no territories smaller than a county but gives detailed information on natural resources and physical features, especially coasts and harbours. The two other maps are less articulated physically but richer in territorial and family names. One is 'A single draght of Mounster';[13] the other, the 'Cotton' map, shows the whole island but is too damaged to be fully legible.[14] All three have east at the bottom, like so many sixteenth-century English maps of Ireland, and all three are on a scale of seven to eight miles to an inch which is about half the probable scale of Lythe's missing plat but nearly double that chosen by Mercator in 1564. Happily these surviving specimens of Lythe's work are sufficient for his influence to be easily identified in the maps of other cartographers.

Lythe deserves credit for ignoring the well-established distinction between land and water surveys. His expenses included the hire of boats along the coast from Kinsale to Dingle as well as in the harbours of Cork and Kinsale, the lower Shannon, Lough Corrib and Lough Ree. This was a sound judgement of the relative extent and potential

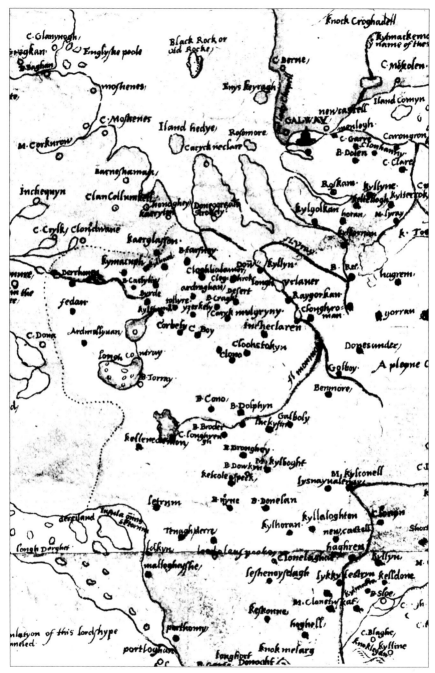

Fig. 3.3   Part of Robert Lythe's map of central and southern Ireland, 1571, West
Sussex Record Office, PHA 9581. County boundaries are shown, but
otherwise this is mainly a map of settlement and economic resources.
Lythe's other maps include more hills, woods, territorial divisions and
dominant families.

importance of the country's main water bodies, Lough Derg being avoided because it bordered on Ely O'Carroll and Ormond, the only areas in the south of Ireland where Lythe had to admit that 'the perambulation of this lordship is not yet travelled'. As early surveys go, this one is quite well documented, not only in the author's expense accounts but in a series of letters which include a signed specimen of his distinctive handwriting. All the same the only clue that he or anyone else let slip about his surveying methods is that in the midlands and south he had 'travelled from five miles to five miles or thereabouts'. However this is interpreted it does not seem to claim very much. Perhaps Lythe meant that there was no square of the size specified in which he had not set foot. But when he did set foot there, what did he do? Like most early maps, Lythe's have the appearance of a finished product. He records no survey stations as such, or any measured lines or angles. He makes no mention of latitude or longitude and although he gives exact values for the mile in his two earliest maps (5000 feet in Belfast Lough and 6000 feet in Co. Down) by the time he reached Munster he was content to leave the 'common miles of Ireland' undefined. As it happens his common mile seems not very different from what became the standard Irish mile of 2240 yards, but this hardly constitutes proof that he ever measured a base line.

In one sense Lythe's covering of tracks had nothing metaphorical about it. Roads are totally omitted from all his maps, a deficiency that surely rules out the traverse as a method of surveying. On the other hand his accuracy along the south-west coast shows that in an environment where linear measurement was impracticable some graduated instrument must have been used to determine angles, and if angles were measured at sea they could also be measured on land, where the requisite instruments would have been easier to manipulate. Unlike England, Ireland had no national system of signal beacons to form the basis of a triangulated map.[15] But it had many hills that were easily identified from a distance, and some of these (like Slieve Coiltia, Mount Leinster and the Great Sugar Loaf) were prominently recorded on Lythe's maps. His coverage of tower houses is also impressive, especially when it is remembered that not all the towers known today had been built before 1571.

Of course it would have been impossible to intersect all the landmarks of central and southern Ireland in two seasons, or even to embrace them in a succession of casual glances. Lythe admitted having drawn on 'the information of the country' as well as his own knowledge and judgement, and guides were one of his heaviest expenses. A guide's duties doubtless included showing the way to the next night's stop, suggesting viewpoints (a service documented in

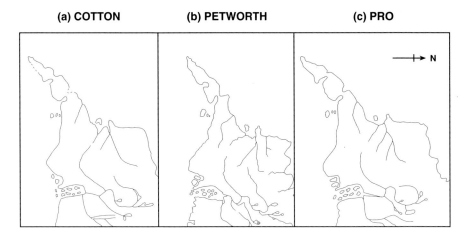

(a) COTTON **(b) PETWORTH** **(c) PRO**

Fig. 3.4   Loop Head, Co. Clare, redrawn from three maps of 1570-71 by Robert
Lythe: (a) British Library, Cotton, Ch. xiii, 42 (b) West Sussex County
Record Office, PHA 9581 (c) Public Record Office, London, MPF 73.
Hills, settlements and names omitted.

Saxton's survey of Wales), helping to find accommodation, and supplying placenames. Guides might also assume a more creative role by
reporting local distance-estimates and by indicating the directions of
places beyond the horizon. There is certainly plenty of cartographic
evidence that Lythe did not see every object he put on his maps. His
work also contains a strong element of personal curvature, best
exemplified where he has left us two or three holograph representations of the same feature (Fig. 3.4).

Lythe's lakes and islands are generally too large, the lakes too lemon-
shaped – evidence of an unstated but apparently common early
cartographer's belief that physical features of the same type in the same
area tend to have the same shape. His rivers are perhaps best
described as wiry-looking, bent rather than curved and with fewer
meanders than in reality. Among his omissions are prominent coastal
features such as Rosslare Point and Raven Point in Co. Wexford, Kerry
Head in north Kerry, and several peninsulas in Connemara. He omitted
the upper courses of many rivers and sometimes the lower courses too:
examples are the Stonestown, Deel and Riverstown rivers in Co. Louth,
the Feale in north Kerry, the Dereen in Co. Carlow, and all the western
tributaries of the Suir. He occasionally linked a tributary river with the
wrong mainstream: his Funshion flows into the Awbeg instead of the
Blackwater, his Triogue into the Barrow instead of the Bauteogue, his
Silver into the Shannon instead of the Brosna. His errors of duplication
are less easily explained, especially where they involved repeating long

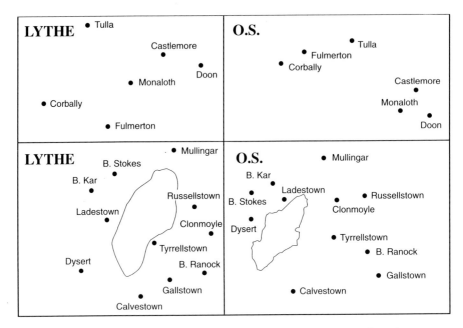

Fig. 3.5   Selected locations from Robert Lythe's map of central and southern
Ireland, 1571 (West Sussex County Record Office, PHA 9581), compared
with Ordnance Survey locations on approximately the same scale.
Above, part of Co. Clare; below, part of Co. Westmeath.

stretches of river like the Nore west of Abbeyleix and the Inny. These
parallelisms might arise from independent sightings of the same feature
on two or more separate occasions, or perhaps from verbal reports of
its existence collected at different places.

Other unusual errors affect the representation of points as opposed
to lines. In most early topographical surveys, inaccuracy increases with
distance and errors between nearby settlements are too small to be
perceptible without a close comparison of early and modern maps,
perhaps close enough to require the application of 'cartometry'. This
generalisation is usually applicable to Lythe, but in some places his
local errors are improbably bad, almost as if he knew nothing whatever
about the relative positions of A, B and C except that they were all
within a few miles of D (Fig. 3.5). All in all, his 'survey' seems to have
had two main constituents: on the one hand his own sketches,
estimates and instrumental readings; on the other, a kind of verbal and
gestural traverse in which he gave graphic form to the information
supplied by his guides. This information may itself have been
sometimes oral, sometimes written, sometimes conceivably sketched.

All that can be said for certain on this point is that at least some of Lythe's spellings are unlikely to have been obtained from local residents. 'Ghildare' for 'Kildare' is the most glaring of his personal idiosyncrasies: most Lythe imitators knew enough to restore the correct form. More pervasive is his cockney's trick of adding an initial 'h' to names like 'Esker' and 'Aghadoe'.[16]

*   *   *   *   *   *   *   *   *

Like several other early cartographers in Ireland, Lythe expressly disclaimed artistic talent. His style was plain and functional, but he knew what a professionally drawn map should look like, and he gradually perfected a neat and legible cartographer's script. His choice of subject-matter – coasts, inland water, mountains, principal settlements, territorial divisions – was characteristic of his time, not unlike Mercator's allowing for the difference of scale, though Lythe judged informal and wide-ranging written notes to be more permissible in manuscript surveys addressed to a small audience than they would be in a published map. The rationale of his and other contemporary surveys was well expressed by Sidney's Irish secretary, Edmund Tremayne, in a note for his master that unmistakably refers to Lythe's map:[17]

> . . . it will be liked for that you shall make a general description of the whole realm. There is not so plain a way to make demonstration thereof as by the view of that perfect cart that your lordship hath caused to be taken in hand . . . whereby you shall have occasion to describe every part of it with their frontiers, and all the borders, havens, creeks, and rivers with other notable commodities. By the same your lordship is able to describe every man his country, of what power he is, and what he hath been, and how it is neighboured, what quarrels he hath, and how every war each of them is affected. [Also] how strait you found the English Pale, and how it is now enlarged. The places that be fortified already will appear. And so may you with good commodity thereupon express what your opinion is for fortification in any other place that your lordship shall think good. And so of the bridge that your lordship hath builded [at Athlone], and any other that you think meet to be builded or repaired. And finally by these means you shall describe what commodity hath grown of such things as are done and what her highness shall embrace by proceeding onward ever abating cost behind as she shall bestow it forward.

This was asking a lot from any map, and no doubt Tremayne meant to imply among other things that graphics are most effective when accompanied by text. But clearly the main preoccupations of an Anglo-Irish cartographer and his clients were military. In a report to Cecil on the contents of his surveys the only settlement-features that Lythe himself specified were towns and castles. The word 'town' in this context was unhelpfully vague. For the Irish historian it is best taken to include every walled settlement and all other places of comparable size. These Lythe identified by profile building symbols, typically a tower with attached 'hall', and by writing their names in capital letters. Castles were not distinctively symbolised, despite his evident interest in them, a non-committal small circle being used for any habitation that was not a town in the sense defined above. Irish settlement history is too badly documented for these symbols to be deciphered with any great confidence. They are unlikely all to have denoted fortifications. Among the thirty-six sites recorded by Lythe in Co. Carlow, for example, fourteen have no castle known to local historians. Nor is it likely that Lythe mapped all the castles standing in his survey area at the time of his visit. His main personal predilection, doubtless strategically motivated, was for those on or near the coast. Otherwise he showed a certain preference for isolated castle-sites, though the distinction between sparsely and densely encastellated regions remained one of the most striking features of his survey.

Lythe marked archbishoprics and bishoprics in the same form as Mercator and perhaps indirectly or directly under Mercator's influence, but he made no claim to notice lesser ecclesiastical sites. Although he identified the names of one-time monastic centres with the prefix 'M', such places were often omitted unless they had some secular importance, and the same seems to have been true of parish centres. Old churches and round towers like Taghadoe, Co. Kildare, or Timahoe, Co. Leix, were evidently not included as of right. At settlements with both church and castle some distance apart, as at Swords, Co. Dublin, it was the castle-site that found a place on the map. For places with neither castle nor church the only long-lasting category available to modern settlement scholars is the townland. Here the selectivity of Lythe's coverage is beyond all doubt. What remains uncertain is whether he chose names at random or to achieve an even distribution of script or whether he considered some townlands more important than others. How to make this last judgement on a small-scale map is a problem that has baffled every generation of cartographers in Ireland and Lythe had little chance of solving it in the time at his disposal. It is however arguable that for these undefended settlements to deserve point-symbols the houses must have been clustered together and not scattered over their respective townlands. This theory has also been applied (without any justification being considered necessary) to the settlement-symbols on Timothy Pont's late sixteenth-century maps of Scotland.[18] Of course it does not imply that Lythe's record of house-clusters was any more complete than that of castles or churches.

Contrary to some modern historical opinion, Elizabethan public servants seldom wasted energy on political propaganda when addressing their own colleagues. Lythe is unlikely to have felt any particular sympathy with Ireland, but he did manage to avoid cartographic jingoism. Thus the legend 'wher Englyshmen first landed' at Baginbun, Co. Wexford, seems subtly to put his fellow countrymen in perspective, as just one incident from Ireland's past, to be matched by his only other historical inscription, an obscure reference to the landing of the 'chief captains of the mahowmets' in Co. Cork.[19] And although at first sight his map seems dominated by densely massed settlements of Anglo-Norman origin, he can be seen on closer inspection to give full weight to the immaterial power of the family, whether native or Anglo-Irish. Gaelic names abound, both personal and territorial. Legends are cited without comment – pasture of mice, speaking stones, devil's bollocks. Unfamiliar names are glossed or translated rather than suppressed, as in 'Knockshebayne, mount of pleasure'. Sometimes indeed the translation process is anti-imperialistically reversed, as where Lythe adopts the Irish form 'B[aile]—' for many names which in every other source are anglicised as '— town'.

Elsewhere Lythe spells the same native name differently on different maps as if edging towards a definitive version, but for elements within a name, like 'Slew' for 'Sliabh' meaning 'mountain', he sometimes makes a deliberate attempt at standardisation. Most important of all, he preserves a multitude of near-Gaelic names for territories, settlements, rivers, lakes and mountains recorded on no other map. In Lythe the past appears indeed as another country, its landmarks and values different from those of today. One remembers T. Jones Hughes's famous reference to 'a timeless world of universal themes'.[20] But Lythe's world was not really timeless. Many of his names were to be totally forgotten except by cartographic specialists, and he himself followed his master Sidney in seeing Ireland mainly as a field for economic development.

Like Mercator before him, Lythe failed to give his readers a united Ireland. As he implicitly confessed to Cecil, the northern section of the Cotton map was not based on his own surveys. It must therefore represent the best outline that he could find on earlier maps, whether those of Sidney in Dublin or Cecil in London. Unfortunately the illegible parts of his Cotton map include a good deal of central and eastern Ulster, but several Lythe-based maps by other artists (including Boazio) show the whole island and most of them agree about the shape of Ulster, a shape that matches the Ulster of Lythe's Cotton map wherever comparison is possible. This northern common denominator is markedly cruder and less accurate than the rest of Ireland, suggesting that it may have been enlarged from a source-map as small as Nowell's or Mercator's. Its main features are an improbably square outline with one corner at Fair Head and the other at a point that modern maps place half-way down the west coast of Donegal. Inland, Lythe chooses a long north-south Lough Neagh and a long west-east Lower Lough Erne in the manner of the 1560s. There are also extensive woodlands, especially beside the lakes, and a notably sparse distribution of settlement by the standards that he himself had set further south.

The main inlets of Lythe's Ulster, recognisable from their names or situations but never from their individual shapes, include Lough Foyle, Lough Swilly, Gweedore Bay, Killybegs Harbour and the mouth of Lough Esk. Despite the prevailing air of wildness, the mountains of Donegal are badly underemphasised, with only two hill masses, Silver Hill and Hawk's Rock, both named in English contrary to Lythe's usual practice. (He was probably the last knowledgeable cartographer in Irish history to signal wildness by extrapolating woods rather than mountains.) This whole northern area resembles Nowell's outline more than any other that survives. Since Nowell's is the best of the earlier maps the similarity is a compliment to both men.

Altogether Lythe transformed the map of Ireland to a degree unequalled by any other cartographer except William Petty. Even when filtered through the inadequate medium of Boazio's *Irelande* his achievement remains impressive. Boazio showed 1861 placenames, as compared with the 388 in Mercator's *Nova descriptio*. Mercator had shown 46 identifiable rivers, 14 lakes and 9 hill masses; for *Irelande* the corresponding figures were 117, 43 and 44. Among the rivers appearing for the first time in Lythe-based maps were the Maigue, Fane, Dee, Clare, Little Brosna, Blackwater (Co. Down), Main, Glyde, Funshion, Awbeg, Goul, Bann (Co. Wexford), Flesk, Newry, Quoile, Camlin, Camoge, Maine and King's. New lakes were Mask, Carra, Ramor, Owel, Lene, Cooter, Graney, Muckno, Guitane, Fea, Doon, Kinale and Gur.

The planimetric accuracy of a map is harder to express than its geographical content. The test used in this book (and described by Matthew Stout in the appendix) is a statistical comparison between the relative positions of a sample of identifiable points in an early map with those of the same points as shown by the Ordnance Survey. The result is expressed as a single number (RMS or root mean square error)

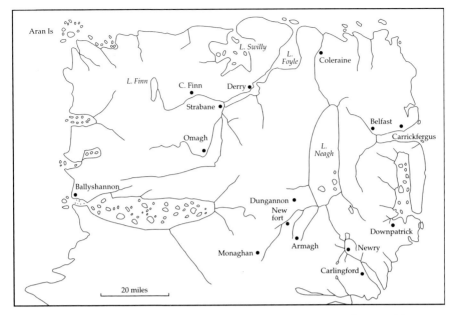

Fig. 3.6   Ulster, *c.*1587, redrawn and simplified from Trinity College, Dublin, MS 743. Probably based on Lythe's map of Ireland, which in most of this area was itself derivative. Spelling modernised. The original has west at the top and also shows tree symbols, hills, a few territorial boundaries and many more territorial and settlement names.

whose magnitude provides an overall measure of inaccuracy. Again Lythe suffers when Boazio is adopted as his surrogate, but Boazio's RMS, at 0.239, is substantially less than the 0.259 scored by Mercator's map of 1564. Other tests relevant to Lythe's accuracy will be given below in chapter 4.

*   *   *   *   *   *   *   *

For all its outstanding merit, Lythe's survey was slow to make an impact in the worlds of international scholarship and cartography. Christopher Saxton had apparently never seen it when he made his map of England and Wales; nor had William Camden when writing the first edition of his *Britannia*. Nor, presumably, had Raphael Holinshed when he praised Saxton's map of England while deploring the absence of good maps for Scotland and Ireland.[21] The breakthrough came when provincial maps of Ireland unquestionably based on Lythe were drawn by various artists to illustrate a treatise on Ireland apparently compiled in 1586 or 1587 (Fig. 3.6).[22] Lythe himself and his achievement were mentioned in print, apparently for the only time until the nineteenth

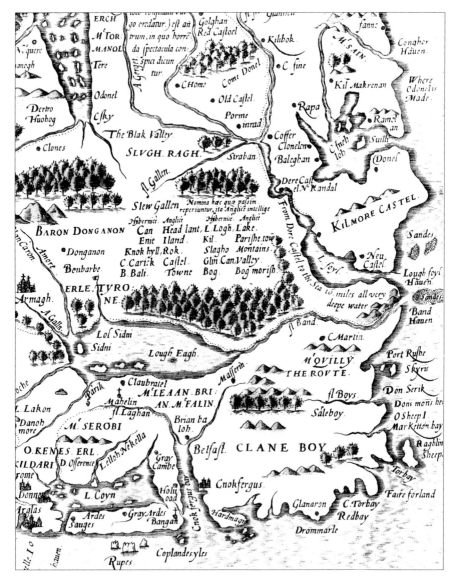

Fig. 3.7   Northern Ireland, from Jodocus Hondius, *Hyberniae novissima descriptio* (Amsterdam, 1591). The first printed map so far discovered to have been based on the work of Robert Lythe, full of gross copying errors but with occasional details not found in other maps, e.g. 'From Dore Castel to the Sea 10 miles all very deepe water'. The table of placename elements anticipates a slightly different list in Boazio's map.

century, in John Hooker's continuation of Holinshed's *Chronicle*, published in 1587,[23] and four years later his map finally reached the public domain in a much-reduced and garbled version for which credit was taken by the Dutch engraver Jodocus Hondius (Fig. 3.7).[24] But

Mercator, in his famous atlas of 1595, was the first cartographer to print a derivative of Lythe (Fig. 3.8) that gave any impression of its character – which needless to say was utterly different from Mercator's map of 1564 – and this was weakened, even in some contemporary eyes, by the author's well-intended effort to incorporate additional information in Ulster.[25] Other mapmakers with debts to Lythe included Petrus Plancius, John Speed and of course Boazio. None of these beneficiaries gave their informant's name. Perhaps they did not know it.[26]

It is impossible to say how Lythe's findings reached his disciples. The three likely recipients of his original maps were the queen's secretary, her lord deputy of Ireland, and the queen herself. The last two must be left out of account. Nothing is known of the royal map collection at this period,[27] but it is unlikely to have been laid open to professional copyists. As for the Irish lord deputies, with the possible exception of Sidney we cannot be sure that any of them maintained a map archive: they were certainly never able to supply duplicates of maps that got lost in London. But Secretary Cecil was a voracious collector. More than anyone else, he had the means of assembling a single master map of Ireland from the best possible materials, of keeping it up to date, and of reproducing it in various suitable formats. He seems to have done none of these things. Instead, he kept the maps he was given, studied and annotated them, apparently over a long period, and met each new crisis by asking for a new map of the area concerned, regardless of the quality of the old ones.[28] None of the maps he acquired between 1571 and his death in 1598 owes anything to Lythe, perhaps a hint that Lythe's results were not yet widely diffused.

Some Cecil items eventually began to turn up in other collections (the Petworth and Cotton maps are probably cases in point) but this is not positively known to have happened until the seventeenth century. At any rate it is hard to picture Cecil in the role of publicist deliberately launching Lythe upon the cartographic community.[29] The maps in the treatise of 1586-7 are more likely to have been made originally for one of his colleagues on the queen's council. Another possible channel for information was Lythe himself. He showed no perceptible interest in cartographic fame, but drafts that he had preserved for future reference may have become available after his death – for which some time in the 1580s is as good a conjectural date as any. Continental cartographers may have been the prime movers here. Mercator's son Rumold was in London at various times during the relevant time-span, including the year 1585, and he is known to have acted as his father's representative. Another son, Michael, lodged in London in 1589. Jodocus Hondius also moved to London in about 1585 and remained there for more than twenty years, associated for part of that time with

Fig. 3.8   South-east Ireland, from *Hibernia australis* in Gerard Mercator, *Atlas* (Duisburg, 1595). Though often described as a version of Hondius (see Fig. 3.7), this is much more detailed and accurate: it derives from Lythe's survey by a line of descent that cannot now be traced.

the Dutch engraver Pieter van den Keere. Data transmitted to Mercator during this period would simply have been added to the Duisburg stockpile, awaiting their turn on the conveyor belt that led towards his great atlas of 1595. If any of this material passed through Hondius's hands, it would have been natural enough for him to seek priority with his own single-sheet map of Ireland.

All this is highly conjectural, but the idea of two streams of Lythe influence, official and private, English and continental, can draw additional support from the purely cartographic evidence, though admittedly the same evidence points to a degree of inter-contamination between the streams. The establishment of causal relations between derivative maps or other artifacts is a difficult task. It is usually achieved through errors – or, more strictly, through differences between representation and referent. The principle involved is that when two maps resemble each other in ways not due to copying from reality it may be unlikely that their authors would have independently made the same decision (especially when this decision entails a choice among many possibilities) and more likely that there is some genetic link between them. A widespread belief among cartographic historians is that if two maps share the same deviations from reality the later has been copied from the earlier rather than both having been copied from a hypothetical third map, on the unspoken premise that if such a third map had existed the historian would know about it. Nowhere is this highly dubious assumption less justified than in the study of Lythe's Irish maps and their descendants. In fact the family tree of Lythe's 'descent' probably includes as many lost as extant members.

One conclusion that does seem well established is that the Hondius and Mercator versions of Lythe, though neither is a copy of the other, share several features not found in most English derivatives. Some of these features probably originated with Lythe's own duplicates, others were introduced by early copyists and propagated by their successors. Boazio may have had some connection with the continental group. He may even have been the 'J.Baptiste' with whom Michael Mercator is known to have lodged in London, but his own map belongs unmistakably in the English stream.

*   *   *   *   *   *   *   *   *

Boazio's scale of about ten statute miles to one inch is considerably smaller than Lythe's but larger than that of any previously published map. He shows fewer names than had appeared in Mercator's *Atlas* (a tribute to the economy of Mercator's style) but many that both Hondius and Mercator had omitted.[30] His closest affinity is with Lythe's separate map of Munster. *Irelande* repeats two highly distinctive inscriptions from that map – 'Carbre begyneth at the haven of Kynsale and endet at myssyne head' (the last name corrupted by Boazio into 'Wisenbias') and, near Tralee, 'Whyt stones poynted lyke dyamonds' (Fig. 3.9). The same relationship appears in the following comparison of certain Boazio spellings with those of Lythe's three most important maps.

Petworth	Cotton	Munster	Boazio
Artullye	Ardtully	Arthully	Arthulli
C none	C noue	C Non	C Non
Donase	donenas	donasse	Donasse
Golden Castell	Golden Castell	C Gold	Ca Gold
lyston	Lystoll	lystoule	Listoule

Yet Boazio's Munster cannot have been copied directly and exclusively from Lythe's surviving 'Single draght' of the province, for it includes several names omitted from that map, among them Kellant in Co. Clare; Capell rocks, Kauerogh, Kinalmega, Mologheden and O Lyre in Co. Cork; Knockseon, McBreen, Monile and The Valei of Goshenoch in Co. Tipperary; and Caruian, Crogay and McThomas in Co. Waterford. Probably the 'Single draght' was closely similar in its depiction of Munster to some lost Lythe map of Ireland as a whole or perhaps to one of a lost regional series.

At all events the prototype of *Irelande* may well have been pieced together (or, as Boazio put it, 'collected') by someone less knowledge-able than its original surveyor. A possible sign of its derivation from two separate maps is the broken line that runs from Olderfleet through the middle of Killultagh between Belfast Lough and Lough Neagh and then past O'Hanlon's Country and into the Fews. This boundary had no existence on the ground, and eventually a not very successful attempt was made to erase it from Boazio's printing plate. More than anything else it seems to mark the limit of Lythe's original survey and to have been drawn as an aid to fitting-on the unsurveyed portions of Ulster and north Connacht. One hint to the same effect is an awkward fictitious bend in the River Suck at the edge of the survey area (some distance north of its nearest real-world counterpart west of Athleague), an error which Lythe himself had managed to avoid perpetrating in the Cotton map. Another possible junction was between Munster and Leinster, where some post-Lythian misunderstanding has created an imaginary 'South Brestnagh' (Brosna) river joining the Shannon from the east at the head of Lough Derg.

Whatever the details of the compilation process, one general inference seems clear. Somehow Boazio must have gained access to

Fig. 3.9   Parts of Kerry and west Cork from Boazio's *Irelande*, 1599. Based on
Lythe, with an especially close relation to his 'Single draght of Mounster'
(Public Record Office, London, MPF 73). This is part of the area that
Lythe surveyed by sea and where he did most to improve upon earlier
maps.

Lythe's work at a comparatively early stage of its 'English' descent (of course this does not mean that he saw any particular map at an early stage in its physical history), because his copy lacks certain errors, illustrated below, that are common to the 'treatise' maps of the 1580s and to John Speed's map of 1610.

Lythe	Boazio	Treatise	Speed
Berde	Birdes	Bore	Bord
Can Boles	Canboles	Can Bolos	Can Bolos
Canleame	Can Leame	Can Leane	Can Leane
C.Arynes	C.Ariens	Carpene	C.Arpenes
Enys Catu	Enis Catu	Enis Catne	Enis Catne

This obviously stands to Boazio's credit: his map would have looked plausible enough even if he had based it entirely on the printed works of Hondius and Mercator. (The credit may be slightly less if he escaped temptation by obtaining his own copy of Lythe before those works appeared.) He also earns thanks from modern historical geographers for preserving certain names and inscriptions which, although they doubtless originated with Lythe, appear in none of Lythe's surviving maps and in no other Lythe derivative. These included hills (Slewbore, Co. Wexford), islands (I. Donecogh, Co. Cork), lakes (Lough Den, Co. Wicklow), rivers (Baltra, Co. Dublin), settlements (Bally Boy, Co. Louth), territories (Tirells, Co. Westmeath), woods (Wood of helgar, Co. Dublin), and finally hydrographic notes such as 'Betweene the Sandes and the Shore is 7 fathom' off the Wicklow coast.

In his dedication to the queen, Boazio stressed the material aspects of geography, promising a map

> Wherein your highness may distinctly see
> What havens, rocks, sands or towns in Ireland be.

This was poetic licence, especially if 'towns' is interpreted in the broadest of its possible senses – the sense chosen by Boazio himself when he defined the word 'bale' as 'small town'. Not only did *Irelande* omit many of Lythe's 'ballys' and other habitation names, but the names it selected were far from being the most significant. A test of early (and no doubt late) Elizabethan settlement-status was to have appeared in one or more of the relatively small-scale maps of Ireland made during the 1560s before the time of Lythe's visit. Thus Mercator in 1564 had noticed Ballyadams (Queen's Co.), Ballyhack (Co. Wexford), Croghan (King's Co.), and Loghill (Co. Limerick). Laurence Nowell's names included Bray (Co. Wicklow), Lea (Queen's Co.), Rathangan (Co. Kildare) and St Michaels (Co. Kerry). John Goghe, most discriminating of the sixties trio, had chosen Adare (Co. Limerick),

Castle Island (Co. Kerry), Fethard (Co. Wexford), Holycross (Co. Tipperary), Jerpoint (Co. Kilkenny) and Tipperary town. All these places were shown by Lythe and all were ignored in *Irelande*. Boazio's real strength, strangely disregarded in his dedication, was in recording personal and territorial names, if strength is the right word for what by 1599 was inevitably a tissue of anachronisms. In this category he copied almost all that Lythe's 'Single draght' had to offer for Munster, despite his own smaller scale, and elsewhere he recorded a number of such names that are otherwise absent from the Lythe family. Some of these were to gain currency as barony or regional names, others had no cartographic future except in the maps of academic historians. Examples from both categories include Ericonagh, Fartollog, Ferigall, Forte, Irrice, Maghery, O'Dempsie and Shellbren. In ranking 'tribalism' and territoriality above buildings and settlements Boazio with all his faults had got to the heart of the matter.

Awareness of the Irish dimension is also signalled by Boazio's marginal note explaining some dozen native name elements. The words defined were Glyn, a wood; Can, a promontory or headland; Carick, a rock; Knock, a hill; Slew, a mountain; B or Bale, a small town; Kill, a village or parish town; Lough, a lake or great pool; Enis, an island; Mo., a monastery; Mc, the son of a chief man; O, the chief man of a race or kindred. Here Boazio had been anticipated by Hondius in 1591.[31] Their tables differ somewhat in content, orthography and lay-out, Hondius defining 'glin' as 'valley' and 'Carick' as 'castle'. On the other hand they both point towards a common source by idiosyncratically translating 'kill' as 'parish town'. Perhaps that common source – presumably Lythe – had provided alternative meanings for 'glin' and 'carrick'. Boazio may have had his own placenames policy, however. (He seems alone among Elizabethan Anglo-Irish cartographers in systematically preferring 'i' to 'y', no doubt a sign of his Italian origin.) If so, it did not save him from errors like the following in Co. Meath.

Lythe (Petworth)	Boazio	Speed 1610
Haghra	Aglira	Agra
Corles	B.Cortus	B.Corlus
Frequones	Fregens	Frequens
Ghyrley	Ghirloy	Churley
B.Monk	Monstron	Monceto[wn]
Myrath	Kildath	Mirath
Myvalla	Menalia	–

* * * * * * * *

What, after twenty-eight years, did Boazio add to Lythe? If he was as diligent a collector as his own words imply, he surely ought not to have ignored the map of Mayo which he himself had coloured in 1584. This was more detailed than Lythe's and therefore apparently better (to us with hindsight its superiority is obvious), and the colourist was believed to have kept a copy of it for himself. How far he should be blamed for disregarding the other excellent manuscript regional maps of Ireland made by Lythe's successors in the 1580s and 1590s is a moot point. Having declared himself a loyal subject of the queen Boazio could at first sight be judged by stricter standards in this respect than non-resident foreigners like Mercator and Ortelius. The truth is simpler and crueller: loyal or not, he had been lucky to get a sight of unpublished official maps by any author; he was not himself a government servant, and he is unlikely to have had any particular claim on Cecil or Cecil's maps, especially if he had some connection with Cecil's enemy, Essex.

As always, it was non-geographical additions that proved easier to 'collect'. Boazio sought to civilise the image of Ireland by the application of decorative rather than utilitarian cartography. His margins describe Elizabeth as its queen and defender of its faith. He flaunts the crown and the royal arms, and sets the harp of Ireland alongside the (more colourful) cross of St George, which also adorns the mastheads of two ships significantly placed off the most remote parts of the coastline, the same saint's name appearing as an alternative designation for the Irish Sea.[32] Lest there be any political misunderstanding, all inscriptions are in the queen's English instead of the Latin still customary among European cartographers.

Within the body of his map Boazio's main additions are territorial. Lythe's omission of provincial names and boundaries was doubtless simply a sign that his maps had not been finished. In fact since 1569 the provinces had been even more worthy of notice than in Mercator's time, for in that year Munster and Connacht were given their own official presidents and councils. Boazio supplied the provinces, but very badly: he put west Kilkenny in Munster, Leitrim and a large part of south Ulster in Leinster. Even Ortelius had done better than that. Boazio's county geography is more reliable, with one major exception: he repeats the town names 'Kingstown' and 'Queenstown' adopted by Lythe (the reigning queen was thought to dislike 'Philipstown' and 'Maryborough') but then spoils the effect by inventing the anomalous forms 'Co. Kingstown' and 'Co. Queenstown'.

Boazio's settlement-symbols show an optimism that went well beyond Mercator's. Substantial-looking spires and towers give an urban, almost metropolitan status to what were probably no more than single churches with a cluster of huddled cabins. Some of these could be explained as victims of the 'episcopal fallacy', for instance Ardfert, Ferns and Kilfenora – a fault compounded in Boazio's key by calling them 'bishops' towns'.[33] Others, like Buttevant and Haghadow, had no very obvious excuse. Lythe's Cotton map had also overdone the bishops' seats and bestowed an unjustifiably large symbol on the purely secular settlement of Castleconnell, Co. Limerick. But there was one oddity that had no precedent in Lythe: in *Irelande* any place with 'castle' in its name was automatically given a massive rectangular tower, coloured red (presumably under Boazio's supervision) and topped with a large flag as if currently in military occupation, a gesture that few English readers were likely to find amusing in the calamitous summer of 1599.

At Boazio's chosen scale the scope for recording recent landscape change was limited. His chief topographical addition to Lythe was the 'new fort' on the north-west bank of the River Blackwater below Benburb, built in 1597 as a gateway to Ulster in succession to a fort of 1575 on the opposite side of the river, and recently notorious as the destination of the English army defeated by Hugh O'Neill (Fig. 3.10). There are no obvious omissions in the military-urban category. Most Elizabethan building operations, such as they were, had been at places like Carrickfergus and Dungannon that could have appeared as important settlements on even the earliest English maps of Ireland. This was a revealing comment on government ineffectiveness since 1571 – and also on the skill shown by the Anglo-Normans centuries earlier in choosing strategic sites. At the lowest level of the settlement hierarchy Boazio's inflationary bias may be represented in his marginal list of subjects by the term 'village', which evidently refers to localities shown on the map by small circles.[34] For English readers this was a somewhat grandiose description of places as insignificant as, for example, the Co. Limerick settlements of B.Bec, B.Laghera, Pallace, Cargonie, Newton and Clograta.[35] Unfortunately there is no means of knowing whether Boazio conceived the village category himself or whether he was following some other Lythe-based classification now lost.

Changes in administrative and proprietorial geography had been easier to effect since 1571. Boazio shows eight new counties in Ulster, including Carrickfergus and Coleraine but not Tyrone or Donegal. He now had to distinguish unshired areas by adding the word 'country' to the names of the appropriate Irish families. In this territorial classification he differs from contemporary official sources. Perhaps he meant to include only those counties that might (on an optimistic view) be regarded as genuinely operational. His judgement on this point if not wholly reliable should at least have been up to date, some of the details in question having been added to the northern plate of *Irelande*

Fig. 3.10   Part of eastern Ulster from Boazio's *Irelande*, 1599. The curved line from
Fuse (Fews) to Olderfleet Haven is not a territorial boundary. It roughly
marks the limit of Lythe's surveys of 1567-8 and may be a 'construction
line' representing the junction of two of Boazio's source maps.

after proof impressions had been printed. Another change noted by Boazio was the transfer of Clare from Munster to Connacht in recognition of the Shannon as a natural frontier. At least he got this right.

Boazio's last-minute administrative revisions should perhaps be credited to his proof-readers rather than himself. With proprietorial changes he was much less effective. Only two of the territorial magnates named on the map had appeared since Lythe's day. One was Thomas Smith in the Ards, publicised by Ortelius in 1573 and consequently an easy catch for later cartographers. The other was Henry Bagenal in south Co. Down, an unfortunate choice in 1599 as he had been killed in the battle of the Blackwater a year earlier. There is no mention of the new land-owning families settled in Munster during the 1580s. On the other hand *Irelande* was still haunted by such long-dead celebrities as Turlough Luineach, Caloe McBrian McMahond, the earl of Clancarre, and Sir Peter Carew; the most eminent of all these ghosts being the earl of Desmond, who had been attainted, defeated and beheaded in the great Munster rebellion of 1583. Proprietorially, then, this is a portrait not of Essex's Ireland but of Sidney's, which is why several good historians have been mistaken about its date. Yet in some fundamental respects the map remained as topical as ever; for example, there was still a real-life difference in settlement patterns between north and south that had been unaffected by all the queen's politicking and war-making.

Most of Boazio's physiographical innovations were among the northern lakes and harbours. Lythe's Cotton map, being unfinished, had shown nothing but water in Lough Erne, a lake whose many islands were its chief claim to attention. Boazio put in the islands, but by a familiar twist of geographical logic, together with a mapmaker's normal preference for land over water, he also took the opportunity of scattering non-existent archipelagoes across Lough Neagh, Lough Foyle, McSwyne Bay, Lower Donegal Bay and the mouth of the River Erne. Here he was extending a policy of 'insulation' common among earlier cartographers like Ortelius and Hondius. Elsewhere his creativity took the even less original form of connecting different river basins. *Irelande's* Lough Cong drains into Blacksod Bay instead of into the Moy; its Lough Mask into the Shannon instead of into Lough Corrib; and its Lough Corrib into the Suck as well as into Galway Bay.

* * * * * * * * *

Any cartographer wishing to perpetuate his own name must hope to see it between the covers of a printed atlas. Boazio lived to enjoy this

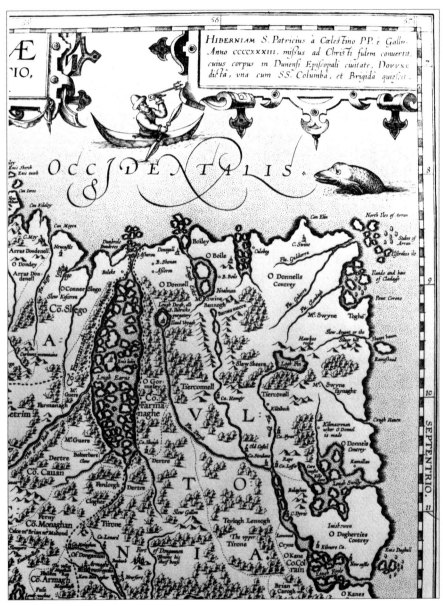

Fig. 3.11   North-west Ireland from Jan Baptist Vrients, *Irlandiae accurata descriptio auctore Baptista Boazio* in Abraham Ortelius, *The theatre of the whole world* (London, 1606). A smaller version of Boazio's *Irelande* and often confused with it, but recognisable from the scale of latitudes and longitudes added by a conscientious atlas-maker. The duplication of Asseroe near the border of Ulster and Connacht suggests that Boazio may have worked by combining provincial maps.

experience when a new version of *Irelande* appeared in the last editions of Ortelius's *Theatrum*, including the English edition published by Jan Baptist Vrients at Antwerp in 1606 (Fig. 3.11).[36] Aesthetically the map gained by the change of engraver, and from a reduction to two-thirds the original scale. Geographically too it was a change for the better, as several blatant anachronisms disappeared – probably by good luck – in the process of scaling-down. Vrients's only major addition was in the margins. Boazio could now claim authorship of the first Englishman's published map of Ireland with its own scales of latitude and longitude (though not with a graticule), but he is unlikely to have supplied these himself and in any case they were not much to boast about. Vrients's projection had the merit of being non-cylindrical; on the other hand his central meridian ran out of sight somewhere in the Atlantic and all his latitudes were too high, no doubt under the influence of Mercator. As it turned out, the life of the *Theatrum* had nearly run its chronological course, though 1350 copies of the new map are thought to have appeared in it,[37] enough to ensure Boazio a place in modern reference books and (occasionally) in modern map dealers' catalogues. Most of his influence on seventeenth-century cartographers was probably exercised through Vrients's *Theatrum*, reaching a maximum when the French cartographer Nicolas Sanson actually named Boazio as his source for Ireland.

This was more than Boazio deserved. The Tyrone war had inspired a new wave of map-making in Ulster which among knowledgeable readers quickly made his rendering of the province out of date. Indeed he himself acted as copyist for at least two regional maps that made nonsense of his own recently published work.[38] We have now met so many divergencies between manuscript and printed cartography that Boazio's failure to revise Ulster for Vrients can hardly seem surprising, especially as such a revision would have damaged the sales that his own larger map might still reasonably expect after only three years. How the original *Irelande* fared with the general public is difficult to say. The fact that only three copies now survive is no proof of failure in a map that never formed part of any atlas.[39] One thing is clear, however: as an evolutionary force its life was short.

References

1. Edward Lynam, 'English maps and map-makers of the sixteenth century', *Geographical Journal*, cxvi (1950), pp 7-28; J.H. Andrews, 'Baptista Boazio's map of Ireland', *Long Room*, i (1970), pp 29-36. It was Lynam who established 1599 as the publication-date of Boazio's *Irelande*.
2. M.J. Blake, 'A map of part of the county of Mayo in 1584', *Journal of the Galway Archaeological and Historical Society*, v (1907), p. 147. The identification of

'J. Baptiste the painter' of the Mayo map with Baptista Boazio seems to be generally accepted.

3. Sudbury in partnership with George Humble was the first publisher of John Speed's *Theatre of the empire of Great Britaine* (London, 1611). See R.A. Skelton, *County atlases of the British Isles, 1579-1703* (London, 1970), p. 242, and chapter 4 below.

4. Boazio's printed explanation promised 'by the rounde pricked Lynes the division or boundes of the 4 Provinces . . . also the division of everi countrye by smaler pricked lynes distinguished in their severall coulours'.

5. Historical MSS Commission, *De Lisle and Dudley*, ii, pp 385, 387, 389.

6. According to R.A. Skelton (in E.M. Tenison, *Elizabethan England*, xi (Royal Leamington Spa, 1956), pp 34-5) the map had been finished by June 1599, but this statement seems to be based on a reference to Boazio datable only by its position in a sequence of payments which is not strictly chronological (Historical Manuscripts Commission, *Rutland*, iv, p. 424).

7. Lynam, 'English maps and map-makers', p. 25. R.A. Skelton agreed that Boazio was 'no surveyor' ('Two English maps of the sixteenth century', *British Museum Quarterly*, xxi (1957), p. 2). Boazio's map of the Isle of Wight, introduced by Skelton in this note, included a scale panel but the engraver had apparently not been given a scale to put in it.

8. J.H. Andrews, 'The Irish surveys of Robert Lythe', *Imago Mundi*, xix (1965), pp 22-31.

9. Peter Barber, 'England II' in David Buisseret (ed.), *Monarchs, ministers and maps: the emergence of cartography as a tool of government in early modern Europe* (Chicago, 1992), pp 67-8.

10. J.H. Andrews, 'Robert Lythe's petitions', *Analecta Hibernica*, xxiv (1967), pp 232-41.

11. Lythe to Cecil, 24 March 1571, Public Record Office, London, SP 63/31/36.

12. West Sussex County Record Office, Chichester, PHA 9581.

13. Public Record Office, London, MPF 73.

14. British Library, Cotton Ch. xiii, 42.

15. William Ravenhill, 'Christopher Saxton's surveying: an enigma' in Sarah Tyacke (ed.), *English map-making 1500-1650* (London, 1983), pp 112-18.

16. J.H. Andrews, 'The maps of Robert Lythe as a source for Irish place-names', *Nomina*, xvi (1992-3), p. 16.

17. Public Record Office, London, SP 63/32/66 (June 1571).

18. Jeffery C. Stone, *The Pont manuscript maps of Scotland, sixteenth century origins of a Blaeu atlas* (Tring, 1989), p. 10.

19. On the only Lythe derivative known to include this reference, by Petrus Plancius, it appears as '7 Castels where ye Mahoundes landed' (Gordon Manley, 'The Plancius map of England, Wales and Ireland, 1592', *Geographical Journal*, lxxxiv (1934), p. 253).

20. T. Jones Hughes, 'Irish landscape studies', *Baile* (1979), pp 5-6.

21. Ralphael Holinshed, 'Epistle dedicatorie', *Chronicle of all the kings of England* (London, 1587).

22. Alnwick Castle, Duke of Northumberland's MS 476; Trinity College, Dublin, MS 743; National Library of Ireland, MS 669. The Alnwick copy includes a map of Ireland as well as the five provincial maps. Another Lythe-based manuscript map of Ireland, in Trinity College, Dublin (MS 1209, no. 2) may also date from about this time, though its descent from the common archetype seems to have followed a different route.

23. *The description, conquest, inhabitation, and troublesome estate of Ireland . . . untill this present time*, in Raphael Holinshed, *The . . . chronicles of England, Scotlande and Irelande*, ii (London, 1587). Hooker was also the author of a plan of Exeter published in 1587. About twenty years earlier he spent some time in Ireland helping Sir Peter Carew pursue a claim to the barony of Idrone, Co. Carlow (J. MacLean, *The life and times of Sir Peter Carew* (London, 1857), *passim*). Lythe's separate map of Idrone (of which there is a near-contemporary copy in Public Record Office, London, MPF 70) was probably a consequence of the government's interest in this claim rather than being commissioned by Carew or his agents, but it may have helped bring Lythe to Hooker's attention.

24. J.H. Andrews, *The* Hyberniae novissima descriptio *by Jodocus Hondius* (Belfast, 1983). Two more impressions of Hondius's map are now known, one in the British Library, the other in a private collection.

25. Mercator's atlas included a general map of Ireland, separate maps of northern and southern Ireland, a more detailed map of eastern Ulster, and a regional map of Idrone. Sir George Carew, who knew Ireland well, annotated his copy of the east Ulster map with the words: 'this mappe is in many places exceeding fallse' (Lambeth Palace, Carew MS 635). The *Atlas*'s maps of central and southern Ireland have been both neglected and misunderstood: they were less influential than those of Boazio and Speed (Vincenzo Coronelli's two sheet map of Ireland in *c.* 1690 is their most spectacular derivative) but are equally important as a guide to the contents of Lythe's survey.

26. It is not known what map of Ireland was referred to in 1596 by Spenser's fictional character Eudoxus as a guide for following his friend Irenius's plan to reform Ireland (W.L. Renwick (ed.), *A view of the present state of Ireland by Edmund Spenser* (Oxford, 1970), p. 99). Several of the places mentioned by Spenser (e.g. Ballinacor, now in Co. Wicklow, and Kilmore apparently in Co. Cork) appear on no known Lythe derivative.

27. R.A. Skelton, 'The royal map collections of England', *Imago Mundi*, xiii (1956), pp 181-3.

28. R.A. Skelton and John Summerson, *A description of maps and architectural drawings in the collection made by William Cecil, first Baron Burghley, now at Hatfield House* (Oxford, 1971).

29. It is not suggested however that this or any other contemporary English map was deliberately suppressed. In England cartographic secrecy does not appear to have been a major Elizabethan preoccupation (J.B. Harley, 'Silences and secrecy: the hidden agenda of cartography in early modern Europe', *Imago Mundi*, xl (1988), p. 60). This impression is confirmed by Sir Richard Bingham's suggestion in 1591 that Lord Burghley should arrange for the printing of John Browne's map of Connacht, 'as it were pity it should be lost' (Public Record Office, London, SP 63/157/120). It would surely be over-subtle to argue that the government permitted the publication of Boazio's map because it was so bad.

30. Mercator's and Boazio's name-counts cannot be compared on level terms because in Ulster Mercator drew many names from sources other than Lythe. Extrapolating from the three other provinces to the whole kingdom gives him a notional Lythe-based total of 1964. Boazio showed 1861 names and Hondius 551.

31. J.H. Andrews, 'The cartography of Celtic placenames', *Ulster Local Studies*, xiv (1992), pp 7-21.

32. The nomenclature of the Irish Sea is a difficult subject. In 1891 Admiral Sir William Wharton, hydrographer of the Royal Navy, admitted his confusion after having looked at 'many old documents' on the subject. The general consensus,

he thought, was that the Irish Channel was 'the whole channel from north to south', St George's Channel was that part from the Tuscar and St David's Head to Holyhead, the North Channel was the two straits formed by the Mull of Kintyre and Galloway with the opposite coast, and the Irish Sea was or should be that part of the Irish Channel between the North Channel and St George's Channel. The Scottish cartographer Keith Johnston had introduced the name 'St Patrick's Channel' for one of the northern straits but the hydrographic department felt unable to accept this (National Archives, Dublin, Ordnance Survey letters 8659.5).

33.   J.B. Harley, 'Maps, knowledge and power' in Denis Cosgrove and Stephen Daniels (eds), *The iconography of landscape* (Cambridge, 1988), p. 294. Harley sees this description as a glorification of ecclesiastical power.

34.   In Mercator's account of the symbols used in his *Atlas* (1595) it is said that 'simple villages [*pagi*] where there are no amenities, are content with a circle alone' (quoted in Catherine Delano Smith, 'Cartographic signs on European maps and their explanation before 1700', *Imago Mundi*, xxxvii (1985), p. 26).

35.   None of these places recorded by Boazio appears in a recent exhaustive history of Co. Limerick towns and villages by P.J. O'Connor (*Exploring Limerick's past: an historical geography of county and city* (Newcastle West, 1987)).

36.   This Boazio-based map of Ireland was one of the few modern maps published in a supplement to Ortelius's *Theatrum* known as the *Parergon*, which was mainly devoted to ancient geography. Its inclusion out of the proper sequence presumably marked a sense of this map's special importance. The Vrients version also occurs in a copy of the Latin edition of the *Theatrum* published in 1603 (Andrew Bonar Law, *The printed maps of Ireland to 1612* (Morristown, New Jersey, 1983), p. 6).

37.   M.P.R. van den Broeck, 'Facts and speculations on production and survival of Ortelius' *Theatrum orbis terrarum* and its maps', *The Map Collector*, xxxvi (1986), pp 2-12.

38.   Map of Ulster (British Library, Cotton MS Augustus I, ii, 30); map of north-west Ireland, redrawn from an original by John Baxter (National Maritime Museum, Greenwich, MS P.39, No. 7); both usually assigned to the period 1601-3.

39.   One copy is in the British Library, one in Trinity College, Dublin, and a third, an earlier state printed on silk, at Knebworth House, Herts. R.A. Skelton considered that a map of Ireland bought by Robert Cecil for 2s 6d in May 1608 was probably Boazio's (Skelton and Summerson, *Maps and drawings of William Cecil*, p. 11).

Chapter 4

The empire of Great Britain: John Speed, 1610

In March 1603 Hugh O'Neill, earl of Tyrone, surrendered to Queen Elizabeth's representative in the forest of Glenconkein west of Lough Neagh. The final stages of his defeat had been achieved in a brilliant campaign by Charles Blount, Baron Mountjoy, soon to be rewarded with the earldom of Devonshire. Now, for the first time, the whole island lay at the mercy of a single governing power, or so it could plausibly be claimed. Throughout the queen's reign, English cartographic activity in Ireland had increased, fitfully but irreversibly, in good times and bad, and it was appropriate that Mountjoy should have been followed through Ulster by Richard Bartlett, the most gifted of all Elizabethan military surveyors. As well as conventional maps, Bartlett drew close-up views of several memorable scenes. His most epoch-making subject was the destruction of a large stone chair in which the O'Neills had been ceremonially inaugurated as territorial chiefs.[1] Politics like map-making were about to enter a new phase.

The work of Ireland's sixteenth-century regional surveyors was now almost complete. Their last frontier was Donegal, and their last standard-bearer was Bartlett. He did not live to see his work in print (he was killed by the people of Donegal in a belated display of Irish resistance) and in any case he would probably never have sought publication; none of the government's Anglo-Irish cartographic heroes had ever been known to penetrate the peaceful metropolitan world of atlases and print shops. But while the first half of the seventeenth century yielded many Irish fort plans and numerous *ad hoc* property surveys, there were no more regional rebellions and there are almost no more manuscript regional maps. Small-scale cartography throughout this period was to be virtually monopolised by editors and publishers.

Queen Elizabeth herself had died six days before O'Neill laid down his arms. Under her successor, James I, the government of Ireland grew stronger. Administrative boundaries were rationalised – as far as this was possible without good maps – and shire government became a reality everywhere, even in the north. Vigorous new English and lowland Scottish communities settled in Ulster, and new borough towns were established in every province. Ireland now began to enjoy some modest social and economic progress. A new university, founded in late Elizabethan times, was soon flourishing, the unpractical and non-scientific character of its scholarship best represented in the famous Biblical chronology of Archbishop James Ussher.

Outside the university it was still early days for Irishmen to start pursuing topographical knowledge for its own sake. The only English immigrant showing any keen interest in such matters was George Carew, president of Munster in 1600-2, and after Carew left Ireland his example was quickly forgotten.[2] In England it was John Speed who brought the Elizabethan topographical tradition to a climax in the maps and text of his *Theatre of the empire of Great Britaine*, published in 1612. Speed was a London tailor who took up history and cartography in his spare time. By the 1590s he had shown enough talent to be encouraged and subsidised, though already well into middle age, by Camden's friend Sir Fulke Greville. Approved by the queen and supported by the Society of Antiquaries, Speed became the first professional cartographer to qualify as a member of the English cultural establishment.[3]

In their final form nearly all the maps in the *Theatre* are dated 1610, but on some proof copies the date is as early as 1605 and the book was probably first conceived in the decade before that. Whatever Speed had originally planned, his ideas must have been modified by the change of monarch. James I was king of Scotland as well as being nominally conqueror of Ireland. An atlas of all three kingdoms would be a fitting recognition of his multi-national stature. Such a project would also differentiate the author's cartographic attainments from the county atlas of England and Wales completed in 1579 by Christopher Saxton, and from the *Speculum Britanniae* that Speed's less successful rival John Norden had been preparing since the 1590s. Points of difference were certainly needed, because Speed's geographical information came mainly from other people's research, much of it already published.[4] Like Ortelius he made no secret of his unoriginality in this respect, the only maps that he claimed to have drawn from his own surveys being those marginal town plans to which he had attached a linear scale of distances. He was less specific about individualising personal debts. Half a dozen predecessors are named as authorities in the *Theatre*. The ones most often mentioned were Saxton and Norden, but even to these familiar mentors the acknowledgements are manifestly incomplete. We cannot therefore argue that because Speed's Irish authorities are unspecified their names must have been unknown to him – though this is a likely enough state of affairs. All the same, his failure to mention Boazio may well have struck contemporaries as a little pointed.

* * * * * * * * *

One of the undated documents relating to Ireland collected by Sir Robert Cotton envisages 'a perfect map generally' and 'a particular map of each province distinguished by counties and possessions'.[5] Perhaps Speed's most crucial decision was to adopt this proposal, publishing Ireland by provinces instead of by counties as English precedent would have led his readers to expect. He was not the first cartographer to take this course. Manuscript provincial maps of Ireland (with Meath as one of the provinces) were already being circulated in the 1580s, and the same arrangement appears in a set of miniature printed maps of the British Isles by the Dutch engraver, Pieter van den Keere. Some of the English maps in van den Keere's atlas are dated 1599. The Irish maps, which carry no dates, may have been engraved later, though probably not later than c.1605, because by that time a knowledge of Speed's bolder ambitions would have discouraged van den Keere from continuing.[6] The Dutchman's scale was so small that every Irish county could have made as good a showing as the English counties, especially given the contemporary engraver's talent for spreading out information to fill the space available. His provincial format therefore deliberately relegated Ireland to second-class geographical status and no doubt reflected his assessment of contemporary interest in the country.

In thus downgrading Ireland van den Keere expressed an English attitude that history has shown to be almost ineradicable. Even Speed could imply in an unguarded moment that his subject in the *Theatre* was the single island of Great Britain. On a conscious level, however, he was anxious to do Ireland justice. This had already been made clear by his treatment of military geography in two printed maps, a small one in 1601 (Fig. 4.1) and a large one in 1603-4, showing the major historic battles fought in the two kingdoms.[7] Britain in these maps was based on a representation by Norden of the same military theme. Norden's map is known to have omitted Ireland.[8] Speed took the trouble to include it. He evidently saw the military histories of the two countries as intertwined. Indeed from this standpoint the Irish Sea was less of a conceptual barrier than the River Tweed, for Speed's battle maps belonged to a cartographic genre, first illustrated by Laurence Nowell, in which a common frame surrounded England, Wales and Ireland while all or most of Scotland was ignored.

The same Anglo-Hibernian bias reappeared in the *Theatre*, where Scotland had one map and Ireland ten, including inset town and fort

Fig. 4.1   Ireland, from John Speed, *The invasions of England and Ireland
with all their civill warrs since the conquest*, first published 1601,
from Speed's *Prospect of the most famous parts of the world* (London,
1627). The events depicted range from the conquest of Wexford by
Robert Fitzstephen in 1170 to the battle of the Blackwater in 1598
and the subsequent invasion of Ulster by English forces, 'for whose
prosperous success', adds Speed, 'with the overthrow of all treasons
and rebellions, let all true-hearted subjects pray'.

plans though not the province of Meath which Speed like most of his contemporaries considered to be part of Leinster. Speed may even have found Ireland interesting enough to visit – Dublin is one of the towns he implicitly claimed by the inclusion of a scale-line to have surveyed himself – though there is no evidence in his maps or elsewhere that he managed to penetrate the interior and his non-cartographic knowledge of the country was unimpressive.[9] Given this generally sympathetic disposition, his motive for combining the Irish counties into provinces should not be taken for granted. Grouping small territorial divisions in a folio atlas may have been a practical necessity, indicating that Speed's Irish source-maps were less detailed than Saxton's and Norden's in England, perhaps not much larger in the original than they appeared in the *Theatre*. The reader's attitude to this decision would depend on whether county maps or national maps were regarded as the norm. In Ireland, where the county map was still virtually unknown, a provincial format could be made to look generous, especially when the scales chosen were the largest at which the country had ever been comprehensively mapped in print. Van den Keere had divided Ireland to suit a miniaturised format. At Speed's larger page-size, it was the relative abundance of material that made the division necessary.

In his two military maps of the British Isles, Speed anticipated a rule of modern cartography (more often acted upon than spelt out in words) that thematic base maps need not be strictly correct, and saved himself trouble by choosing outlines for Ireland that were already available in print.[10] Both were ultimately derivatives of Lythe: the small map seems to have come from Hondius's *Angliae et Hiberniae nova descriptio* of 1592, the large from Boazio's recently-published *Irelande*. After researching for the *Theatre* Speed was better informed. The dawn of this enlightenment is difficult to date. His 'card or map of the whole empire of Great Britain' is known to have existed as early as June 1607 and it is clear from his later work that he counted Ireland as part of the empire.[11] A reference to Ireland by one of Ortelius's editors in the following year was more definite: 'Baptista Boazio hathe described it in a map by itself . . . and my good friend M. Speed hath done the same in his *Imperium Britannicum*, lately set forth and dedicated to his highness'.[12] The word 'lately' seems to distinguish the *Imperium* from Speed's battle maps; so does the implication that this newer map was independent of Boazio's, though just as good. The most economical hypothesis is that the Ireland of the *Theatre* already existed in 1607, if not as a separate map then as part of 'The kingdome of Great Britaine and Ireland', a title which other writers may have refrained from quoting on the good constitutional ground that the area in question was actually not one kingdom but three.

One reason for dwelling on the chronology of Speed's general maps is to clarify his relationship or lack of relationship with John Norden. In an undated letter to Robert Cecil, earl of Salisbury, Norden claimed to have made three successive maps of Ireland. Two of them survive, both addressed to Salisbury as lord treasurer of England and therefore both finished in or after May 1608.[13] Norden was still doubtless seeking support for his proposed atlas of England, and such gestures may have seemed a useful way of keeping his name alive, even though he was no better informed about Ireland than Boazio or Speed and even though he must have known that Speed was now mapping Ireland independently. In fact Norden's own Irish maps are disappointing. The first is based mainly on Boazio, the second on Boazio with a nod in the direction of Richard Bartlett's Ulster and north Connacht – apparently the only use of Bartlett by any other regional cartographer – and a limited if interesting admixture of names from sources not otherwise recorded (Fig. 4.2). But the results were too small and sparse to give Speed any serious competition, and we may safely eliminate Norden as ghost-cartographer behind the *Theatre*. Of the two, Speed would have been more justified in making Norden's famous claim to have tediously conferred many disagreeing plots together.

*   *   *   *   *   *   *   *   *

There remains the problem of identifying the plots 'conferred' by Speed. The important distinctions here are between Ulster and the south, and between his general map (entitled *The kingdome of Irland . . . newly described*: Fig. 4.3) and the four provincial maps. In the three southern provinces most of Speed's knowledge ultimately came from Lythe, but it reached its destination through several different routes. The *Theatre*'s general map has some points in common with Mercator's maps of 1595, some in common with Boazio, and some that can be matched in no known earlier printed source. It is of course possible that all these features derived not from three separate maps, but from a single ancestor, now unknown, that also influenced Mercator and Boazio. However, these eminent cartographers belong to different streams of Lythe's descent, and features that they and Speed had found in some common archetype would be expected to occur on other Lythe-based maps. This does not happen. For instance, Speed's multi-directional drainage of the Connacht lakes appears in Boazio but nowhere else.

Speed's most likely borrowings from the *Atlas* of Mercator are his scales of latitude and longitude, which carry Ireland to nearly 57 degrees north. (The text of the *Theatre* quotes Mercator by name as its

94

Fig. 4.2   From 'The plott of Irelande with the confines', by John Norden, c.1610,
                Public Record Office, London, MPF 67. Based on Boazio with additions.
                Some of these, such as Ardenglass and Collowny, appear in Richard
                Bartlett's map of north-west Ireland (MPF 37). Others, such as Croagh
                Patrick, may have been supplied by Sir Francis Shane, whose help
                Norden acknowledged in his brief account of the map (MPF 117).

Fig. 4.3   From *The kingdome of Irland*, 1610, in John Speed, *Theatre of the empire of Great Britaine* (London, 1612). The midlands and south derive from Lythe, central and eastern Ulster from Francis Jobson, the rest of Ulster from more recent sources. Latitudes and longitudes are probably based on Mercator (1595). Speed's extreme latitudes are 51° 29′ (Fastnet Rock) and 56° 55′ (Malin Head).

authority for the latitude and longitude of Limerick city.) Like his more illustrious predecessor he chose a non-cylindrical projection and a central meridian apparently situated at 11 degrees east of Mercator's datum at St Mary's in the Azores, though unlike Mercator he included no coordinates in his regional maps.[14]

Also revealing are those name-forms, sometimes much distorted, that seem to link Speed with either Boazio or Mercator but apparently with no one else. Examples are:

O.S. map	Lythe	Speed	Mercator	Boazio
Doonlicka	Downelykey	Downdekey	Doune Likey	Downdekey
–	Kyllone	Killaus	Killane	Killaus
Sl. Aughty	Slewhargty	Knock Hagg	Knok Baght	Knock hagg
Elphin	Helphyn	Elpin	Helphen	Elpin
Kilfenora	Kylfenrogh	Killynerock	Kylfenerog	Killynerock
–	–	Cologmore	Calogmore	Cloghmore
Inishsharke	Enys Sarke	Herk	Herk	Enis Sherck
Killowen?	Kelkone	Kylkone	Kylkone	Kicone
–	Polnydragh	Polirsdragh	Polirsdragh	Polidragh
–	–	Terancy	Terraney	Terraner

Sometimes it is the name itself and not just the spelling of it that seems to point in one of these two directions. Examples apparently borrowed from Mercator are Annax, Brandyron, Fastenay, Fleneker, Incolagh, Kattirin, Kylcorbre, Lacalon, Lemgore, Lesteren, L. Glaninay, Stakki, Synag, and Triperain. Speed may have turned to printed authorities because his manuscript source for Ireland was not detailed enough to suit his chosen scale. But why should he draw from two such maps when one would have been enough? Perhaps Speed was simply displaying his erudition, or anticipating critics who might wish to display theirs.

The natural course for any cartographer working on more than one scale is to prepare his largest map first and then use it as the basis for his smaller maps. This was evidently how Mercator treated Ireland in his atlas of 1595. A surprising feature of the *Theatre*'s coverage is that even in areas derived from Lythe the sources of its general map (including manuscript sources) are different from those of its provincial maps. No other conclusion is possible from the replacement of 'Kildare' in the map of Ireland by 'Ghildare' in Leinster and Munster or from the respelling of the above-mentioned names Killaus and Polirsdragh in Ireland as 'Killone' and 'Pollydragh' in Munster. The most probable reason for reversing the normal course of events is that Speed discovered a new body of Lythe material after his general map was either finished or too nearly finished to be given up. The time and place of this discovery are unknown. The only archival source mentioned by Speed (in a general acknowledgement forming part of his preface) was the private collection of Sir Robert Cotton. To judge from the evidence of placenames, he did not use the one complete Lythe map of Ireland that now forms part of that collection, but of course Cotton may well have possessed other Lythe-based maps which do not survive – perhaps because someone like Speed failed to return them. On the other hand Speed was certainly respectable enough to be given direct access to official archives, and here some beneficial chain-reaction may have been set off by Norden's inquiries, perhaps contemporaneously with the emergence of hitherto unused Lythe material. At any rate the *Theatre*'s provincial maps unquestionably belong to the 'English' rather than the 'continental' family of Lythe derivatives.

In the provinces Speed abandoned a number of names shown on his own map of Ireland. Since the discards included nearly all the Mercator borrowings listed above, this decision looks like a belated dismissal of secondary in favour of primary sources. (An interesting exception is Mercator's fictional but apparently irrepressible name 'Pontoy', revived in Speed's Connacht – though not his *Irland* – perhaps because in that region names of any provenance were relatively scarce.)[15] In quantity the omissions were no great loss, for even without them the *Theatre*'s provincial maps show more Lythe names than had been recorded by any other copyist. This in itself suggests that its author had got closer to the fountainhead than all the master's other descendants. So does the example of 'Ghildare', which occurs in no other known Lythe derivative. At Kildare, of course, moving closer to Lythe meant moving further from the truth, insofar as any placename can be true, but that is only because this name was so famous that even an otherwise ignorant copyist could be expected to amend it. In most cases, certainly in Ireland, copyists have been too ill-informed to make corrections and derivative maps are consequently inferior to their sources.

In separating the four provinces Speed faced a problem not yet familiar in relation to Ireland, the adjustment of scale to page-size. Fortunately the range of variation was not excessive: about 8.7 statute miles to an inch in Leinster, 10.0 in Munster and 11.6 in Connacht, expressing an order of precedence among the provinces that later became traditional in a variety of non-cartographic contexts. These scales were not much larger than Boazio's, but Speed made more economical use of the available space. In particular he is a better guide to variations in settlement density, though in the fashion of the time his design tries to give an appearance of uniformity. Being larger, his selection of names also looks somewhat less arbitrary: he includes eleven of the fourteen 'test-case' names which in a previous chapter Boazio is admonished for having left out. But Speed's knowledge of the country was apparently little better than Boazio's: among his omissions are several places which for various reasons one would expect to see on a Lythe-based provincial map, for instance Ballymore Eustace (Co. Kildare), Ballymore (Co. Westmeath), Castledermot (Co. Kildare), Elphin (Co. Roscommon), Kilconnell and Knockmoy (both Co. Galway).

Speed follows Boazio in transcribing a large number of Lythe's territorial and personal names, some of the latter now even more obsolete than they had been in 1599. At first sight Boazio does better justice to such names by writing them consistently in roman characters, allowing the absence of correlative settlement-symbols to distinguish them from the similarly-written names of large towns. Speed rashly complicates the picture by switching from roman to italic within the same thematic category as an indication of relative importance. But in the end Speed scores more points for intelligibility, partly by the superior neatness of his engraver's script and partly by integrating names and point-symbols more closely. He also gains in clarity if not in liveliness by omitting almost all inscriptions other than names.

All this begs the question of whether Speed's transcriptions may have been done at least in part by one or more assistants working independently. An odd feature of the *Theatre* is that the whole of Co. Clare appears on the maps of both Munster and Connacht. It was in some respects a natural mistake. When Lythe included the county in his 'Single draght of Mounster' he was evidently unaware that it had been moved to Connacht in the previous year. In 1602 it was said to have been restored to Munster, but the subject remained a source of confusion and it is doubtful whether this transfer can be used either to date Speed's general map (which puts Clare in Connacht) or to establish a time-sequence for the two overlapping provincial maps. The point is rather that Speed himself was too methodical to hedge his bets on such an issue by double-counting. The duplication of Clare suggests a failure of personal supervision.

Another such lapse is Speed's treatment of minor settlement symbols. In Munster, lesser settlements are shown by small circles (Fig. 4.4), in Leinster and Connacht by towers. The difference might have originated with Lythe, whose 'single draught' of Munster is not known to have been matched by separate maps of any other province, but this does not relieve Speed of an editor's responsibilities. Worse still from an editorial point of view, the compiler of Leinster, having perhaps become habituated to working on the *Theatre*'s English sheets, describes the province as a 'county' and gives its scale in simple miles,

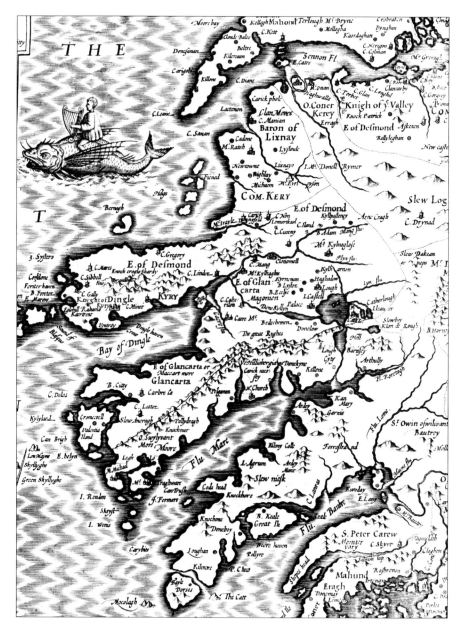

Fig. 4.4   From *The province of Mounster*, 1610, in Speed's *Theatre*. Though
following the same ultimate source as Boazio (Fig. 3.1) Speed's names
are more numerous and his coasts, rivers and hills more articulated.
He edits out a number of Boazio's (and Lythe's) idiosyncrasies but
introduces a new error by connecting the lakes of Killarney with Dingle
Bay.

as in most of Speed's English county maps, instead of in the Irish miles specified for Munster and Connacht. Leinster is also out of step in using lower case instead of capitals for all but two of its county names.

It is not clear how much Speed or his assistants added to Lythe in southern Ireland. Some un-Lythian features may have been introduced by other copyists at an earlier stage in the transmission process, for example the inappropriate use of an extra-large settlement-symbol for villages named 'Palace', a word which in travelling from its Latin origin through the Irish language into Anglo-Irish had lost all implications of grandeur. The *Theatre's* territorial divisions are more numerous than those of Mercator and Boazio but they seem likely to have come from Lythe even where they are not shown on any Lythe maps that now survive. These units present their own problems, one of which is the rarity of subdivisions smaller than a county. It was natural for Speed to notice minor territories within the large county of Cork, but he had no special reason to single out Westmeath for the same treatment, or to make a point of distinguishing Idrone and Ossory (Fig. 4.5). At least it can be said with confidence that none of these divisions had been created since Lythe's time. The most important post-Lythe territorial development, the creation of Co. Wicklow in 1606, was nowhere recognised in the *Theatre*.

Tests of planimetric accuracy have been applied to Speed's map of Ireland and to each of his provincial maps. In Munster his error is only 0.134 (thanks no doubt to Lythe's special survey of the western peninsulas), in Leinster 0.175. His superiority to Boazio's score of 0.239 need not surprise us, for the Boazio figure is vitiated by those areas in the north and west that Lythe had not surveyed. This regional influence is underlined by the weakness of Speed's performance (0.364) in Connacht, suggesting that neglect of the 'bulges' in Galway and Mayo was the most serious error to be found in any standard Tudor map of Ireland. For the country as a whole Speed stands comfortably ahead of Boazio at 0.196.

These results do not make the *Theatre's* rendering of Ireland the best that was possible at the time. Several cartographers had already mapped some parts of the centre and south better than Speed did. One was Francis Jobson, a professional land surveyor active in the official admeasurement of estates confiscated after the Desmond rebellion who later tried to establish himself as a freelance cartographer.[16] Jobson's provincial maps of Munster corrected all his predecessors in Tralee Bay, Kerry Head and a few other areas, and some of his minor place-names are not known to have been mapped before. Taken as a whole, however, this plantation-based mapping showed a degree of over-simplification obvious even to readers without first-hand knowledge,

Fig. 4.5   From *The countie of Leinster*, 1610, in Speed's *Theatre*. The margin of
this Lythe-based map includes as an inset a more up-to-date plan of
Dublin, but in the rest of the province Speed shows no evidence of
first-hand knowledge later than *c.*1570.

and since Lythe had given a convincing and well-filled outline for the
whole province anyone with access to him could have been forgiven
for ignoring Jobson.

John Browne's map of Connacht was in a different category. This was not a plantation exercise but a topographical survey done for the government by a gentleman-amateur. Browne's official position was sheriff of Co. Mayo; he died in mid-survey fighting a local war, but the map was finished in 1591 by a nephew who also bore the name John Browne.[17] It improved on Lythe's treatment of south-west Connacht and was creditably accurate in areas that Lythe had been unable to visit. The omission of the Brownes' findings from all printed maps may well have been the worst Anglo-Irish cartographic failure of the century but Speed's alibi was reasonably watertight. Jobson lived to copy and distribute his own works, even though they were never published. The Brownes had neither motive nor opportunity to do this. No copies of their map are known apart from the one supplied to the government, and that was acquired by Sir George Carew at a fairly early stage in its uneventful life, possibly before Speed had started work on Ireland.

It was in north Connacht that Speed ran out of excuses. From around the dawn of the seventeenth century there are several maps combining the coasts of Donegal, Sligo and north Mayo in a new and realistic portrayal.[18] As will be noted later, Speed's representation of western Ulster was almost certainly based on such a map. Yet south of the provincial border he stayed unthinkingly close to Lythe, another split-minded decision suggestive of multiple authorship.

*   *   *   *   *   *   *   *   *

In Ulster Speed's strongest claim to respect is for ignoring the Lythe model, despite its recent acceptance by Mercator and Boazio, and despite apparently himself having access to original Lythe material of the kind that had helped to justify his predecessors' choice. That this was an early decision on Speed's part is shown by the identical treatment given Ulster, scale difference permitting, in his general and provincial maps. An early date may also follow from his inclusion of Co. Louth in the northern province as confirmed by William Camden. (Most later authorities placed Louth in Leinster.) Another chronological pointer may be the failure of the *Theatre* to notice Bartlett's excellent manuscript map of *c.*1602, which included some noteworthy information for south-east Ulster not available elsewhere – though here the argument is complicated by having to estimate how long it would take for Bartlett's work to become accessible.

However in eastern Ulster Speed did follow one of Bartlett's most important sources, an unpublished map of the province by Francis Jobson (Fig. 4.6). This was a by-product of an attempt to pacify the Ulster heartland in 1587 by making Hugh O'Neill an earl and Tyrone a

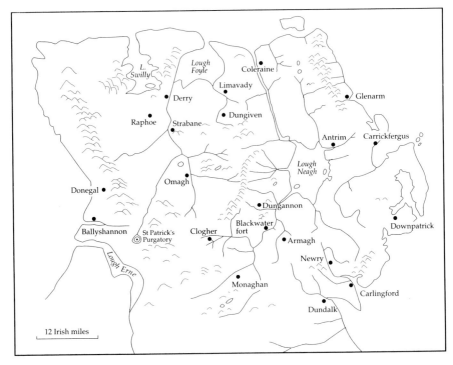

Fig. 4.6   Ulster, 1591, redrawn and simplified from Francis Jobson, 'The provence of Ulster', Trinity College, Dublin, MS 1209, no. 15. Spelling modernised. The original also shows major territorial boundaries and many more names. The blunt western projection of Donegal is a feature of several maps originating from the period between Robert Lythe and Richard Bartlett.

county. At that time the only available maps of northern Ireland showed little or no advance on Lythe, who himself had been following earlier authorities in this region.[19] Nevertheless it was some time before Jobson started work, no doubt because he was fully employed in the plantation of Munster. Like other surveyors he said nothing about his methods, simply recalling how he had been directed to 'make description of Ulster inhabited with a most savage and rebellious people from whose cruelty at that time God only by his divine power delivered me being every hour in danger to lose my head which service I performed as far as I could obtain guides to assist me.'[20] Fears of decapitation were by no means unwarranted at this period, as Bartlett was to learn a few years later. Not surprisingly Jobson's field work, like Lythe's, was done with all convenient speed. The map of Ulster as it survives (for it can be identified beyond reasonable doubt) gives 1590 as the date of his describing and plotting.[21] A letter from the lord deputy makes clear that work had still not yet been started in August of that year.[22] The map was delivered to the privy council in 1591, presumably before the issue of a concordatum authorising payment of Jobson's fee on 23 May.[23] Later in the same year Jobson spent six more weeks on a separate map of Co. Monaghan, but there is no evidence that Speed ever saw this.[24]

Jobson's coverage is more elaborate than Lythe's and also messier (causing him to be undervalued by posterity) but his choice of subject-matter was broadly similar. Coastlines and rivers are both prominent. Trees and hills are drawn in profile, the hill symbols being sometimes massed together in upland blocks like the Antrim Plateau and the Mournes and sometimes left as single summits with individual names. Small settlements are shown not by simple circles but by either towers, churches or courtyards, with 'T' meaning 'temple' added to the familiar initials used for 'castle' and 'monastery'. Roads as usual are omitted, except for a few short passes through forest. Small territorial divisions are delimited within the counties and there is an abundance of Irish family names. Such resemblances do not imply that Jobson had ever seen Lythe's maps (in fact he gives no sign of having studied any other Irish cartographer), only that both men were drawing from a common sixteenth-century cartographic heritage. For Speed this meant that the switch from Lythe to Jobson on the margins of Ulster could be effected without disharmony.

Several major features of the Ulster landscape, physical and human, had made their cartographic debut on Jobson's map. Previously unrecorded settlements of current or future importance included Augher, Ballymoney, Dungiven and Maghera. There were new hills at Knocklayd, Mullaghcarne and Sawel, new lakes at Creevelough and Loughs Guile (Co. Antrim), Aghery, Begney, Brickland and Knok Iorney (Co. Down). And like so many early mapmakers Jobson does especially well with rivers, his additions being the Agivey, Camon, Coalisland, Faughan, part of the Main, the Owenkillen and the Sixmilewater.

Of the various similarities between Speed and his predecessor there is one that has no topographical content. Ulster is the only map in the *Theatre* that gives two scales, with five English miles equal to four Irish. Jobson had done just the same. Their chosen ratio roughly matches the one prevailing in the middle seventeenth century, but in 1610 the metrological situation in Ireland was still so fluid that no two independent surveyors were likely to adopt the same units. The scale evidence therefore suggests that Speed was following Jobson's map or a copy of it. More convincing are the common features, listed below, in which the *Theatre* differs not just from all earlier cartographers except Jobson but also from reality.

(1) Lough Neagh is shaped like a shield. Though closer to its true north-south and east-west proportions than on any earlier printed map it has been over-corrected and is now slightly too short latitudinally instead of too long. Besides Coney Island (called Island Sidney by both Jobson and Speed) the lake contains 'Enis Garde', which is apparently Rams Island exaggerated in size and misplaced southwards.

(2) Rathlin Island is a broad east-west trending rectangle with a small 'pan-handle' at its south-east corner.

(3) The Lower Bann is improbably straight, and twisted anticlockwise from its true alignment by about ten degrees.

(4) The Carlingford peninsula points south-south-east instead of east-south-east.

(5) The River Lagan traces a large northward-looping meander centred on the town of Dromore.

(6) Four streams converge at the same point on the Ballinderry River west of Lough Neagh.

Speed also follows Jobson closely along the coastline of Down and Antrim and across the Ulster hinterland as far west as Coleraine, Tyrone and Cavan. He avoids confusion however by omitting Jobson's second tier of small territorial units, a wise decision even if inconsistent with his own policy for parts of Leinster and Munster. His omissions of Jobson's names are probably accidental – this is certainly true of 'Cryne', which the *Theatre* shows in Ireland though not in Ulster – but they also raise the question of whether Speed's copy of Jobson was necessarily the copy that now survives. As it happens, this is not very likely, for the extant version is known to have been acquired by George Carew – probably at the same time as the Brownes' map of Connacht, which (as already noted) Speed is not likely to have seen. Although the omissions in question are not numerous, the map still looks rather sparse compared with those of the southern provinces. The difference is partly masked by judicious placing of inscriptions and, less creditably, by a redistribution of hill symbols (always fair game for copyist's licence in the sixteenth and seventeenth centuries), which has the result of spoiling some of Jobson's happiest strokes.[25] For his own part, Speed's only concession to geomorphology is a wall-like feature appropriately called Knockcragge apparently derived from a misunderstood territorial boundary. Probably for the same cosmetic reason a number of regional names have been allowed to float out of position.

* * * * * * * * *

As often happens when manuscript maps are adapted for printing, a number of Jobson's longer inscriptions were edited out of the *Theatre*. His two Spanish Armada wrecks had lost their topicality; so had the Scottish signal fires near Fair Head. But no map of Ireland could omit St Patrick's Purgatory, and Speed also retained a 'parley hill' or place of assembly at Knockmullagh in Antrim and 'ye stone where O'Neill is chosen' at Tullaghogue, Co. Tyrone, the latter expanded from the 'O'Neill's chair' of the general map. One of Speed's own additions in the same vein is 'the ancient seat of the kings of Ulster' at Owen Maugh near Armagh, doubtless derived from Camden's *Britannia*.[26] At first sight, references to chiefs, let alone kings, might have seemed politically tactless in the new Ireland. Perhaps they are evidence, if further evidence is necessary, that Speed's map originated during a conciliatory interlude in the government's relations with Ulster Gaeldom, after the pardon of Hugh O'Neill in September 1603 and before his attainder for treason following O'Neill's famous 'flight' to Rome almost exactly four years later.

Speed's personal view of Irish national identity is perhaps best illustrated in the marginal portraits of 'civil' and 'wild' Irishmen and Irishwomen in his general map.[27] (He did not tempt fate by giving heraldic recognition to individual families as on his English maps, not even to families of unquestioned loyalty and impeccably non-Irish origin.) The 'wild' representative carries a spear and looks surly enough to use it. His civil compatriot extends the hand of friendship, presumably welcoming the 'empire of Great Britaine'. The empire now looked strong enough for Irish traditions to be sanitised as historical phenomena – strong enough too for its geographers to follow international custom by drawing maps with north rather than west at the top. Speed shows a province under subjugation, its forests (what was left of them) divided by passes, a warship patrolling its largest lake, its rebellious spirit curbed by a network of military strongholds. The forts, sixteen in number, were indicated either by inscriptions or as schematic angle-bastioned enclosures. Four of them – the Blackwater, Toome, and two nameless sites in Down and Tyrone – belonged to Jobson's cartographic legacy. The others, built by the English army in 1600-3, were the latest of Speed's chronological markers. The most interesting name in this respect was 'Fort Charles', which among the general public soon gave way to 'Charlemont' and may therefore help to anchor the map within a short period of toponymic uncertainty immediately after the war.

New forts were a predictable innovation in any map of Ireland from around the beginning of the seventeenth century. As symbols of imperial power they were Speed's strongest psychological selling-point.

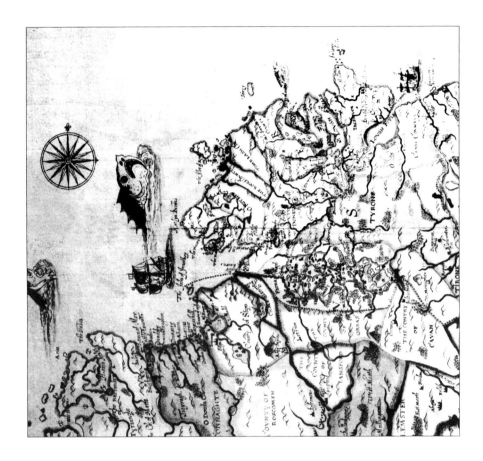

Fig. 4.7   North-west Ireland, c.1601, Trinity College, Dublin, MS 1209, no. 14. The
             first recognisably modern representation of the Donegal coastline on a
             surviving map, based on observations from the warship *Tramontayne*. A
             number of recently built forts are included, and Lough Erne is shown to
             be more complicated than previous cartographers had supposed, but in
             much of interior Ulster the information is up to forty years old.

More surprising are the numerous well-established but relatively
unimportant non-military names that he added to Jobson's stock within
the Elizabethan surveyor's own sphere of cartographic influence. Some
of these, admittedly, could have come from a lost variant of Jobson's
map that has already been postulated, the most likely examples being
Kells and 'Connor a bishop's see'. But this explanation fails where
Speed directly contradicts Jobson, for instance by giving different
names to some of the Copeland Islands off the coast of Co. Down. The
names most probably attributable to Speed himself rather than to

Jobson are commonest on the coastline immediately north and south of this archipelago. Here Jobson's extant nomenclature is notably deficient, and there is no reason why the lost versions of his map should have been any better. After all, his main commitment had been to the current focus of official anxiety further west in Tyrone.

Speed, his eye on the general reader, knew that coastlines were expected to have plenty of names. Most of his presumed additions seem to come from the oddest of the five Irish maps published by Mercator in 1595, *Ultoniae orientalis pars*. Admittedly some of these names also occur in certain official English manuscript maps that Speed might conceivably have seen, but no such map is known to include them all; the least improbable source therefore remains Mercator, especially as his *Atlas* can be seen to have left some other traces on Speed's general map. What clinches the argument is that by a strange aberration Speed ignores Jobson's Killegh on the eastern shore of Lough Neagh and instead follows Mercator in writing the word 'Scots': it must have been a long time since pre-plantation Scottish settlements were identifiable this far inland. Mercator's Scots had perhaps been carried forward from his own map of 1564, a source that no Englishman is likely to have taken seriously at this late stage. It was bold of Speed to use anything from *Ultoniae orientalis pars* when so much of it was now clearly incorrect. His implicit assumption seems to have been that while precursors might have invented their own shapes they were unlikely to have coined their own language, and that so long as a coastline was based on the best available source there could be little harm in filling otherwise empty space behind it with names drawn from inferior maps.

* * * * * * * * *

Jobson had admitted not daring to survey Fermanagh and Donegal. Here, as in the unconfiscated parts of Munster, he did the best he could – probably by 'graphicising' verbal information rather than by finding the best available maps. The result was to give north-west Ireland a Jobsonian version of an early Elizabethan square outline, pulling it westwards to make the unsurveyed area larger and so more dangerous and punctuating it with a handful of well-known castles and monasteries arranged in topological order. In Speed's *Theatre* the square is finally broken and the Donegal coastline modernised. Its two main constituents, an east-west 'base' and a 'hypotenuse' from south-west to north-east, are correct, and they incorporate a number of recognisable if still anonymous minor features including Fanad Head, Horn Head, Bloody Foreland, Burtonpoint Head, Croly Head, Rossan Point, St John's Head, Tory Island and Rathlin O'Byrne Island.

Fig. 4.8   From *The province Ulster described*, 1610, in Speed's *Theatre*. In the area shown, Speed was mainly following Jobson's map of 1591. A number of later forts are included, but 'ye stone where Oneale is chosen' had been removed by the English army in 1602.

110

Only one survey of the Donegal coastline is known to have been completed before Speed's time. In July 1601 Captain Charles Plessington of the patrol vessel *Tramontayne* reported finding a new and unnamed bay in Co. Mayo (probably either Broadhaven or Blacksod Bay, both mapped by John Browne in 1584 without Plessington or Speed becoming aware of the fact) which he promised to show Sir Robert Cecil on a forthcoming original chart of the Irish coast.[28] No other contemporary mentions this chart, though Plessington and his ship reappear in the caption to a manuscript map of northern Ireland said to have been made by 'Mr Griffin cocket master' (Fig. 4.7). This map is a rare hybrid of information from sea and land, the latter including several forts and castles recently occupied by English troops. Plessington's Donegal is by no means the same as Speed's or for that matter Bartlett's, but with a generous allowance for personal curvature they may just conceivably be derived from the same 'field notes': after all, this was not a coastline that anyone would willingly survey if he knew that someone else had done it. On all three maps the Malin Head peninsula is divided from the rest of Inishowen by a narrow thread of water. None shows any trace of Dawros Head or Loughros Bay; all twist the alignment of Sheep Haven through ninety degrees, and all place Tory Island too far from the mainland. This similarity does not extend to nomenclature. As in eastern Ulster (Fig. 4.8), so in Donegal, Speed was apparently content to combine a unitary coastline with names culled from various sources: Ancraga, All Mallallen and Misha Meagh from Jobson; Silver Hill and Hawks Hill from Boazio; Enyspyk, Bay of Ballewilly, Ballewilly Castle and the Moan River from Mercator.

Finally the *Theatre* effected a long overdue reappraisal of the Fermanagh lakes. Despite the endorsement by Mercator and Boazio of the time-honoured Lough Erne 'cigar', students of recent Irish history already knew that the lake contracts to a narrow ford exactly where the cigar of the maps was at its widest, near the Maguire castle of Enniskillen besieged by English forces in an engagement fore-shadowing the Tyrone war. The sequence of cartographic events here seems to be as follows. A regional military map of 1594 had distinguished the upper and lower lakes and separated them by a right-angled bend.[29] William Camden before writing his *Britannia* had evidently seen this map or had it described to him. He introduced both its new features, though with different shapes, in the map of Ireland illustrating the 1607 edition of the *Britannia*, a map otherwise based mainly on Mercator's *Atlas* (Fig. 4.9). No doubt Speed was already alert to the difficulties of this area. The marginal inset in his map of Ulster featured not a town, as in his other provincial maps, but a view of Enniskillen Castle which, while seriously out of date, at least avoided

Fig. 4.9   From William Hole, *Hiberniae* . . . , in William Camden, *Britannia* (London, 1607). The first printed map to distinguish upper and lower Lough Erne. Otherwise it is based mainly on Mercator's maps of 1595, with more recently built forts in Ulster and antiquarian information derived from Ptolemy.

putting the castle in the middle of a broad lake.[30] So the cigar had to be given a firm squeeze half-way along its length. The problem is to explain why Speed contradicted the most recent maps by making the upper lake larger than the lower and by bringing it too far north. This left the Erne system as the least accurate of his major features in Ulster but it was good enough for his few settlements in this area – Lisgoole, Castle Skea and Enniskillen – to appear in their correct topological relationships. His only serious combinatorial error was to move the abbey of Clones from Monaghan to Fermanagh. Speed's good fortune in Ulster was that conflicts between the Jobsonian and post-Jobsonian elements in his map were muffled by broad cushions of featureless, sparsely populated and therefore virtually unmappable countryside.

* * * * * * * *

Although the Ulster of the *Theatre* was far from faultless, it had at least brought the province up to Lythe's standards, actually scoring a little better – RMS 0.172 – than Speed's wholly Lythe-based Leinster.[31] In fact altogether this must rank as the most carefully considered and internally harmonious synthetic map of any part of Ireland to be published since 1564. To that extent it deserved the distinction of a larger scale (about eight statute miles to an inch) than the other provincial maps; its junction with the rest of the country was also a remarkable feat. Further south, Speed's representations of Leinster, Munster and Connacht, for all their anachronisms, surpassed every earlier published map. His maps of these provinces showed 2142 names compared with Boazio's 1610. For basic geographical features his all-Ireland scores, with Boazio's shown in brackets, were rivers 136 (117), lakes 45 (43), hill-masses 53 (44).

Like Boazio, though with more justification, Speed was quick to win public acceptance, the summit of approval being reached when all four provincial maps were displayed by George Carew upon his study walls.[32] He also resembled Boazio in being quickly overtaken by real-world events – some of which, as with the formation of Co.Wicklow, he might have been expected to register, while others like the Ulster plantation came too late. He was especially unlucky to miss by such a narrow margin the adoption in 1613 of 'Londonderry' as the official name for both the city of Derry and the county of Coleraine. Apart from the extent of country involved here, the linking of Thames and Foyle in Irish nomenclature was a change of deeply emotive significance which Speed the imperialist, who was proud to call himself a citizen of London, would undoubtedly have welcomed. A few cartographers otherwise dependent on Speed did add the prefix

'London' later in the seventeenth century,[33] but it was in an unmodernised form that his image of Ireland enjoyed its widest circulation, being distributed from Amsterdam throughout the civilised world (after some heavy-handed editing) in two gigantic atlases by Jan Jansson from 1636 and Willelm Blaeu from 1654.[34] More ephemeral, but perhaps also more revealing, was an English map of Ireland depicting the rebellion of 1641 on a base entirely derived from *The kingdome of Irland.*[35] Even in a tract written for Cromwellian settlers the index of placenames was unmistakably based on Speed, placing Arklow in Co. Carlow, Wicklow in Co. Dublin and Limavady in Co. Coleraine.[36]

Other publishers were still copying from the *Theatre* with no sense of anachronism until almost the middle of the eighteenth century. This was perhaps unremarkable in faraway Augsburg, where Matthaus Seutter's map of the British Isles paid homage to Speed as late as 1744; but surely not in James Grante's *Chart wherein are marked all the different routs of P[rince] Edward* (Edinburgh, 1749), though admittedly this was a thematic map and therefore less open to planimetric criticism.[37]

The *Theatre* itself became an international atlas in 1627 when Speed enlarged it to form the *Prospect of the most famous parts of the world,* a work that continued to appear in successive editions for almost fifty years. Neither the author nor his posthumous editors had any objection to amending their copper plates, and changes were made in due course to several English counties. But there was never a Londonderry in either *Theatre* or *Prospect* and never a Co. Wicklow. This looks like an object lesson in the difference between being published and being read. Or had Irish map-users already formed the habit of addressing their criticisms to everyone but the person who deserved them? At any rate the earliest known complaint about Speed's Ireland, that some of his woods no longer existed, came in 1645 not from an Irishman but from a Dutchman. This was the naturalist Gerard Boate, anticipating the more rigorous approach to cartography cultivated by European scientists in the later seventeenth century.[38]

References

1. G.A. Hayes McCoy, *Ulster and other Irish maps,* c. 1600 (Dublin, 1964). Bartlett's 'A generalle description of Ulster' (Public Record Office, London, MPF 35) is perhaps the best map of any large region of Ireland that never got into print.
2. William O'Sullivan, 'George Carew's Irish maps', *Long Room,* xxvi-xxvii (1983), pp 15-25.
3. R.V. Tooley, 'John Speed, a personal view', *The Map Collector,* i (1977), pp 4-9.
4. No doubt this is the basis for Edward Lynam's over-hasty dismissal of Speed as 'no cartographer, though a good historian' ('An atlas of England and Wales: the maps of Christopher Saxton, engraved 1574-1579' (1939), reprinted in Lynam's *The mapmaker's art* (London, 1953), p. 90).

5.   British Library, Cotton MS Titus B xii, f. 523.

6.   This suggestion is advanced in Helen Wallis's introduction (p. [iiii]) to *Atlas of the British Isles by Pieter van den Keere* c. *1605* (Lympne, 1972).

7.   Gunter Schilder and Helen Wallis, 'Speed military maps discovered', *The Map Collector*, xlviii (1989), pp 22-6.

8.   D.W. Rannie (ed.), *Remarks and collections of Thomas Hearne*, iv (Oxford, 1898), p. 407.

9.   Speed's selection of names for his general map of Ireland does not include such well-known places as Kilmallock, Loughrea, Maynooth, Mullingar and Raphoe. Nor has his claim to have visited the towns for which he gives scale lines been universally accepted (J.H. Andrews, 'The oldest map of Dublin', *Proceedings of the Royal Irish Academy*, lxxxiii C (1983), p. 208). One of his plans, of Newcastle in Northumberland, carries both a scale and an attribution to another cartographer.

10. The basis of this rule appears in Jacques Bertin, *Graphics and graphic information-processing* (Berlin and New York, 1981), p. 145 and in J.S. Keates, *Understanding maps* (New York, 1982), pp 80-81.

11. Heather Laurence, 'Permission to survey', *The Map Collector*, xix (1982), p. 20.

12. R.A. Skelton, 'Bibliographical note' to *Abraham Ortelius, The theatre of the whole world, London 1606* (Amsterdam, 1968), p. xv. Skelton gives reasons for thinking that this edition of Ortelius's atlas was not published until 1608.

13. Public Record Office, London, MPF 117. Norden's surviving maps are in Trinity College, Dublin, MS 1209, no. 1, and Public Record Office, London, MPF 67, the latter reproduced in *State papers, Henry VIII*, II, iii.

14. Marginal coordinate-scales appear on Mercator's maps of Ireland, northern Ireland, southern Ireland, and eastern Ulster, the last with a cylindrical projection, but not on his map of the barony of Idrone. For the high reputation and wide influence of Mercator's longitudes see John Gregory, *The description and use of the terrestrial globe*, in *Gregorii posthuma: or certain learned tracts written by John Gregorie, M.A. and chaplain of Christ-Church Oxford* (London, 1649), pp 276-7.

15. See above, ch. 2, note 27.

16. J.H. Andrews, *Plantation acres, an historical study of the Irish land surveyor and his maps* (Belfast, 1985), pp 33-46. This account omits the National Library of Ireland's copy of Jobson's map of Munster (16.B.13), reproduced in Noel Kissane (ed.), *Treasures from the National Library of Ireland* (Dublin, 1994), pp 182-3.

17. Trinity College, Dublin, MS 1209, no. 68. Browne was an ancestor of two aristocratic modern families, the Brownes of Westport and the Brownes of the Neale (M.J. Blake, 'A map of part of the county of Mayo in 1584', *Journal of the Galway Archaeological and Historical Society*, v (1907), p. 146).

18. Examples are the Plessington map of c.1600 (below, note 28), the Baxter-Boazio map of north-west Ireland (above, ch. 3, n. 38) and Richard Bartlett's map of the same area (Public Record Office, London, MPF 37).

19. The best example is Public Record Office, London, MPF 90.

20. Public Record Office, London, MPF 312; *Calendar of State Papers, Ireland, 1598-9*, p. 445.

21. Trinity College, Dublin, MS 1209, no. 15.

22. Public Record Office, London, SP 63/154/3.

23. *Analecta Hibernica*, i (1930), p. 100.

24. Public Record Office, London, AO1/286/1079. Trinity College, Dublin, MS 1209, no. 31; Public Record Office, London, MPF 76, MPF 79.

25. For the indefinite meaning attributable to hill symbols at this period see J.B. Harley, 'Meaning and ambiguity in Tudor cartography' in Sarah Tyacke (ed.),

English map-making 1500-1650 (London, 1983), p. 32.

26. The 'ancient seat' had also been identified on Richard Bartlett's map of south-east Ulster in 1600 (British Library, Cotton MS Augustus I, ii, 37).

27. For a comment on the influence of these pictures see Harley, 'Meaning and ambiguity in Tudor cartography', plate 33.

28. *Calendar of State Papers, Ireland, 1600-1*, pp 436-7; Trinity College, Dublin, MS 1209, no. 14.

29. Map of Lough Erne by John Thomas, 1594, National Maritime Museum, Greenwich, MS P.39, no. 21.

30. Speed's view of Enniskillen is similar to that of John Thomas in 1594 (British Library, Cotton MS Augustus I, ii, 39), a resemblance first noted by R.A. Skelton in 'Tudor town plans in John Speed's *Theatre*', *Archaeological Journal*, cviii (1951), p. 113. It is fair to add that in an English context Speed has been praised for 'commendable selectivity in rejecting out-of-date material in Cotton's collection' (D. Smith, 'The enduring image of early British townscapes', *The Cartographic Journal*, xxviii (1991), p. 174, n. 45).

31. For other tests of Speed's map compared with earlier maps of Ulster see Joan Murphy, 'Measures of map accuracy assessment and some early Ulster maps', *Irish Geography*, xi (1978), pp 88-101.

32. Trinity College, Dublin, MS 1209, nos 7, 19, 38, 70. O'Sullivan, 'George Carew's Irish maps', p. 17. Speed's map of Munster was copied in *Pacata Hibernia* (London, 1633), an account of the late Elizabethan war in that province based on Carew's papers. It also seems likely that Speed's was the 'new map of Ireland that is so well known to your lordships and most statists here' mentioned by an author of 1623 (George O'Brien (ed.), *Advertisements for Ireland* (Dublin, 1923), p. 3).

33. Examples are maps of Ireland by Frederick de Wit (undated, a revision of de Wit's earlier map which lacked 'London'), and of the British Isles by Pierre du Val in 1665 and by A.H. Jaillot in 1689. For the addition of 'London' to a map not originating with Speed see *Angliae et Hiberniae nova descriptio veteribus et recentioribus distincta ad . . . Camdeni Britannii* (1643, apparently derived from Jodocus Hondius's map of 1592).

34. According to R.A.Skelton (*County atlases of the British Isles, 1579-1703* (London, 1970), p. 109), Blaeu copied from Jansson rather than directly from Speed, but some of his marginal features were wholly original, including his supposedly Irish names for Munster ('Moun et Woun') and Ulster ('Cui-Guilly'). Apart from predictable changes in decorative style (with Blaeu introducing some characteristically Irish livestock), the Dutchmen's editing comprised new latitude and longitude values, new linear scales with new units of measurement, latinised titles and marginal inscriptions, and a somewhat free interpretation of Speed's symbols for hills, woods and settlements. They seem to have contributed no extraneous topographical information, however: these are not the 'continental maps based on Speed's' in which Liam Price found the new name 'L.Lodeste' applied to Lough Dan in Co. Wicklow (*The place-names of Co. Wicklow. I, The barony of Ballinacor North* (Dublin, 1945), p. 30). Price's reference was probably to maps deriving from Mercator's *Hiberniae pars australis* (1595).

35. *A map of ye kingdome of Ireland with perticular notes distinguishing the townes revolted taken or burnt since the late rebellion* (sold by William Webb, 1642?), with distinctive symbols for towns taken by the rebels, towns besieged, and towns burnt.

36. *The map of Ireland, with the exact divisions of the provinces . . .* by John Woodhouse (London, 1653). The British Library copy of this work contains a

placename index and a list of baronies with their acreages but no map.

37. R.W. Shirley, *Printed maps of the British Isles, 1650-1750* (Tring and London, 1988), pp 63-4, 132.

38. Gerard Boate, *Ireland's natural history* (London, 1652), reprinted in *A collection of tracts and treatises illustrative of the natural history, antiquities, and the political and social state of Ireland, at various periods prior to the present century* (Dublin, 1860), p. 101. Boate did not mention Speed by name, but Speed's was the only published map to show woods in the area (round Newry) to which he drew attention.

Chapter 5

Eight times round the world:
William Petty, 1685

There is a depressingly cyclical character to Irish history as seen through English eyes. Each uprising leads to a conquest, each conquest to an uprising. In 1641 it became clear that the Tudors' last and seemingly irreversible victory had failed to break this rule. What Elizabeth and James had done, a new generation of Irishmen now tried to undo. Their efforts were frustrated by Oliver Cromwell; later their sons and grandsons rose to support the Catholic King James II and were duly put down by the Protestant William of Orange. Alongside this alternation of revolt and defeat there ran a parallel series of related landscape changes involving destruction, counter-destruction, forfeiture of land, redistribution of land, immigration, habitation and 'improvement'. The only unpredictable feature of these events was their precise location within the country, though most parts of Ireland were affected sooner or later. Colonial cartography followed a similar course, progressing from regional sketches to fort plans, and thence to plantation surveys and estate maps. This repetitive schema is not inconsistent with an overriding evolutionism, because at each turn of history's wheel the maps became larger, better, more numerous and more carefully preserved.

Genuine events are never as tidy as historical models. One anomaly in the real world of seventeenth-century Ireland was that the colonisers could no longer wait for the natives to rebel. Instead they found legal excuses to seize lands that were still more or less peaceful, thus elaborating the sequence of plantation surveys between one war and the next until by Cromwell's time it had included estates in Munster (first mapped in the 1580s), Ulster, Wexford, Longford and Leitrim, parts of King's County and neighbouring counties, Wicklow and finally in the 1630s Connacht together with Clare and north Tipperary. Most of the lands under forfeiture were measured by professional surveyors or by military engineers in a series of traverses around the boundaries of townlands or blocks of townlands occupying several hundred acres. Each parcel was treated as a polygon in which the sides were perambulated with a chain and the angles taken from numerical compass

bearings observed on an azimuthal instrument known as a c\
ferentor. The results were plotted at scales of 40 or 80 Iris
'plantation' perches to an inch, the perch containing 21 feet instea\
16.5 feet as currently in England. It was a method that absolved the
surveyor from following rivers or roads except where these features
happened to coincide with a townland boundary. He was however
expected to show substantial buildings that might enhance the value of
an estate (not a very numerous category in Ireland) and also to
separate profitable from unprofitable land. Townlands not included in
the current programme of confiscation would be left alone, so that
where patterns of ownership and alleged disloyalty were discontinuous
the maps, however accurate, would be interrupted by irregular patches
of empty space. Anything less like the regional cartography of Lythe
and Jobson would be hard to imagine, and indeed the plantation
surveys had little to do with either geography, strategy or politics: their
purpose was simply to help divide the victors' spoils. This meant that
they had no counterparts in England, where small-scale national maps
continued to depend on ageing regional surveys of Elizabethan date.

The same could easily have been true of Ireland: to assemble a map
of Europe's second largest island from scattered cadastral surveys was
an act of courage and imagination not to be taken for granted. The gap
between the country's largest and smallest maps was bridged by two
ideas. One was the hierarchy of scales, reflecting different levels of
geographical interest and exemplified by several great seventeenth-
century atlases in which the world was followed first by the continents
and then by individual countries, and in which important kingdoms
and empires were further subdivided into separately-mapped provinces
or counties. Ireland and its townlands were the two extremes of such a
hierarchy, mediated by the descending orders of the provinces,
counties, baronies and parishes. Within such frameworks, it has always
been common for one map-scale to call other scales into existence, a
process of emulation and imitation well illustrated in the history of the
British Ordnance Survey. A second concept relevant to cartographic
progress, more specific and more narrowly utilitarian, was that of the
index map, not meant for study in its own right but guiding readers to
the appropriate page of an atlas. There were indexes to several of the
Irish plantation surveys; probably few of them seemed accurate or
detailed enough to be worth including in a published map-hierarchy,
but all were suggestive of future possibilities.[1]

The Irish government had employed its own permanent surveyor-
general since the sixteenth century,[2] but despite the archival responsibilities appurtenant to this office few of the country's early plantation
maps were available to surveyors employed after 1641. The exception

Fig. 5.1   Counties, baronies and parishes in part of western Ireland from 'A mappe of the province of Connaght', c.1640, Trinity College, Dublin, MS 1209, no. 69. The best outline of Connacht since John Browne's unpublished map of 1591, it was probably intended as an index to the areas surveyed by direction of the earl of Strafford in the 1630s.

was the admeasurement of Connacht, Clare and north Tipperary generally known as the Strafford Survey after the lord deputy who ordered it in 1636, but actually conducted by 'an able scholar and in particular a very good mathematician' named William Gilbert.[3] Strafford's intended plantation of Connacht never came about, but that was not the fault of his surveyors. In a country where experts have the reputation of seldom speaking well of each other, the official verdict on their work, some twenty years later, was that 'nothing could be expected more exact'.[4] It was a remarkable compliment in a region that the Elizabethans had considered particularly dangerous: a long-standing gradient in Irish cartographic quality, from poor in the east to very poor in the west, had been suddenly though not permanently reversed. (Socio-economic gradients on the ground were unaffected.) The Strafford Survey included both parish maps and county maps, which left only one step to a single map of the province and its outliers. And although most of the large-scale Strafford coverage has been lost there does survive a small map of the entire survey area – inevitably unsigned and undated – that is best interpreted as a by-product of Gilbert's activities (Fig. 5.1).[5] Since it shows the plantation borough of Jamestown in Co. Leitrim this map must be later than 1622, while its old-fashioned style of decoration would seem to place it earlier than the mid-century. It was probably intended only as an index, but since the whole region had become eligible for forfeiture the result was a portrait of the province with no blank spaces which on merit deserved a high place in the history of mainstream Irish cartography. Instead it has remained almost unknown. Gilbert and his colleagues were soon to be lost in a single giant shadow.

*   *   *   *   *   *   *   *

Outside Ireland few people think of William Petty as a mapmaker. English scholars in particular are so conscious of their country's poor cartographic performance at this period that such a role for a mid seventeenth-century man of genius would surely strike them as too improbable to be contemplated. And there were plenty of more exciting parts for Petty to play – youthful university professor, headline-making anatomist, co-founder of the Royal Society, respected member of parliament, to say nothing of pioneer economist and statistician.[6] In Ireland none of these achievements cuts any ice: there, Petty is famous only as director – and beneficiary – of the unprecedentedly extensive land survey that followed the Cromwellian confiscations. He secured this appointment in 1654 by criticising the dispositions of the current Irish surveyor-general, Benjamin Worsley, and by offering to conduct the survey more cheaply than anyone else thought possible. At thirty-one years of age Petty had no special qualifications for the task, his most recent employment having been that of physician-general to the Cromwellian army in Ireland.

In fact Worsley's surveying technique was inherited from the

Strafford Survey and Petty did little to change it. Their dispute turned on problems of organisation and finance that were exacerbated by the magnitude of the work in hand. In three counties the Cromwellian settlement could use the Strafford Survey itself. Elsewhere Petty's new 'Down Survey' would employ a thousand hands and embrace an area that was later estimated at nearly 8,400,000 acres, being all the land in Ireland held by Catholic proprietors at the outbreak of the rebellion in 1641.[7] The forfeited estates would go partly to soldiers who had served in the reconquest and partly to 'adventurers' who had invested money in Cromwell's cause. When a government's debts are being paid in acres the measuring needs to be done correctly. Petty's areas were on average more than ten per cent below the truth, but they were better than anything previously available. His survey was certainly good enough to underpin the most comprehensive land transfers of the whole plantation period. It then retained a privileged status for an indefinite future in the authentication of Irish land titles. Petty's later reputation in small-scale cartography must have owed much to his success on the cadastral level.

The issue of most geographical interest in the Petty-Worsley disagreement was the surveying of administrative as opposed to property boundaries. Territorial divisions had been involved in each successive attempt to pacify Ireland. Two of the four provinces had been given separate administrative status under Elizabeth I. Twenty of the thirty-two counties had been created since the reign of Henry VIII. Baronies ceased to be purely baronial when each acquired its own local constable. It was a weakness of English government policy that these administrative reforms had never been integrated with the business of land forfeiture and colonisation and while cartography had been part of the plantation apparatus at every stage there are hardly any surviving regional maps expressly devoted to local government boundaries.[8] An achievement of Petty's generation was to combine these two kinds of geographical record.

True, the Strafford Survey had shown every kind of territorial division from the parish upwards, but this coverage followed almost automatically from the unbroken continuity of the townland network set out for cadastral purposes in Connacht. It was different when county and barony boundaries ran through extensive unforfeited areas outside the jurisdiction of the plantation authorities. Before Petty's takeover his employers found it hard to make up their minds on this subject. In 1653 they decided to base the whole survey on baronies (perhaps anticipating Petty's scheme for a general map of Ireland) which would be divided into planters' estates by other surveyors at a later date. In May 1654 this policy was overturned: now property boundaries would be surveyed and barony boundaries ignored. Then Petty, followed by the committee examining his views, took exception to this neglect of 'the ancient bounds of baronies, parishes etc.' The word 'ancient' comes as a surprise from one whose disrespect for history was otherwise ultra-Cromwellian, and in any case the antiquity of the bounds in question had nothing to do with their modern administrative role. The really old boundaries were the frontiers of the various Os and Macs and nobody in the 1650s wanted to map those. Parishes and baronies were simply the current official divisions and therefore a necessary datum plane on which to draw and record whatever changes Cromwellian authority might now initiate. Their boundaries could themselves be questioned as uncertain, but no better method of locating information was feasible. A numbered rectangular reference grid is the kind of twentieth-century idea that Petty might well have put forward in his later theoretical writings, but as director of the Down Survey he was too level-headed to envisage anything so impracticable.

Instead he proposed a synthesis of proprietorial and administrative mapping with the addition of a physical element; the whole country, in his own words, being 'measured both according to its civil bounds, *viz.*, by baronies, parishes, townlands, ploughlands, balliboes etc., and also by its natural boundings by rivers, ridges of mountains, rocks, loughs, bogs etc. as answering not only the very ends of satisfying the adventurers and soldiers then in view, but all such other future ends whatsoever as are usually expected from any survey'. Petty was thus moving towards the idea of a complete topographical map, and his casual reference to 'any survey' was more significant than it looked. Since the only recent surveys familiar to most contemporary readers would have been topographical close-ups of relatively small estates, the new map of Ireland was evidently being conceived on a generous scale.

Unfortunately these ambitions turned out to be unrealistic. Petty instructed his Down Survey staff to map a number of features that could not be taken for granted in a normal Irish plantation survey, among them towns, churches, castles, 'known' houses, hills, raths, highways, rivers, islands, rocks and harbours, but in the rush to help settle the government's immediate obligations many of these details were disregarded; when it came to the point the Down Survey differed little in topographical content from previous plantation surveys, and many landscape changes of the early seventeenth century went unrecorded as a result (Fig. 5.2). All the same, when Petty's contract was drafted in December 1654 the distinction between plantation and non-plantation surveying stood clear in the government's account

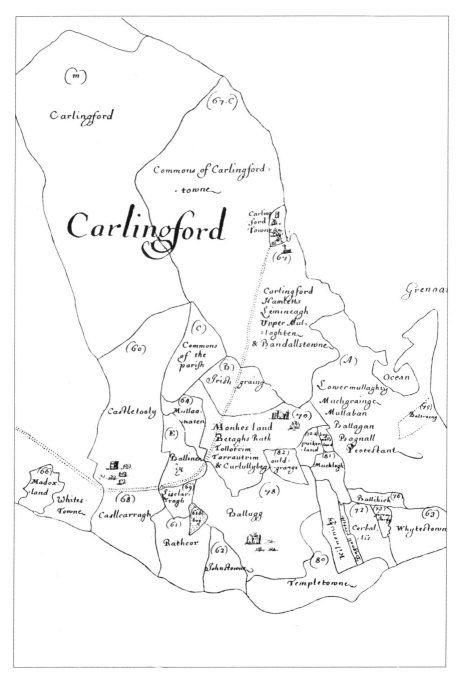

Fig. 5.2   From the Down Survey, part of the barony of Dundalk, Co. Louth, by
Captain William Morgan, [1657], original in Bibliothèque Nationale, Paris,
printed by the Ordnance Survey (Southampton, 1908). Numbers refer to
an accompanying terrier. The representation of roads and small houses
is obviously incomplete.

books. For mapping the forfeitures he was to be paid according to the acreage measured. The barony and county maps were a separate item, important enough to carry their own fee of one thousand pounds. In all this one is struck by the prominence of the barony as a bridge between local and national cartography, a role that was never shared by the equivalent territorial divisions in England. It is true that eventually baronies came to play some practical part in Irish local government at a time when the hundreds and wapentakes of England were obsolete, but it was Petty's example that caused them to appear on quite small national maps of Ireland until well into the nineteenth century.

Petty was typical of early cartographers in preferring not to publicise his methods. However, it went without saying that his sources would be accurate large-scale surveys, unadulterated by the 'conferring' of inferior earlier maps. The difficulty in compiling national maps from regional surveys is that each regional surveyor achieves consistency by pushing his errors towards the edge of his allotted territory, which thus becomes harder to dovetail with adjoining territories.[9] Petty had to overcome this tendency. He knew that a good survey must proceed from greater to less, and urged his staff that 'as often as conveniently you should protract your large surrounds before you do the inwork of the same'. The largest surrounds were the baronies. Their boundaries were to be surveyed 'with the instrument by two distinct measurers at once, their respective servants keeping double reckoning of the chains also'. These and other common lines were to be checked and where necessary corrected by a superior class of surveyors known as examiners. It was the separate surveying of barony boundaries, even where they ran through unforfeited land, that justified the director's fee of one thousand pounds. Within the baronies, parish boundaries were to be measured where 'the most part' of the land was forfeited, but where a detached parcel of forfeitures lay more than one mile inside the barony boundary and could not be seen from it the position of that parcel would have to be estimated. This was the only concession to non-instrumental methods in the Down Survey programme.[10]

In any study of Irish surveying techniques the argument from silence grows more convincing with the passage of time. If Petty had ordered any kind of triangulation or other mathematical control survey he would have said so, and we would know that he had said so. In his system the barony outlines played the part of triangles. They were self-checking to the extent that a traversed boundary would reveal at least part of the surveyor's error by failing to close upon itself, though the errors in a triangle are easier to locate and correct. In theory, or perhaps one should say in fantasy, the positions of all Petty's traverse

Fig. 5.3   Thomas Taylor, '3 provinces of Ireland described', 1659, British Library, Harleian MS 4784. Lands belonging to the auditor-general of Ireland, Edward Roberts: another example of an index map (see also Fig. 5.1) becoming the earliest surviving small-scale record of a major survey.

points could have been calculated trigonometrically, working outwards from a single national datum line and extending a method once proposed for a single enclosure by a member of the Down Survey staff.[11] In practice the baronies of each county must have been plotted separately and then pieced together jigsaw-fashion. Either before or after being joined they would have been reduced in scale. We know that Petty made use of a printed square grid for calculating areas, and no doubt such grids could also serve for copying maps on different scales, though it is no surprise that the processes of trial and error consumed more than six times as much paper as the final product. The only other check on the jigsaw would be to assemble a ring of peripheral territories before filling in the middle – and thus to carry Petty's maxim about 'inwork' to a higher territorial level.

Outside mid-seventeenth-century Ireland, no cartographic theorist has ever suggested that a national map should be made by Petty's method.[12] It did offer one advantage, nonetheless. Even the best triangulation can yield no more than an array of points which give no safeguard against local errors inside the triangles – as the Ordnance Survey was to discover in the immediate neighbourhood of its scrupulously accurate base-line nearly two centuries later. In the Down Survey many landscape details, and especially the coastline and numerous major rivers, became part of the control network by virtue of being barony boundaries and therefore had to reach the highest attainable level of accuracy. For the moment, 'personal curvature' was no longer an issue.

*　*　*　*　*　*　*　*　*

The process of synthesising larger from smaller units could be carried upwards through the territorial hierarchy, albeit with increasing risk of error, building provincial maps from county maps, and then a national map from the provincial maps. For Petty it was on the higher levels and at the smaller scales that destiny put down its challenge. There was no question of disseminating 252 barony maps, let alone 2278 parish maps, as contributions to geographical knowledge.[13] But with larger regions publication became a practicable possibility and as early as 1659 he was promising that 'maps of each county and province, as also of the whole island, will be published in print'.[14] There was already something to offer. From the same year we have a map of Connacht, Ulster and Leinster on one sheet drawn as an index to a collection of Down Survey extracts showing the estates of Edward Roberts and also unveiling in casual throwaway fashion the new outline that was to revolutionise the map of Ireland (Fig. 5.3).[15]

But with the Down Survey safely and remuneratively behind him Petty had begun to withdraw from active cartography. Henceforth most of his time was spent either in London, enjoying the knighthood conferred on him in 1661 and pursuing his career as man of science, or in Kerry looking after his new estates. His cartographic *alter ego* was Thomas Taylor, formerly a senior member of the Down Survey staff and now working in Dublin as deputy surveyor-general responsible among other things for preserving the maps that Petty had delivered to the Irish government. Taylor's superior officer was Petty's cousin John Petty, who also seems to have abandoned practical cartography by this time. It was Taylor's signature that appeared on the Roberts map, which to judge from later events had needed little if any direct supervision from anyone else. In January 1660 Petty asked his cousin to visit Taylor from time to time and 'observe the progress of the map' – evidently a more complete and more elaborate map of Ireland than Roberts's.[16] His own contributions in this year, apart from further words of encouragement for Taylor and a thank-you for the finished product, were to secure a monopoly of future sales a few months after the restoration of King Charles II and to promise Taylor 'satisfaction for all his pains in this business and his faithfulness to me'.

It may have been the framing of his request for copyright protection that prompted Petty to consider publishing an atlas as well as a single map. By the following year, at any rate, 'map' in his correspondence had become 'maps'. The main preoccupation was now engraving. Petty did not wish his work to be reproduced by etching, a technique recently applied to maps by Wenceslaus Hollar,[17] but otherwise showed no desire to concern himself with practical details. Indeed he wrote of being 'pestered' by engravers in London and perhaps it was to escape this harassment that he resolved to find an engraver in Dublin. It seems an extraordinary decision. Dublin was due to grow and prosper in the restoration era as a centre of many arts and crafts, but it still had no engravers of note, and the only good reason for Petty's choice was that in Ireland Taylor's editorial services would be available. This was spelt out in a letter to John Petty dated 23 March 1661: 'I have written to T.T. about our maps which pray peruse and agree with him. In brief he preparing all the maps within mentioned and overseeing and correction of the graver. Shall have £60 out of the first year's profits and £30 per annum for seven years after'. An earlier letter may help to identify the maps 'within mentioned':

Tell T.T. that I would have a convenient size of paper pitched upon such as might contain the largest county, and two of the smallest according to the present scale, upon which account bid him send me word how many sheets will hold the map as it now is. (2nd) I would have these loose sheets capable of making four large provincial maps to match which (as to size) I would have a new general map done at half the present scale: for so shall we have five maps of near one size to hang a room with. (3rd) I would have four provincial maps and the general reduced to a

Fig. 5.4   Parts of Cos Antrim and Down from an anonymous printed map of
Ireland probably by Willam Petty, *c.*1663, British Library, K.51.9.11. A
graticule has been added in pencil by an unknown hand. The blank
spaces represent lands not forfeited in the Cromwellian settlement and
therefore omitted from the Down Survey, though some additional detail
not forming part of that survey is incorporated in the Hillsborough district.

single sheet also, that those five small ones and the county sheet
maps may together make a book, whereunto shall be added the
description of each map.

Unfortunately this correspondence comes to an end without
recording whether Taylor accepted Petty's terms. But at least we know

that the first and third items in the programme were eventually carried out. So should the strictly cartographic part of Petty's achievement be credited to Taylor? It is a penalty of high office to be accused of stealing other people's glory, and a perquisite of high office that posterity seldom finds such accusations wholly convincing. The matter is best smoothed over with words from a later phase of Irish cartographic history: to Petty belongs the design, to Taylor the execution.[18]

'The map as it now is' was presumably the one received from Taylor in August 1660. It figures in a later list of Petty's achievements written by himself as 'the grand map of Ireland 1663',[19] the date probably a reference to engraving rather than drawing. This map was apparently never published, for only one copy containing all fifteen sheets survives and that is an unfinished proof (Fig. 5.4).[20] Petty may well have changed his mind about where to have it engraved: the map's maturity and elegance of style are consistent with the testimony of his friend John Evelyn that it was done in Amsterdam.[21] Some of its features certainly suggest an ignorance of Irish geography – as where names common to parishes and townlands are written twice in the same script, producing an effect of pointless duplication, instead of in different styles for parish and townland as the original authors had intended.

Stage three, the 'book' of national, provincial and county maps, was later to be famous as Petty's *Hiberniae delineatio* (Figs 5.5-5.7). This he did manage to publish, though not until 1685. One proof that it was engraved more than twenty years before publication is the decorative motif on several of its maps depicting Petty's invention, the double-bottomed boat, first announced in 1662 but not likely to have been advertised after 1666, when the prototype was ignominiously wrecked.[22] Atlas and grand map are broadly similar in style and substance, but typologically they are not contemporaneous. The atlas contains many more names, as would be expected from its larger scale. It also falsely connects four pairs of river systems which on the grand map are separated; somebody must have drawn attention to these errors after the atlas had been finished. Another sign that the grand map cannot have been simply taken from the atlas as printed is its inclusion of several features peculiar to itself, among them the town of Donaghadee, the buoy known as the Perch in Dublin Bay, the town of Arklow, the nearby 'shires of Wicklow', and the name 'Mountkennedy' in the same county, substituted for the atlas's 'Balligarne'. Perhaps both atlas and grand map were derived from an even grander manuscript map, a theory supported not just by *a priori* probability, but by several freakish scribal errors common to both versions, such as the merger of

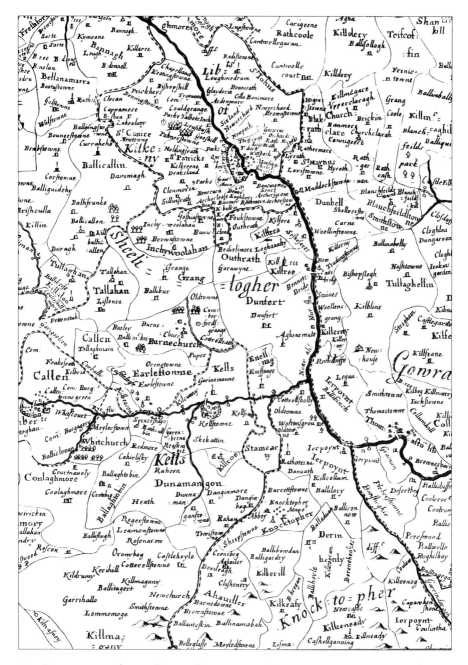

Fig. 5.5   Part of Co. Kilkenny, from Petty's *Hiberniae delineatio* (London, 1685).
The scripts for barony, parish and townland names are easily
distinguished, but some of the numerous symbols used for single
settlements are unintelligible.

131

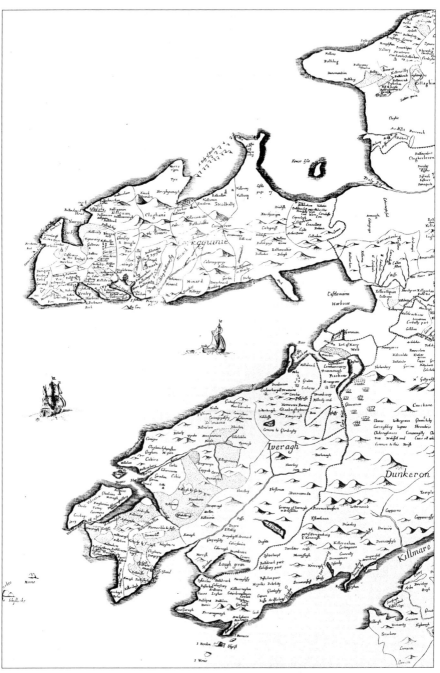

Fig. 5.6   Part of Co. Kerry, from Petty's *Hiberniae delineatio*, 1685. In its
representation of coasts, islands, rivers, lakes, mountains and woods the
Delineatio here testifies to the value of the Down Survey as a
geographical source, and as the first important advance on Lythe's
outline of the south-west.

:Fig. 5.7   Part of Co. Fermanagh, from Petty's *Hiberniae delineatio*, 1685. Petty's
worst failure, omitting much of the coastline of Lough Erne and (despite
his promise to the government) a considerable length of barony
boundary. The *Delineatio*'s provincial map of Ulster is similarly
defective, but in Petty's large map of Ireland (Fig. 5.4) the lake is
completed by a diagrammatic east-west line.

'Fethard' and 'Tintern' in Co. Wexford to make 'Feathearn'. This may help to determine whether all Petty's engravers worked in the same place. It is difficult to picture a single manuscript being passed from one atelier to another – perhaps from one country to another – and the sum of one thousand pounds quoted by Evelyn for Petty's engraving costs seems enough for an atlas as well as a map. On the other hand the two works sometimes give conflicting interpretations of the author's wishes, for instance in the matter of parish and townland name-sizes already mentioned. Furthermore the *Delineatio*'s styles (clearly different artists worked on different pages) were generally rougher and uglier, and certainly no credit to Amsterdam. The nationality of its engravers must remain an open question.

Wherever the engraving was done, it cannot have been under Petty's own direct supervision. An author of his originality and modern-mindedness would surely have found some way of giving his maps a new look, perhaps by anticipating eighteenth-century or (more probably in Petty's case) nineteenth-century ideas. But on this level *Hiberniae delineatio* is soporifically conventional. Its cartouches, though up-to-date in decorative style, are unnecessarily elaborate, clumsily executed, and without allegorical point, satisfying neither mind nor eye with their frozen-faced marine creatures and wizened little cherubs. Similarly hills, woods and buildings appear in traditional profile. Titles and length-units are in Latin, exactly the kind of antiquarianism that Petty should have disliked. The only personal touch in the whole decor is the cartographically irrelevant double-bottomed boat.

*   *   *   *   *   *   *   *   *

If *Hiberniae delineatio* was engraved in the 1660s why did it remain unpublished until 1685?[23] The usual cause of delay in such cases is lack of external finance. But Petty acted as his own publisher, and it is clear from his offer to Taylor that he never had any intention of sharing the profits with a commercial firm. He could certainly afford the luxury of vanity publishing; by his own calculation the profits from the Down Survey had been nine thousand pounds, a satisfactory source of income when invested in Irish land.[24] On the other hand he may as a matter of principle have expected the government to finance the *Delineatio* and been willing to wait for this eventuality. A monopoly of future sales did nothing to get the work printed, and in 1665 Petty petitioned Charles II for more practical help. On the king's advice, parliament responded in a statute that belatedly finalised the Irish land settlement begun by Cromwell. The act urged Petty's Down Survey debtors to pay him but that was all.[25] This may well have been a good enough reason for giving up in disgust. At any rate he did give up and suddenly, with the engraver of Co. Roscommon stopping short in mid-map.

Or Petty could have simply lost interest in the organisation of cartography, just as he had already lost interest in its practical details. There were certainly enough other calls on his time, and his later writings seldom refer to maps of any kind. Moreover, as restoration science gathered momentum he must have felt increasing regret that his own maps were fundamentally unscientific in their lack of latitudes and longitudes and of a proper mathematical control. Accurate techniques for connecting astronomical and terrestrial measurements were already well known before Petty was born. Willebrod Snell in Holland had measured a degree of latitude by astronomical observations at the extremes of a triangulation network in 1617-22.[26] In 1635 Richard Norwood did the same at the ends of a traverse survey from London to York.[27] Admittedly these methods had not yet been integrated into any otherwise normal mapping project, but such a consummation was inevitable sooner or later.

The 1650s or at a pinch the 1660s were the last decade in which anyone calling himself a natural philosopher could hope to pass muster with a survey by chain and circumferentor. After the foundation of the Royal Society in 1660 and the French Academy six years later, the problems of geodesy were constantly before the educated public. Jean Picard's measurement of a degree was reported to the Royal Society in 1672, and its cartographic implications became evident in the following year when Jean Dominique Cassini was appointed to reform the map of France.[28] Nearer home, John Adams in 1682 proposed a new map of England built around three accurately laid-out meridians of longitude.[29] In this rarefied context the merit of the *Delineatio* was purely negative: its author had at least refrained from drawing a retrospective graticule across his map with the unwarranted facility made respectable by Gerard Mercator in a less demanding age. Petty must have had mixed feelings when others tried to remedy this omission on his behalf.[30] The fact was that the longer he put off publication, the stronger became the reasons for continued postponement. The problem would have seemed less serious with the county maps than with the national map, for it was generally understood that graticules could not be accurate enough for maps of small areas at large scales – where in any case they were less useful to the ordinary user. Perhaps this explains why in the end Petty published the *Delineatio* but not the 'grand map'.

The most probable reason for hesitancy was one that Petty admitted himself in 1673. All his maps, he said then, 'could the defects of them be supplied with the yet unmeasured lands, could be exposed to public view'.[31] The unmeasured lands made up about half the surface area of Ireland, but when the maps were engraved he was still hoping that the gap could somehow be filled. The normal practice in map design was euphemistically to mask the blanks in an author's knowledge by spreading out names and symbols, but Petty's engravers always left a sharp edge between densely packed detail and empty space – an aesthetic solecism that no member of their profession would have committed except under direct orders. To begin with, Petty may have taken comfort from his expectation of official assistance, and in December 1660 he warned Taylor almost jauntily to 'take a view of our surveying instruments, for there will be work'.[32] When government help failed to materialise, hiring surveyors at his own expense was evidently out of the question.

To solicit private estate maps for Petty's purpose was equally impracticable: in the whole of Irish history there is hardly one recorded case of landed proprietors commissioning joint surveys of their estates. We may wonder whether Petty ever considered roughing out the necessary maps from the Civil Survey of 1654-6, which took in unforfeited as well as forfeited land but which gave only names, acreages and verbally-described boundaries with no cartographic support. 'Graphicisation' of this kind had been used for the escheated lands of Ulster in 1609,[33] but Petty would surely have scorned it as too inaccurate to be contemplated. His best hope was that the county authorities would independently adopt the Down Survey as a basis for local taxation and then make their own surveys to fill the gaps. In some places this actually happened, parts of Antrim outside the Down Survey area, for instance, being newly measured at county expense in 1661.[34] Sure enough, hitherto unknown material from south Antrim was duly incorporated into *Hiberniae delineatio,* and another patch of new information, including the town of Hillsborough, was printed for Co. Down. Here perhaps was an early sign of superior Ulster initiative in practical affairs, for elsewhere such *ad hoc* local-authority surveys did not become common until the eighteenth century; at any rate these seem to have been the only specimens that came into Petty's possession.

Thomas Taylor, as deputy surveyor-general in Dublin, might have been expected to collect and process county or part-county surveys like those of Antrim and Down. But Taylor, like Petty, was becoming a person of consequence, with less time and energy to spare for the minutiae of map-making. In any case, relations with his former chief appear to have deteriorated. In 1681, writing in his official capacity about the custody of the government's surveys, he took exception to fees charged for access to maps still held by Petty. He went on, gratuitously, to revive an old dispute about Petty's use of Strafford Survey information where this overlapped with the Down Survey. According to Taylor, Petty had been given the Strafford maps to help him with the Down Survey, but instead of acknowledging them he 'left out here and there a line' to disguise the work and to make absolute and unprofitable, and Patrick Raggett the surveyor did it, as I remember, and never surveyed the land and yet was paid for it'.[35] These were not the words of a loyal and willing collaborator, whatever Taylor had been in the past.

Did Petty also charge a fee for access to his maps of baronies and larger areas? Without doubt they were known to a surprisingly wide circle of readers long before he published them. Sir Alan Brodrick had his own proof copy of the whole atlas at some time during his tenure of the Irish surveyor-generalship in 1660-67 (another pointer towards its engraving date)[36] and Sir Henry Piers had already seen the 'great map' when he wrote an account of Co. Westmeath in 1682.[37] The national and provincial maps even became a source for several commercial publications, notably *A new mapp of England Scotland and Ireland* by Robert Morden and Robert Greene in 1674.[38] Given their availability for so long through various private channels, we may well ask why Petty bothered to publish his maps at all. One influence may have been the misfortunes of the London bookseller Moses Pitt. In the early 1680s Pitt hoped to make his name with the first English multi-volume world atlas, for which maps of Ireland were to be supplied by William Molyneux, the energetic secretary of the new Dublin Philosophical Society. Molyneux planned a national map and four provincial maps. Encouraged no doubt by the generosity shown to earlier compilers like Morden and Greene, he hoped to base these maps on Petty's. Like so many atlases this one was never completed.[39] It seems to have been Pitt's failure, rather than the threat of his success, that finally brought Petty into the open. If no one else could publish a good-sized map of Ireland, he might as well do it himself.

It is also possible that government interest in the project now belatedly revived and that publication in the first months of a new reign was something more than a coincidence, especially since printed maps from *Hiberniae delineatio* were used to illustrate a military survey of Irish towns and forts produced at this time for James II by Captain Thomas Phillips.[40] In fact the decision was probably taken at least two years earlier, for the date engraved in the portrait of Petty that prefaces the atlas in its published form is 1683. This was also the year of the author's sixtieth birthday, a time of life when delays begin to seem imprudent. In fact he beat the clock quite comfortably, not dying until 1687. No doubt printing, collation and binding brought their own problems, but otherwise Petty did little to make up for lost time. As a vehicle for 'production values' the *Delineatio* was a disappointment. There was no preface, no dedication, no text, no key, and no attempt to finish what had been left so glaringly incomplete twenty years earlier. Half of Roscommon was still blank, Achill Island was still missing from the map of Connacht (though present in that of Mayo), and Lough Erne still had no northern shoreline in the map of Fermanagh. Nor had there been any improvement to the interconnecting rivers that Petty had corrected on his grand map as early as c.1663.

No one ever complained of these defects. Petty had made up for everything by the extraordinary accuracy and comprehensiveness of what he did get right. The *Delineatio's* RMS errors (Leinster 0.063, Munster 0.056, Ulster 0.049, Connacht 0.077) show a greater improvement on the best of its predecessors than do those of any other map tested in this study. And even for the most basic physical features he managed to increase Speed's coverage substantially: of rivers from 136 to 166, lakes from 45 to 59, upland masses from 53 to 75. In broader terms his achievement remains beyond precise quantitative assessment, except that the number of placenames in his surviving manuscript barony maps has been estimated at about 25,000.[41] But by depending almost entirely on incomplete surveys he inevitably failed to show all that his scale was capable of accommodating. Of rivers exceeding twenty miles in length the *Delineatio* ignores no less than ten, among them the 42-mile Annalee in Co. Fermanagh. As Charles Smith remarked in an early contribution to Petty criticism, it sometimes omits detail that had been shown on earlier maps: three of the above-mentioned rivers are marked in Speed's *Theatre*.[42]

*   *   *   *   *   *   *   *   *

If Petty was not a truly scientific cartographer he could at least avoid being totally commercial. In the context of ordinary map-publishing, *Hiberniae delineatio* was an act of defiance. Its most fundamental break with tradition was the author's choice of scales. Earlier atlas-makers had taken pains to achieve a uniform sheet-size. Typically they would devote each page to a single political or administrative division, with the size of that division determining the scale of the map. Not only did different scales appear on different pages, but to fit a map snugly within its page the chosen scale-ratios were often awkwardly lacking in 'roundness'. It was reasonable enough that this awkwardness should be . particularly characteristic of small scales: a user was less likely to measure lengths on small-scale maps, not least because their statements of ground distance were especially vulnerable to the contraction and expansion of the paper. In such circumstances it was preferable to think in terms of latitude and longitude, and on small-scale maps the requisite graticule was more likely to be provided. An atlas of uniform page-size was also convenient to handle and aesthetically pleasing. Geographically however the scale differences necessitated by this arrangement were illogical and misleading – except on the argument (perhaps over-sophisticated in this case) that large administrative areas are generally less densely populated than small ones and therefore do not deserve such detailed mapping.

Unlike every other Irish county-atlas maker of whom anything is known, Petty preferred a single scale for each territorial order, with a simple ratio of ground units to inches on the paper, and simple relationships between the scales of different orders. For maps not immortalised by printing, the first of these rules could be waived provided the waiving was done methodically, with the result that in the Down Survey parishes were mapped at either 40 or 80 Irish perches to an inch, and baronies at either 80, 160 or 320 perches. In the *Delineatio* all counties were at two Irish miles to an inch, all provinces at six miles, and Ireland at twelve miles.[43] The mile and the perch were left undefined, a further rebuff to scientific method. Petty doubtless felt that the Down Survey had standardised the Irish perch at twenty-one feet and the Irish mile at 2240 yards, and with any other interpretation his hierarchy of scale-ratios loses much of its point. On this premise an English mile can be identified from his double scale-bars as the 'statute' measure of 1760 yards – still a comparative rarity on English maps of the 1660s and therefore another claim to originality for the *Delineatio*.

Nearly all Petty's atlas maps are in either 'landscape' or 'portrait' format with north at the top; only the general map is slightly twisted, in a clockwise direction, probably by accident. The most awkward result of an uncompromising scales policy was that the largest counties needed more than one plate. Part-counties were not given their own sheet lines in the manner of, say, Mercator's northern and southern Ireland. They had to be pasted together and folded.[44] Another implication of uniform scales was that theoretically the counties could have been cut out and assembled as they stood to form an unbroken map of Ireland eleven feet long and seven feet wide. This is a good enough reason for treating the entire atlas as a cartographic unit, a necessary fiction considering the smallness and inadequacy of its introductory map of Ireland at twelve miles to an inch (Fig. 5.8). Of course it would have been even more radical to publish Ireland in rectangular sheets filled up to their edges like those of the Ordnance

Fig. 5.8   *A general mapp of Ireland*, from Petty's *Hiberniae delineatio* (London, 1685). The only single-sheet map of Ireland to be published by Petty himself. Though modern in general outline, its minor details and cartographic design do less than justice to the merits of his survey.

Survey. But the ordnance map had a military purpose. In a country whose conquest seemed to be complete, Petty chose to prefigure the growing civil importance of the county as local-government expenditure increased throughout the next two centuries. He was also,

140

no doubt consciously, taking his place beside Saxton, Speed and other county mapmakers in the mainstream of English cartography.

* * * * * * * * *

Another of the *Delineatio*'s surprises is a lack of editorial control so blatant that it must almost be taken as some kind of manifesto. Other atlas-makers had sought balance and harmony through evenness of texture and uniformity of subject-matter, and in Ireland some unfortunate geographical implications of this policy can be seen by comparing Robert Lythe's holographs with their printed derivatives. Petty was steadfast in varying his line-character for different kinds of boundary and his script for different orders of territorial name. Otherwise all was confusion. He cannot be blamed for the large blank spaces marking unforfeited land: no one would expect him to have re-engraved the whole atlas in 1683 with names and symbols spread out. But he could have softened the contrast by not crowding so many words into the forfeited areas to begin with. Most of them were the names of townlands whose boundaries had to be omitted, and for which there were no appropriate settlement symbols. The floating territorial name was already a familiar device for large areas like Brefni or O'Donnell's Country. Now it was proliferating at the lowest level, and by some process of contagion names of the same kind were invading unforfeited territory and capturing middle-rank settlement nucleations such as Kilkea and Rathangan in Co. Kildare.

Many of Petty's successors, including the Ordnance Survey, would feel obliged to admit names without symbols, but they managed to keep the floaters evenly spread. Petty stacked them up like sandwiches on a plate, with other names crammed sideways or aslant between one pile and the next. As a result his writing was necessarily reduced in size, making even important places awkwardly hard to find, the county towns of Cavan and Monaghan being among the most elusive cases in point. In this calligraphic jungle, words and parts of words could easily fuse together, with pseudo-names emerging from their dismembered fragments, or from such tightly written descriptive phrases as 'hereafight' in Co. Meath. And Petty made the worst of both worlds by omitting many names that had appeared in the manuscript Down Survey parish and barony maps. In a sample of sixty-four townland names on the parish maps of northernmost Co. Tipperary, twelve are missing from the *Delineatio*. Not all the names that did appear were well chosen. Many of the parcels in the manuscript maps were clusters of townlands combined within a single boundary, and the names of individual members of these clusters were often written prose-fashion in horizontal lines with no attempt to locate them correctly – thus reviving a medieval genre known to some historians as the 'list map'. The transcription of such lists on to a smaller scale by uncomprehending engravers would inevitably give a false impression of spatial explicitness.

The *Delineatio* also retained many symbols and inscriptions that a more vigilant editor would have eliminated as unhelpfully random and defective gleanings from what had begun as a well-stocked thematic display. The printed industrial sites, for instance, are so few that they might just as well have been omitted; the same is true of antiquities like the 'steeple' at Antrim. Other legacies from the Down Survey were what might be called plantationisms. Some of these were harmless enough, the names or titles of landowners for instance. Others, such as the words 'diff[erence]' and 'contro[versy]', had lost all meaning in the change of milieu. Purists might also object to certain longer entries like 'The Thurlogh being Markes' (the last word a misreading of 'marshes') in Co. Roscommon and 'A place where the water howls' at what was later known as McSwine's Gun on the coast of Donegal, though future map-historians would value the howling water as a clue to Petty's influence on a number of later maps.[45]

Part of the editing process was to distribute information among three sets of maps representing three territorial orders. A useful rule of map history, often forgotten, is that small maps sometimes contain information not to be found on the larger maps from which they purport to derive. This seeming anomaly is both inevitable and desirable: a regional name like 'The Fens' may suit a small-scale map of eastern England, but could hardly appear on any of the 1:2500 Ordnance Survey sheets that cover the area in question. On the same principle, Petty can be forgiven and even congratulated for using less accurate sources in his national and provincial maps than he would have tolerated at the county scale. For instance, in the county and provincial maps of the *Delineatio*, as in the Down Survey, roads appear only as occasional short detached lengths. In the *Delineatio*'s small map of Ireland they form an integrated network. Given an engraving date in the early 1660s, this could well be the earliest national road system to be shown on any British map. As it happens, Petty's accuracy and comprehensiveness in this field are open to serious doubt. He shows no road from Dublin to Maynooth, or from Cork to Kinsale, and several major towns like Longford, Maryborough, Naas and Navan are left inaccessible. There are also many differences from near-contemporary sources like John Woodhouse's Irish road-list of 1647 (Fig. 5.9)[46] and the record of postal services compiled by Henry van der Heyden in 1659 (Fig. 5.10).[47] The fact remains however that at a scale

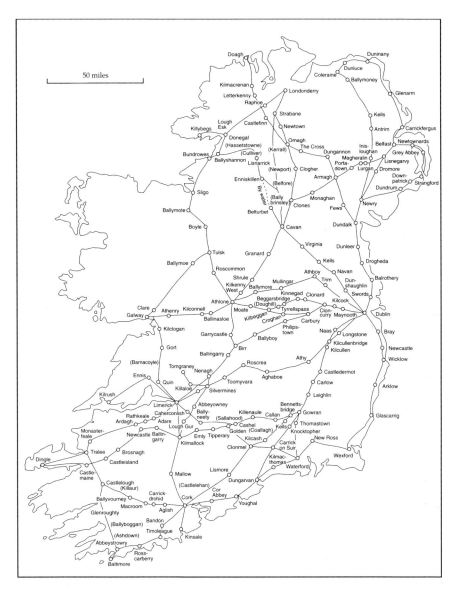

Fig. 5.9   Mid seventeenth-century roads, freely and diagrammatically interpreted
from John Woodhouse, *A guide for strangers in the kingdom of Ireland*
(London, 1647). Spellings modernised where possible. Unidentified
places (shown in brackets) have been located in accordance with
Woodhouse's mileage figures. The inclusion of minor settlements and
physical features (e.g. Glenroughty and L. Esk) suggests that the author
was following a map rather than a list of post towns.

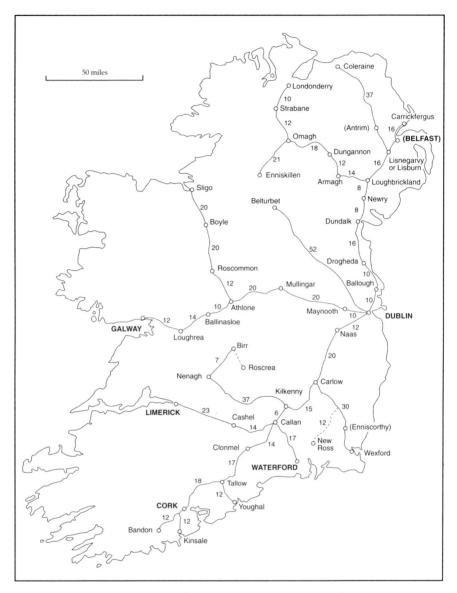

Fig. 5.10   List of post roads, 1659, British Library, Add. MS 32,471 (8). Figures give
distances in miles (presumably Irish) between places with unbracketed
names. Roads are shown by broken lines where their point of junction
with other roads is unknown.

as small as twelve miles to the inch it was justifiable in principle for roads to be mapped by 'graphicising' a verbal source.

On the coast the cadastral antecedents of the *Delineatio* produced some unusual results. Whatever interest and romance may attach to small islands, they pose difficult logistical problems for any farmer or businessman seeking to exploit them, and most of the Cromwellian government's creditors would have preferred to be paid in acres of mainland. Consequently islands were under-valued and under-represented in the plantation surveys, including the Down Survey, despite Petty's special instructions on the subject. On his small maps, however, he remembered his economist's concern for trade and navigation. No doubt he also remembered the general cartographic principle that coasts need more attention than interiors. At any rate he now filled some of the hydrographic gaps in the Down Survey, even at the cost of breaking his own unwritten embargo on non-plantation sources. The obvious authorities were existing maps. John Speed, for instance, is the most likely source for Petty's Makenton Bay, Bishop's Seat, Anguish Rock, Tuskard, Ferriter and Inishbofin. Perhaps he reasoned that, as with roads, this less accurate information should be confined to smaller scales. All the same the results were confusingly unpredictable. With three territorial orders, a given feature could appear on all three levels, on any two, on any one, or on none, a total of eight possibilities. But in practice there seems no reason why the Mullets and Dundalk Bay (or Harbour) should be absent only from the provincial map, or Glenarm Bay only from the county map; or why Bimena and Duffin should be present only on the provincial map, and Lambs Island and Cow and Calf (near Cork Harbour) only on the national map. And of course this leaves aside all irregularities in the transmission or non-transmission of Petty's own survey material from county to province and from province to kingdom, an issue best evaded by forgetting that the *Delineatio* is not in fact a single map.[48]

It is hard to know whether to blame Petty or Taylor for these editorial weaknesses. Perhaps their draughtsmen were simply told to reduce the barony maps as best they could and perhaps each drawing was then passed to an engraver without further scrutiny. Alternatively the *Delineatio* might be seen as a deliberate protest against editorial meddling and an insistence on giving the most direct possible access to primary sources, the cartographic equivalent to the modern novelist's slice of life. Petty would surely have sympathised with this idea.[49]

* * * * * * * *

Petty's merits and his faults combine to give a clear but misleading picture of seventeenth-century Ireland. Most previous mapmakers, like most early topographical writers, preferred to put the best face on God's creation. Among the Elizabethans, for instance, the map of England evoked a countryside 'with shadowy forests and with champains rich'd, with plenteous rivers and wide-skirted meads'. This was also the effect of Saxton's county maps. It was an impression enhanced by cheerful colours – red for buildings, blue for water, green for trees and sometimes rather optimistically for mountains. Petty too preferred to see colour on his maps,[50] but we may guess that this was probably to define the territorial hierarchy by tinting boundaries rather than for any aesthetic reason. Most surviving copies of his atlas are uncoloured and the feature that first catches the eye is its only area-convention, an engraved stipple denoting bogs – not many people's favourite landscape. Elsewhere a heavy shade darkens most of his coastlines and many of his hillsides.

Petty's trees are too few to be very shadowy in an agreeable or any other sense. Before the conquest woods had been an enemy landscape in the Englishman's Ireland, ruthlessly destroyed when opportunity allowed to root out the rebels who took shelter in them. In the ecologically misnamed plantation era they were cut down for more peaceful uses – house and ship building, barrel staves, tanning, iron smelting – but older attitudes remained influential and there was no attempt at coppicing or replanting. By the time of the Civil and Down Surveys timber-woods were a scarce resource, to be bounded and measured at least as carefully as arable land. No longer could cartographers hide their ignorance of Ireland by scattering forests across it like savage pictures on an Afric map.

Politically the *Delineatio* is more neutral than its author. Native power has disappeared. There are none of the old territorial and family names that dominate Elizabethan maps. The population, though large, is helpless and divided. Its density is shown by the close spacing of habitation names, not only in the old English Pale but in remote places like Rathlin Island, Sheep's Head and the western end of the Dingle peninsula. The dispersal of settlement is suggested, paradoxically, by a shortage among the names of point symbols that might have been taken to denote villages. The symbols that do occur are bewildering in their unedited variety – towers, rectangles, crosses on circles, houses, a mixture of realism and convention symptomatic of a disorganised and fragmented society. No clear hierarchy of settlement emerges and few towns were deemed worthy of special emphasis. The tangle of parish and barony boundaries speaks of confinement and segregation, a feeling strengthened on the county maps by the almost complete absence of roads.

Petty's neutrality also has a historical dimension, ignoring modern achievements in favour of a quintessential Irishness. This unprogressive disposition, at first sight strange in one so modern-minded, can be assigned to several causes. The most obvious was the delay in publication already discussed and the consequent omission of all developments later than about 1660. Now that Ireland had started to modernise itself such time-lags were becoming more noticeable. For instance eighteen places had received their first borough charters during the reign of Charles II and some of them, like Charleville, Lanesborough, Midleton and Portarlington, had failed to qualify for even the *Delineatio's* smallest size of script. Also easily explained is the under-recording of pre-Cromwellian geographical change. This partly reflected the emphasis that Petty gave to townlands and parishes, for many post-medieval settlements had not yet given their names to either of these divisions. In any case, much new early seventeenth-century settlement had been in areas of recent Protestant immigration on land omitted from the Down Survey (and therefore from the *Delineatio)* because it had escaped forfeiture. Though nobody said so, this was essentially an atlas of Catholic Ireland.

The *Delineatio* shows little sympathy either with Ireland's native past or for that matter with historical studies in general. Its neglect of antiquities has already been mentioned. St Patrick gets some recognition but only as a placename element, once at his famous Purgatory and again at his (exceptionally high) mountain in Co. Mayo; and there is no special acknowledgement of Tara (except as an anonymous 'mount'), Glendalough, the Hill of Uisneach, Navan Fort, or Rathcroghan. At the same time Petty did seem to be looking backward in his choice of style and subject-matter. His towns were defended by curvilinear walls with closely-spaced towers, more medieval than modern (even at Londonderry) and sometimes probably defunct or non-existent as at Mullingar, Callan, Ballymoe and Carrigrohame. Lesser settlements were arranged along streets but always without the regularity of the modern town-planner, and country roads were all of the 'evolved' variety, never straight. Where individual houses were drawn realistically, they were tall, narrow and unwelcoming. This was in many ways a truthful picture, as Thomas Dineley had shown in his drawings of the Irish landscape a few years earlier.[51] But a differently minded cartographer could have done more to highlight the exceptions. For instance, why not draw Beaulieu House near Drogheda in the latest Caroline fashion (as it had been rebuilt in 1663) instead of as a medieval moated grange? In the same spirit, Petty's constitutional landscape was littered with medievalisms like 'manor', 'liberty' and 'lordship', as well as with innumerable commons, many of them doubtless appropriated by private owners before the atlas was published. Was this more neutralism, or perhaps an implicit plea for modernisation?

Off the map, at any rate, Petty was very far from neutral. He made no secret of believing that Irishmen would be happier if they could become more like Englishmen. But his attitude to placenames was less straightforward than this general philosophy might suggest. In his *Political anatomy*, written in about 1673, he stressed the need for names to be backed by state authority, with equivalences between official and earlier versions properly recorded. The same book also quoted a recent statute recommending that barbarous and uncouth names should be replaced by new ones. But it was only near the end of his life and with the impatience of advancing age that Petty expressly recommended introducing English names for all places in Ireland. The *Anatomy* simply proposed that the 'significant parts' of Irish names should be 'interpreted, where they are not, or cannot be abolished'.[52] Despite his ignorance of the Irish language Petty hoped to compile his own explanatory table of 'significant parts' – perhaps as a step towards standardising recurrent prefixes and suffixes in anticipation of the Ordnance Survey.

Petty's table never appeared, and none of the names on his maps are new translations. When it came to the point the orthography of the Down Survey was like that of most earlier mapmakers – as nearly phonetic as contemporary English spelling habits (and listening habits) would allow. The *Delineatio* however made numerous alterations. Many of these were obviously accidental; others showed the somewhat haphazard application of a definite if unspoken principle, which was to shorten a name where this could be done without seriously affecting its pronunciation. Thus terminal 'e's' were dropped, double letters were made single, and 'agh' was reduced to 'a'. Shortening could be vertical as well as horizontal, for instance when 'y' gave way to 'i'. This suggests that Petty's motive was simply to save space on a crowded map. He betrayed his illiberalism by defying orthographic custom in pursuit of this aim.

*   *   *   *   *   *   *   *   *

Perhaps the strongest tribute to Petty's cartographic influence comes from the German map historian Johann Georg Kohl in 1844: 'It is scarcely credible, yet it is not the less true, that all the maps of Ireland which were made during the last century, were based on an old one, drawn towards the close *[sic]* of the seventeenth century'.[53] Kohl might have felt less incredulous if he had recognised the map in question as

148

the first of any country (according to another continental authority) to have been made 'from direct protractions'.[54] But despite its importance the *Delineatio*'s bibliographical history was mercifully simple. The 1685 printing eventually became scarce and in 1732 Petty's son, the earl of Shelburne, authorised the re-use of the original plates by the Dublin bookseller George Grierson. Though not without cartographic ambitions of his own, Grierson made no changes of substance except that his plate for the small map of Ireland was different from that of 1685 without being in any sense more up to date. Perhaps it was old work intended for the first edition but then rejected. The appearance of an unrevised edition after nearly half a century was a comment on the low state of Irish cartography in the post-Petty era as well as a tribute to the master himself. But Grierson had chosen about the latest possible opportunity for getting the *Delineatio* taken seriously in its own right. (The second reprint of 1875 can be dismissed as an antiquarian curiosity.) Ireland would soon be changing too fast for Petty's defects to be tolerable. For features that did not change, he remained a high authority, the equivalent on his own ground of Ptolemy in fifteenth-century Europe except that in most countries the eighteenth century was a time for discarding and replacing established cartographic authorities rather than venerating them. Kohl's testimony was supported by the next three maps considered in this book and by innumerable others. The reasons for the longevity that so impressed him were simple enough. There were no more Down Surveys until the 1830s, and no more Pettys ever.

References

1. Examples are Francis Jobson's map of Munster in c.1589 (National Library of Ireland, 16. B.13; National Maritime Museum, Greenwich, MS P.39, nos 18, 20, 27; Trinity College, Dublin, MS 1209, nos 36, 37); two maps of the escheated counties of Ulster in 1609-10 (Hatfield House, Cecil maps, 4/1; British Library,Cotton MS Augustus I, ii, 44); and a map of Co. Londonderry by Thomas Raven in 1622 reproduced in D.A. Chart (ed.), *Londonderry and the London companies* (Belfast, 1928), frontispiece.

2. J.H. Andrews, *Plantation acres, an historical study of the Irish land surveyor and his maps* (Belfast, 1985), pp 55-6.

3. *Calendar of State Papers, Ireland, 1633-47*, p. 353.

4. T.A. Larcom, *A history of the survey of Ireland commonly called the Down Survey, by Doctor William Petty, A.D. 1655-6* (Dublin, 1851), p. 57.

5. Trinity College, Dublin, MS 1209, no. 69.

6. The best account of Petty's cartographic work is still Y.M. Goblet, *La transformation de la géographie politique de l'Irlande au XVIIe siècle dans les cartes et essais anthropogéographiques de Sir William Petty*, 3 vols (Paris, 1930).

7. For Petty's estimates of the total distance measured (using the earth's circumference as a unit) see Andrews, *Plantation acres*, p. 80, n. 67.

8. The only surviving early map directly associated with the shiring of Ireland is a sketch of Wicklow and Ferns in 1579 (Public Record Office, London, MPF 69).

9. Aaron Arrowsmith, *Memoir relative to the construction of the map of Scotland published by Aaron Arrowsmith in the year 1807* (London and Edinburgh, 1809), pp 8-9.

10. Larcom, *Down Survey*, pp xiii, xiv, 6, 8, 28.

11. Henry Osborne, *A more exact way to delineate the plot of any spacious parcel of land* (Dublin, 1654).

12. For a general judgement on the impossibility of compiling national maps from uncontrolled local territorial surveys see Roger J.P. Kain and Elizabeth Baigent, *The cadastral map in the service of the state: a history of property mapping* (Chicago, 1992), p. 231.

13. These are Petty's own figures (William Petty, *The political anatomy of Ireland* (London, 1691), p. 117).

14. Larcom, *Down Survey*, p. xviii.

15. British Library, Harleian MS 4784.

16. Bowood papers, vi, first series, no. 7, 28 January 1659[-60], microfilm, Bodleian Library, Oxford.

17. Helen M. Wallis and Arthur H. Robinson (eds), *Cartographic innovations: an international handbook of mapping terms to 1900* ([Tring], 1987), p. 297.

18. Adapted from a reference by Thomas Larcom to the parts played by two of his fellow-officers in the invention of the Ordnance Survey's base-measuring apparatus (J.H. Andrews, *A paper landscape, the Ordnance Survey in nineteenth-century Ireland* (Oxford, 1975), p. 51).

19. Edmond Fitzmaurice, *The life of Sir William Petty, 1623-1687* (London, 1895), pp 317-18.

20. British Library, K.51.9.11. The Bodleian Library, Oxford, has three sheets of this map (Gough Maps, Ireland, 2), one with an engraved compass rose absent from the British Library copy.

21. E.S. de Beer (ed.), *The diaries of John Evelyn*, iv (Oxford, 1955), p. 58.

22. The best account of this venture is in P.G. Dale, *Sir W.P. of Romsey* (Romsey, 1987), pp 36-9.

23. The publication date is fixed by an entry in E.S. Arber, *The term catalogues, 1668-1709* (London, 1905), ii, p. 126. Later editions were produced by George Grierson (Dublin, n.d., 1732), the Marquis of Lansdowne (Bowood, 1875), Frank Graham (Newcastle, 1968), and the Irish University Press (Shannon, 1969, with introduction by J. H. Andrews).

24. Fitzmaurice, *Life of Petty*, p. 62.

25. Irish statutes, 17 and 18 Charles II, c. 2; Larcom, *Down Survey*, pp 398-401.

26. N.D. Haasbroek, *Gemma Frisius, Tycho Brahe and Snellius and their triangulations* (Delft, 1968), pp 59-115.

27. Richard Norwood, *The sea-man's practice, contayning a fundamentall problem in navigation, experimentally verified* (London, 1637); G.L. Evans, 'Richard Norwood, surveyor, of Stevenage', *Hertfordshire Past and Present*, viii (1968), pp 29-31.

28. 'A breviate of Monsieur Picart's account of the measure of the earth', *Philosophical Transactions of the Royal Society of London*, x (1675), pp 261-72.

29. Edward Heawood, 'John Adams and his map of England', *Geographical Journal*, lxxix (1932), pp 37-44; E.G.R. Taylor, 'Notes on John Adams and contemporary map makers', *Geographical Journal*, xcvii (1941), pp 182-4.

30. William Molyneux intended to add coordinates to Petty's maps and apparently

did add latitudes to his map of Ulster (J.H. Andrews, 'Sir William Petty: a tercentenary assessment', *The Map Collector*, xli (1987), pp 36-7). For further details see J.H. Andrews, 'Science and cartography in the Ireland of William and Samuel Molyneux', *Proceedings of the Royal Irish Academy*, lxxx C (1980), pp 231-50.

31. Petty, *Political anatomy*, p. 59.

32. Bowood papers, 22 December 1660, vi, 1st series, 61.

33. J.H. Andrews, 'The maps of the escheated counties of Ulster, 1609-10', *Proceedings of the Royal Irish Academy*, lxxiv C (1974), pp 133-70.

34. *Calendar of State Papers, Ireland, 1647-60*, pp 641, 660-61, 665, 684.

35. Historical Manuscripts Commission, *Ormonde*, new series, vi, p. 119. Dr Patrick Raggett was a member of Petty's Down Survey team charged with revising part of the Strafford Survey. He signed various Down Survey barony maps in King's Co., Co. Limerick and Co. Tipperary (Earl of Kerry, 'The Lansdowne maps of the Down Survey', *Proceedings of the Royal Irish Academy*, xxxv C (1920), pp 398-9), as well as copies of Strafford Survey maps now lost. Nothing else is known of Raggett except that in 1655 he gave his address as Thurles, Co. Tipperary (Larcom, *Down Survey*, pp 61-2, 327).

36. Sarah Tyacke and Helen Wallis, *British Library Journal*, v (1979), p. 187.

37. Of the supposed junction of the Inny and Brosna rivers Piers wrote: 'This is a remark, not observed in any chorographical map I have seen of this county; no, not in Sir William Petty's great map of Ireland' (*A chorographic description of the county of West-meath* (Dublin, 1786), p. 18).

38. R.W. Shirley, 'Two lost wall maps by Robert Morden', *International Map Collectors' Society Journal*, v (2) (1985), pp 35-9.

39. Andrews, 'Science and cartography in the Ireland of William and Samuel Molyneux', pp 236-7.

40. National Library of Ireland, MS 2557, MS 3137. It seems clear from the contemporary list of contents that the Petty maps were an integral part of Phillips's submission and not inserted afterwards.

41. Y.M. Goblet, *A topographical index of the parishes and townlands of Ireland in Sir William Petty's MSS barony maps and* Hiberniae delineatio (Dublin, 1932), p. v.

42. Charles Smith, *The antient and present state of the county and city of Cork* (Dublin, 1750), i, pp xvi-xvii.

43. This had been one of the issues discussed in John Norden's essay on county atlases, *Nordens preparative to his Speculum Britanniae* (London, 1596), pp 2, 13. Norden preferred to vary the scale and keep the page-size constant.

44. In the second edition of 1732 county names were added as catchwords for the binder in the margins of previously unidentified plates.

45. Examples are John Rocque's map of Ireland in *c.*1760 and Bernard Scalé's *Hibernian atlas* of 1776. In George Grierson's *New and correct Irish atlas* of *c.*1818 the water is said to howl 'at McSwine's gun'.

46. John Woodhouse, *A guide for strangers in the kingdom of Ireland* (London, 1647). Woodhouse is described as a contributor to *The map of Ireland, with the exact dimensions of the provinces therein contained* (London, 1653) but, as Andrew Bonar Law informs the author, the only map found in this work is derived from Boazio and shows no roads.

47. List of post roads, B.L. Add. MS 32,471 (8), a document misleadingly described as 'plans' in Historical Manuscripts Commission, *Various collections, Jersey*, viii (1), p. 99. For non-cartographic road descriptions see H.G. Fordham, *The road books*

and itineraries of Ireland, 1647 to 1850, Bibliographical Society of Ireland Publications, ii, 4 (1923).

48. Petty's manuscript copies of his provincial maps (formerly held by his descendant, Lord Shelburne, at Bowood, Wiltshire) have evidently been cut from a single map of Ireland before being separately mounted.

49. For all his apparent indifference to the final version of the atlas Petty did seemingly recover and preserve the drawings supplied to his engravers. The evidence for this deduction is a hole in his manuscript map of Ulster (formerly at Bowood) which causes Scotchgate, Carrickfergus, to appear as 'chgate'. The same error appears in the *Delineatio,* suggesting that the hole already existed in the 1660s and was duly copied by the engraver.

50. In the summer of 1685 Petty arranged for colours to be added to some maps (presumably the newly published *Hiberniae delineatio*) that he was presenting to Edward Southwell (Marquis of Lansdowne, *The Petty-Southwell correspondence* (London, 1928), p. 139).

51. National Library of Ireland, MS 392.

52. Petty, *Political anatomy,* pp 108-9; Goblet, *Transformation,* iii, pp 26-30.

53. J.G. Kohl, *Travels in Ireland* (London, 1844), p. 289.

54. Goblet, *Topographical index,* p. vi.

Chapter 6

On the road:
Henry Pratt, 1708

Yet another Irish war began in 1689. This time the rebels could claim to be loyalists, assisting their fellow-Catholic James II against a heretical usurper. The war between king and king lasted two years. After James's defeat many of his Irish supporters lost their lands in the customary way, though for various reasons the process of redistribution did not begin until 1700. The reign of William III brought a stock-taking of forfeited estates – the 'Trustees' Survey', conducted in much the same way as earlier plantation surveys – but this time there was no organised plantation, most of the confiscated properties being sold by auction to existing Irish residents or to absentees. Socially and economically, as well as cartographically, the turn of the century marked a transition from war to peace. It was some time before Protestant landowners felt safe enough to invest much money in their Irish estates, but a rising class of surveyors was kept busy in both public and private service delimiting and dividing landed property throughout the 1690s and 1700s.[1]

William's campaigns had brought the usual demand for geographical information, but one difference from earlier wars was that more foreigners were now taking part, with English, French, Danish, Dutch and German personnel engaged on both Catholic and Protestant sides. No doubt this helped to raise the level of literacy and 'graphicacy' among the combatants. There had also been a considerable expansion of the map trade since the mid-century in several metropolitan centres of western Europe, with London – though not yet Dublin – emerging as a nursery of energetic publishers like William Berry, Christopher Browne, Francis Lamb, Herman Moll, Robert Morden, John Overton and John Seller.[2] These men were not surveyors, or even geographers in any academic sense, but entrepreneurs. Competition among them was keen, and partnerships, though common, were short-lived. Cartography formed part of the new coffee-house culture and there was much deployment of newspaper advertisements, trade cards and published catalogues, few of which gave credit to the technicians, scientists and artists who supplied the publisher with his copy. In a world where maps were beginning to function like newspapers rather than works of literature, the single sheet was starting to gain ground on the atlas. Kingdoms and empires would find a ready sale through this medium, but counties, non-metropolitan towns and other small areas had little chance of publication unless made newsworthy by war. Ireland though small could qualify as a kingdom. From 1689 to 1691 it was also a theatre of war.

*　*　*　*　*　*　*　*　*

William Petty died too soon to see the extent of his influence during this period of cartographic ferment. His *Hiberniae delineatio* was fresh in the public mind and in its first four years of life showed no signs of being superseded. It must also have been obtainable without difficulty, for its price, originally fifty shillings, soon came down – at one time to as little as seven shillings.[3] Of course contemporaries could not perceive its superiority to Speed, as we can, by matching both outlines against a mental image derived from the Ordnance Survey. The best they could do as an independent test was to compare rival land-based maps with early seventeenth-century Dutch charts, which probably owed nothing to English models and which looked much more like Petty than Speed, especially in Connacht.[4] But even without this endorsement Petty would have flattened all critical doubts by the large size of his maps and the sheer quantity of their information.

Not that this information could be said to leap from the page. Even before events in Ireland had brought Petty's maps under the spotlight, William Molyneux had seen how much editing would be needed to adapt them for a non-Irish general reader.[5] Modern general readers can verify this statement by trying to plan a journey from say Dublin to Sligo entirely on the basis of *Hiberniae delineatio*. The book was even less suitable for fighting a war or for studying warfare at a distance. Not only was it too large and heavy for a campaigner's luggage, but most of its emphasis was on invisible legal boundaries and unpronounceable local names – two categories of information notoriously unhelpful to soldiers in the field. However, publishers quickly responded to a demand which at first they must have found startlingly enthusiastic. 'The new map of Ireland I cannot live without and therefore send it immediately', wrote Robert Molesworth from Dublin in March 1690.[6] In fact nine separate maps of Ireland, excluding new editions and reprints, were issued by Berry and the other publishers named above between March 1689 and May 1691. There was also a new miniature atlas of Ireland by Francis Lamb, 'very useful for all gentlemen, and military officers, as well for sea, as for land service'. No one attempted to conceal the main source of these publications. Petty's name was everywhere accepted as a selling point – it figured in nine out of ten advertisements – and no doubt his knighthood was felt to add a certain lustre.

But except for Berry, whose maps were said, ambiguously, to be 'exactly engraven from Sir William Petty's survey', all the new ventures promised at least a modicum of originality. They were all smaller than the eleven feet needed for a map of Ireland at Petty's county scale; even the largest, advertised by Robert Morden in March 1691, was to be not more than seven feet 'deep', and several publishers preferred to make a virtue of compactness and portability. Smallness is a merit easy to achieve, and Petty had shown one way to select from his mass of inscriptions by naming parishes more prominently than townlands. Half the publications under review claimed to be not just more convenient but more informative. The most immediately relevant new item of information was roads, but in the competitive atmosphere of the London publishing industry every map aspired to serve as many purposes as possible. Bishops' seats for instance had been a staple of European cartography since the sixteenth century, in the British Isles since Mercator had included them in 1564. They were now ripe for revival in Ireland where (apart from the hiatus of James's reign) the Protestant episcopate was gaining power and influence.

On the secular plane, the political balance had shifted since Speed had filled his margins with royal pedigrees. Robert Greene's map of England in 1682 had distinguished parliamentary boroughs, and at about the same time William Molyneux promised a similar service when listing his intended additions to Petty's maps of Ireland.[7] This showed foresight in a country whose legislature had not met for sixteen years; but after the English revolution of 1688 parliament in Dublin as well as London could be expected to carry more weight in national life. Another timely reminder of the bond between the two kingdoms was to map the geographical relationship of one to another as well as mapping them separately. Petty had neglected this obvious point by omitting the Mull of Kintyre from the corner of his map of Ireland. Now the Mull and other western extremities of Britain were being generally restored, and some maps of Ireland went further with insets of the whole British Isles disguised as miniature sea charts, which also provided an excuse to revive the patriotic name 'St George's Channel'.

One effect of competition was to lift a carefully chosen corner of the veil that so many cartographers had drawn across their methods and sources. Lamb's atlas of Ireland was 'corrected and amended by the advice, and assistance, of several able artists, late inhabitants of that kingdom'. Lea and Moll's map was 'an improvement of Sir W. Petty's, by the help of a new survey of particular persons' estates, which are not inserted in his [map], or any other'. Morden's seven-foot map had been 'supplied with many additions by the assistance and encouragement of several ingenious gentlemen of that kingdom'. All this looks like ad-man's licence; but given a good (though incomplete) original like Petty's it was not difficult, if space allowed, to insert roads and other information 'by eye', either from other maps or if necessary from non-cartographic lists. On the other hand the likelihood of private estate surveys being discovered, borrowed, copied and 'dropped in' to a one- or two-sheet map of Ireland was no greater in Morden's time than in Petty's. The yield of new material from such sources, especially given the skeletal style of current Irish estate mapping, would hardly have repaid the necessary effort, except perhaps as an occasional token to justify advertisements like those quoted. In this connection the apparently total loss of Morden's large map is particularly unfortunate. Morden was a cartographer with scholarly aspirations;[8] but if he had collected as much new information as his 'seven-foot' announcement suggests, it would surely have left its mark in the map of Ireland that he contributed to Camden's *Britannia* five years later. There is a great deal of Petty in this map, and hardly anything attributable to 'ingenious gentlemen'.

* * * * * * * * *

In the long run the commercial revolution in cartography was irreversible. Single-sheet maps of Ireland would saturate the market in England, with overspills into France and Germany, for nearly all the eighteenth century. But in the first few years of post-Williamite peace a pause was needed for map-users to digest the fruits of wartime overproduction. The silence was broken in the public sector, and in a non-cartographic source: 'To Henry Pratt in part for making a map of Ireland £30'.[9] This entry, which apparently refers to the first seven months of the new century, comes from a list of royal warrants to the lord lieutenant and lords justices of the exchequer of Ireland. No other payments to Pratt have been brought to light, and an instalment of thirty pounds gives little scope for speculative extrapolation about the precise range of his activities, apart from being too much for a straightforward copy of someone else's map.

But at least there is no doubt about Pratt's identity.[10] He was not an organiser of other men's labours like Petty, but a practical surveyor and draughtsman in his own right, successful enough by 1700 to attract and to reject an offer of employment in the Trustees' survey. Between 1697 and 1703 he worked successively for the earl of Kerry, the Irish court of exchequer, the clergy of Christchurch cathedral, and the provost and fellows of Trinity College, Dublin. Land surveyors of this type generally showed little interest in the making of national maps, but the only other candidate for such a task in 1700 would have been a military engineer, and given the small number of engineers likely to have been stationed in post-war Ireland it would hardly be surprising if none were available: map-making is not such a pleasurable pastime that volunteers for it will always be on call. The real question is why the authorities suddenly needed a map. For three-quarters of a century, including the Cromwellian and Williamite wars, there had been very little official regional and national cartography of the kind commissioned by Queen Elizabeth's ministers from Lythe, Jobson, Browne and Bartlett.[11] If more recent generals had fought their wars with published maps, or with out-of-date manuscript maps, why should they not manage equally well in peacetime?

One answer lies in the size of Ireland's new standing army, fixed in 1698 at 12,000 men. The country had few inns capable of quartering soldiers, and few private householders willing to do so. Expensive ramparted and bastioned enclosures were no longer economic. The remedy was an unfortified but sturdy building known as a barrack – still an unfamiliar term at this period. Barracks became a popular institution both for the security they brought to isolated upper-class households in their vicinity and for the stimulus they gave to traders in a still impoverished countryside. To meet these needs they were widely distributed: accommodation was provided initially for about 270 companies of foot and troops of horse in over a hundred localities, some of them places that even an Irishman could be forgiven for never having heard of, such as Ninemilehouse, Rosscastle, Bryansbridge and Colecormuck.[12] A cartographic record of these obscure demands on the public purse was clearly expedient. In fact two such maps survive in manuscript from the year 1700, both on a Petty-style outline, and both signed by the overseer of Irish barracks, Sir William Robinson, who had himself chosen the sites depicted (Fig. 6.1).[13] Though trained as a military engineer Robinson had spent most of his career in various administrative posts and in his late fifties was about to retire, no longer in the best of health. Little could be expected from him by way of original cartography. His representations of the barracks and the main roads connecting them were undoubtedly effective; they can even be praised as early thematic maps, their simplicity a welcome corrective to the clutter of Petty's *Delineatio*. But they were too simple to give their theme a regional context and the government did well to call for something more ambitious.

Fig. 6.1   William Robinson, 'The kingdome of Ireland with the distribution of the barracks for quartering the armey 1700', British Library, K.51.15. An early thematic map on a base derived from Petty. The difference between guidons (cavalry) and flags (infantry) appears to have been introduced to Irish cartography by Robinson. The coloured original is more comprehensible, using different boundary tints for counties (green) and 'spheres of influence' (carmine).

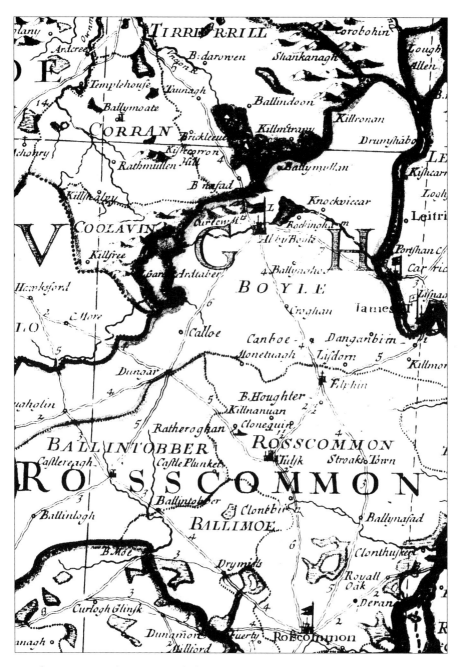

Fig. 6.2   Part of east Connacht from Henry Pratt, *Tabula Hiberniae novissima et*
emendatissima (London, 1708). Pratt's main source was evidently
Hiberniae delineatio, to which he added roads, road distances, and a
large number of settlement and other names. In the parts of Cos Sligo
and Mayo shown here, for example, only eleven out of twenty-one
minor names had appeared in the *Delineatio.*

Pratt may have helped Robinson with these maps, or been recommended by him as a possible successor in the field of barrack cartography. At any rate there are hints of a link between the two men. One of Pratt's last known Irish estate maps, in 1703, was of land belonging to Robinson in Co. Louth. More tenuously, they both left Ireland around the middle of the decade, apparently to spend the rest of their lives in the London area, where Pratt surveyed land at St Marylebone in 1708. Pratt was probably going home. The favourable references to new English plantations in the commentary he wrote for his map of Ireland seem enough to establish the author's place of upbringing: people born and raised in Ireland, even in loyalist Protestant families, are seldom unfeignedly enthusiastic about the English. Judging from the lack of references to Pratt in 1703-8, much of his time was now being quietly devoted to the map of Ireland. Part of it must have been spent in London overseeing the final stages of publication, which took place in April 1708 (Fig. 6.2).[14] His engraver was John Harris, a Londoner not known for any familiarity with Ireland, so the map's remarkable freedom from copying errors suggests an unusual degree of personal supervision by the author.

No doubt it was during Pratt's stay in London that his map was 'corrected' by a fellow land surveyor in Dublin, Thomas Moland,[15] who may have suggested some of the interpolations observable in Pratt's placenames. That still leaves several years for field work and research in Ireland, added to whatever Pratt had done for his thirty pounds in or before 1701. How he supported himself during this later period (assuming that there are no lost estate surveys) is not clear. He seems to have kept some official standing, for one source of the marginal town plans in his map of Ireland is the unpublished military survey made by Captain Thomas Phillips for James II. Pratt may have used the version of this survey belonging to the duke of Ormond, who was lord lieutenant of Ireland from 1703 to 1707: besides copying Phillips's town plans he obtained an anonymous and previously unpublished view of Kilkenny, where the castle was the duke's principal residence, and his commentary gives special attention to the town. This is not much of a foundation for a theory of continued government patronage, but it seems unlikely that any cartographer of Pratt's day would have been subsidised at the compilation stage by a private firm.

There is one other sign that Pratt's researches may have occupied him for more than a few weeks. At some time between May 1705 and January 1707 a new map of Ireland was published by a quite different kind of artist, the Dublin engraver Edwin Sandys (Fig. 6.3).[16] It was Sandys who had provided the portrait of Petty for *Hiberniae delineatio*, and who had been chosen by William Molyneux to engrave the maps

Fig. 6.3   Part of eastern Ireland, from Edwin Sandys, *A general map of the kingdom of Ireland* (n.d., *c.*1707). Four grades of settlement are shown: plain circle (lowest grade), circle plus tower (market town), circle with two-storey tower (city or large town), more than one tower (highest grade).

of Ireland for Moses Pitt's abortive atlas. But Sandys was not known as an independent cartographer. Why should he now produce what seems to have been the first separate map of Ireland ever published in Dublin? One possible answer is that he knew of Pratt's intentions and decided to anticipate them. Perhaps indeed Pratt had first proposed to employ Sandys for his own map and then had second thoughts; he would not have been the only Anglo-Irish cartographer to transfer his custom from Dublin to London in mid-project.

The real author of Sandys's map remains unknown. Whoever it was, he had less ambition than Pratt. His scale of about eight statute miles to one inch was considerably smaller. He showed fewer names of settlements (but spelt them in his own way) and none of baronies. He depended heavily on Petty's maps for physical geography but interpreted and amplified them differently from Pratt and not always with equal accuracy. His map even included a few names not shown by either Petty or Pratt, such as 3 Mile Bush and Killrush, both in Co. Louth, and an apochryphal River Blackwater in Co. Wicklow. Its road system repeatedly diverges from Pratt's. In many particulars, then, the two maps were independent, but their sources may well have overlapped. Both made the same major correction to the *Delineatio's* rendering of the upper Bann in Co. Armagh and their additions to Petty's stock of placenames were remarkably similar. More interestingly, their general conception was virtually identical. It was to make Petty's Ireland simpler, more coherent, more up-to-date, and more 'relevant', notably by the inclusion of roads, roadside settlements, market towns and barracks.

*   *   *   *   *   *   *   *   *

Pratt's scale of about 5.5 statute miles to one inch, though large for a single eighteenth-century map of Ireland, was less than half that of Petty's county maps. Indeed on the principle that a map should first be drawn at about double its intended final size, Pratt may have begun by treating the *Delineatio* as a base on which to plot his own design. In that case, it might be thought, all he had to do was choose a plausible selection from Petty's abundance of printed detail. But like most of Petty's disciples he felt obliged to make some innovations of his own. In the event these were so numerous and so important that he can be forgiven for breaking with recent tradition and omitting to mention the master's name. His chief contribution, apart from an array of barracks almost identical with those of Sandys (Fig. 6.4), was a road network more elaborate than that of any earlier map, too elaborate to have been wholly derived from any non-cartographic source (Fig. 6.5). Roads

Fig. 6.4   Barracks from Pratt's *Tabula*, 1708. Spelling modernised.

were the dominant cartographic fashion of the early eighteenth century: to omit them, said a new generation of pundits, was to deny that they existed.[17] But in what sense were Pratt's 'surveyed'? The numbers marked alongside most of them are said in his title to be 'common reputed miles by inspection'. No doubt by 1708 travellers

Fig. 6.5   Roads from Pratt's *Tabula*, 1708. Spelling modernised. Except for his
occasional use of broken lines in the far west, Pratt does not distinguish
different kinds of road.

were sufficiently well educated for a common reputed mile to be the
same as a surveyor's standard mile. Sure enough, the English and Irish
miles in Pratt's scale bars stood like Petty's in the ratio of about 1 to
1.27 and were therefore almost certainly equivalent to 1760 yards and
2240 yards respectively. But if he had measured the roads with the

164

kind of odometer or chariot mensurator used by John Ogilby in England some thirty years earlier, we should surely have some evidence for this.[18] At least he could then have avoided that dangerously weak phrase 'by inspection'.

Pratt's *Tabula Hiberniae novissima et emendatissima* stands near the threshold of the coaching era, a period when English cartographers began to be exercised by the problem of classifying roads. Hitherto the only distinction in maps of Ireland had been between those roads that were worth including and those that were not, but Pratt's network was almost dense enough to create a need for differentiation, even in the consciousness of a casual browser. For the intending road user the need was more evident, especially where there were two or more routes of approximately equal length between the same two towns. Most of these questions were settled by the *Tabula's* roadside mileage figures: at least there was a classification that recognised longer and shorter. Except in one kind of situation, the occasional absence of such figures is probably an oversight rather than a negative judgement on local travelling conditions. The exceptions are three short lines of road without mileage figures each indicated by pecks rather than the usual continuous double line. One runs westwards from Currarevagh (Claremore on the *Tabula*) at the west end of Lough Corrib in Co. Galway; one westwards from Kilfenora in Co. Clare; one westwards from Dromore on the south side of the Iveragh Peninsula in Co. Kerry (Fig. 6.6). Use this road at your own risk, seems to be the message here. Few and inconspicuous as they are, these pecked lines could be the first map-conventional hints of a distinct regional personality in the far west of Ireland.

Pratt's roads look too rough to have been properly measured. They are not straight in the manner of a diagram or a Roman road – most real-life straight roads in Ireland belong to a period later than 1708 – but their curves have the conventional wobble already familiar in early cartographers' rivers. Altogether it seems not impossible that Pratt himself travelled many Irish roads (or arranged for collaborators to do so), estimating the distances as he went. No doubt the results of such an operation would be patchy, and it may be significant that his written commentary suggests a personal knowledge of the midlands as far south as a line from Killarney to Enniscorthy, but not of Ulster or the western peninsulas. In any case his concern was only with the main highways, as he admits by showing numerous bridges with no roads leading to them.

Any traveller in Queen Anne's Ireland must have been struck by a number of other features that cartographers had hitherto ignored or misrepresented. It was plainly impracticable for all this defective detail

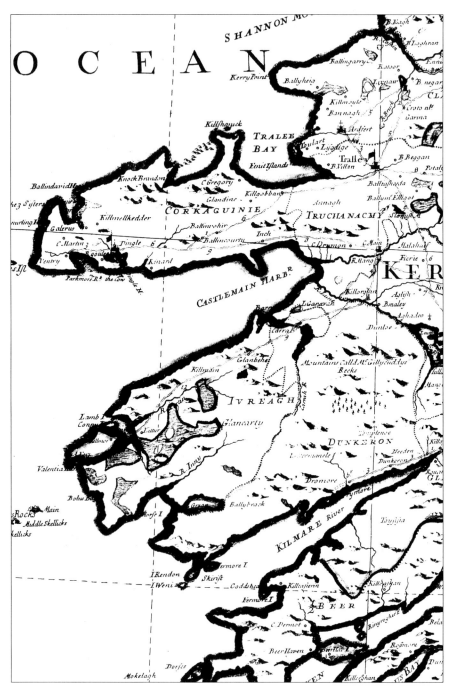

Fig. 6.6   South-west Ireland, from Pratt's *Tabula*, 1708. Among the features not
derived from Petty are the Fenit peninsula west of Tralee, the Bruck
River, and several placenames, including B.Villan and Lissodige, from an
estate survey made by Pratt for the earl of Kerry in 1697.

to be accurately measured or remeasured in the kind of quick recon-
naissance here postulated, but Pratt was too conscientious to settle for
Petty-with-roads. It is the skill with which he steered a course between
slavish copying and *de novo* surveying that makes him the most under-
rated cartographer in eighteenth-century Ireland – perhaps in the whole
British Isles, for no English or Scottish compiler had to face the mixture
of good and bad that Petty had left for posterity. In deviating from
Petty, Pratt seems to have been moved by three considerations. The
first was the intrinsic importance of the available data, based on a
commonsense estimate of contemporary map-using opinion. Another
was the *a priori* likelihood that Petty was wrong in cases where he
could not readily be checked and corrected. A third was the amount of
time and effort needed to put Petty right.

The territorial divisions of *Hiberniae delineatio* could be accepted
ready-made because it had been part of Petty's contract with the
government to survey them exactly. At first sight his seacoasts deserved
the same respect as his interior boundaries but there was one
exception to this rule, noticed in the previous chapter, and that was his
inadequate treatment of islands. Pratt added to the *Delineatio*'s store in
west Donegal, Antrim, Down, Louth, Wexford, Cork and Mayo. None
of the additions are imaginary, but some of their shapes and alignments
are poor, not surprisingly if they were observed from the mainland
without being circumnavigated. Elsewhere he accepted the existence of
Petty's islands but corrected their positions, notably at Lambay, Aran
(an over-correction that makes the South Passage too narrow), the
Inishbofin group in Co. Galway, and Fenit in Co. Kerry. He could copy
Fenit from the survey that he himself had made for the earl of Kerry in
1697 – a rare case of estate cartography contributing identifiably to a
national map. Elsewhere he followed the charts in John Seller's *English
pilot* of c.1690 and in Greenvile Collins's *Great Britain's coasting pilot*
of 1693. These sources also supplied Pratt's inset maps of Cork and
Kinsale harbours; on the main map they contributed soundings and
shorelines in Lough Foyle, Belfast Lough, Carlingford Lough with its
adjoining coasts, and Galway Bay. Most of this information originated
with surveys made by Collins in 1687[19] or with Dutch surveys first
published by Willem Blaeu. Only Pratt's improvements to Inishbofin
remain untraceable to any known source.

Another boundary for which Petty could claim to be trusted was the
line between profitable and unprofitable land which had been such a
crucial element in the Down Survey. At Pratt's scale, the assumption
that no bogs had been drained since the 1680s was safe enough, and
he did a good job of selecting and simplifying Petty's outlines. The
manuscript Down Survey parish and barony maps had also put a

boundary around the mountains as well as showing them by hill profiles. At their smaller scales neither the *Delineatio* nor Pratt attempted to reproduce this boundary, but both of them kept the hills. These of course were an ancient convention, but since the sixteenth century the individual symbols had generally got smaller and flatter, sometimes indeed being barely recognisable as hills and perhaps reflecting the international dominance of cartographers educated in the Low Countries.[20] Pratt was a child of his time in this respect. His Irish landscape was too low and too smooth, improbably ripe for agricultural development in a new age of politico-economic optimism. It could even have been his fault that the Irish parliament in 1715 recommended making a canal from Cork to Mallow through country that later surveys showed to be unsuitable.[21] Pratt does show some interest in particular hills, but except at Croaghpatrick he identifies the better-known summits by name rather than by enlarging the appropriate symbols. Among the hill names he adds to Petty's stock are Ben Bulben, Carrantogher, Devil's Bit (also shown by Robinson in 1700), Slemish Mountain, Slieve Bloom, Sperrin Mountain, Taragh Hill (Wexford), and Usny (Uisneach) Hill. Without the anchor of a name he attached no individual significance to Petty's hill symbols and did not hesitate to move them aside where they got in his way. He also introduced some totally new ones, for instance in Queen's County around Timahoe.

Despite the warning implicit in the Cromwellian surveys, Pratt's contemporaries were living through a period of sustained and ruthless deforestation. By the end of the seventeenth century woods survived only in the remoter parts of Ireland and a national timber surplus was fast becoming a deficiency. Pratt showed no particular awareness of this problem. His treatment of Petty's tree symbols (and for that matter his own on the earl of Kerry's estate maps) was free-handed. Some were necessarily left out when Petty's scale was reduced, for Pratt unlike Sandys disliked condensing a whole wood into a single tree, but in other areas the proportion of wooded land was somewhat exaggerated, either as a result of not noticing changes on the ground (like the clearing of a large area east of Lough Neagh: Fig. 6.7) or simply by over-liberal generalisation.

Rivers had not yet begun to lose their cartographic importance in the early eighteenth century, except in the purely relative sense that more attention was now being paid to roads. It was the impracticability of a new survey that led Pratt to copy Petty's rivers wherever he could. If he felt that change was unavoidable, the least complicated way to effect it was by adding whole rivers that Petty had omitted, and in areas exempt from Cromwellian forfeiture he had of course omitted many.

Fig. 6.7   Part of Ulster from Pratt's *Tabula*, 1708. Additions to Petty include a patch of forest north-east of Lough Neagh and a considerable amount of detail in the baronies of Castlereagh and north Ards. Pratt's additions and deletions in Belfast Lough are derived from Greenvile Collins's chart of 1693.

Pratt may have taken compass bearings along the streams he saw while tracing the roads, but he is unlikely to have followed them to their sources with or without an instrument. Rivers like the Bredagh in Inishowen and the Moyola in Co. Londonderry he must have sketched more or less conjecturally without seeing more than a minute fraction of their length. This practice could clearly lead to trouble: Pratt's Annaclor River in Co. Down, for instance, runs due south through Kilmore to Dundrum, whereas in truth the river turns east into Strangford Lough without ever reaching Dundrum. He also prolonged rivers that Petty had left too short, some of them major streams like the Lagan and the upper Bann, others less obviously defective like the Clabby in Fermanagh.

Several of the new rivers flowed out of new lakes, such as Loughs Finn (dropped by Petty after an eventful career on Elizabethan and Jacobean maps) and Reagh in Co. Donegal. The opposite process was to unravel streams that others had intertwined, for instance the Crumlin Water and Sixmilewater in Co. Antrim, which Pratt separated at the cost of defying all Petty's maps as well as Lamb's atlas. This reform was not complete, however. In the south-west, Mount Gabriel was still insulated and the Rivers Laune and Blackwater were still commingled. Most difficult were stretches of what might or might not be the same river that had to be integrated into some larger drainage system. Some of Petty's smaller fragments could be simply disregarded under cover of generalisation. Of those impossible to ignore, the largest and most famous rivers were generally the easiest to deal with: Pratt could hardly go wrong in Co.Waterford by continuing the Bride eastwards into the Blackwater; between King's and Queen's Counties he was less successful, carrying water uphill across the highest part of the Slieve Bloom. Occasionally he broke his own unwritten rule and corrected some feature of Petty's that was not self-evidently wrong. Examples, in common with Sandys, were his enlargement of Lough Erne and his translocation of the upper Bann outflow several miles westwards from the south-east corner of Lough Neagh.

* * * * * * * *

Pratt's most notable achievement was to bring order from the chaos of Petty's human geography. His main objective was apparently to establish a settlement hierarchy, and his marginal key is set out in descending order of centrality: cities and large towns; boroughs; market towns; gentlemen's seats and villages. These categories and their symbolism reveal the transitional character of Pratt's Ireland as a peacetime society haunted by thoughts of war. Armed force was still being deployed, but not as part of the hierarchy – either standing outside it altogether, as with the small squares used for still-functioning forts, or superimposed upon it as rectangular flags or cavalry guidons (introduced by Robinson to distinguish foot and horse barracks and given printed expression by Sandys) flying above the civil settlement symbols. The military theme was pursued outside Pratt's margins with a tabulated list of barracks as well as with large separate fort-plans of Charlemont, Charlesfort and Duncannon and town plans of Athlone, Belfast, Carrickfergus, Coleraine, Cork, Dublin, Galway, Limerick, Londonderry and Waterford (all except Charlemont being chiefly derived from Thomas Phillips)[22] and with the two exceptions of Cashel and Kilkenny Pratt allowed Phillips to dictate his definition of a 'large town' in the main map. He knew enough about these places to up-date his model at several points, but Dublin was the only town he showed to have grown very far beyond its medieval walls. (Town walls also figure prominently in the commentary printed under the map.) Only the anonymous view of Kilkenny looks almost utopianly peaceful, with its cathedral, three parish churches, and apparently still-flourishing monasteries. In the main Pratt takes little notice of religion. Bishops' seats like barracks are excluded from the settlement hierarchy and marked by disrespectfully small crosses (doubled for archbishops as in Mercator) above the appropriate secular symbol, a method that allowed some seats, like Achonry and Ardagh, to be correctly identified as villages rather than towns.

The foundations of Pratt's settlement scheme, as any English reader would have expected, were politics and economics. A borough was a place with a member of parliament. Some boroughs had earned their status by genuine post-medieval population growth, especially in plantation Ulster, but others, like Bannow, Clonmines and Harristown, were no more than demographic nullities. The economic qualification for hierarchy-membership was a market. Here for the first time one begins to wonder about Pratt's sources. (Barracks, bishops and boroughs posed no problem for the early eighteenth-century researcher.) His reference to including 'many market towns omitted in former maps', though justified as an aspersion on Sandys, made no claim to completeness. His total of 270 market towns, which included the higher grades in his urban classification, nevertheless compared impressively with Sandys's 245 (Fig. 6.8). It allowed him to illustrate several previously undocumented geographical trends of the post-Petty era, such as the growth of economic activity in north-east Ireland and the ability of landlords to establish market rights at estate centres like Brookeborough, Edgeworthstown, Eyrecourt and Manor Hamilton. However, in the absence of independent verification some of Pratt's markets look a little improbable: examples are Maghereveely (Co. Fermanagh) and Coronery (Co. Cavan), neither of which he places on a road.

Villages were not a new subject for cartographic symbolism in Ireland, but their essence was no easier to define in 1708 than at any

Fig. 6.8   Boroughs and market towns from Pratt's *Tabula*, 1708. Spelling
modernised. Boroughs omitted are Harristown, Co. Kildare, and St
Canice, Co. Kilkenny. The map shows many more market towns than
are listed in Pratt's letterpress description of Ireland mounted outside
its lower margin. The market of Newtownbutler is included in the
description but not in the map.

other period, except in the wholly negative sense of not necessarily being parish centres, a point that map-readers could check by comparing Pratt with Petty. With the whole kingdom as his subject, an Irish cartographer could hardly follow the English natural historian Robert Plot in granting the title of village to any settlement with more than a specified number of houses.[23] Pratt gave no definition. Instead he blurred the issue by combining villages with gentlemen's seats. The seat, peacetime successor to the rural tower house, was a settlement-form not previously recognised in maps of Ireland. Pratt's merger shielded him against probing criticism from future settlement historians. Given the high value that he obviously set on visual clarity, it may also have marked a last-minute refusal to muddle his map with two low-grade symbols that might have been hard to distinguish, a theory consistent with our earlier hypothesis of different scales for compilation and engraving. In any case, grouping country seats with villages was less odd than it would become later, for Anglo-Irish gentlemen had not yet started to distance themselves from their social inferiors by living in the middle of otherwise empty parks. The village-seat symbol, whatever Pratt's reason for choosing it, made enough sense to be copied in more than one mid-eighteenth-century county map, including those of Walter Harris and Charles Smith discussed in the next chapter.

This brings us to the small open circles that mark the lowest level of the territorial hierarchy.[24] Of course no map at six miles to an inch could accommodate all the townlands shown by Petty. But Pratt deserves praise for the care with which he built his own alternative system of minor names. His first principle was that settlement should count for more than territoriality. Places qualifying as villages or seats were thus preferred as space-fillers to the floating townlands of the *Delineatio*. In the context of plantation-based cartography this was perhaps the most radical of Pratt's innovations. It meant that in adopting one of Petty's names he might have to supply the corresponding symbol himself and so assume responsibility for its location. Elsewhere, even at places of considerable importance, he would have to supply the name as well. A few of his additions to Petty had been published on earlier maps – for instance Baginbun and Glascarrick in Co. Wexford – though of course that is not necessarily where Pratt found them. Of his new names many were of native Irish origin, historically timeless to all but a handful of experts. Of the new English names many are unmistakably post-medieval. This is perhaps most obviously true of 'seat' names, some featuring the word 'Hall' (Crump Hall, Hill Hall), others introducing a modern 'ascendancy' family as at Castlepollard, Hamilton Bawn, Manor Cunningham and Newtown Gore. Others again are topographical names whose instant intelligibility suggests that they had as yet had little time in which to be corrupted. Examples are Green Mount, New Grove, Roundwood, Spring Hill and Summerhill. A small class of industrial names includes Bushmills, Colepit Hill, New Forge, New Mills, Obers Mills and Silvermines.

But the great majority of Pratt's new-looking names are associated in some way with travel. Blew Bell, Royal Oak and Two Pot House were evidently inns, a rare category of name in Ireland as one would expect from the complaints of early travel writers. River crossings are naturally abundant, among them Broadford, Ferry Bank, Ferry Carrick (Pratt revived the sixteenth-century convention of a boat to represent a ferry), Foxford, Hawksford, Longford and Millford. As befitted an age of improvement, forms like Kilcullen Bridge and New B[ridge] were even more common: whether they were all villages as well as bridges is perhaps doubtful, though all of them were given a settlement symbol. 'Pass' in Irish names like Pratt's Milltown Pass and Lamb Pass typically meant a road between bogs rather than mountains. The self-explanatory McTaggart's Cross occurs in Co. Antrim, but 'Cross' was less common in settlement names than it became in the nineteenth century, partly no doubt because there were not yet so many roads and therefore not so many intersections. Finally there is the interesting class of mileage names already encountered at 3 Mile Bush and Sixmilewater, most of them denoting either bridges or houses (the latter presumably inns), with designated distances of between three and nine miles. Such numerical specificity is perhaps surprising in 1708 before the introduction of milestones and signposts. In fact some of the names in question may already have existed for a considerable time but not been noticed in Petty's maps, or in seventeenth-century documents relating to landed property, as they were neither parishes nor townlands. All of which increases the probability that Pratt did most of his own travelling.

Apart from a preference for settlements over territories, two principles seem to have governed Pratt's choice of minor names. One, accepted by most mapmakers at most historical periods, was that no large space should be without script. This justified his retention of the floating townland, a mark of identity unimportant – and unhelpful – in itself but still the most significant item of information that many areas had to offer. He was sparing in his use of floaters, too sparing in the opinion of some later cartographers, but this was a natural reaction against Petty. Another rule was that lines and points should reinforce each other, causing minor settlement-names to be spaced at reasonably short intervals along roads and rivers, and territorial boundaries to be made more comprehensible by their proximity to named points. With so many townlands on offer, floaters must have been difficult to choose. It is true that Petty had dropped plenty of hints. Apart from emphasising parishes, his engravers had written some townland names more clearly than others. Their horizontal names were more immediately eligible than those written sideways, and so were names that caught the copyist's eye by standing alone. And of course Petty had applied his own presumably authoritative tests of importance when copying selected detail from his county to his provincial maps. For good or ill Pratt preferred to take his own decisions, often rejecting the obvious choice and sometimes extracting names that lay almost invisible in the scriptorial confusion of the *Delineatio*. Like any cartographer in this situation he sometimes had to choose at random, but at least the randomness did not extend to Petty's 'plantationisms': all Pratt's names are genuine proper nouns.

If Pratt had any toponymic bias it was towards user-friendliness. At first sight he seems to have favoured words of English origin, but this apparent chauvinism probably just reflects the history of nodal settle-ments in post-plantation Ireland, most of which had been founded and named by English-speakers. His real prejudice, common among expatriate cartographers but rarely acknowledged, was for names that were easily spoken by the copyist's inner voice and readily visible to his inner eye; or at least for monosyllables, and for words whose syllabic structure is quickly apparent. Such predilections were doubtless largely unconscious. Pratt is unlikely to have worked out any theory of names as distinct from the places they denote. He is not known to have invented any new ones, for example. On the other hand his spellings often differ from Petty's, at every level from the county (Sligoe, no longer Slego) to the smallest and most obscure townland. Indeed there can be few authors of the post-Petty era who did more to modernise the spelling of Irish placenames than Pratt. He corrected numerous glaring scribal errors in the *Delineatio,* and he caught up with changes in orthographic fashion that must have been spread over many years. Both tasks required access to supplementary sources. Thomas Moland is known to have consulted at least one collection of Down Survey parish maps on Pratt's behalf, presumably to recover spellings that had not yet been misrepresented by Petty's engravers. But some of the available authorities were doubtless non-cartographic, including lists of barracks, boroughs and market towns, while for the less familiar names Pratt must have simply listened to the current pronunciation.

* * * * * * * *

Pratt's crucial advantage over Lamb, Morden and the rest was his personal knowledge of Ireland. Yet he was also determined to achieve a high professional polish and a broad international appeal. As recent London publishers would have agreed, this meant supplying the geographical coordinates that Petty had so scrupulously omitted. Accordingly he drew meridians and parallels thirty minutes apart on a non-cylindrical projection – the longitudes unattributably reckoned from London, the central meridian apparently at eight degrees west – and divided his margins at one-minute intervals. There were three possible sources for these latitudes and longitudes: furnishing a new and original outline with coordinates inherited from earlier geographers; converting original linear distances into degrees; or making original astronomical observations. Each hypothesis presents its own difficulties. The only known precedent that Pratt accepted without deviation is 53° 20' for the latitude of Dublin, which by now was so widely accepted that it proves nothing.[25] His other coordinates differ from those of all earlier published maps, and apparently from every average calculable from any two or more earlier maps. They also differ from the values supplied to William Molyneux by some of his Irish fellow-scientists. If Pratt had derived his graticule from an agreed position for Dublin and from the dimensions of Ireland as measured on the *Tabula*, he should (according to his own equation of fifty Irish miles with one degree of latitude) have made Ireland 4.80 degrees long from north to south instead of about 4.09 degrees. If he had observed any latitudes for himself, he should have discovered that there are more than fifty Irish miles to a degree. In fact the ordinary land surveyor of this period had no equipment for measuring stellar altitudes and it was not until the mid-eighteenth century that a few members of Pratt's profession in Ireland began to study field astronomy. And if latitudes were an unlikely element in his repertoire, longitudes would have been virtually impossible. So Pratt must have used a mixture of methods. Such fudging (as a later generation would have called it) was no doubt thoroughly unsound by any scientific standard, but in this case it somehow gave coordinates that no earlier cartographer could rival.

Scales were not the only bonus provided in Pratt's margins. His separate plans of towns, forts and harbours have already been mentioned. So has his twelve-column letterpress description of Ireland. Here a reminder of Pratt's estate-surveying experience was the acreage figures given for each of the thirty-two counties, with an all-Ireland total of 11,067,712 Irish acres – like most contemporary estimates well short of the truth. He also felt the usual loyalist cartographer's desire to connect the sister kingdoms. There was the now-customary inset map of the British Isles, a comparison of the latitudes of various places in

Ireland and England, and a statement of relative areas (Ireland 18, England and Wales 30) apparently taken from the early seventeenth-century statistician Gerard de Malynes rather than the more recent work of Gregory King.[26] Elaborate baroque compositions surround the title of the map, its scale panel, and its dedication to the queen's consort Prince George of Denmark. Two figures (Neptune and an anonymous ploughman) represent Pratt's combination of maritime and terrestrial sources. The key is grandiosely written in both Latin and English, and a tabloid-sized headline rings with appropriate superlatives. As a wall-mosaic of cartographic and textual information Pratt's work recalled an earlier 'Tabula', that of 'totius Angliae' published by John Adams, another mapmaker long neglected by posterity. Unfortunately Pratt did not follow Adams in adding an informative autobiographical preface.[27]

Pratt's cartographic juggernaut was launched with all appropriate ceremony. Subscriptions were invited through separately published proposals – an unusual practice for a single national map – and advertisements appeared in the *London Gazette* and *Daily Courant*. The price of one guinea was, justifiably, about four times what readers were accustomed to paying for a map of Ireland. The publisher, William Berry of Charing Cross, was sufficiently impressed to enter into competition with his own earlier maps of Ireland, and his judgement was backed by three partners – B.Linfoot, J. Hide and Mrs Luttrel – attracted from outside the normal cartographic milieu. Another breakthrough, early in the following year, was the first map advertisement yet discovered in an Irish newspaper.[28] Sales in Dublin were handled by R. Fleming of Ormonde Quay, but it was a sign of Ireland's inferior status in the map world that copies were to be coloured, backed and mounted in London before shipment.

*   *   *   *   *   *   *   *   *

The effect of this publicity is hard to estimate. Copies of the *Tabula* are now extremely rare, and although this is normal with very large maps, it seems not unlikely that in Pratt's case sales were restricted by a high price and a cumbersome format, as well as by the variety of smaller maps of Ireland still available. Critically, however, the author soon became a hero, even among the scientific elite. Printed map reviews were still unknown to the English-speaking world at this period, but in private Samuel Molyneux, son of the philosopher William Molyneux, praised this map in the year after its publication as 'the most exact that hath hitherto appeared' and chose a smaller version of it to illustrate his never-to-be-published account of Ireland.[29] A few years later

Archbishop William King, another prominent member of the Irish scientific community, was one of the first map-users to adopt Pratt's value for the area of Ireland – a value that continued to be quoted until about 1780.[30] In contrast, not a single contemporary reference has been found to the most like-minded of his predecessors, Edwin Sandys. Despite the excellence of Sandys's ideas, his reputation was evidently suffering from inadequate publicity and, it has to be said, inferior execution. Sandys was also unfortunate in having ostentatiously dedicated his work to the second duke of Ormond, who fell from grace in 1715 as a result of supporting the Jacobite rebellion.

So Ireland was lucky to have Pratt, or perhaps we should say Pratt and Moland. Without them, Petty would have held the floor virtually unsupported for several more decades. New national maps that copied from the *Tabula* directly or indirectly were those of the partnership Charles Price, John Senex and John Maxwell in 1711, John Senex acting alone in 1712, Herman Moll in 1714 and John Overton in 1715. Of these Moll seems to have been the most popular, thanks to the international reputation he had won with his elegant style. He did nothing to improve on Pratt, apart from adding marginal views of St Patrick's Purgatory and the Giant's Causeway, and like his contemporaries he omitted much that Pratt had shown. In 1720 Lamb's small atlas of Ireland took on a new and more creditable lease of life with the first of three editions based on the *Tabula* and its commentary (instead of on the *Delineatio* as hitherto) by the London publisher Thomas Bowles. Eight years later Moll recycled his own version as a small atlas of Irish counties and groups of counties; he gave more names in 1728 than in 1714 but most of them came from the same source. Higher standards among his readership were now making Moll more vulnerable to criticism, though the only map that critics could suggest as a check on his was Pratt's.[31]

Altogether it was not surprising that a second edition of the *Tabula* should appear in 1732.[32] The body of the map was now on four sheets, anonymously re-engraved and published in Dublin by George Grierson to coincide with his edition of the *Delineatio*. Grierson recognised the metropolitan supremacy of Dublin with a new index of towns showing distances from the capital as well as references to his own system of grid-cells. He also included a certain amount of new geographical information, much of it in north Antrim, and some of it apparently added at the last minute as if under pressure from independent proof-readers. In general, however, he kept close to the original. That this was not much of an accolade for Pratt became clear when Grierson revealed his own catholicity of taste by republishing Moll's map.

As travellers in Ireland grew more venturesome, so the errors that

Grierson had copied from Pratt began to reveal themselves. Some of them were noticed by Dr Richard Pococke, bishop of Ossory, who took a number of maps (including a 'large' one that must have been Pratt's: no other recent cartographer had earned this description) on a journey through the north and west in 1752. Among other criticisms he noted a non-existent abbey at Muckish in Donegal, a non-existent river crossing the Inishowen peninsula, and a non-existent lake near Ballinrobe.[33]

It was evidently time for a change, but not even the most ambitious mid-century map-publisher was ready to do without Pratt. The most ambitious of all in volume of output and range of interests was the Anglo-French cartographer John Rocque, who maintained an office in Dublin from 1754 to 1760, producing town plans, county and regional maps and at least one major estate survey.[34] His map of Ireland in four sheets was advertised in 1759 as 'not only drawn from the surveys of Sir William Petty and others, but corrected from all the late surveys'.[35] It was published soon afterwards under the London imprint of Robert Sayer and again in 1794 by Robert Laurie and James Whittle. Rocque knew from his own experience that early eighteenth-century town plans were now impossibly out of date, so instead of reproducing Pratt's marginal insets he enlarged the scale of the main map by about one-third. In fact Rocque's canals and other new information were quite inadequate to fill the extra space, and he made do by resurrecting a large number of late seventeenth-century names not used by Pratt from Petty's apparently inexhaustible store. In most other respects Rocque's map was flattery at its sincerest. His marginal inset of the British Isles was almost identical with Pratt's in both content and position; so were his English and Latin keys, compass rose, meridians and parallels, sheet lines, road mileages, names of seas, provinces, counties and baronies, and (after more than fifty years) harbour depths.[36]

Through the medium of Rocque, Pratt was a major source for an incomplete set of small Irish county maps published by Peter Wilson as illustrations to magazine articles in 1764.[37] Twelve years later he played the same role in the *Hibernian atlas* of Rocque's brother-in-law and former pupil Bernard Scalé. This was a collection of small national, provincial and county maps with scales varied to fit the page size (Fig. 6.9). It was heavily criticised in its own time, mainly it seems for scribal errors; as an estate surveyor without experience of printing, Scalé had not learned to discipline his engravers, a difficult task for any author when they were in London and he was in Dublin. But as an estate surveyor he could also draw on a personal archive of unpublished information, especially the names of numerous country seats, for which

Fig. 6.9　　　County Cavan, from Bernard Scalé, *Hibernian atlas* (London, 1776).
Although his outlines derive from John Rocque's map of Ireland (Fig.7.7)
and therefore ultimately from Pratt, Scalé includes a number of names
that do not appear in either of these maps.

he has never been given credit.[38] Among his innovations were Burtonhall and Sherwood Park in Carlow, Farmley and Snowhill in Kilkenny, Charleville in King's County, Beauparc and Mount Tisdall in Meath and Belvedere in Westmeath.

For the historian all this is an impressive testimonial to Pratt, but his achievement stopped well short of personal immortality. The only plagiarists who condescended to reveal his name were Moll and Bowles, and Moll had forgotten it between 1714 and 1728. (Perhaps Pratt died during this interval.) Grierson named the original author in his 1732 edition, but somehow this failed to register with the public: things might have been different if Pratt had spent more time in Dublin. Outside Ireland his reputation was never more than patchy. He was ignored in mid eighteenth-century France, for example, where Moll's and Senex's maps of Ireland were singled out for commendation.[39] This makes it surprising to find twelve copies of 'Ireland in six sheets including the plans which go along the sides' being ordered from Paris in 1779, though once again nobody remembered Pratt's name.[40] Worse still, both the *Tabula* and its author remained unknown to England's most eminent contemporary map historian, Richard Gough, until the Irish antiquary Joseph Cooper Walker, belatedly put him right. 'You inquire about the best general map of Ireland', wrote Walker in 1787. 'Grierson's four sheet map is said to be the best'. This was an undeserved dismissal of Rocque. It also looks like faint praise for Grierson, especially as Walker added his own personal recommendation of a quite different map. But 'said to be' may mean only that he himself had never seen the *Tabula*, which he warned Gough was 'not easily to be procured'.[41] Walker also reported that Grierson was preparing a new edition, but this was never heard of again. Grierson decided on a new atlas instead, perhaps taking a hint from Walker's attacks on Scalé. In the event, the race to please the critics was won by an outsider, the Revd Daniel Augustus Beaufort. He had never heard of Pratt either.

References

1. J.H. Andrews, *Plantation acres, an historical study of the Irish land surveyor and his maps* (Belfast, 1985).
2. For these and many others see Sarah Tyacke, *London map-sellers, 1660-1720* (Tring, 1978).
3. 28 October 1722 (D.W. Rannie (ed.), *Remarks and collections of Thomas Hearne*, viii (Oxford, 1907), p. 110).
4. See especially Willem Janszoon Blaeu's *Zeespieghel*, first published in the 1620s (Andrew Bonar Law, *Three hundred years of Irish printed maps* (Belfast, 1972), pp 1, 31). The original surveys on which the Dutch charts were based appear to be undocumented.

5.   J.H. Andrews, 'Science and cartography in the Ireland of William and Samuel Molyneux', *Proceedings of the Royal Irish Academy*, lxxx C (1980), pp 237, 241-3, 248-9.

6.   Robert Molesworth to Mrs Molesworth, 18 March 1690, Historical Manuscripts Commission, *Various collections, Clements*, viii, p. 215. This was probably William Berry's map advertised in February 1690 (Tyacke, *Map-sellers*, no. 179).

7.   Robert Greene, *The royal map of England* (London, 1682), reproduced in R.W. Shirley, *Printed maps of the British Isles 1650-1750* (Tring and London, 1988), p. 65. Andrews, 'Science and cartography', p. 249.

8.   Laurence Worms, 'Mapsellers at the Royal Exchange, part two: 1666 to 1714', *The Map Collector*, xxxv (1986), p. 16.

9.   *Calendar of state papers, domestic, 1702-3*, p. 78.

10.   J.H.Andrews, 'Henry Pratt, surveyor of Kerry estates', *Journal of the Kerry Archaeological and Historical Society*, xiii (1980), pp 5-38.

11.   The only manuscript regional map from this period listed among official collections is of the country between Drogheda and Dundalk (*Calendar of state papers, domestic, 1689-90*, p. 385). It is not mentioned in *Maps and plans in the Public Record Office, 1. British Isles, c.1410-1860* (London, 1967).

12.   Barracks were shown in Pratt's map of Ireland, in Edwin Sandys's map of c.1707, in Charles Price, John Senex and John Maxwell's map of 1711, in Herman Moll's map of 1714 and in Moll's county atlas of 1728. For non-cartographic lists see R.W. Jackson, 'Queen Anne's Irish army establishment in 1704', *Irish Sword*, i (1949-53), pp 134-5; H.P.E. Pereira, 'Barracks in Ireland, 1729, 1769', *Irish Sword*, i (1949-53), p. 142; Trinity College, Dublin, MS 1179, f. 61. See also Paul M.Kerrigan, *Castles and fortifications in Ireland, 1485-1945* (Cork, 1995), pp 130-33.

13.   British Library, K.51.15, K.51.16. These presumably include the original or the copy (or both) mentioned by the earl of Galway in a reference to Robinson's work on 'a map of our barracks' in June 1700 (British Library, Add. MS 9718, f. 105). See also Rolf Loeber, *A biographical dictionary of architects in Ireland 1600-1720* (London, 1981), pp 88-97.

14.   *Daily Courant*, 14 April 1708; Tyacke, *Map-sellers*, pp 90-91.

15.   J.H. Andrews, 'New light on three eighteenth-century cartographers: Herman Moll, Thomas Moland and Henry Pratt', *Bulletin of the Irish Georgian Society*, xxxv (1992-3), pp 18-19.

16.   *A general map of the kingdom of Ireland: giving an exact account of the several cities, towns, barracks, redoubts, roads, boggs, loughs woods and mountains therein contained . . . by Edwin Sandys*, n.d., n.p.

17.   John Green, *The construction of maps and globes* (London, 1717), pp 137-8, 151-3.

18.   D.A. Woodward, 'English cartography, 1650-1750: a summary' in N.J.W. Thrower (ed.), *The compleat plattmaker: essays on chart, map, and globe making in England in the seventeenth and eighteenth centuries* (Los Angeles, 1978), p. 171.

19.   Coolie Verner, *Captain Collins' Coasting pilot*, Map Collectors' Series, lviii (1969). Information on Pratt's maritime sources has been kindly supplied by Professor Richard Clarke of Belfast.

20.   According to one authority, hills should be shown on maps by 'a black clouded figure, in shape like a bell' (William Alingham, *A short account of the nature and use of maps* (London, 1698), p. 24). Pratt is one of many early mapmakers who might have been surprised to read that relief representation has 'always' been among the hardest problems in cartography: for quotations to this effect from several modern writers see Denis Wood, *The power of maps* (London, 1993), p. 145.

21.   Irish statutes, 2 George I, c.12. However, many of the placenames mentioned in this statute are not in Pratt's map.

22.   The National Library of Ireland has two copies of Phillips's survey, MS 2557 and MS 3137. The former was acquired from the Ormonde collection at Kilkenny, but the two versions are too similar for either of them to show a closer relationship with Pratt than the other. The *Tabula* generalises Phillips's outlines and omits most of his extra-mural cabin suburbs – perhaps for 'ideological' reasons, perhaps because Pratt regarded them as impermanent. Pratt's additions include a number of placenames and several new projected lines of fortification. Phillips also included small-scale maps of the more important estuaries but Pratt does not appear to have used these.

23.   In Plot's account of Oxfordshire the minimum number of houses in a village was ten (S.A.E. Mendyk, *Speculum Britanniae: regional study, antiquarianism, and science in Britain to 1700* (Toronto, 1989), p. 196). A little-known precedent for settlement-selection by numerical criteria was Mikolaj Krzysztof Radziwill's *Magni ducatus Lithuaniae* (Amsterdam, 1613) which claimed to record all localities with more than fifty households (Michael J. Mikos, 'Monarchs and magnates: maps of Poland in the sixteenth and eighteenth centuries' in David Buisseret (ed.), *Monarchs, ministers and maps: the emergence of cartography as a tool of government in early modern Europe* (Chicago, 1992), pp 173-4).

24.   At Dunamase, a prominently sited castle in Queen's County, a tower is added to the circle, but this seems to have slipped through the editorial net. Other conspicuous castles such as Blarney (Co. Cork), Castleroche (Co. Louth), Lea (Queen's County), and Narrow Water (Co. Down) are shown simply as villages.

25.   The latitude of Dublin is expressly marked as 53° 20' in a map of Ireland by William Robinson (British Library, K.51.15) which gives no other information about latitudes or longitudes. This value also appears in Alingham, *Nature and use of maps*, p. 58 and E. Hatton, *A mathematical manual; or delightful associate* (London, 1728, p. 103). For other examples see Andrews, 'Science and cartography', p. 240, n. 36.

26.   Gerard de Malynes, *Consuetudo, vel lex mercatoria: or, the ancient law-merchant* (London, 1686), p. 49.

27.   John Adams, *Index villaris* (London, 1680), preface, reproduced in V.C. Norman, 'John Adams flourished 1680', *UCLA Library Newsletter*, iv (1984), p. 17.

28.   *Dublin Intelligence*, 5 November 1709.

29.   Samuel Molyneux, 'Hiberniae notitia, or the present state of Ireland', 1709, Trinity College, Dublin, MS 888/1, f. 4 and MS 888/2, f. 277.

30.   William King to Samuel Molyneux, 25 February 1715[-16], Trinity College, Dublin, MS 2533/137. Pratt's acreage was certainly not considered too small in the eighteenth century. From 1737 to 1803 the area of Ireland was given in John Watson's annual *Gentleman and citizen's almanack* (Dublin) as 11,042,642 Irish acres. This is about 85.95 per cent of the truth; Pratt's value is about 86.15 per cent.

31.   Andrews, 'New light on three eighteenth-century cartographers', pp 18-19.

32.   Grierson's advertisement refers to 'a new large general map of Ireland, of six sheets, very much improved beyond any that have been before sold' (*Faulkner's Dublin Journal*, 22 February 1732). The map itself is undated but the list of barracks accompanying it is headed 1731-2.

33.   G.T. Stokes (ed.), *Pococke's tour in Ireland* (London, 1891), pp 50, 54, 61, 91, 94, 100. But the tourist who accused cartographers of omitting the King's River (Co. Kilkenny) and the River Bride cannot have been using Pratt ([W.R. Chetwood], *A*

tour through Ireland in several entertaining letters (London, 1748), pp 130, 146).

34. J.H. Andrews, 'The French school of Dublin land surveyors', *Irish Geography*, v (1967), pp 275-92.

35. Rocque's map of Ireland was advertised before publication in *Faulkner's Dublin Journal*, 18 December 1759.

36. It is not surprising to find a copy of the *Tabula* in a volume of maps apparently bound to Rocque's order (and consisting with this one exception of his own publications) in c.1758 (Weinreb & Douwma Ltd, London, 'John Rocque (c.1704-1762)', typescript catalogue, 1970, p. 9).

37. *The Dublin Magazine for the Year 1764*, pp 37 (Cork), 325 (Limerick), 331 (Waterford), 392 (Kerry), 445 (Wexford), 557 (Roscommon), 669 (Down).

38. Editions of Scalé's work are dated 1776, 1788, 1798 and 1809. J.C. Walker told Richard Gough in October 1787 that Scalé's errors were innumerable (J. Nichols, *Illustrations of the literary history of the eighteenth century*, vii (London, 1848), pp 702-3). Edward Ledwich complained to Walker in April 1789, 'Scalé has no sort of merit; it is a bad transcript of Petty's maps, and on such a scale as gives no information' (Trinity College, Dublin, MS 1461 (2), f. 141). An anonymous and undated early nineteenth-century essay on 'maps, surveys and charts' among the Templemore memoir material at the Ordnance Survey Office, Dublin, accused Scalé of 'intolerable ignorance or negligence', mentioning in particular orthographic errors and the omission or misplacement of mountains.

39. G. and D. Robert de Vaugondy, *Atlas universel* (Paris, 1757), p. 14. However, Napoleon is known to have possessed a copy of 'Prott's' map (Henri Berthaut, *Les ingenieurs géographes militaires, 1624-1831*, i (Paris, 1902), p. 284).

40. Mme J. Lattre to William Faden, 17 June 1779: Jefferys-Faden letter book, vol. i, no. 46, William L. Clements Library, Ann Arbor, Michigan. This reference was kindly supplied by Dr Mary Pedley.

41. J.C. Walker to Gough, 26 September 1787 (Nichols, *Illustrations of literary history*, vii, p. 699). Nichols prints 'Grienon' as the cartographer recommended by Walker, but Grierson seems more likely to have been intended. The only other possibility, much less likely, is the contemporary London engraver Reynolds Grignon (d. 1787), who executed a cartouche for Thomas Jefferys but is not known to have produced any complete maps (Coolie Verner, 'The Fry and Jefferson map', *Imago Mundi*, xxi (1967), p. 78). Contrary to Walker's suggestion, Pratt's map was said in 1788 to be obtainable for 10s 6d (Robert Sayer, *Atlases, both ancient and modern, books of maps and surveys, and catalogues of single maps, of all the empires, kingdoms, states, etc. in the universe* (London, 1788), p. 30). Gough's *British topography* (London, 1780) had included maps of Ireland, despite its title. The other map recommended by Walker was 'Andrews's', presumably a reference to John Andrews (1736-1809) of London.

184

Chapter 7

Surveys of a later date:
Thomas Jefferys, 1759

It was shortly after the middle of the eighteenth century that London
became the world's leading emporium for good maps, not just of the
British Isles but of most other countries. Its emergence was due in part
to indigenous causes, and notably to economic and technological
progress that gave British mapmakers a whole new subject-matter on
their own doorstep in the farms, fields, settlements, industries and lines
of communication created by the accelerating industrial and agrarian
revolutions. At a broader scale London map-publishers found a new
stimulus in Britain's closer involvement with the world at large, and
especially with those parts of Asia and America where Anglo-French
rivalry was most acute. There followed another rise in the demand for
maps and charts, and among the new generation of cartographers that
satisfied it Thomas Jefferys is usually considered the first and one of the
best. Jefferys began in the 1730s as an engraver, a capacity in which he
maintained a number of non-cartographic interests until the end of his
career.[1] (On one occasion, in an unlikely exchange of national stereo-
types, he was arrested by the French police for selling obscene prints.)[2]
His first maps were highly derivative and he was fortunate in 1746 to
be awarded the title of geographer to Frederick, prince of Wales. After
Frederick's death it seems to have taken Jefferys some time to receive
the same honour from the next prince, an enthusiastic and perhaps
more critical student of maps who later became King George III.[3]

By the 1760s Jefferys had made himself an industrious cartographic
compiler in the tradition of Morden and Moll.[4] This was a progression
that apparently owed much to his alliance with a geographer named
Bradock Meade, later known as John Green. This somewhat
disreputable character is said to have 'successfully achieved obscurity',
but that was not a difficult feat at a time when hardly anyone was
bothering to write or read about the theoretical side of cartography and
when Green for one had to support himself by book-editing, gambling,
and contracting profitable marriages.[5] As it happened Green was a
Dubliner: he may well have been living in the city when Henry Pratt
published his map of Ireland and when he himself was preparing a

book on the construction of maps and globes.[6] His main contribution to the latter subject was an insistence that mapmakers should explain their techniques and their sources. Given the methods still considered professionally acceptable, this doctrine was less ambitious, intellectually, than the more general belief in scientific publication that had inspired the first of England's learned journals half a century earlier. Admittedly cartographic performance would soon be starting to improve – most markedly perhaps through the use of more accurate instruments – but it would be a long time before these advances left much mark on published small-scale maps. For Jefferys's generation, the new spirit can be defined quite modestly by admitting that sometimes the only scientific course of action is to confess oneself unscientific.

Occasionally Green's principles could be applied within the body of a map – as with his proposal for underlining the names of towns whose latitudes and longitudes had been determined astronomically. More often they needed to be spelt out in some kind of ancillary statement. Such statements might be squeezed into what Green called 'some corner of the map'[7] but their natural culmination was the separately published explanatory memoir. Many geographers since Ortelius had written prose commentaries that filled as much space as the correlative graphics, but these were almost invariably simple descriptions of countries that remained blandly silent about how the accompanying maps had been made. Green sought to break the taboo with his 'remarks' on a new chart of North and South America in 1753 and two years later with his explanation of Jefferys's map of Nova Scotia and Cape Breton.[8] Meanwhile *in-situ* cartographic explanations started getting longer, especially for remote countries on the frontiers of knowledge where a mapmaker could claim to be drawing on original research. This new enthusiasm for communication (or perhaps rather meta-communication)[9] was a welcome change for all concerned, including future map historians, but it also brought its own dangers. As one of Jefferys's colleagues, Robert Sayer, wrote in 1775, 'It is a custom that has been introduced for some years of annexing to maps and charts, remarks and minutes which give some account of the labours, the methods, and facts upon which they are grounded.' Then came the warning that 'we ought to be cautious not to abuse it by making a parade of our geographical erudition'. Every student of early maps will know what Sayer was getting at.

* * * * * * * *

By Jefferys's time cartography, like literature and journalism, had created its own closely-related and inward-looking community of

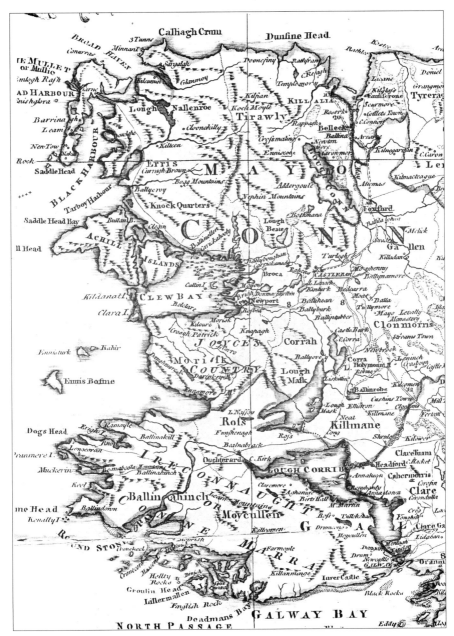

Fig. 7.1   West Connacht, from Thomas Jefferys, *A new and accurate map of the kingdom of Ireland* (London, 1759). Mainly based on Henry Pratt's *Tabula Hiberniae novissima et emendatissima* with the addition of several coastal names, e.g Dunfine Head, 3 Tunns, Broad Haven, Conurris, and numerous changes of spelling, e.g. Corrah for Carah and Killmane for Killmain.

practitioners in which each member sought to emulate his predecessors and contemporaries irrespective of non-cartographic or non-literary events. In other words, no publisher needed an excuse for a new map of any particular country. Ireland was still a considerable kingdom (though starting to look smaller as European horizons widened) and still independent enough to maintain its own parliament, its own civil service and its own army. By general European standards its economic progress was nothing to be ashamed of. The trade in livestock and livestock products was buoyant. Spinning and weaving were widely distributed and the Ulster linen industry had already grown to international stature. (Bales of cloth were a prominent marginal feature of the map described in this chapter.) Rural and urban populations were increasing, with the city of Dublin at about the 100,000 mark. The life-style of the country house was well established, and more people were travelling the roads on business and pleasure. A small minority of them, as we shall see, were students of Irish history and topography. Such were the benefits of pacification. But the danger or reality of international conflict would always be a stimulus to mapmaking, and in the Seven Years' War of 1756-63 Ireland could easily be pictured, like North America, as a theatre of operations against the French, with the locals joining in on both sides. In Dublin the threat of hostilities set off a mild invasion scare in which the country's coastal defences were inspected, surveyed and mapped by military engineers.[10] And in London Jefferys embarked on a new map of Ireland (Fig. 7.1), with an appropriate emphasis on barracks as well as on internal and external communications (Fig. 7.2).

There was nothing particularly 'colonial' about this burst of activity. Jefferys also mapped various other seats of war, including a number of German principalities and duchies where the English had no peacetime ambitions for planting either themselves or their national flag. The one frontier-like element in the new map of Ireland was a long 'advertisement' near its lower right-hand corner. Jefferys took pride in this application of Green's ideas and found room to summarise it at some length when compiling a catalogue of all his maps.[11] Here is the full text:

> This map of Ireland is drawn from the original surveys of the several counties made by Sir William Petty, compared with all the surveys of a later date, particularly those of the counties of Cork, Down, Kerry and Kildare, the counties and harbours of Dublin, Waterford and the River of Kenmare; it is also corrected and improved from all the drawings in the admiralty relative to Ireland, and includes an exact delineation of the post roads as

Fig. 7.2   Barracks from Jefferys's map of Ireland, 1759. On the original the names of barracks currently out of use are underlined. Unlike earlier cartographers Jefferys does not distinguish horse and foot barracks.

well as the chief called the great roads, as those distinguished by the names of the branch and by roads and the situation of all the barracks as well those now subsisting as those called cast barracks that are now disused. The delineation of the roads was communicated from the post master general of Ireland and an account of the barracks sent from the barrack office by the order of his grace the duke of Bedford, who also obtained leave of Lord Anson, first lord of the admiralty, for the editor to inspect the MS drawings and maps in that office. His grace was also pleased to communicate the other materials and to contribute a very considerable sum towards the expense of drawing and engraving the work.

According to a Dublin newspaper,[12] Jefferys mapped Ireland at the duke's command as well as under his patronage, and although this claim had no official standing it does not seem inherently improbable. Bedford was appointed lord lieutenant of Ireland in January 1757, seven months after the declaration of war. He did not leave for Dublin until September and in the intervening period he or his staff may well have been requesting London publishers for a good map of the country and noting that none of the first rank had appeared for more than thirty years.[13] As owner of a much-mapped estate in England it would not have been out of character for the duke to take this kind of cartographic initiative.[14] Alternatively he may have been nudged by pressure emanating from Jefferys into commissioning a new map of Ireland. At any rate the 'advertisement' suggests that no serious effort was put into this one until Bedford's support had been ensured. The only secure landmark in a mist of uncertainty is Jefferys's footnote. Under an act of the Westminster parliament passed in 1734 publishers seeking copyright protection were required to put a date on their work.[15] The act was not always complied with, perhaps because such dates could too easily become a confession of obsolescence. But on this occasion Jefferys was obligingly specific: his map came out on 13 November 1759, a few days after copies had been presented to King George II at Kensington and to the prince and princess dowager of Wales at Kew.[16]

* * * * * * * *

In common with all the most original cartographers of Ireland, then, Jefferys enjoyed at least a measure of government backing. But his map was less ambitious, and less of an advance on its predecessors, than most of those considered in this book. For one thing it is comparatively small – about 12.5 statute miles to an inch, less than half the size of Pratt's *Tabula*. But among his contemporaries Jefferys scored by exercising more influence on articulate map-users than either John Rocque or Bernard Scalé, and also by virtue of achieving two kinds of originality. The precedent of incorporating material from independently published single-county surveys into a national map had been set in England at least as early as 1700 by Christopher Browne. Jefferys carried the same idea across the Irish Sea and thereby set the tone for national mapmaking over a period of seven or eight decades. Another new fashion, for writing explanatory notes, unfortunately never became popular in maps of Ireland. But here too, for what it is worth, Jefferys's advertisement has a good title to priority. All the same, he is lucky to find himself flanked by Pratt and Beaufort on the highest level of Irish cartographic achievement.

The advertisement is long enough to be interesting for what it leaves out. The author makes no claim to have visited Ireland, or to have organised any new surveys as he did later in several English counties. Another notable absence is the newly fashionable practice of citing 'astronomical observations'.[17] Instead Jefferys pays the standard tribute to Petty, made more impressive by not attaching personal names to any of his other authorities. His ad-man's boast of having studied 'all surveys' later than Petty's is, like Rocque's claim to the same effect, an implicit repudiation of Pratt. Petty's achievements were now nearly seventy-five years old (more if the truth were known), Pratt's nearly fifty. These were venerable sources for a map that pronounced itself both accurate and new, but as the most recent original all-Ireland surveyor in sight Petty was still the name-dropper's first choice while Pratt was no doubt dismissed, with some injustice, as a secondary source whose followers would necessarily brand themselves as tertiary. The fact remains that outside the areas of his indebtedness to local and regional surveys Jefferys was heavily dependent on Pratt for both physical and human geography and especially for minor placenames.

Thus Jefferys follows the *Tabula* in running a river diagonally across the Inishowen peninsula. Both cartographers connect the Bray and Liffey rivers. In Co. Limerick both show a seven-mile tributary running past Newcastle West south-eastwards into the River Deel. Both make Lower Lough Erne more than half as broad as it is long, and in the same lake both place 'C.Aghy' (presumably the Ordnance Survey's Crevinishaughy Island) north of Boho Island. In themselves there is nothing odd about these errors. They are typical of Pratt, typical of Jefferys, and typical of eighteenth-century mapmaking in general. The point is that none of them occurs in Petty's *Hiberniae delineatio*: as always, the best proofs for or against a genetic relationship are shared and unshared deviations from the truth. As would be expected, the edition of Pratt known to Jefferys was the one published by George Grierson in 1732: this is evident from his substitution of Grierson's

'Newport' in Mayo for Pratt's original 'Westport' (a change from right to wrong) and from his inclusion of a cluster of Grierson-based names in Co. Antrim (Dundermol, Dunsholigiss, Glenwhirry, Kinslea and Leminary) that had been omitted in 1708.

Jefferys's graticule is the same as Pratt's, simplified to show two-minute rather than one-minute marginal divisions, and apparently drawn on the same projection. He was typical of his time in counting longitudes explicitly from London – not just by implication, like Pratt – and also in leaving London undefined. If pressed, he might have said that it meant St Paul's Cathedral (a Londoner is unlikely to have called Greenwich 'London' at this period) or he might have argued that at this scale it made no difference what London meant.

Like Pratt, Jefferys stated his scale in both Irish and English miles, though writing in a more enlightened age he took greater care with his definitions. Now that the union with Scotland had penetrated national consciousness Pratt's English miles were changed to 'British statute miles', even though the statute in question had actually been passed in 1593 as an attempt to restrict the growth of London. In the absence of similar legislation from the Dublin parliament the Irish mile was rather less determinate. As recently as 1750 the well-known land surveyor Gabriel Stokes had published a map of Co. Dublin repeating Petty's identification of 14 English with 11 Irish miles but at the same time confusing the issue with an equation of sixty English miles and one degree of latitude. Jefferys's definition is pretentiously – but for ordinary readers unhelpfully – astronomical. An Irish mile was a distance which if multiplied by 54.5 (plus the equivalent of 14 perches) would be equal to one degree. On the usual contemporary reckoning of 2,240 yards to each of such miles, this value for a degree improves considerably upon the fifty Irish miles accepted by Pratt and many of his generation, but it is most unlikely to have been derived from geodetic operations in Ireland or anywhere else. More probably it had been calculated from the corresponding distance in statute measure. In that case there should have been 69.42 English miles in a degree, but if the 14 perches is an engraver's error for say 34 perches, the assumed English value is more likely to have been a rounder 69.5: this was a common mid-eighteenth-century estimate, quoted in Jefferys's own map of Cumberland (1760) and again in his posthumous atlas of America.[18]

Of course none of this had anything to do with Petty, and by now some cynics may be doubting whether Jefferys 'drew from' Petty's surveys at all. At a scale so much smaller than Pratt's he certainly had no real need to do so, except that if he wished to gain credit by 'parading' a famous name he had at least to know that Petty was the source behind his own source. In fact he does include a small number of names which are in the *Delineatio* but not in either edition of Pratt. One of them is Glenlelane in Co. Donegal. This was at the west end of Ireland's northernmost county: did Jefferys start transcribing his names in serial reading order and then immediately abandon Petty for the more user-friendly Pratt? If so, the abandonment was not quite total: other such names are Liscanor (Co. Clare), Ballinakill (Co. Galway), Templemory and Sargarlah (both Co. Mayo). Not all the cynics may be satisfied by this reply. The places just listed are within a few miles of the sea. Perhaps that is where Pratt's names seemed most in need of eking out – further testimony to the special value attached to coastal names by early cartographers in general. But these names could also have been transmitted through an intermediary or intermediaries, one of them perhaps a sea chart, which remain to be identified by future research. Differences between Petty's and Jefferys's treatment of the names in question may seem to support this suggestion: none of their spellings is the same, and in Mayo the name Sargalah (Sergaltagh in the *Delineatio*) has been moved from one side of Benwee Head to another through a distance that Petty would have reckoned at more than five miles, a bad mistake for a generally careful cartographer like Jefferys.

* * * * * * * * *

Rather more effective was Jefferys's exploitation of both script and graphic symbols in the representation of geographical hierarchies (Fig. 7.3). Rank and degree had always been the tokens by which mapmakers could recognise a well-ordered society. In the *Tabula* this theme had been somewhat muted. Ireland was making a fresh start, Pratt seemed to be saying, and the processes of differentiation still had some way to go: hence his non-committal choice of small italic writing for many different kinds of feature. Jefferys, like Green, was a believer in 'marks ... which distinguish places on account of their rank, opulence, or any other remarkable occasion',[19] though in practice his differentiations were no more than moderately successful.

One hierarchy that left little scope for change was that of local government. Jefferys's subtitle, 'Divided into provinces, counties and baronies', had appeared on almost every large map of Ireland since 1690, and the units in question remained virtually identical until certain large baronies were subdivided towards the end of the eighteenth century.[20] Settlement was a more promising field for innovation. Here he chose a four-tier structure, with categories different from Pratt's.

Fig. 7.3   East-central Ireland, from Jefferys's *New and accurate map*, 1759. The
use of sources more recent than Pratt is especially evident in Co. Kildare,
where several names (e.g. Carbury Hill, Castlebrown, Cell Br and
Timolin) are derived from John Noble and James Keenan's county map
of 1752. The Grand Canal, cutting through the name 'Newcastle', is
evidently a late addition: the real canal had not yet penetrated west of
the Liffey, and when it did so passed south of Millicent and not north as
shown here.

Pratt	Jefferys
Cities and large towns	Cities and bishops' sees
Boroughs	Boroughs
Market towns	Post towns and places of note
Villages and gentlemen's seats	[Undefined lesser places]

It was hardly the ideal solution. For one thing, contrary to what is normally expected from an urban hierarchy, the higher categories did not necessarily include the lower: some bishops' seats and boroughs were post towns, others were not. Jefferys also revived the 'episcopal fallacy' whereby Achonry, Old Leighlin and Raphoe were made to seem comparable as settlements with Dublin and Cork.[21] And since boroughs for him meant places represented in parliament, one might also speak of an electoral fallacy now that places like Bannow, Harristown and Knocktopher had manifestly failed to grow into towns or even into considerable villages. The whole point of these 'rotten boroughs' was that it did not matter where they were located.

The third settlement-entry in Jefferys's key showed two different symbols, each combining a small location-circle with a conventionalised elevation – one a large tower surmounted by what looks like a modern television aerial and accompanied by a featureless out-building, the other just a small tower. Readers were left to infer that the first signified a post town and the second merely a 'place of note'. Post towns were a welcome innovation and long overdue: places where mail could be collected or left for collection had been shown on maps of England since the 1660s and on maps of France for even longer.[22] This category embraced several minor settlements ignored by both Petty and Pratt but included by Jefferys, notably Castle Blakeney in Co. Galway and Colehill in Co. Longford. On the other hand the 'aerial' appears in several places without postal services – at least according to John Watson's *Almanack*, where the list of the post towns was impressively said to have been 'compared with the post office books'. Jefferys's post towns included Magheralin in Co. Armagh, Waringstown in Co. Down, Altmore in Co. Tyrone and Ballinafad in Co. Sligo, all omitted by Watson; and for Watson's post town of Ballitore, Co. Kildare, he gives neither name nor symbol.[23] To complete the impression of disharmony, the *Almanack* yields no explanation of the 'notability' found by Jefferys at such insignificant places as Broca (Co. Mayo), Blackbank (Co. Armagh), Conovery (Co. Cavan) and Inver Castle (Co. Galway).

The lowest grade of all Irish settlements, marked only by small circles and ignored in Jefferys's key, were presumably the 'principal villages' which are promised (along with cities, boroughs, post towns and barracks) in his main title. This at least is how the circles were understood by a subsequent mapmaker and map-critic, the Revd Daniel Augustus Beaufort. On this interpretation Jefferys cannot be blamed for omitting 'noted places' mentioned in Watson's *Almanack,* many of which were little-known gentlemen's seats such as Cooksville near Youghal, Hermitage near Kilcoole, and Purcell's Inch near Kilkenny. (In any case there were far more 'noted' placenames in the *Almanack* than could fit into a medium-sized map, especially a map as well designed as Jefferys's.) More serious was Beaufort's complaint that more than 175 of what he knew to be true villages had been ignored by every all-Ireland cartographer earlier than himself. Given what has been called the dynamic quality of Irish rural settlement, this was a somewhat dangerous line of criticism. Several of Beaufort's examples were obviously too recent to be eligible; and there were very few for which he could have produced irrefutable evidence of eligibility from the 1750s.[24] More sympathetic readers will pardon Jefferys for ignoring villages later than the publication of Pratt's *Tabula* in 1708.

These doubts about classification detract from what would otherwise be one of Jefferys's main achievements, which was to out-do Pratt in matching script with subject-matter. His four settlement categories are represented in descending order by roman capitals, italic capitals, roman lower case and italic lower case. With less self-evident justification, the four-tier script sequence was also applied to coastal features, creating a fussy, restless effect with the Mullet, Broad Haven, Achill Head and Black Rock all in different styles. Without the italic capitals, the same principle appears in the names of lakes and rivers, and in one example of a mountain name: Mangerton ('supposed to be the highest mountains in Ireland') is roman, all other hill names italic.[25] Lettering style is not the only way of distinguishing an inscription. The underlining of barrack names, with the dotted line a useful refinement for establishments evacuated after several decades of peace, was an ingenious idea that Jefferys may have adopted from Green.[26] At the same time it would have been fatally confusing to represent more than one or two kinds of information by this method, which may be why Jefferys made no attempt to show markets.

*   *   *   *   *   *   *   *   *

It was in the sphere of communications that Jefferys showed most originality, and it was here too that Ireland was changing fastest in ways that could be accommodated in a small-scale map. Canals had yet to justify the optimism expressed by the Irish parliament in 1715. The Newry Canal had been opened in 1731-2 in the forlorn hope of exporting coal from Co. Tyrone. The Grand Canal from Dublin to the

Shannon (known to Jefferys as the 'New Canal') was an exercise in anticipatory mapmaking, for in 1759 there were only a few miles of it on the ground and the line as finally built was different from Jefferys's forecast. Perhaps it represented one of those last-minute impulses which on further reflection an author often comes to regret: at any rate the engraving of the waterway was obviously done later than that of the nearby names.

Land routes were harder to deal with. Jefferys shows many of Pratt's roads in Pratt's style but also adds many of his own, achieving a closer network than any previous cartographer (Fig. 7.4). In fact it may have been with Jefferys in mind that Arthur Young wrote his famous commendation of Irish roads and incidentally of Irish maps: 'I found it perfectly practicable to travel upon wheels by a map. I will go here; I will go there; I could trace a route upon paper as wild as fancy could dictate, and everywhere I found beautiful roads without break or hindrance, to enable me to realise my design.'[27] This was hardly true of the whole country. If contemporary maps were as good as Young seemed to think, western Ireland had been disappointingly unresponsive to the eighteenth-century transatlantic trade boom, many of its harbours being still portrayed as inaccessible by road and many of its uplands as impassable.

In most areas however the road system was complex enough to raise some awkward problems of classification. This was also an aesthetic issue: a close network of undifferentiated roads always looks untidy and confusing, as is immediately evident from several of Bernard Scalé's county maps. From a practical standpoint, the more alternative routes there are between any two places, the more help the reader needs in choosing from them. In any case a hierarchy of settlement-sizes implies a hierarchy of roads, even if this is defined only by volume of traffic. In eighteenth-century Irish road administration the main difference was between roads maintained by the county authorities (the grand juries) from the proceeds of local taxation and those where tolls were collected from travellers at turnpike gates set up by statutory trusts. The turnpike system had been introduced in 1729 and during the next thirty years was applied to a number of well-frequented roads radiating from Dublin. These were too few to count as the main roads of Ireland, either in Jefferys's time or later. Nor, as Young discovered, were they always the best roads. In most parts of Ireland the turnpike system was a failure, traffic being insufficient to give the trusts an adequate income. In short there was no objective basis for grading Irish roads as major or minor.

Jefferys's remedy, unfortunately not open to modern historians, was to obtain a 'delineation' of the roads from the postmaster-general. This

197

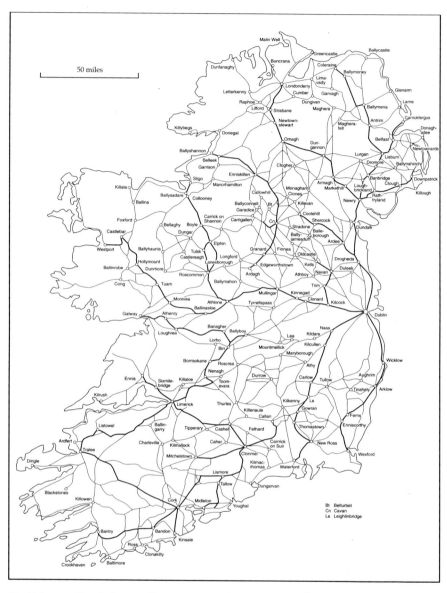

Fig. 7.4   Roads from Jefferys's *New and accurate map*, 1759. Some of the minor roads are too fine to be easily deciphered on surviving copies.

may have been the map of post roads by 'Mr Stokes' (probably the Gabriel Stokes mentioned above) which was missing in 1755[28] but which had presumably been recovered or replaced before Jefferys started work. Perhaps Stokes was also the source for some of Jefferys's post towns and even the odd non-postal centre situated on a main road like Newbrook (Co. Mayo) and Shankill (Co. Kilkenny). But all we know about this map is that it was thought good enough to deserve a finder's reward of two guineas; and it has to be admitted that most of the lines taken by Jefferys from sources other than Pratt are unrealistically straight, a good example being the road from Monivea via Tuam to Castlebar.

Whatever their provenance, Jefferys's roads are graded in his key as either grand post roads (double lines, one thick and one fine), branch post roads (fine double lines) or bye post roads (one continuous and one broken), non-post roads being mapped without explanation as single lines. The post roads are also distinguished by distance-numerals in Irish miles at appropriate points between towns – more widely spaced than the corresponding figures on Pratt's map and not always yielding the same totals. Whether the postal categories were based on the speed, frequency or bulk of the traffic (the last presumably with implications about vehicle sizes) remains uncertain. At any rate this classification is not very closely related to the list of principal Irish roads in Watson's *Almanack*.[29] Some of Watson's 'principal' arteries, like the one between Limerick and Charleville, are given only fourth-class status by Jefferys. Others he omits altogether, for example the line from Cabra to Shercock. On the other hand some of Jefferys's major routes are unrecognised by the *Almanack*: for instance his road from Wicklow to Arklow hugs the coast instead of taking Watson's more direct and altogether more probable course inland through Redcross. In any case the general utility of any post-road classification seems somewhat dubious. Did the eighteenth-century post office's customers have any more interest in the exact route followed by their mail than do their present-day descendants? It was nearly the end of the century before mail coaches began to assume a wider public significance by carrying passengers as well as letters.

*　*　*　*　*　*　*　*　*

The postmaster-general's delineation was the only land map of the whole island mentioned in Jefferys's advertisement. Was it also the source, or one of the sources, for his highly idiosyncratic representation of relief? On mid eighteenth-century maps in general, continuing a long-established trend, hill symbols took the form of profile drawings, uniformly small in size and often distributed more or less at random.[30] Jefferys adds another peculiarity. His hills form long strings, one symbol in width, suggesting either esker ridges (misplaced by scores of miles) or perhaps some kind of scarpland topography that is actually almost unknown in Ireland. The nearest he gets to a hill mass is a bunch of parallel strings. In a more sophisticated milieu these linear forms might be interpreted as watersheds; or as a neat device for 'cancelling' impracticable canal routes set at right angles to the relief. Neither theory is supported by the map itself. Nor is this habit likely to have been picked up from Gabriel Stokes or any other local cartographer. The hills on Stokes's map of Co. Dublin have all the faults of their time, but there is nothing stringy about them. On the contrary, stringiness seems more characteristic of an artist habituated to very small scales. That description certainly fits Jefferys, though he had already published at least one English county map. The strings remain a mystery.

John Green in 1717 had blamed cartographers for their neglect of sea charts. As an Irishman, it is just conceivable that he was thinking of Petty among others: this was certainly a fair criticism of the *Delineatio*. It was also a comment that Jefferys evidently took to heart when mapping Ireland, at least in the prominence that his advertisement gives to the records of the admiralty office. Yet when it came to the point his map conveyed less purely hydrographic information than Pratt's. Its harbours were too small to have soundings written in them, and outside the areas for which he advanced particular claims (to be discussed below) it is hard to find any stretch of coast where he altered either Pratt's configuration or his geographical coordinates. He did make changes in the corner of the map to Galloway and the Mull of Kintyre, but those are unlikely to have come from materials 'relative to Ireland'. The only obvious accessions are a small number of coastal names such as Kilcoridon Bay (Co. Clare), Enis Basson (Co. Donegal), Malin Bay (Co. Donegal) and Dunfine Head (Co. Mayo). Altogether the absence of identifiable admiralty input in Jefferys's map can hardly surprise us, for there is little evidence of major official hydrographic surveys along British or Irish coastlines in the early eighteenth century. Most charts at this period were products of private enterprise, and like contemporary land surveys they were mainly restricted to small areas.[31] It is his treatment of this more localised material that makes Jefferys especially interesting.

But before exploring his references to regional authorities we must consider one other category of information. The most noticeable absentees in Jefferys's advertisement are the 'inhabitants' or 'gentlemen' so glibly acknowledged by older cartographers such as Francis Lamb and Robert Morden. Perhaps these anonymous contributors had been discredited by the failure (critical if not commercial) of Herman Moll's *Set of twenty new and correct maps of Ireland* in 1728.[32] But Jefferys did have his own personal links with Ireland (apart from Green he was at one time friendly with the Revd Richard Dobbs of Lisburn, Co. Antrim)[33] and he did manage to include a number of features for which it is hard to find an origin in any earlier map or in any official document. One example is Dillonstown, a 'place of note' in Co. Louth; others are the 'villages' of Castle Bellingham (Co. Louth) and Castle Caldwell (Fermanagh), neither of them obtainable from either Petty or Pratt. Then there are the regional names Ire Connaught and Connemara, which Jefferys wrongly treats as synonymous, and Joyce's Country which he wrongly locates in Mayo instead of Galway. Lacking the administrative status of the province, county and barony, territories of this kind had hitherto been studiously ignored by all cartographers of the post-plantation era. (No government or government-supporter would want an insurgent Joyce laying claim to his ancestral domains.) In a more historically-minded age a non-political interest in regional nomenclature could be expected to make itself felt.

The most common 'gentleman's' preoccupation was orthography and it may be significant that Jefferys showed less deference to Pratt in spelling placenames than in choosing them. Given the amount of printed matter now available relating to counties, baronies and boroughs, it is not unexpected that he should modernise familiar names like Athenry, Carlow, Cashel, Cork, Kinsale and Mallow. More interesting in this connection are the names of villages and townlands. Among a hundred randomly chosen townland names of Irish origin that occur in both Pratt and Jefferys, twenty-four appear to have been re-spelt by editorial decision rather than by miscopying. The changes are not perhaps of great significance to placename scholars, but it seems unlikely that Jefferys made them on his own initiative. Like Petty, he or his advisers evidently favoured simplification: in half these twenty-four cases he replaces a double by a single letter (e.g. Pratt Bannada, Tinnehinch; Jefferys Banada, Tinehinch). Elsewhere he seems to have been influenced by pronunciation, as when changing Cloonekille to Cloonekilly and Sharcock to Shircock. There were no concessions to written Irish, however: on the contrary, preferring 'agh' to a Latin-looking 'a' may be seen as a form of anglicisation, despite the latter's association with Petty. But at least the orthography of Irish names was being treated as a matter for careful thought.

Finally, as with most maps of any complexity, there is an inevitable residue of idiosyncrasies that can be neither classified nor explained. For instance, having eliminated all but one of Pratt's nineteen woodlands, why did Jefferys insert a new cluster of tree symbols in the unlikely neighbourhood of Lough Finn, Co. Donegal? And who supplied him with the fictitious tributary of the upper Liffey that he shows running south-westwards from a point near Ballinastoe in Co. Wicklow?[34]

* * * * * * * * *

Throughout the British Isles, the normal unit of eighteenth-century regional mapping was the county, and no separately published county map could expect a welcome from the critics unless drawn from an original survey. Modern standards were set by the 'six years of indefatigable pains, with almost insuperable difficulties' endured by Joel Gascoyne in preparing a map of Cornwall which he published in 1699 at a scale of nearly one inch to one statute mile.[35] Nine more counties in England and Wales had followed by 1740 at the same scale or larger.[36] In Ireland progress at the county level was slower, but by the middle of the century two streams of development had become distinguishable. The first, unprecedentedly, flowed from the world of scholarship. The Dublin Physico-Historical Society was founded in 1744 with a view to publishing county surveys of natural history, antiquities and topography. Petty's contemporaries had planned a similar venture in the 1680s, with almost no visible results. Their successors were more productive.[37] By 1756 the society had published four counties, all written in whole or part by Charles Smith, an apothecary from Co. Waterford with a degree in medicine. The physico-historians took a realistic attitude to cartography. They wanted each county volume to have its own map, but they knew that few Irish gentlemen-amateurs were likely to do much outdoor measuring. The most they could expect was for roads, towns, villages and gentlemen's seats to figure in some kind of cartographic half-way house between a proper survey and a compilation.

The society was able to adopt or adapt two earlier surveys. One of these appeared in 1744 as an illustration to *The antient and present state of Co. Down*, written by Walter Harris in collaboration with Smith. This map was superseded eleven years later by a much larger and more ambitious survey of Down. Its author, a certain Dr Kennedy, is not known to have been in touch with the society, indeed he is not known to have done anything except make his map, but presumably his doctorate put him into the same socio-intellectual category as Smith. The other cartographer sponsored by the society was Gabriel Stokes in Co. Dublin, but here no prose text was forthcoming and this map appeared as an independent publication in 1750. Then there were the three maps that Smith included in his own books on Waterford (1746), Cork (1750) and Kerry (1756). Smith criticised Petty for not determining latitudes, for not marking roads and, more pertinently, for neglecting the seacoast, but in the development of topographical surveying he himself was no more than a transitional figure. Instead of laying out a straight base-line for the triangulation of Co. Cork, he fixed his scale by plotting a traverse road survey from Cork to Limerick (apparently not his own work) and then measuring the distance between the two towns on paper. He also surveyed certain roads and certain stretches of

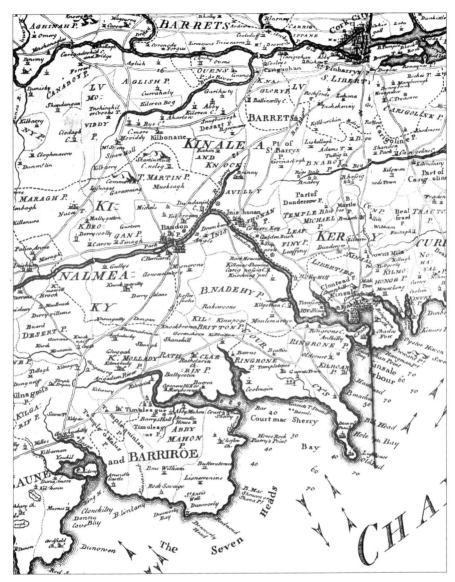

Fig. 7.5   From Charles Smith's map of Co. Cork in *The antient and present state of the county and city of Cork* (Dublin, 1750), showing names and boundaries of baronies and parishes. Angled crosses represent ruined churches, upright crosses decayed abbeys, crossed circles spa wells. The smallest settlement symbols are for 'seats and villages'.

coastline but with no attempt at all-inclusiveness. In style and presentation Smith's maps were even more evidently out of date, though at least this fault had the advantage of making them easier to absorb into a Pratt-based national framework (Fig. 7.5).

Private maps like Smith's were soon to be overshadowed by a more vigorous growth. This was the product of a new cross-fertilisation between professional land surveyors and grand jurymen, sometimes with the involvement of a commercial publisher. The first such official survey, of roads in Co. Down, provided the basis for the map in Harris's *Antient and present state*.[38] Later operations proceeded independently. A grand jury survey was commissioned for Meath in 1749-52, for Tipperary and Queen's County in 1752, and for King's County soon afterwards. But apart from Kennedy's Down the only free-standing county map to have been published before Jefferys went to press was a survey of Kildare by John Noble and James Keenan, crude enough even to contemporary eyes but still the earliest full record of an Irish county's roads to appear in print.[39]

As usual, placenames provide the clearest evidence of derivation. Examples found by Jefferys in sources other than Pratt's *Tabula* are: Kilcully, Lisgoold, Mogeely (Smith, Co. Cork); Ballee, Breda, Seapatrick (Harris, Co. Down); Briggs, Leestone, Woodgranges (Kennedy, Co. Down); C. Kelly, Rathmitchell, Rath of Killosery (Stokes, Co. Dublin); Derryhannan, Gowlane, Ratass (Smith, Co. Kerry); Bert, Davidstown, Old Connel (Noble and Keenan, Co. Kildare); Aglish, Fox's Castle, Rathgormuck (Smith, Co. Waterford). All the county maps in Jefferys's advertisement have now been accounted for. He had found as many as could be expected. A Londoner could hardly be blamed for not pursuing unpublished specimens to their various places of concealment in the Irish hinterland.

In eighteenth-century chart-publishing the equivalent of the county was the bay or harbour. Knowing that hydrography changes faster than topography, Jefferys could not creditably draw information from the charts of Greenvile Collins or John Seller even though these were slightly more recent than Petty's land maps. Had he done so, he should have added Carrickfergus, Cork and Kinsale to the three harbours named in his advertisement. Two of the latter present no problem. Waterford Harbour and Tramore Bay had been mapped by William Doyle in a well-advertised survey of 1737.[40] Doyle claimed among other achievements to have made observations of both solar and lunar eclipses and to have taken the latitude of Hook Head with a good astronomical quadrant. Besides anticipating Smith's outline for east Co. Waterford this chart gave information for adjoining parts of Wexford. (Neither Smith nor Jefferys showed the fishing ground discovered by Doyle on the Nymph Bank, presumably because it was submerged at low tide.) Another reference in the advertisement is unmistakably to William Irvine's survey of the Kenmare River, Co. Kerry, in 1748. This had been criticised and allegedly corrected by

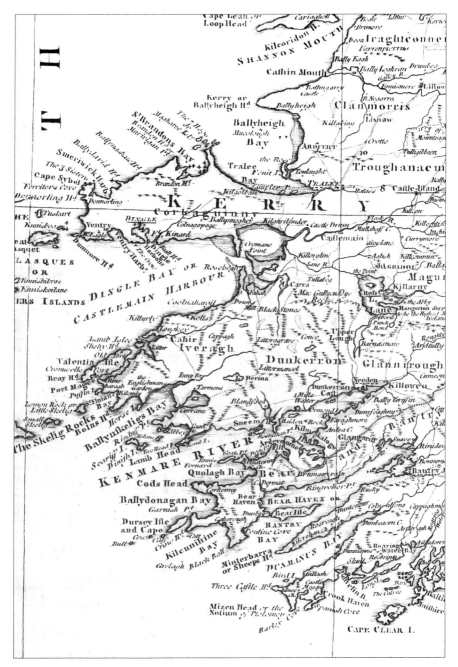

Fig. 7.6   South-west Ireland, from Jefferys's *New and accurate map*, 1759. The
debt to Charles Smith's map of Kerry (1756) is shown by idiosyncratic
names such as The Abbey and The Point.

Charles Smith, so there was a touch of 'parading' in Jefferys's citation of both Smith and Irvine without saying which he had preferred. For Dublin harbour there were several published charts, but the most likely model for a cartographer of 1759 was that of George Gibson dating from only three years earlier.

Jefferys's treatment of regional maps throws valuable light on his own cartographic personality. First, like many mapmakers he disliked unearthing a possible source and then not finding any use for it. About the only feature he seems to have derived from charts of Dublin Bay, for example, was the Candle Sticks at Howth Head, but even one such small and little-known feature was better than nothing.[41] This impulse brought a certain widening of thematic range. Jefferys's borrowings from regional maps included not just settlements and roads but aliases (Notium or Mizen Head, Co. Cork), antiquities (Strongbow Fort, Co. Wexford), bays (Stradbally Cove, Co. Waterford), bridges (Spence's Bridge, Co. Down), commons (the Curragh, Co. Kildare), corries (The Devil's Punchbowl, Co. Kerry), headlands (Mine Head), hill masses (Ardmore mountains, Co. Waterford), islands (Rockabill), lakes (the Upper Lake at Killarney, Co. Kerry), lighthouses (Copeland Islands), parks (the deerpark near Lismore, Co. Waterford), peninsulas (Cromane Point, Co. Kerry), rivers (the Greece and the Lerr, Co. Kildare), rocks (Kid's Rock, Co. Cork), territorial divisions (the baronies of Decies within Drum and Decies without Drum in Co. Waterford),[42] valleys (Glen Flesk, Co. Kerry) and various coastal features too small to carry names. Nor did Jefferys scorn such diagnostically useful oddities as the seignory of Mount Eagle and the Englishman's Garden in Co. Kerry (Fig. 7.6). Not when using recent regional surveys, anyway: he refrained from copying inscriptions that might have linked him to Pratt, such as 'Sallmon fishery' in Mayo and 'Hook tower now a lighthouse' in Wexford.

Secondly and more importantly, where national and regional maps disagreed preference usually went to the latter, no doubt because as a general principle the accuracy of any given feature is likely to depend on how much of a cartographer's attention that feature has received, in other words on what proportion of his total map-space it occupies. The most significant example of this propensity in the counties under review was a new willingness to twist and push a whole coastline into harmony with the latest geographical coordinates, a clean break with the seventeenth-century policy of correcting obsolete placenames while leaving obsolete outlines unchanged. In the southern counties for instance Jefferys's latitudes and longitudes often differ from Pratt's by two or three minutes, and in several places the difference is signalled by boldly moving a settlement across the nearest meridian, as at Ardmore, Bandon and Clonmel, or the nearest parallel, as at Castle

206

Drum, Mallow and Mohaliffe. Such concern for exact geographical position doubtless reflects Jefferys's experience with charts, and also with maps of whole continents where a cartographer's raw material sometimes included latitude and longitude data with no accompanying graphics or verbal descriptions.

Jefferys's blending of his sources did not always take a predictable form. Cartographers can differ in their choice of information without actually contradicting each other; and by a kind of 'scale-inversion' mentioned in an earlier chapter it is not uncommon for a small-scale map to include features absent from larger-scale maps of the same area. So numerous are Ireland's townlands, and so hard to rank in order of importance, that they have always been especially vulnerable to this kind of anomaly. Thus in north Kerry Jefferys sometimes followed Pratt's map of Ireland in choosing townlands that Smith had not considered worth recording in a county context, for instance Bally Eagh, Brimore and Farrenpierus, while elsewhere he ignored several settlements, like Ballybunion and Lick, that Smith had made a point of singling out. So much for Jefferys's claim to recognise 'principal villages'. Perhaps he had worked his way across the county border from Limerick some distance into Kerry before remembering to change sources. On the other hand he showed good judgement in retaining Pratt's road north-eastwards from Killarney through Brewsterfield and Fivemilebridge despite its omission by Smith. Individual features apart, he gave an overall impression of editorial balance that would have won praise from Mercator or Speed, making it impossible to tell from the map alone which counties had been drawn from Pratt and which from larger-scale authorities. In particular, he resisted the temptation to show too much. This was part of the professionalism that brought Jefferys his success.

* * * * * * * * *

One early threat to that success was the map of Ireland announced by John Rocque just over a month after Jefferys's publication date, doubtless in an effort to pre-empt some of his rival's market (Fig. 7.7).[43] There is no newspaper record of Rocque's announcement being followed by any tangible results, but like Jefferys he was the holder of a royal appointment, and when it did appear his map described the author's patron as the prince of Wales, thus dating itself before the prince's accession to the throne in October 1760. Rocque's advertisement looked like a close paraphrase of Jefferys's, but the maps themselves were quite different – not always to Rocque's advantage despite his superior personal knowledge of Ireland. Rocque charged a

Fig. 7.7   From John Rocque, *A map of the kingdom of Ireland* (n.d., London, c.1759). The outline is derived from Pratt, but Rocque shows more names. In the baronies of Ibrican and Moyarta he has 25 (Pratt has 15), most of the additions apparently being drawn from Petty's *Hiberniae delineatio*.

much higher price, 5s 5d (9s 9d coloured) as opposed to Jefferys's two shillings. On the other hand his map was considerably larger, though as always size brought its own disadvantages, the chief of these being that Rocque's apparently new infill was for the most part unbecomingly old. He could and did claim to have drawn on two surveys unknown to Jefferys (his own county maps of Dublin and Armagh, not published until 1760), but the areas affected were too small to make much impact, and even within their boundaries Rocque invited criticism by remaining unnecessarily dependent on Pratt. Elsewhere, despite his acknowledgement to 'numerous other actual surveys in many parts of the kingdom', he made little use of recent work by Smith, Kennedy, and Noble and Keenan. His most impudent gesture was to borrow a few details from Jeffreys, including the misplaced Joyce's Country.

Another of Jefferys's rivals was his contemporary Thomas Kitchin, whose career followed a very similar course to his own.[44] Their maps of Ireland are identical in almost every respect, including errors not found elsewhere like 'Lillermalin', 'Moyfenarth', 'Slime Head', 'Swadlingar' and 'Tertullagh'. Since at least one copy of Kitchin's version lacks a date and since it is not known to have been advertised, the genetic relationship between these two maps cannot be taken for granted.[45] Even the fact that Kitchin's map appears to be slightly less correct is inconclusive: by the mid-eighteenth century a good editor might just be capable of making a few amendments to the map he was copying. What seems to clinch the matter is that it was Jefferys and not Kitchin who gave a list of sources. This was not a performance that could be easily faked, and it is more likely that Kitchin was plagiarising Jefferys than vice versa.

Kitchin's map was popular but in the circumstances this cast no reflection on Jefferys. In any case Jefferys was popular as well, and with a better class of clientele. It was his map that found a place in the royal collection, printed both on paper and on satin.[46] Having originated with one lord lieutenant of Ireland, it was chosen in 1770 by another, Viscount Townshend, to illustrate an important despatch on Ireland's military defence, and this military connection was still in place when Colonel Charles Vallancey marked out the districts of his proposed survey on what may have been a new edition of Jefferys's map in 1776.[47] Vallancey's was only one of several projects that made the seventies a revolutionary period in Irish map history. However, all the major operations of this decade were in some sense regional, and it would clearly take some time for general maps of Ireland to catch up with them. 'Jefferys is by no means an unsafe guide', Joseph Cooper Walker could still write in 1787, 'his errors are but few'.[48] This was a backhanded compliment, reflecting both the obsolescence of the map concerned and the prevailing Irish attitude to English authors in general, but it was a compliment none the less. It found an echo three years later when another new edition of the map was issued in London by Jefferys's business successor William Faden.

Jefferys was still prominent in Irish map-consciousness when the Revd Daniel Beaufort wrote the memoir that accompanied his own new map of Ireland in 1792. Beaufort was determined to work from maps that were wholly original and 'not to pay the slightest attention to those of Moll, Jeffreys, Kitchin, Rocque, Bowles etc.'[49] He did however pay these authors enough attention to make numerous criticisms of them. After the disclaimer just quoted, he named Jefferys twenty-one times, Bowles four times, the others not at all. That Jefferys was here acting as a scapegoat for all derivative cartographers (except Beaufort himself, of course) is clear from his appearance several times in the *Memoir* as 'Jefferys etc.' This makes Beaufort's strictures a kind of unintended tribute, for it would have been merely vindictive to keep picking on a single victim unless it was to puncture an apparently solid reputation. Beaufort pounced on a number of editorial slips, like 'Monastere' for 'Monasterevan', and as already noted found fault with his predecessor's treatment of villages. A more interesting ground of complaint was the incorrectness of Jefferys's latitudes and longitudes, and his erroneous lengths and breadths for the various counties.[50] Here Beaufort was bringing an unwonted rigour to Irish cartographic criticism: ever since *Hiberniae delineatio*, map-users had been more concerned with the character and nomenclature of geographical features than with the mathematics of location. Beaufort had a right to be critical, as we shall see, but with the advantage of hindsight we can now recognise Jefferys as one of his worthier forerunners.

References
1. The best summary is J.B. Harley, 'The bankruptcy of Thomas Jefferys: an episode in the economic history of eighteenth century mapmaking', *Imago Mundi*, xx (1966), pp 27-48.
2. Mary Pedley, 'Gentlemen abroad: Jefferys and Sayer in Paris', *The Map Collector*, xxxvii (1986), pp 20-23.
3. Frederick died in 1751. According to Harley, citing the *Gentleman's Magazine*, xxvii (1757), p. 581 ('Bankruptcy of Thomas Jefferys', p. 35, n. 44), Jefferys again became geographer to the prince of Wales in 1757, but he had been so described on the title page of John Green's *Remarks in support of the new chart of North and South America* in 1753.
4. An unprofessional degree of conscious falsification has been found in a set of road maps entitled *Jefferys's itinerary*, but this was not published until four years after the nominal author's death and may have been the work of the unnamed editor mentioned in its preface (Gordon Dickinson, 'The deceit of Thomas Jefferys', *The Map Collector*, 1 (1990), pp 32-4). For a tribute to Jefferys's integrity from the contemporary Scottish surveyor John Ainslie see Gwyn Walters, 'Thomas Pennant's map of Scotland, 1777: a study in sources, and an

introduction to George Paton's role in the history of Scottish cartography', *Imago Mundi*, xxviii (1976), pp 126-7.

5. G.R. Crone, 'John Green, a neglected eighteenth-century geographer and cartographer', *Imago Mundi*, vi (1949), pp 85-91. As he probably would have wished, Meade will here be identified by the name under which he wrote the most important of his books. Crone withdrew his reference to Green's obscurity after discovering that he had been involved in a notorious abduction case, that his brother had been lord mayor of Dublin, and that he had ended by throwing himself from a third-storey window (G.R. Crone, 'Further notes on Bradock Mead, alias John Green, an eighteenth century cartographer', *Imago Mundi*, viii (1951), pp 69-70). It is interesting that John Greene was also the name of an eminent near-contemporary Dublin land surveyor.

6. The only facts known about Green's non-literary life before the 1720s are that he was over forty years old in 1729 and that he had married a Dublin woman in about 1714 (*The whole case and proceedings in relation to Bridget Reading, an heiress* (London, 1730)).

7. John Green, *The construction of maps and globes* (London, 1717), p. 149.

8. *Remarks in support of the new chart of North and South America* (London, 1753); *Explanation of the new map of Nova Scotia and Cape Britain . . .* (London, 1755).

9. For metacommunication see J.H. Andrews, 'Map and language: a metaphor extended', *Cartographica*, xxvii (1990), pp 1-19.

10. *Faulkner's Dublin Journal*, 29 November 1755; Paul M. Kerrigan, *Castles and fortifications in Ireland, 1485-1945* (Cork, 1995), p. 145. No maps or plans of forts are known to survive from this episode.

11. Facsimile in Harley, 'Bankruptcy of Thomas Jefferys', p. 34.

12. *Sleater's Public Gazetteer*, 17 November 1759.

13. Patricia Kernaghan of the Public Record Office of Northern Ireland kindly confirms that no reference to Jefferys's map has been found in the duke of Bedford's lord lieutenancy papers (T.2915).

14. A. Sarah Bendall, *Maps, land and society: a history, with a carto-bibliography of Cambridgeshire estate maps, c. 1600-1836* (Cambridge, 1992), pp 162, 170 and *passim*. The agent for the Bedford estates was a noted land surveyor, John Wing.

15. British statutes, 8 George II, c.13.

16. *Sleater's Public Gazetteer*, 17 November 1759. As in Rocque's map of Ireland, King George III (who acceded on 25 October 1760) was soon to replace the prince in Jefferys's reference to his patron.

17. See for example Emanuel Bowen, *A new and accurate map of Ireland laid down from the best authorities extant* (London, c.1760).

18. The value of 54.5 miles and 34 perches to a degree was also adopted in George Taylor and Andrew Skinner's *Maps of the roads of Ireland* (Dublin, 1778: see introduction by J.H. Andrews (Shannon, 1969), p. x) and in William Wenman Seward's *Ireland according to the best authorities* (London, 1795). To complicate matters further, the relative lengths of Jefferys's scale bars are not quite the same as Pratt's, being more consistent with a value of 20 feet than 21 feet for an Irish perch; but this difference is surely too slight to be significant.

19. Green, *Remarks in support of the new chart*, p. 6.

20. Jefferys omitted the baronies of Warrenstown in King's County and Bantry in Co. Wexford. In Westmeath his erroneous barony name 'Mullingar' (noted in D.A. Beaufort's *Memoir of a map of Ireland* (Dublin, 1792), p. 65) was copied from Pratt.

21. Jefferys's use of a cross for bishops' seats was as prescribed by Green (*Construction of maps and globes*, p. 11).

22. John Carr, *A description of al* [sic] *the post roads in England* (London, 1668); R.W. Shirley, *Printed maps of the British Isles, 1650-1750* (Tring and London, 1988), pp 10, 12, 40; Werner Elias, 'Road maps for Europe's early post routes 1630-1780', *The Map Collector*, xvi (1981), p. 33.

23. John Watson, *The gentleman and citizen's almanack . . . for the year of our lord 1759* (Dublin, 1759), pp 85-92.

24. Beaufort, *Memoir, passim*. Beaufort also interpreted Jefferys's 'notable places' as towns (p. 77). He conceded that his own predecessors would not have been able to show Rutland in Co. Donegal (p. 32), but still blamed them unfairly for omitting settlements as new as New Geneva (Co. Waterford), Prosperous (Co. Kildare) and Warrenpoint (Co. Down). He was also unreasonable (p. 46) in expecting such small maps to show satellite villages of Dublin like Clontarf, Crumlin and Glasnevin.

25. Jefferys's note on Mangerton was taken from a reference to the same mountain (singular, not plural) in Charles Smith's map of Kerry, discussed below. According to the Ordnance Survey, the height of Mangerton is 2766 feet above sea level. Ireland's highest mountain is now known to be Carrauntoohil, Co. Kerry, 3414 feet.

26. Underlining was also used in Jefferys's map of Jamaica, for the names of negro towns.

27. A.W. Hutton (ed.), *Arthur Young's tour in Ireland (1776-1779)* (London, 1892), ii, p. 79. Some of Jefferys's roads, especially in north Donegal and west Connacht, were to be omitted from George Taylor and Andrew Skinner's generally authoritative *Maps of the roads of Ireland*.

28. *Faulkner's Dublin Journal*, 7 January 1755.

29. Watson recognised only one class of road. His list (*Almanack . . . 1759*, pp 81-5) was stated to be 'corrected, either from Mr Senex's map; by the late Mr John Gibson: or from the information of gentlemen'. The London cartographer John Senex had been author or co-author of three maps of Ireland between 1711 and 1720. John Gibson was an Irish mathematician and land surveyor. His road distances had appeared in Watson's *Almanack* as early as 1736 (J.H. Andrews, *Plantation acres: an historical study of the Irish land surveyor and his maps* (Belfast, 1985), pp 291-2).

30. An expert pronouncement from the year of Jefferys's death was that 'mountains are sketched on maps as on a picture' (William Guthrie, *A new geographical, historical and commercial grammar* (London, 1771), p. 45).

31. The only general review of this subject is A.H.W. Robinson, *Marine cartography in Britain, a history of the sea chart to 1855* (Leicester, 1962), especially chapters 4 and 7.

32. For some of Moll's gentleman-informants see J.H. Andrews, 'New light on three eighteenth-century cartographers: Herman Moll, Thomas Moland and Henry Pratt', *Bulletin of the Irish Georgian Society*, xxxv (1992-3), pp 17-22.

33. This is the most likely identity of 'the Revd Dr Dobbs' mentioned by Jefferys in 1767, though at that time he did not know whether Dobbs was still alive (Crone, 'Further notes on Bradock Mead', p. 69).

34. Jacob Nevill's map of Co. Wicklow was not the source for this misinformation: Nevill shows the Ballinastoe district correctly as draining to the Vartry, which debouches at Wicklow. He published his map in 1760 after working on it since 1754. Donald Hodson believes that it may have been one of the sources for *A new map of the kingdom of Ireland divided into its several provinces*, engraved by J.Bayley and apparently published in c.1763 (*County atlases of the British Isles*

     published after 1703, i (Tewin, 1984), pp 116-17).

35.   J.B. Harley and William Ravenhill, 'Proposals for county maps of Cornwall (1699) and Devon (1700)', *Devon and Cornwall Notes and Queries*, xxxii (1971), p. 34.

36.   Paul Laxton, 'The geodetic and topographical evaluation of English county maps, 1740-1840', *The Cartographic Journal*, xiii (1976), Fig. 1.

37.   G.L. Herries Davies, 'The making of Irish geography, IV: the Physico-Historical Society of Ireland, 1744-1752', *Irish Geography*, xii (1979), pp 92-8.

38.   Printed as *A map of County Down, drawn by Oliver Sloane, 1739* (Linen Hall Library, Belfast, 1992) with an introductory note by R.H. Buchanan.

39.   Andrews, *Plantation acres*, ch. 11.

40.   William Doyle, *A new chart, being an actual survey of the harbours of Rineshark and Waterford* . . . (Dublin, 1737); *Dublin News-letter*, 15 July 1738; William Doyle, *A letter to every well wisher of trade and navigation containing a relation of the author's discoveries on the Nymph-Fishing-Bank* (Dublin, 1739).

41.   According to D.T. Flood ('Dublin Bay in the 18th century', *Dublin Historical Record*, xxxi (1978), p. 137) 'The Candlestick' (in the singular) originally referred to a navigational light rather than to a rock as later supposed.

42.   Jefferys's authority for this early example of post-Petty administrative geography, Charles Smith (*The antient and present state of the county and city of Waterford* (Dublin, 1746), p. 68), was unable to say when the subdivision of Decies had taken place.

43.   *Faulkner's Dublin Journal*, 18 December 1759.

44.   Laurence Worms, 'Thomas Kitchin's "Journey of life": hydrographer to George III, mapmaker and engraver', *The Map Collector*, part 1, lxii (1993), pp 2-8; part 2, lxiii (1993), pp 14-20. Worms describes Kitchin as perhaps more cautious and more pragmatic than Jefferys (part 1, p. 6).

45.   A copy in the British Library from which the imprint appears to have been trimmed off (10805(35)) is catalogued as 1755, a date tentatively accepted in Trevor Stafford, *A study of twelve eighteenth century maps of Ireland*, B.A. Mod. dissertation, department of geography, Trinity College, Dublin, 1980, p. 21. The earliest edition with a publisher's imprint is dated 1777, and the design of the title-piece is more characteristic of this later period.

46.   British Library, K.5l.23a, K.51.23b.

47.   British Library, K.5l.31.2., trimmed to remove imprint.

48.   John Nichols, *Illustrations of the literary history of the eighteenth century*, vii (London, 1848), p.701.

49.   Beaufort, *Memoir*, p. iii. Several maps of Ireland were published by members of the Bowles family, for whom see Hodson, *County atlases*, i, pp 186-90. Beaufort was probably referring to Carington Bowles's *New and accurate map of Ireland divided into its several provinces, counties and baronies* (London, 1782, later editions published in 1796 and 1800). This was on a larger scale than Jefferys's map (about 6.4 statute miles to an inch) and was in some respects a more worthy representative of pre-Beaufort cartography. It drew on Taylor and Skinner's road surveys of 1777 as well as on Jefferys and Rocque.

50.   An extreme case was Beaufort's criticism that the 'old maps' made Donegal too wide by one mile, an error of less than two per cent. It might seem arguable that Jefferys had provoked this kind of metrical scrutiny by entitling his map 'accurate' (a term coming into fashion in map-titles since around 1720) rather than 'correct', but to judge from Samuel Johnson's *Dictionary of the English language* (London, 1755) the two words were too nearly synonymous to justify this interpretation.

Chapter 8

A churchman's Ireland:
Daniel Augustus Beaufort, 1792

Most maps of Ireland have been severely practical in concept and character. However unimpressive to the academically minded, their utilitarianism is in no way surprising. Poverty, hatred and violence must all be enemies of disinterested scholarship, the more so if the scholar needs to undertake extensive field work. In the eighteenth century Irish hatreds went underground. On the surface – and cartography deals in surfaces – this was the quietest period in the country's history. It also happened to be the most British period, despite the increased activity of the Irish parliament and (after 1782) its increased constitutional authority. But it is hard to see the culture of Georgian Ireland as colonial, if only because there was so much of it in quantity and quality. Demographically Dublin could now claim second place among the urban centres of the English-speaking world, a safe assertion even if one could exclude those of its inhabitants who spoke only Irish. The city was producing more than enough literature and art to match its population, and from Swift's time onwards Dubliners cultivated the uncolonial habit of out-writing the conqueror in the conqueror's own language. In a European metropolitan community of this magnitude surveyors, engravers and publishers could all prosper, and several of the publishers were willing to become involved with maps, especially after John Rocque had spent six years in Ireland setting them an example.

This was an age when English culture and England's official religion were not thought incompatible with Irish patriotism. Whatever their ideological differences, most educated Irishmen were eager for national improvement, a desire attested in the proceedings of the Dublin parliament, in numerous pamphlets and newspaper articles, and in several all-Ireland institutions of which the Dublin Society, founded in 1731, was the most businesslike and down-to-earth. On a more elevated cultural plane Trinity College was still trying to educate the Anglo-Irish ruling class, but original scholarship remained a matter for personal initiative throughout the period between the demise of the short-lived Dublin Physico-Historical

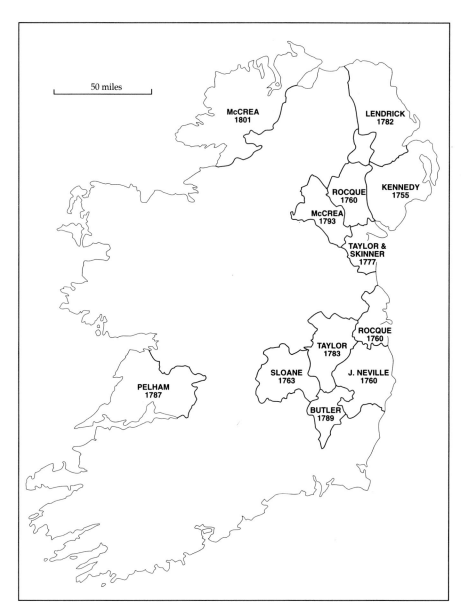

Fig. 8.1   County surveys, 1752-92. Dates are those of publication, which was
            sometimes considerably later than the date of survey. For further details
            see J.H. Andrews, *Plantation acres: an historical study of the Irish land
            surveyor and his maps* (Belfast, 1985), p. 350.

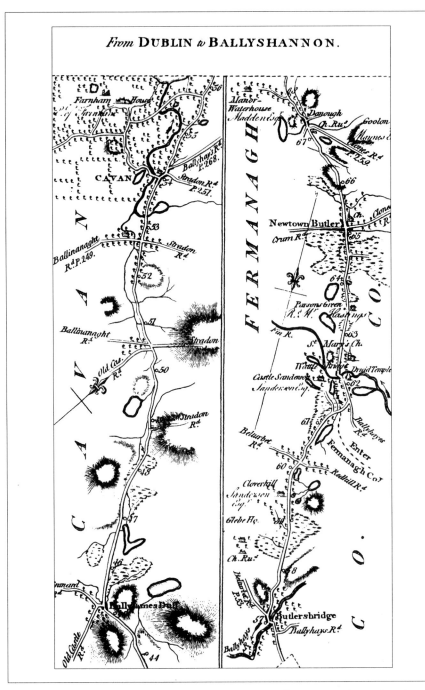

Fig. 8.2　From the second (Dublin, 1783) edition of George Taylor and Andrew Skinner, *Maps of the roads of Ireland* (first published in 1778), p. 46. The distances, in Irish miles reckoned from Dublin Castle, continued to be treated as authoritative until the advent of the Ordnance Survey.

Society in the middle fifties and the foundation of the Royal Irish Academy in 1785. The Academy unlike the Society never published any important maps of its own, but one of its earliest members was the military surveyor Charles Vallancey and another was Daniel Augustus Beaufort, the first Irish cartographer to treat his own researches as a subject for scholarly memoir-writing. Meanwhile the progress of industry and settlement observable in the Ireland of Thomas Jefferys continued at an accelerating pace. One trend especially relevant in the present context was the improvement of travel facilities with the introduction of the first Irish mail coaches in 1789. Another was the increasing number of British and foreign visitors to Ireland, and their growing disposition to write books about their experiences.

The problem of national mapmaking at this period was defined in Beaufort's comment of 1792: 'A perfectly correct map cannot be expected, until every county has been completely surveyed'[1] – exactly what William Enfield had written about England nearly twenty years earlier.[2] Cartography in Ireland was indeed now becoming dominated by the county map at a scale of one or two inches to an Irish mile. There may even have been visions of a national atlas based entirely on regional surveys of more recent date than Petty's,[3] though such hopes remained well short of realisation with the newly measured counties confined to an east-coast 'pale' and two Atlantic outliers (Fig. 8.1). Outside the county framework, cartographic specialisation had been proceeding apace. In 1777 the strip road map was imported to Ireland by George Taylor and Andrew Skinner more than a hundred years after making its debut in England (Fig. 8.2).[4] Their 300-page *Roads of Ireland* may well have brought more practical benefit to Irishmen than any other map or atlas of the century.

Meanwhile estate maps remained a flourishing minor art form and a proving ground for the surveyor's talent; and under Vallancey's direction military surveying, once confined to the immediate vicinity of forts, sieges and battlefields, had begun to take in broad tracts of open country, though it was not until the next century that its results became widely known. Even more than in Jefferys's time, charts of coasts, rivers and canals were needed in sufficient numbers to be printed, advertised and retailed in the same way as ordinary maps, thus encouraging the combination of hydrographic and non-hydrographic material in new kinds of cartographic amalgam. The dominant influence here was Murdoch Mackenzie's *Maritim survey* of Ireland, published in 1776 to crown a long career of chart-making among the western British Isles. Finally there was the thematic element that now began to colour almost all maps of Ireland in varying degrees. In particular the national passion for Irish history inspired several distribution maps of ancient territories and families.[5] Another possible subject for thematic mapping in the land of Protestant versus Catholic was religion. In the new atmosphere of enhanced map-consciousness any churchman might need cartographic help to appreciate how it could be possible for a single Irish county to fall among five dioceses – even if, like Daniel Beaufort, he had lived until middle age without making any maps himself. What all these new ventures had in common was to be totally independent of William Petty. It was time for a fresh synthesis.

* * * * * * * *

Though born in England, Beaufort was a member of the Protestant Irish nation.[6] He graduated from Trinity College, Dublin, at the age of twenty in 1759 (the same institution gave him an honorary doctorate in middle age) and later succeeded his father as Church of Ireland rector at Navan, Co. Meath. Without neglecting his clerical duties he also became librarian of the Royal Irish Academy, a keen educationist, an energetic practical farmer and a gifted amateur architect. In private life he was a successful father and father-in-law and one of eighteenth-century Ireland's most observant and articulate diarists. Yet the *Dictionary of national biography* introduces him simply as a geographer. There can be no quarrel with this description, even though Beaufort published no more than three maps – a civil and ecclesiastical map of Ireland (1792), a small map of the country's river systems (1792),[7] and a map of the diocese of Meath (1797) (Figs 8.3-8.5).[8] He illustrates the cartographic principle that high quality and low productivity often go together.

Cartographically Beaufort did as much as anyone could to free his country from English domination. In one major respect, however, his principal map was not very Irish, for neither in planning nor execution did it so much as hint at the existence of the Catholic faith. Its author could indeed be caricatured as a sectarian propagandist foisting a totally Protestant ecclesiastical geography on an island that was three-quarters indifferent to it. More sympathetically considered, the map helped to inaugurate a late efflorescence of official Christianity that was soon to find expression in the numerous new church buildings financed by the board of first-fruits. On a purely personal interpretation it could have been an ambitious cleric's aid to ecclesiastical preferment, identifying desirable benefices that might one day fall into his own hands. Beaufort himself, it must be said at

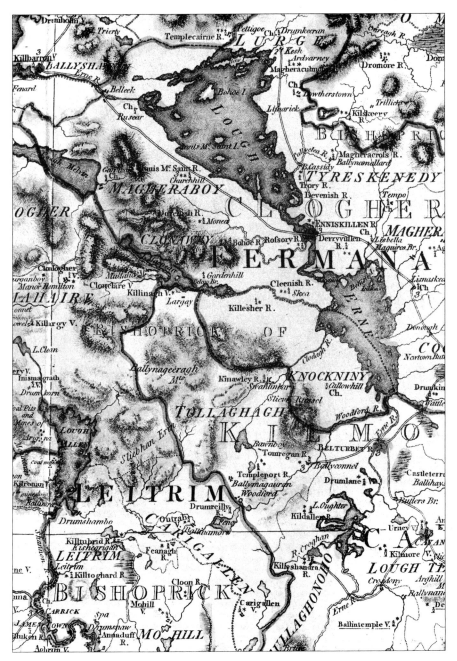

Fig. 8.3   Upper and Lower Lough Erne from Daniel Augustus Beaufort, *A new map of Ireland, civil and ecclesiastical* (London, 1792). One star denotes a glebe, two stars a parsonage house, Ch a chapelry, R a rectory, V a vicarage, single underlining an impropriate rectory, double underlining a wholly impropriate parish. Figures show the number of post-days per week.

Fig. 8.4   *Sketch . . . of the groups of mountain[s], the extent of the greater bogs, and the influence they have on the origin and course of rivers*, in D.A. Beaufort, *Memoir of a map of Ireland* (Dublin, 1792). The first printed all-Ireland thematic physical map.

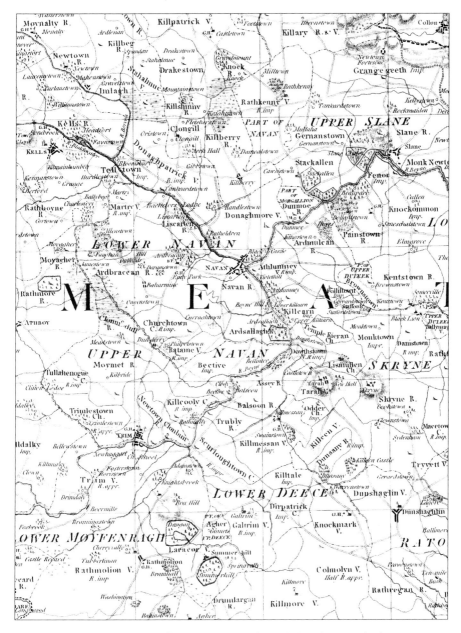

Fig. 8.5   From D.A. Beaufort, *The diocese of Meath* (London, 1797), showing
baronies, parishes, churches, glebe houses, parks, gentlemen's seats and
round towers. Beaufort was rector of Navan from 1765 to 1818.

once, felt no particular desire for professional advancement (though he did eventually pick up another living at Collon, Co. Louth) and quickly made his map available to every potential competitor by publishing it with all the salesmanship he could command.

His first objective was a simple boundary map of dioceses, parishes and counties on a scale of ten Irish miles to an inch or 1:806,400.[9] Later he experimented with even more selective concepts, substituting church sites for parish boundaries.[10] Of course even the most abstract thematic map is expected to include a coastline, but it was still tacitly understood among cartographers that base maps for thematic distributions could be simpler and therefore less accurate than ordinary geographical maps on the same scale. Yet there have always been a few conscientious thematic cartographers attracted by the requirements of their base map into the realms of general geography and even geodesy. In restoration England, for instance, John Adams had started by mapping markets for fish and ended by trying to measure an arc of longitude. Geologists like Ireland's Richard Griffith have also sometimes found themselves in this position.

Beaufort was another geographical perfectionist. In his own words, his original design 'went no further, at first, than to insert [the dioceses and parishes] in a faithful copy of one of the best and most modern maps of this country and it was not until after I had employed much time and pains on it, that I found the … maps which I intended to follow, so full of errors and defects as to require almost total correction'.[11] Thus Beaufort like several of his contemporaries was led towards what might be called the frontier theory of cartographic progress, lamenting that 'the astronomer and engineer have been so much less employed in settling the geography of the British Islands, than in ascertaining that of our distant possessions'.[12] In their day, the excellence of Petty's surveys could have been held to prove that colonies are generally better mapped than metropolitan countries. Beaufort and his generation aspired to higher cartographic standards and did not recognise Ireland as a colony;[13] for them what justified the frontier theory was the inferiority of Petty's maps to the best of their new-world counterparts.

*   *   *   *   *   *   *   *   *

Beaufort's solution was 'to set about my work, as if no general map of Ireland had been extant'. This gave short shrift to a few good maps as well as to many bad ones, with Petty treated as a necessary if not wholly justifiable exception. It was not general or small-scale maps as such that now seemed objectionable, but derivative maps. Of course Beaufort's own map could not be truly original – he was never going to put the whole of Ireland into one surveyor's field book – but at least it would not be derivative to the second or any higher degree. A preference for first-hand sources was no longer unusual among aspiring national mapmakers. In 1777 Taylor and Skinner hoped to make a general map of Ireland from field observations connecting their own original road measurements[14] and, as the next chapter will show, Vallancey was planning to do the same with his regional military surveys. The Taylor-Skinner map never appeared – unless we treat the index to their *Roads* as a miniature version of it[15] – and Vallancey's though more or less finished was never published in full. According to Beaufort, in 1785 the Revd James Whitelaw of Dublin, a scholar not unlike himself in abilities and background, was planning a new description of Ireland 'with the same idea of maps as mine'.[16] Whitelaw made one map, of Tyrawley in Co. Mayo, but then conceived and executed the even more original idea of a Dublin population census; his atlas was never heard of again.

Another national map, this time in the not very original form of a county atlas, was begun in 1789 by William Beauford on behalf of the bookseller George Grierson, grandson of the Grierson who had republished Petty and Pratt.[17] Beauford was an artist and antiquary, with both historical and estate maps to his credit. He has often been confused with Daniel Beaufort, and in fact their methods were not entirely different. Beauford began with a skeleton based on Petty's Down Survey and then augmented and corrected this from more recent sources, each county requiring about three and a half weeks' work. For reasons that await discovery this scheme soon fell into abeyance: the Grierson atlas was not printed until about 1818, and then with a minimum of publicity and no known effect on other cartographers (Fig. 8.6).[18] Beaufort differed from these would-be rivals in the quality of his achievement and the speed with which it took shape.

Beaufort was thus not alone in his disenchantment with the standard contemporary maps, but it is not known exactly when his own loss of innocence came about. One clue may be found in his rather unhappy relationship with Vallancey. When they met in May 1785, apparently for the first time, Beaufort was already planning some kind of ecclesiastical map, and Vallancey upstaged him by claiming to have had the same idea several years earlier and to have satisfied himself that it was not worth pursuing. It was on this occasion that Beaufort first saw Vallancey's great military map of Ireland, to be more fully described in the next chapter. He saw it

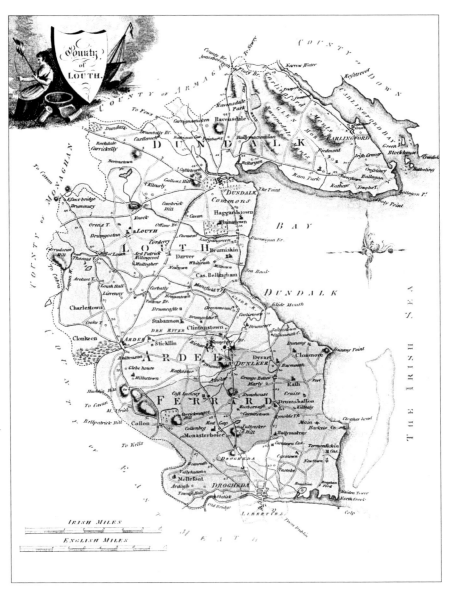

Fig. 8.6   *County of Louth* from George and John Grierson and Martin Keene, *New and correct Irish atlas* (Dublin, n.d., *c*.1818), probably compiled by William Beauford. Distances are in Irish miles: those reckoned from Dublin provide a means of identifying main roads. Original features include the use of Dublin as an alternative prime meridian, also a number of names for country houses and physical features that had not appeared in previously published maps.

again seven months later, on the day that Vallancey was due to take it to London for presentation to the king. If Beaufort had been seeking original material at this stage he would surely have asked permission to study Vallancey's map, or at least mentioned this possibility in his diary, instead of simply noting the map as an object of admiration.

The fact was that Beaufort spent much of the period 1785-6 mapping not the whole country but the much smaller area occupied by his own home diocese of Meath. At the end of 1786 he arranged for the results of this endeavour to be shown to the assembled bishops of Ireland. He also showed them to Vallancey, who expressed polite approval but nothing more. The bishops seemed more enthusiastic, but their final verdict was that Beaufort would do better to work on 'the general map'.[19] Commercially they were right: the diocese never sold well in either of its two editions.[20] Aware of his amateur status, Beaufort was always a seeker and taker of advice, a useful habit in one whose social position and personal qualities made him widely acquainted with the great and the good. He now lost no time in redefining his priorities. By March 1787 he was issuing advertisements and soliciting orders for a map of all Ireland, discussing arrangements for the publication of such a map with William Allen, Dublin's leading printseller, and making inquiries about the cost of having it engraved.[21] All this was before he had started serious work. Indeed the advertisement hinted as much by inviting readers to contribute 'authentic information'.

At this stage the map was described as 'ecclesiastical and civil'. In the final title these adjectives were transposed, but in either order they jointly laid claim to the whole field of cartographic discourse not covered by Vallancey's military survey. They also absolved Beaufort from including forts and barracks, but not from incorporating Vallancey's improvements (if any) in the representation of civil subjects. Unfortunately Vallancey took offence at Beaufort's published claim to be rectifying 'the gross defects which occur in all the present maps of this kingdom'. This was over-sensitive considering that Vallancey's map had not been published, but it meant that little more could be expected from him. From now on, his only gestures towards Beaufort were a warning that the civil and ecclesiastical map would not do well in France, a refusal to divulge the distance between Loop Head and Kerry Head, and a 'sneer' when the two men happened to meet at Dublin Castle. Beaufort retaliated, if only in Vallancey's absence, at a dinner in Killarney where the party 'amused ourselves correcting the numerous errors in Colonel Vallancey's map of the lake'.[22] On his own map he expressed a contrary view of the French market by including a separate scale of French leagues. It is a pity that these two talented cartographers could not be friendlier. As it was, the streams of map history that they represented were not to be fully brought together until the coming of the Ordnance Survey.

Beaufort's publicity campaign of 1787 did well enough for him to start work almost at once. Wisely his first decision, on 16 April, was to fix a scale, six miles to one inch. The miles were of the Irish variety, but although Beaufort thought as an Irishman, London was still the obvious place of publication for any part of the British Isles, and in July he reached an agreement with William Faden of Charing Cross, Thomas Jefferys's successor as geographer to the king.[23] Evidently William Allen was not yet thought sufficiently well established to be given sole responsibility for an Irish masterpiece, though in due course his name was to appear on the map as Faden's co-publisher. Back in Dublin the pace began to quicken. Years later, the German map historian J.G. Kohl published the disapproving comment that Beaufort was 'not even a mathematician or a geographer by profession'.[24] But pride in amateurism is one of many non-Teutonic qualities common to the Anglo-Irish and the English. Beaufort obtained appropriate surveying instruments from the distinguished Irish astronomer Henry Ussher and set forth on travels that were intended partly to carry out first-hand observations and partly to collect written and oral information not available in Dublin. He made two such journeys, in 1787 and 1788 (Fig. 8.7).[25] He also spent much time on indoor research in Dublin, and during the summer of 1790 in London. The map was finished in manuscript on 14 September 1790, personally presented to King George III on 9 May 1792 and effectively published towards the end of the same month, though the date in Beaufort's printed footnote was 1 March.[26]

*   *   *   *   *   *   *   *   *

Memoir of a map of Ireland was published at the same time as the map it describes. Like most works of the same kind it was no blockbuster, and 71 of its 235 pages were devoted to indexing the names on the map, but in an Irish context it commands admiration as a vastly expanded successor to Jefferys's 'advertisement' of 1759. More probably it was inspired by cartographers of the post-Jefferys generation like J.B. D'Anville, Murdoch Mackenzie, whose *Treatise on maritim surveying* in 1774 urged cartographers to publish explanatory essays, and James Rennell, who followed this advice when mapping Hindustan in 1783. Beaufort's *Memoir* first describes the making of the map and then gives a brief geographical description of Ireland. Allowing for changed standards, the description is not much more

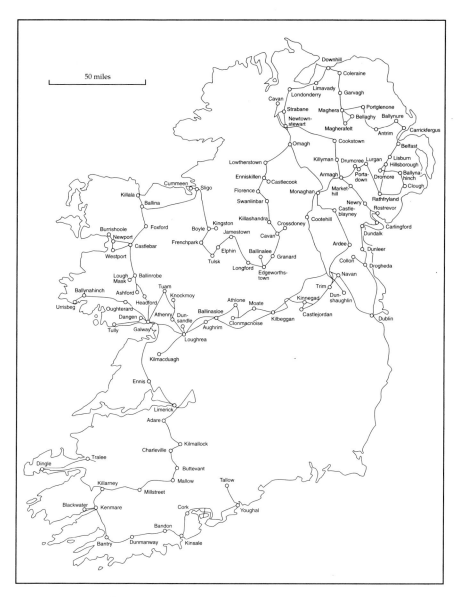

Fig. 8.7   Beaufort's journeys in 1787 and 1788, from a more detailed list in C.C. Ellison, *The hopeful traveller: the life and times of Daniel Augustus Beaufort 1739-1821* (Kilkenny, 1987), pp 122-4. Routes are approximate and in some cases wholly conjectural. There appears to be no surviving record of Beaufort's 1788 tour after he left Tallow, Co. Waterford.

substantial than the text accompanying Henry Pratt's map of 1708, and immeasurably inferior as a portrait of the Irish landscape to Beaufort's unpublished diaries. Its most original and important features were peripheral to the main theme. They were, for contemporary geographers, the acreages of counties, provinces and dioceses, the first authoritative figures of their kind since Pratt's time; for modern social historians, an estimate of populations in the same areas; for cartographic historians, the small map of Irish river systems, representing a quasi-thematic approach pioneered in early seventeenth-century France by Melchior Tavernier but still uncommon in Beaufort's day; for placename students, the table of Gaelic-derived prefixes, fulfilling a promise made but never kept by Petty more than a hundred years earlier.

The *Memoir*'s account of Beaufort's cartographic methods is harder to assess. He seems to have hesitated about how much to say, for in print his treatment is arbitrarily and confusingly divided, with seventeen separately numbered pages of preface and 'description of the map' followed by eight pages on the 'construction of the map' which are paginated as part of the main text – doubtless a hint that Beaufort enlarged his technical coverage after sending part of it to the printer. Today judgement is made difficult by the shortage of contemporary or earlier specimens of the memoir genre to serve as a standard. This fact alone must make us pathetically grateful to Beaufort for writing anything at all. What he said, and left unsaid, will emerge from the following narrative.

Perhaps surprisingly, there is no reference in either memoir or diaries to any scheme of major triangulation of the kind proposed for Ireland many years earlier by William King and more recently made familiar in England by the Royal Society's plan for connecting the observatories of London and Paris.[27] The only clue to Beaufort's original intentions in this sphere comes in one clause of one sentence confided to his diary for 1 September 1787: 'for if Dr Usher comes and takes the latitude of Athlone it will answer still better'. This was written after two hot and uncomfortable days of abortive measuring and levelling in the south-west corner of Co. Meath. Beaufort can hardly have been laying out the base-line for a triangulation in this area; for that purpose he would have chosen flatter terrain. Nor was he trying to measure the east-west width of Ireland, because then he would surely have started from either Dublin or Galway. It seems more likely that he accepted the existing maps of Co. Dublin (by John Rocque in 1760) and Co. Kildare (by Alexander Taylor in 1783) as accurate and was planning to link the western border of Kildare via the Meath 'pan-handle' with Athlone and later with the west coast, probably by means of a road traverse rather than as a straight line. Whatever their purpose, the measurements were quickly abandoned, and the only figure quoted in the *Memoir* for the distance between Dublin and Athlone was derived from Taylor and Skinner's road-book.

The Dr Ussher mentioned in Beaufort's diary was Henry of that name, professor of astronomy at Trinity College, Dublin. This reference to him suggests, and the *Memoir* confirms, that when it came to the point the mathematical control for the new map was to be based entirely on independent determinations of latitude and longitude. Beaufort had little trouble in mastering the astronomical theory involved, but he made no observations of the sun or stars himself. The latitude of Athlone was taken not by Dr Ussher but by one of his pupils who happened to be Beaufort's fourteen-year-old son Francis, later famous as hydrographer to the Royal Navy but on this occasion modestly nameless.[28] Francis also made provisional observations at Galway, and values for a number of other stations were supplied by some of Ireland's leading astronomers. The latitudes were well distributed except in the west. Longitudes, being so much harder to determine, were inevitably fewer: west of the Cork meridian there were none, leaving more than forty per cent of Ireland's longitudinal extent unverified. For many towns the only available method was a form of dead reckoning derived from road and canal surveys, and the positions of critical features like Loop Head, Mizen Head, Cape Clear, Slyne Head and Rossan Point had to be deduced from earlier maps, mainly Petty's. Beaufort was rightly proud of having done as well with his coordinates as anyone could expect. He wanted to graduate the margins of his map in single minutes, as Pratt had done, but the engraver, Samuel Neele, persuaded him that this would look 'paltry and ugly' so he settled for a three-minute interval.[29]

Beaufort's table of latitudes and longitudes[30]

	Observations	Old maps
	Latitudes	
By the Revd Dr Ussher:		
Dublin	53.21.02	53.21.00
Wicklow Pier	52.59.00	52.58.00
By the Revd Dr James Archibald Hamilton:		
Armagh	54.20.30	54.20.00
Cookstown	54.38.20	54.40.00

Ardee	53.50.30	53.52.00
Portarlington	53.39.30	53.11.00

By the Revd William Hamilton:

Bengore Head	55.15.00	55.15.00
Ballycastle	55.12.00	55.14.00
Londonderry	55.00.00	54.58.00

By Mr Mason:

Cavan (Donegal)	54.51.41	54.49.40

By Dr Longfield:

Cork city	51.53.54	51.45.00

By Mr Mackenzie:

Cape Clear	51.19.00	51.11.30

By a pupil of Dr Ussher:

Athlone	53.23.30	53.22.30
Galway	53.16.00	53.10.30

Longitudes

By Dr Ussher:

Dublin	6.15.00	6.30.00

By Dr Hamilton:

Cookstown	6.40.00	7.06.00

By Mr Mason:

Cavan (Donegal)	7.23.00	7.52.00

By Dr Longfield:

Cork city	8.30.00	8.37.30

For purposes of comparison Beaufort scaled distances from Jefferys's map (presumably that of 1759) and today the same can be done from the Ordnance Survey's one-inch map. In eighteen latitudes there was only one for which his value was less accurate than the 'old maps' and one where old and new values were identical. On average he had reduced the old-map latitude error from 2.96 minutes to 0.77 minutes. All four of his longitudes were better than Jefferys's, the average error being reduced from 16.79 minutes to 3.25 minutes. In planimetric terms he shows up just as well. The average RMS error for Petty's four provincial maps is 0.061: the corresponding figure for Beaufort's map is 0.039.

Beaufort's memoir anticipated the Ordnance Survey's self-descriptions in saying much more about his control survey than about the treatment of local detail, but even allowing for this bias his exposition fails to meet the highest scientific standards. He does not date the observations or specify the methods and instruments employed, nor does he define his stations with reference to local landmarks. He also says nothing about his choice of projection, a subject on which the diary is equally silent except for the single entry (as if to show that here too Beaufort was capable of managing for himself), 'All day calculating logarithmically curves of latitude parallels'.[31] Criticisms of his reticence may seem to miss the point by applying nineteenth- or even twentieth-century standards to the 1780s. But no sooner was the *Memoir* in print than the Royal Irish Academy received a proposal from two mathematicians, Thomas Harding and Benjamin Workman, to make 'astronomical, nautical and geometrical observations' that would constitute a 'survey of the coasts and principal towns of this kingdom, their longitudes, latitudes etc.' This was a reflection on the *Memoir* and its associated map, but as so often in such cases the reply springs readily to mind: Beaufort's work was finished and published, Harding and Workman's was not.[32]

* * * * * * * * *

Otherwise the main value of the *Memoir* was to list the original surveys used in Beaufort's map. His thoroughness is impressive. In fact the omission of any published regional map from his review can be confidently taken not as an oversight but as a negative judgement of its quality. Thus he evidently shared the prevailing low opinion of Bernard Scalé's *Hibernian atlas*, and ostentatiously failed to mention the Physico-Historical Society's county maps of Down, Waterford, Cork and Kerry that Jefferys had taken credit for consulting. His only reference to Charles Smith was to note a bad error in Smith's astronomical calculations.

Beaufort was not content with printed sources. Throughout his travels he hunted down manuscript maps and other relevant documents in public offices and private houses, sometimes having to exercise considerable tact and persistence. An example from 1788 was his success in eliciting unpublished county maps of Armagh, Donegal and Tyrone from their reluctant author, William McCrea of Lifford.[33] Beaufort found maps in the gallery at Dromoland Castle, Co. Clare, in the library of Trinity College, Dublin, and in the office of the Londonderry estate surveyor David McCool. No repository was too unpromising to be explored. He mentions several maps of which modern historians would otherwise know nothing, like [Oliver?] Sloane's Co. Meath of 1752 and Harvey's Inishowen, Harvey perhaps being the Revd John of that name resident at Malin Hall, Co. Donegal. Rocque and Jefferys had understood that any map corrupted in the process of publication must be set aside by subsequent compilers in favour of its original manuscript. With Beaufort this preference for primary sources is more specifically documented. He found the manuscripts of both John Cowan's chart of the Shannon and Henry Pelham's map of Co. Clare, and through the kindness of Ireland's deputy surveyor-general, Matthew Handcock, he gained admission without payment to the parish and barony maps of the Down Survey in Dublin Castle.[34]

With manuscript maps it is harder to draw conclusions from the *Memoir's* silences, because there could obviously be more than one reason – including an owner's unhelpfulness – for not using unpublished sources that were worthy of attention. (Beaufort did not anticipate the modern habit of publicly criticising private individuals for not opening their archives.) No doubt the *Memoir* had good reasons for omitting Neville Bath's map of Co. Cork, for example, which the diary describes as 'very well done'. And it may have been embarrassment over Vallancey's hostility that kept out any reference to the military sketch of southern Ireland by William Roy which Beaufort's diary shows him to have studied in 1790. Perhaps most significant, considering Beaufort's original aim, is his apparent neglect of diocesan and other ecclesiastical maps. A few of these are known to have existed, and he certainly saw two, supplied respectively by the bishops of Cloyne and Limerick. But apparently no comprehensive and accurate record of ecclesiastical boundaries was held by the church authorities at this period, as Beaufort shows by making special acknowledgement to Petty, of all people, for the ecclesiastical part of his map. Since Petty had not delimited dioceses as such and Beaufort did not delimit parishes this must refer to parish boundaries that Beaufort knew to form parts of diocesan boundaries. Non-spatial information about the church – rectories, chapelries, curacies, impropriations etc. – was doubtless obtainable from diocesan registries and by word of mouth.

Of the manuscript maps he consulted, Beaufort borrowed some and traced others *in situ*, reducing them to the required scale with a 'pantographer'.[35] Some sources he carried into the field, notably Taylor and Skinner's *Roads* and Mackenzie's charts (both of which he held in high esteem), adding and correcting as he went. He took bearings to one or more points in the Aran Islands from the main-land, and to various other landmarks from Knockmoy in Co. Galway. Without further observations to complete a triangle these angles would have been unhelpful except as a check on existing maps. On the other hand when Beaufort inserted Keeper Mountain in Tipperary on Taylor and Skinner's map it may have been by intersection from two determinate positions in their road system. It may also have been simply by sketching, for after September 1787 the diary makes no mention of instrumental readings and Beaufort is likely to have decided that on his very small scale they were not worthwhile.[36]

The bulk of the diary's record was non-mathematical. For instance, 'the little village of Douglas' in Co. Tyrone was pronounced worth marking in the map (it was duly marked) and Cahermorris in Co. Mayo, though shown by Jefferys as a town, was found to consist of one cabin and one ruined castle with a quarter of a mile's distance between them. Sadly for the map scholar, though happily for the historical geographer, Beaufort's travel notes are such as might be expected from any alert and educated observer, with very few cartographic technicalities. The same is true of the diary he kept at home. We learn little of how the various existing county and regional surveys were spliced together. The survey of Donegal by William McCrea, for example, could be pinned onto Beaufort's mathematical framework in just one place, the observatory at Cavan near Lifford on the very edge of the county, and since McCrea seems to have inserted no meridians this left an infinite number of possible alignments for the rest of his map. How could a compiler make his choice? Such questions are more than a diarist can be expected to answer at the end of a hard day. In any case Beaufort was a sociable character and seldom wrote in detail about activities that did not involve other people.

* * * * * * * *

We may now turn from the documents to the map, or rather the maps, for Beaufort is unusual among cartographers in recovering his manuscript from the engraver and preserving it for posterity (Fig. 8.8).[37] There is no need to worry about identifying the draughtsman: by 'my drawing' Beaufort meant what he said in every sense. The only part of the map attributable to another hand was the title piece, designed by his daughter Frances to embody a number of family allusions, including a dunce's cap, though no doubt a dedicated semioticist could find some ideological significance in it as well.[38] For first-class engravers, as for publishers, London was the

Fig. 8.8   Part of Ulster, from D.A Beaufort, manuscript map of Ireland, British
            Library, Add. MS 53,711A. Copied with the addition of roads and various
            minor corrections in Beaufort's printed map. In style and layout the
            manuscript and printed versions are closely similar, the main change
            introduced by the engraver being the simplification of the ornamental
            capitals used here for town names.

Fig. 8.9   Co. Kilkenny and adjoining areas, from Beaufort's *New map of Ireland*,
1792. The coal pits are one of four mining areas shown on the map, but
the hachures fail to bring out the form of the Castlecomer Plateau. One
of Beaufort's few outright errors is to place a round tower at Dysert
instead of Timahoe.

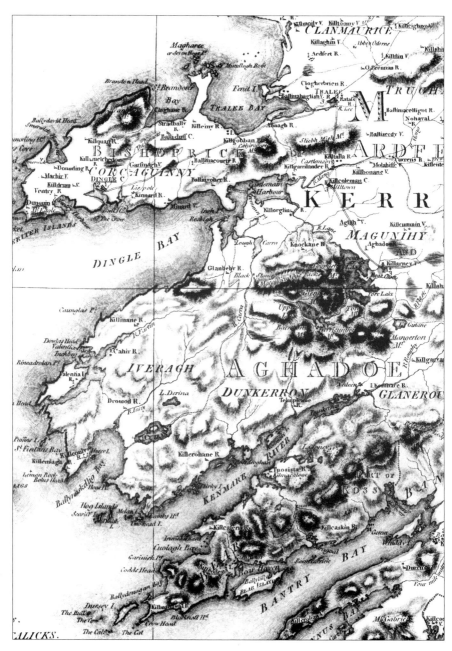

Fig. 8.10   The south-west peninsulas from Beaufort's *New map of Ireland*, 1792. An
excellent representation of coasts, rivers and placenames, less
satisfactory for relief: mountains over 2000 feet high are omitted near the
north coast of the Iveragh peninsula. On present-day maps the
peninsulas extend about six statute miles further west than Beaufort's
ten-degree meridian implies.

obvious hunting ground. On his own publisher's advice, Beaufort chose Samuel Neele of the Strand. It is not often that we know an early cartographer's opinion of his engraver, or vice versa. The *Memoir*'s praise of Neele was almost unqualified: on the subject of hill shading he was said to have coincided with Beaufort's drawing 'except in very few instances'. Privately, actions spoke at least as loudly as words. Neele's services were retained for the diocese of Meath in 1797 and Beaufort later claimed credit for recommending him to a number of county cartographers.[39] Neele for his part remembered Beaufort not just as a customer but as one of his oldest friends.[40] Their collaboration certainly achieved a good match between manuscript and print, and Beaufort emerges not as an innovator (differing in this respect from many amateurs) but as a designer of professional standard, especially successful in exploiting the sizes, styles and underlines of names to convey information, and in limiting detail to just the right density (Figs 8.9, 8.10).

Like most maps, even in the austere Augustan age, this one was meant to be coloured. Colours were still applied by hand in the late eighteenth century, an operation that gave Beaufort a humiliating experience when he was pursued through the streets of London by a colourist demanding to be paid.[41] For those who preferred do-it-yourself colouring the *Memoir* gave advice (followed in the author's own manuscript version) which emphasised the map's ecclesiastical purpose: 'The limits of every diocese may be illustrated by a broad pale colour, while the counties and baronies in each province, are coloured in the usual manner.' The last phrase was not very helpful, but in fact any consistent colour scheme will improve legibility if not too aggressive, while no scheme can hope to make a highly complex map look simple.

Beaufort's map was undeniably complex, both in the minute articulation of his line-work and in the low degree of generalisation applied to both physical and human features. He wisely decided not to show parishes or (as he was later said once to have proposed)[42] church property, but he did delimit the liberties of towns, baronies, and counties, including urban counties and numerous county enclaves. In the physical realm his concern for hydrology was shown not only by the separate fluvial map in the *Memoir* but by the elimination of many false river-junctions perpetrated in earlier maps and by a special symbol for the subterranean rivers flowing into Galway Bay. He depicted relief by hachures, which are closely spaced lines of varying thickness showing the directions followed by imaginary streams on mountain and hill sides. Hachures had been made familiar in Irish regional cartography by Rocque's county maps and later by the work of surveyors with military antecedents like Alexander Taylor. Beaufort was the first Anglo-Irish cartographer to publish them on a national map, beating Taylor by just one year. He claimed to have shown both the relative heights of the hills and the areas they occupied, the former no doubt by the width of the hachure lines and the latter by their length. In fact his uplands are rather too lumpy – more so in the engraving than the manuscript – as if the individual 'sugarloaves' of a seventeenth-century map had each been separately translated into the new medium. Perhaps he was reacting against the excessive linearity of Jefferys's hill features. In the portrayal of land cover there was no need for change. Ireland's woods were still dwindling, its bogs still largely unreclaimed. Beaufort ignored what was left of the woods, and distinguished the bogs by a reed-and-water symbol (though admitting in the *Memoir* that Ireland had no true marshes) which was changed in the engraving to a pattern of horizontal lines. Another contribution to physical geography was a generous quota of previously unmapped names for both mountains and rivers. The *Memoir* was justified in complaining about the omission of Mount Leinster on earlier maps.

In one way Beaufort's approach to settlement geography was unoriginal. Cities and boroughs were named in capital letters. Contemporary readers may have accepted his implicitly electoral definition of a borough as a tribute to the constitutional strengthening of the Irish parliament after 1782, but cartographers would have recognised a habit as old as the generation before Pratt's. There had been no geographical dimension to the latest reforms, either in the creation of new constituencies or the abolition of old ones. The only novel feature in Beaufort's treatment was to emphasise the gap between population and representation by showing the actual extent of both boroughs and non-boroughs, as far as his scale allowed, by a realistic lay-out of streets and building blocks.

There were equally serious discrepancies between religious and secular geography. Parishes, though not delimited, were prominently named in roman print. Beaufort improved on Petty by classifying their ecclesiastical status (rectory, vicarage, curacy, chapelry) with under-lines and initial letters, and also by marking the exact location of each parish church with the cross-on-tower symbol later made famous by the Ordnance Survey. His unexpected inclusion of 'ancient round towers peculiar to Ireland' might be interpreted politically as the annexation of a heroic native past by an alien state religion, for most of the towers stood in what were now Protestant churchyards. On the other hand he surrendered a good deal of the present by admitting how many of the later buildings in these churchyards were already in ruins. The distinction between ruined and intact parish churches had been suggested by Sir Francis Hutchinson[43] and could therefore be an illustration of Beaufort's propensity to take advice, but he might just as well have adopted it of his own accord as a long-familiar element of Irish topographical maps with undiminished way-finding relevance for the traveller.

Some other weaknesses of the established church were exposed in Beaufort's separate provision for 'names of towns and villages, not being parishes' (Fig. 8.11). He collected some 615 of these names, almost all accompanied by one or more planiform house-symbols as an indication of relative size – without of course attempting to record the exact number of buildings on the ground. Many of the settlements in question, it is true, were centres of Protestant worship, either as chapels of ease or as parish churches at new or renamed sites. But there were also innumerable church symbols without adjacent building blocks while the names of several rising towns like Carrickmacross, Castleblayney, Tullamore and Westport had to make do with the smallest size of italic script because they were not parishes.

An impressive number of Beaufort's minor names, like Pratt's, appear to mark the influence of secular factors. Black Rock, Courtstrand, Cove, New Geneva, New Pier, O'Callaghan's Mills (a rare industrial example) and Parkgate, for instance, are all offered as the names of villages. The most important of these influences was still the building of new roads and the intensification of road traffic. Although Pratt's suffix 'bridge' had now been dropped at Crumlin, Golden and various other river crossings identified in 1708, a new generation of settlements had entered the same stage of toponymic evolution at Beggars Bridge, Newbridge (one each in Cork and Limerick) and Goresbridge. There were also one or two previously unrecorded 'passes' such as Pass If You Can in Co. Westmeath, and even a few seemingly new 'fords'.

Another aspect of road use was represented at Glenn Inn (Co. Donegal), Man of War (Co. Dublin), New Inn (Co. Galway) and elsewhere. And of course many road-based settlements must simply have retained their pre-modern townland names. The same was doubtless true of certain estate villages, though family pride dictated otherwise at Villierstown, Newtown Fortescue, Newtown Saville and Frenchpark. Some putative members of this category, like Sandford (Co. Roscommon) and Colehill (Co.Longford), had shrunk to single houses by the time they were mapped by the Ordnance Survey and occasionally we may doubt whether such places had ever deserved the name of village. However, at least it is clear that Beaufort had

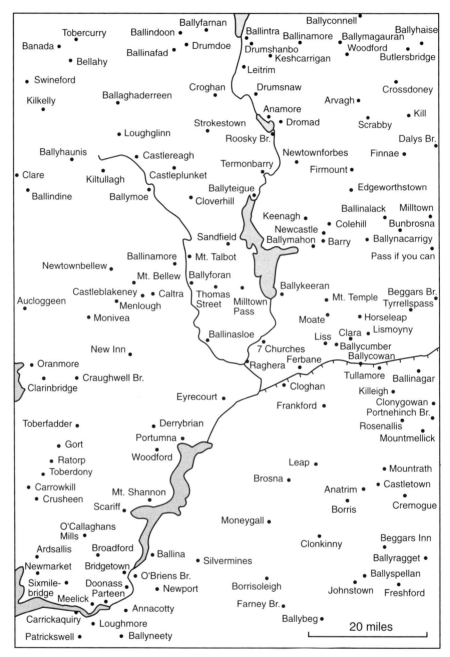

Fig. 8.11   Towns (other than cities and boroughs) and non-parochial villages in the
mid-Shannon region, from Beaufort's *New map of Ireland*, 1792.
Spellings modernised.

none of the deference towards gentlemen's demesnes that one associates with an estate surveyor like Bernard Scalé, despite himself enjoying a higher social status than most estate surveyors and despite having included a number of great houses in his travels. Otherwise he would not have omitted such illustrious examples as Carton, Curraghmore, Emo and Julietstown.[44] In general, at this neglected end of the settlement spectrum Beaufort's views deserve attention from historical geographers even where they seem unlikely. Cartographic specialists for their part can congratulate him on almost completely eliminating 'floaters' from the map of Ireland.[45]

The roads on the *civil and ecclesiastical* map strike a revealingly discordant note: they are cruder than the other detail even in counties that already had accurate grand jury maps, and are easily recognisable as an afterthought, the last stage in the author's metamorphosis from ecclesiastical to general cartographer.[46] They do not appear on Beaufort's manuscript, are not mentioned in his key, and were not engraved until all the writing was in position, to judge from the awkwardness with which they cut through many placenames. Perhaps they were copied from a smaller map: if he was in a hurry Beaufort might not have had time to assemble, select and edit source materials with his usual care and precision. At any rate he gives less impression of a serviceable road network than do many early eighteenth-century cartographers. It is disconcerting to find busy midland towns like Kilbeggan, Mountmellick and Oldcastle treated as outposts of civilisation, and there seems to be little point in distinguishing two kinds of road (identified in the *Memoir* as 'Dublin roads' and cross roads) when there are so few of either kind. The fact is that Beaufort, even more than Jefferys, was describing postal services rather than roads as such, though admittedly this could have been useful information for those of his fellow country churchmen who saw themselves as exiles from a metropolitan culture. Beaufort's neglect of the travelling public was underlined when Alexander Taylor published a specialised road map of Ireland in the following year.

As a man of learning and a contemporary of Samuel Johnson, Beaufort may be assumed to have had some definite policy for the spelling of placenames, but the *Memoir* does not tell us what it was. He was also a contemporary of Charles O'Conor, William Beauford, Edward Ledwich and Charles Vallancey, who with different degrees of competence were all promoting the study of the Irish language. The glossary of placename elements in the *Memoir* marks at least a slight interest in linguistic matters as well as a desire for consistency, and Beaufort's choice of standard or semi-standard forms shows a carefully limited deference to native orthography, reversing the trend towards phonetic spelling followed by so many earlier cartographers.[47] Thus 'agh' is preferred to 'augh' (Irish 'ath', ford), 'inis' to 'inish' ('inis', island), 'kill' to 'kil' ('cill', cell or small church) and 'tobar' to 'tubber' ('tobar', well, though the glossary admits 'tubber'). Irish aspiration appears in 'Bindubh' (Co. Tipperary) and 'Slieve Dham' (Co. Sligo). As the map progressed Beaufort became slightly more responsive to current scholarly fashion and readier to Gaelicise or re-Gaelicise his names. A note addressed to the engraver in the margin of his manuscript reads: 'Where rivers begin with Owen they are to be altered to Awin', evidently a gesture in the direction of the Irish 'abhainn'. Another last-minute decision, not universally enforced, was to write 'Sliebh' (Irish 'sliabh', mountain) instead of the familiar 'Slieve'.[48] Such cases were exceptional. In general Beaufort went no further towards re-hibernicisation than did the Ordnance Survey forty years later. For many modern Irish readers it was nowhere near far enough.

Beaufort's achievement was widely praised but seldom analysed. Few if any contemporary verdicts probed more deeply than the comment by Richard Colt Hoare in 1807 that Alexander Taylor's map of Ireland was 'the best for travellers, but that by Dr Beaufort, annexed to his memoir, is much fuller, and contains the names of more places; it is more properly an ecclesiastical map'.[49] The uncertain tone of Hoare's final qualification expressed an important truth. During its composition the map had drifted away from the thematic category and towards the general, arguably finishing with the worst of both worlds. A purely thematic map might just have found room for parish boundaries. A purely topographical map (if any topographical map can be pure) would certainly have shown more roads. Here, too, twentieth-century standards may seem inapplicable. But a simple yet effective map of Ireland's Quaker meeting houses in a manifestly thematic style was published in 1794 and seems to have existed in manuscript for many years earlier.[50] Twentieth-century standards were not quite irrelevant after all.

* * * * * * * * *

However Beaufort's map is classified, contemporaries were glad to have it, and after five years of advance publicity they were quick to respond. It was sold in superior London bookshops like Debrett, Edwards and Hookman, reviewed in the *Gentleman's Magazine*, given pride of place in Trinity College, Dublin (the 'old map' it replaced on the college library wall had ceased to be worth identifying by name),[51] and acquired by the totally non-ecclesiastical

242

Bureau Topographique in Paris.[52] This popularity is hard to translate into pounds, shillings and pence, because in Beaufort's accounts map and memoir are inextricably combined.[53] No doubt a true geographer would consider this financial 'synthesis' wholly appropriate, but for the map-historian it presents problems unless he happens also to be a chartered accountant. The largest expenses were engraving (£186 14s 9d), a supply of Whatman's double elephant paper (£64 15s), colouring, casing and pasting (£77 16s), and printing at between 6d and 7d a copy (£41 7s). A thousand copies were printed in 1792, of which 480 went to William Allen in Dublin for the Irish market. This presumably represents Faden's and Allen's initial estimate of the number required.

Another four hundred copies (including a hundred for Allen) were printed in 1793 after some small alterations to the plates, and a further hundred in 1794. Since there was more than one price, it is difficult to make an independent calculation of the number sold. Beaufort records that £280 was collected in advance subscriptions. On the face of it this represents 492 copies, as the subscription rate was 11s 4.5d or 10s 6d sterling. The post-subscription price was 17s 4d (16s sterling) for a coloured copy, £1 3s if cased. Politically the most interesting item in the receipts column was a government grant. The lord lieutenant told Beaufort that but for the king's illness the whole cost of publication would have been met from public funds.[54] As it was, the grant amounted to no more than £56 17s 6d – barely enough to uphold the rule that Irish cartographic progress has always depended on the state.

Beaufort's accounts may have been slightly 'massaged'. For instance, did 'sundry expenses' include the cost of his visit to London in 1790, and if so were accompanying family-members included as a charge on the map? And did he deduct the living expenses he would have incurred by remaining in Ireland? On his own figures the map had almost broken even by 1794. Perhaps this is why he sold the plates (and presumably his whole interest in the map including twenty-six years' unexpired copyright) on 1 September of that year, though more probably this decision just reflected the author's chronic impecuniosity. The transaction introduces an element of uncertainty into the number of copies printed. The figures quoted above amount to 1500; in December 1795 Beaufort's estimate was 2000.[55] The difference might be explained by assigning the balance of 500 copies to the period after Faden had become owner of the plates, but Beaufort was to recall later (admittedly in extreme old age) that 2000 copies had been printed in the first year and a half after publication, in other words before the end of 1793.

At any rate sales continued buoyant. Faden published a second edition in 1797, with extensive re-engraving, and a third in 1813. The latter made an interesting attempt at the kind of civil and military synthesis that had defeated the original author, adding numerous roads and associated settlements drawn from Alexander Taylor's map of 1793; it was a tribute to Beaufort that the new settlements were comparatively few. A series of later editions by Faden and his successor James Wyld continued well into the railway age.[56] Perhaps this longevity in part reflected the map's thematic character, for patterns of ecclesiastical geography change more slowly than those of settlement and industry. Its specialised content may also have discouraged plagiarism, though more than one cartographer followed Beaufort's lead in the representation of round towers.

Beaufort's influence was thus embodied mainly in his own map. There is no record that he made any contribution to the last two editions published before his death in 1821, though he did collect material for a new set of Irish county maps to be accompanied by a new memoir (neither of them ever published) and true to his original notion for a control survey was still seeking better latitude and longitude values at the age of eighty-one.[57] At this time, according to Richard Lovell Edgeworth, the civil and ecclesiastical map had not yet been superseded.[58] Admittedly Edgeworth was the cartographer's son-in-law but his judgement found support in the *Encyclopaedia Britannica* and again when John Wilson Croker, secretary to the admiralty, confirmed that Beaufort's map was generally thought to be 'the most accurate we have'. Croker was speaking in 1824,[59] so Beaufort's reputation had survived until the advent of the Ordnance Survey. After that no reputations were safe.

References

1. D.A. Beaufort, *Memoir of a map of Ireland* (Dublin, 1792), p. iii.
2. Quoted by J.B. Harley, 'William Yates and Peter Burdett: their role in the mapping of Lancashire and Cheshire in the eighteenth century', *Transactions of the Historic Society of Lancashire and Cheshire*, cxv (1963), p. 116.
3. In about 1770 the Dublin printer Boulter Grierson had prepared separate maps of Armagh, Down, Dublin, Louth, Kildare and Wicklow, based upon county surveys of the period 1752 to 1766, reduced to a common size (though not to the same scale) and a common style. The author is indebted to Andrew Bonar Law for a sight of these rare maps.
4. George Taylor and Andrew Skinner, *Maps of the roads of Ireland* (London and Dublin, 1778, second edition 1783), reprinted with introduction by J.H. Andrews, Shannon, 1969.
5. J.H. Andrews, 'Mapping the past in the past: the cartographer as antiquarian in pre-Ordnance Survey Ireland' in Colin Thomas (ed.), *Rural landscapes and communities: essays presented to Desmond McCourt* (Dublin, 1986), pp 31-63.

6.   C.C. Ellison, *The hopeful traveller; the life and times of Daniel Augustus Beaufort, LL.D., 1739-1821* (Kilkenny, 1987).

7.   Beaufort, *Memoir*, pp 10-11: *Sketch [of] the position of the groups of mountain, the extent of the greater bogs, and the influence they have on the origin and course of rivers.* Unfortunately the geomorphological discussion half-promised by this title does not appear in the text of the *Memoir*. This map was copied in *A map of Ireland principally intended to shew the position of the chief groups of mountains and the courses of the greater rivers, copied with some additions from Beaufort's small map, by permission*, National Library of Ireland, 16.B.4.

8.   E.M. Rodger, *The large scale county maps of the British Isles, 1596-1850* (Oxford, 1972), pp 43-4.

9.   Beaufort, *Memoir*, p. ii. Parish boundaries were shown on Beaufort's map of the diocese of Meath (1797), described in its dedication as a 'parochial map'.

10. Beaufort's diary, 2 July 1788. The diaries cited here and below are Trinity College, Dublin, MSS 7941 (August 1781 to November 1786), 4031 (November 1786 to April 1790) and 7942 (May 1790 to August 1792).

11. Beaufort, *Memoir*, p. ii.

12. Beaufort, *Memoir*, p. iii. Beaufort may have been influenced by Sir Joseph Banks's comparison in 1791 between current British cartography and the most recent maps of India (Charles Close, *The early years of the Ordnance Survey* (reprinted Newton Abbot, 1969, with introduction by J.B. Harley), p. 37).

13. Though note the word 'even' in Beaufort's statement that 'The coasts and harbours of India and America are better known, and more correctly laid down, than those of Ireland or even of Great Britain' (*Memoir*, p. iii).

14. *Proceedings of the Dublin Society*, xiii (1777), p. 145. This map was to measure eight feet by six feet at a scale of three Irish miles to an inch (1:241,920) and to show hills, woods, flour mills and objects 'either of natural curiosity, of note in the history of the country, or otherwise important'.

15. The scale of the *Roads* index was only about 1:1,330,000. Its inappropriately pretentious title – *A new and accurate map of the kingdom of Ireland made from actual surveys* – was perhaps a legacy of the authors' scheme for publishing a larger map.

16. Diary, 23 April 1785; Beaufort to J.C. Walker, 23 November 1795, Trinity College, Dublin, MS 1461 (4), f. 6.

17. Edward Ledwich to J.C. Walker, Trinity College, Dublin, MS 1461 (2), f. 141. The early stages of this project are documented in letters of 1789-90 in the same series and in Trinity College, Dublin, miscellaneous autographs, 335.

18. For watermark and other internal evidence on this point see D.A. Smith, *Imago Mundi*, xxxix (1987), pp 91-2.

19. Diary, 2 May 1785, 29 November 1785, 1 December 1786, 7-30 March 1787.

20. Beaufort to Francis Beaufort, 5 March 1821, Trinity College, Dublin, Non-TCD mic. 2.

21. *Dublin Evening Post*, 5 April 1787; Diary, 24 March, 29 June 1787.

22. Diary, 7 July 1787, 20 January 1788, 26 August 1788, 27 July 1789. Vallancey's map of the Killarney lakes, described by Beaufort in his next day's diary as 'incorrigible', had been published by William Faden in 1786.

23. Diary, 16 April 1787, 27 July 1787.

24. J.G. Kohl, *Travels in Ireland* (London, 1844), pp 288-9.

25. These tours are in Trinity College, Dublin, MSS 4026 (26 August to 1 October 1787), 4027 (1 October to 4 November 1787), 4028 (5 November to 14 December 1787), 4029 (3 July to 14 August 1788), 4030 (17 September

1788). See also Ellison, *Hopeful traveller*, pp 122-4; Ellison here misdates the 1788 journey to 1786 but gives the correct year on page 57.

26.   According to Beaufort's report (Diary, 9 May 1792) the king asked 'When did you publish it?' and he replied, 'It is but just now ready for publication, sir'.

27.   William Roy, 'An account of the measurement of a base on Hounslow-Heath', *Proceedings of the Royal Society of London*, lxxv (Pt. 2) (1785), pp 3-8.

28.   Diary, 31 August, 1 September 1787; 30 January 1789.

29.   Francis Beaufort to D.A. Beaufort, 6 [June 1790], Trinity College, Dublin, microfilm, R.276 (original in Huntington Library, California).

30.   Beaufort, *Memoir*, pp 7-8.

31.   Diary, 16 April 1787.

32.   Royal Irish Academy, Dublin, council minutes, i, p. 250 (1 December 1792), p. 252 (15 December 1792). Harding and Workman did record a precise latitude (52° 43' 46") and longitude (6° 4' 20") for Croghan Mountain in their mineralogical map of the Goldmines district of Co. Wicklow in 1801 but both were somewhat less accurate than the values quoted by Beaufort for other places (British Library, Add. MS 32,451 F).

33.   J.H. Andrews, *Plantation acres: an historical study of the Irish land surveyor and his maps* (Belfast, 1985), p. 352.

34.   For these and other references to Beaufort's use of earlier maps see Diary: 24 May 1787; 8, 13, 16 November 1787; 5 December 1787; 11-13, 15 July 1788; 3, 4 August 1788; 15 September 1788.

35.   A pantograph (to use the modern form of this word) is a drawing instrument with which the same outline can be simultaneously traced in two different places on different scales.

36.   Beaufort's silence on the subject of bearings is an especially striking feature of his visit to Kerry and west Cork in 1788, for this region afforded many opportunities to check the positions of small islands instrumentally as he had done with the Aran Islands in the previous year.

37.   Beaufort's manuscript map passed through the private book trade before reaching the British Library, where it is now Add. MS 53,711 A.

38.   *The late Mrs Edgeworth, of Edgeworthstown* (privately printed, n.d., n.p.), p. 5 (Royal Irish Academy Pamphlets, 1865, no. 34).

39.   Beaufort to Francis Beaufort, 22 April 1820, Trinity College, Dublin, Non-TCD mic. 2.

40.   Neele to Francis Beaufort, 14 August 1821, Trinity College, Dublin, microfilm RP 276.

41.   Diary, 29, 30 May 1792.

42.   *Memoirs of Captain Rock* (4th ed., London, 1824), p. 137.

43.   Diary, 21 April 1787.

44.   This was partly a matter of scale: gentlemen's seats are numerous in the diocesan map of Meath.

45.   The apparent exceptions, where not physical features (also shown by Beaufort in small italics), are probably intended as district names, e.g. The Fews in Co. Armagh and Poles in Co. Meath.

46.   In Beaufort's diocesan map of Meath, the last words of the title ('to which is added a sketch of the principal roads') seem to confirm the unimportance of roads as a constructional framework for his maps.

47.   The clearest contemporary expression of phoneticism had been, surprisingly, that of a chart-maker: 'The names of the places in Ireland are, for the most part, spelled in the charts . . . agreeable to the common pronunciation; it may

246

not therefore be altogether unnecessary to observe to an English reader that, in order to pronounce them intelligibly (ch) and (gh) must always have a guttural sound, that (g) is pronounced hard before e and i, as well as before a, o and u; that (a) is pronounced open as in (war) or in (add); and (i) sharp, as in (image) or in (sin), with very few exceptions' (Introduction, Murdoch Mackenzie, *Maritim survey of Ireland and the west of Great Britain* (London, 1776)).

48. These trends are continued in the index printed with the *Memoir*, which sometimes goes further than the map in the modernisation and standardisation of orthography. Thus the map gives Abbyfeale, Ballyconnel, Slieve Russel and Tamlaghtocreely, the index Abbeyfeale, Ballyconnell, Slieh-russell and Tamlaghtocrely. 'Sliebh' also appears in the diocesan map of Meath.

49. Richard Colt Hoare, *Journal of a tour in Ireland, A.D. 1806* (London, 1807), p. xv. For other notices of the map see J. McParland, *Statistical survey of Mayo* (Dublin, 1802), p. viii; Nicholas Carlisle, *A topographical dictionary of Ireland* (London, 1810), p. xi; Alexander Jamieson, *A treatise on the construction of maps* (London, 1814), p. 160.

50. *A map of Friends meetings in Ireland 1794* showed the days of Quaker meetings and market days. It also gave the approximate distances between towns in Irish miles from Taylor and Skinner's *Roads*. See also Richard Shackleton to Mary Shackleton, 24 May 1779, quoted in *Journal of the Kildare Archaeological Society*, ix (1918-21), p. 152.

51. Trinity College, Dublin, library minute book, 13 March 1793.

52. H.M.A. Berthaut, *Les ingénieurs géographes militaires, 1624-1831* (Paris, 1902), i, pp 258-9.

53. National Archives, Dublin, IA.37.96.

54. Diary, 6 February 1789.

55. Beaufort to J.C. Walker, 23 November 1795, Trinity College, Dublin, MS 1461 (4), f. 6, apologising for the poorer quality of the most recent impressions.

56. Andrew Bonar Law lists editions of 1821, 1824, 1829, 1833, 1836, 1838, 1851 and 1862.

57. Edward Ledwich to Bishop Thomas Percy, 12 January 1803, John Nichols, *Illustrations of the literary history of the eighteenth century*, vii (London, 1848), p. 828. Beaufort to J.C. Walker 14 October 1803, Trinity College, Dublin, MS 1461(5); Beaufort to R. Phillips, 25 June 1805, National Library of Ireland, MS 8778. A two-volume 'sketch of the present state of Ireland, statistical and picturesque' by Beaufort was advertised in *Leinster Journal*, 24 November 1802. Beaufort to Francis Beaufort, 17 March, 22 April, 4 May, 19 June, 11 July 1820; 5 March 1821, Trinity College, Dublin, Non-TCD mic. 2. Beaufort's own copy of the *Memoir* contains some (though disappointingly few) additions and corrections evidently intended for future editions of both book and map (British Library, Add. MS 53,711 B).

58. *Memoirs of Richard Lovell Edgeworth, Esq.*, ii (London, 1820), p. 193.

59. *Report from the select committee on the survey and valuation of Ireland*, House of commons sessional papers, H.C. 1824 (445), viii, p. 37.

Chapter 9

A soldier's Ireland: Aaron Arrowsmith, 1811

A political merger between Great Britain and Ireland had often been discussed in the eighteenth century. When it came in 1800 the act of union was a panic measure inspired by a French threat to the British Empire and by the reality of an Irish rebellion that had been largely unforeseen. The rebels were defeated with surprisingly little delay. Integrating the two kingdoms was a slower process, still unfinished when part of Ireland became independent again after the first world war. One immediate result of the union was the dissolution of the Irish parliament and the Irish army but many branches of the Dublin civil service remained in place, including several with cartographic connections such as the post office and the surveyor-general's department. Improved communications by land and sea brought an increase of British influence in several of these ostensibly autonomous agencies – a significant cartographic by-product of that improvement being the surveys of Irish mail-coach roads ordered by the post office after 1805.[1] To complicate the story, departments with wholly Irish jurisdictions continued to be established after the union, among them the general valuation and boundary survey, while some offices concerned with the whole united kingdom made separate arrangements for the two islands, as was eventually done with considerable success by the Ordnance Survey. Throughout the nineteenth century, much parliamentary business and much official literature were exclusively devoted to Ireland, an early cartographic example being the reports of the Irish bogs commission in 1809-13.

All this showed a new sense of responsibility towards the Irish. Indeed absorption in the metropolitan heartland made their country look more colonial than when it had really been a colony. There was a strong feeling in London, and even in Dublin, that Ireland's affairs should now be conducted more methodically, energetically, economically and expeditiously than heretofore and that its public servants should be subjected to stricter discipline and more rigorous accounting procedures. For a quarter of a century the exact opposite of all these ideals had been personified by the director of Ireland's military survey, Charles Vallancey. His life, work and finances were unorganised, disputatious and perpetually out of control.[2] As we shall see, this did not prevent him from making a valuable map.

For commercial publishers the union brought little change. London had been the cartographic capital of Ireland at least since the time of William III, and there had been many mapmaking enterprises that embraced all parts of the British Isles. With Aaron Arrowsmith this tradition was carried into the new century. Arrowsmith had no close links with Ireland. He was born in County Durham in 1750 and surveyed land for a living before setting up as a publisher in London.[3] His mapping of England and Wales was interrupted by an official request that he should turn his attention to Scotland. There his method was similar to Beaufort's in Ireland except that Scottish cartographers had more source-maps for their homeland and a larger number of accurately determined points on which to fit them.

In the absence of a Down Survey the main source for 'Scotland at this period was the 'magnificent military sketch' begun in the Highlands by William Roy in 1747 and later extended to the whole country. Arrowsmith's map was published in four sheets at four miles to an inch in 1807. Perhaps in anticipation of possible copyright problems its title was laboriously explicit: *Map of Scotland constructed from original materials obtained by the authority of the parliamentary commissioners for making roads and bridges in the Highlands*. To match this prolixity Arrowsmith also wrote of 'the permanent advantage which would accrue to geography in general, if those who have it in their power to make a good map, would at the same time publish such notices of their authorities as might inform future geographers how far to rely on it, and in what proportion further materials remain to be sought elsewhere whether from actual survey, or celestial observations of latitude and longitude'.[4] In short, he wrote a memoir. This volume, slim in the manner of its kind, still wins praise as a classic of map history, though it also proves that primary sources will triumph in the end by being cited more often as a source for Roy's military survey than for the author's own compilation.

Scotland was only the beginning. Arrowsmith's *Ireland*, engraved by Edward Jones on the same scale, appeared on 4 January 1811, with England and Wales following in 1816. England as so often was given pride of place at three miles to an inch instead of four miles as in Scotland and Ireland. Otherwise the three maps were generally similar in format and identical in price at £3 13s 4d. No doubt this parallelism seemed enough to establish a sense of unity. At any rate Arrowsmith felt no need to give Ireland its own scale-statement or key, let alone add any overtly political graphics. He simply wrote the name of the country against a sun bursting through dark clouds and let readers draw their own conclusions. Nor did he produce an Irish memoir, despite his known enthusiasm for the memoir principle. The fact that England was similarly passed over does little to excuse this omission, for Scotland and Ireland, as seen from London, shared the 'frontier' quality that was traditionally thought to call for written explanations of a country's maps. (In any case, an English memoir may well have been part of Arrowsmith's original design: his map of England includes a projection diagram which in the absence of a commentary is quite unintelligible.) No doubt some sensitive Irish readers felt the slur of second-class citizenship. Arrowsmith for his part was probably afraid of being disadvantageously compared with Beaufort. After all, his recommendation of memoir-writing had been addressed to those able to make a *good* map.

Discovering Roy's Scottish maps must have left Arrowsmith primed for the unearthing of similar materials elsewhere. Whether he embarked on Ireland before encountering the Irish equivalent of Roy's surveys or vice versa is not known. Perhaps the two events were more or less contemporaneous. At any rate it is in a letter of 25 March 1809, less than three months after the completion of the Scottish memoir, that we first hear of his new cross-channel venture and of its association with Charles Vallancey. The informant, writing from London, was John Foster, a notable Irish statesman and enthusiast for economic development; the recipient was Daniel Beaufort, equally notable as a cartographer. 'Arrowsmith has been with me', wrote Foster. 'He is publishing a map of Ireland in which he has got all office assistance here . . . . He praises your map and memoir. He has got Vallancey's maps, the large one particularly.'[5] Arrowsmith's capture of the last-mentioned source was verified for contemporary readers by the economist Edward Wakefield writing in 1812.[6] But neither Wakefield nor any other writer of his time has much to tell us about Vallancey's cartographic accomplishments.

*　*　*　*　*　*　*　*　*

Like his rival Beaufort, Charles Vallancey was French by origin and English by upbringing. Another resemblance was that despite having regular professions both men were always short of money. The Irish military survey was important to its author mainly because it earned him fifteen shillings a day plus expenses and gratuities. His real interest, indeed his violent passion according to one acquaintance, was to be considered 'a great orientalist'.[7] Vallancey's orientalism was not quite as exotic as it seemed at first sight, for it was mainly devoted to finding a place of origin for the Irish language. But it must surely have distracted him from his maps. He began the military survey of southern Ireland in 1776 and worked on it with many interruptions, orientalist and other, for twenty years assisted by a number of civilian draughts-men and military engineers of whom the most prominent was Lieutenant Alexander Taylor. The survey started as a series of road strips at the cumbrously large scale of four inches to one Irish mile, tracing the probable routes of a French invasion force from Waterford Harbour to Dublin. In later instalments the scale was halved and the maps given a less elongated shape, covering the south and south-west of Ireland to a distance of about forty statute miles from the coast (Fig. 9.1).

Despite these changes of format, the general style and content of Vallancey's military survey remained much the same; so, no doubt, did the surveyor's methods, though as usual we have no direct knowledge of these. There was certainly no general triangulation in the scientific sense, and Vallancey maintained the Irish field-worker's customary silence about latitude and longitude. Main roads were probably traversed with chain or wheel and theodolite. Landmarks off the road were fixed by theodolite intersection, and many linear features must have been sketched. Besides roads, the survey took in streams, towns, villages, and selected single habitations, with special emphasis on hachured hills, bogs and woodlands, this last category now being dominated by the ornamental plantings around large houses that had come into fashion since the middle of the century. Improved farmland appeared as a network of diagrammatic hedges.

The essence of Vallancey's style was his modern planiform conventions for relief, woodland and settlement. His brushwork hachures give a powerful effect of solidity, revealing the essential unity of extensive hill masses instead of over-emphasising individual summits as so many earlier hill artists had done. One remembers that in another area of his complex intellectual life Vallancey had noticed the physiographic wholeness of the British Isles and the continuity of upland axes from one island to the other.[8] All in all he captured the landscape of a large region more effectively than any previous government surveyor in Ireland, though his coverage was less exact than the best grand jury maps and less detailed than the best estate maps.

The sequence and layout of the military survey were dominated by fear of the French. Dangers from any other quarter, including the interior of Ireland itself, seemed less acute, and at the end of his active career Vallancey admitted that 'the whole of what has been surveyed particularly and accurately lies to the south of a line from Arklow to Limerick'.[9] But in 1782, with the support of 'many of the principal gentlemen of this kingdom', he was seeking the king's permission to

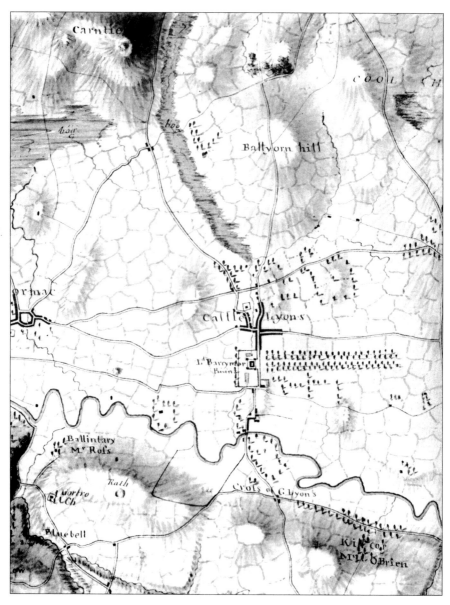

Fig. 9.1   Part of north-east Co. Cork from Charles Vallancey's military survey of Ireland, 1782, British Library K. Top. 6 Tab. 38. Scale of original two inches to one Irish mile. Orientation to contemporary magnetic north, here given as 24 degrees west of true north. Field boundaries are diagrammatic.

publish a general map of Ireland (at an unstated scale) from which he unrealistically hoped to make a profit of four thousand pounds.[10] Despite its origins the proposed map would not show 'military points', perhaps because it was too small for this omission to be noticeable, and its publication was duly recommended by the lord lieutenant and approved by the king.[11] But official minds changed in the course of the next two years and Vallancey's four thousand pounds melted away like fairy gold.[12] As often in his cartographic career he had been too slow off the mark; or perhaps his proposals had grown more ambitious and militarily more revealing.

Confounding the confusion, and no doubt to Vallancey's annoyance, a map of Ireland based on the military survey (but omitting barracks) was eventually published by his subordinate Alexander Taylor without overt signs of official displeasure (Fig. 9.2). At a scale four times smaller than Vallancey's smallest, and a third smaller than Beaufort's, this failed to give much impression of either Vallancey's hachures or his settlement pattern. As a travelling map it was more successful – good enough to be re-engraved and republished in Paris with French-language marginal text.

But at least Vallancey's own version was reproduced in manuscript. Two versions of it survive: the 'royal map' of Ireland dated 1785 (Fig. 9.3), and a copy of 1795 that describes itself in the course of a long marginal note as a 'civil' map. At present there is little point in trying to identify either of these with any of the five or six general maps of Ireland, actual or proposed, that are mentioned in Vallancey's correspondence as his own work.[13] The scale of both extant maps is half an inch to one Irish mile. In their surviving form they are cut into panels and mounted on cloth for folding but give continuous coverage of the whole country. One of them may actually have been consulted 'in anger' at the time of the French landing in Mayo but if not white elephants they were certainly elephantine in conception, and to unfold their nine feet by seven feet for display purposes in a vertical plane is an operation of considerable difficulty. They may even be the largest known maps of all Ireland constructed as single physical objects until late in the nineteenth century. Royal and civil maps are closely similar in outline and physical geography but as so often with manuscript 'duplicates' each has many details absent from the other. In 1795 Vallancey did a modest amount of up-dating and also made good a few of his most obvious deficiencies, but in general the later version is less careful and less complete, omitting many of the smaller settlements that had been included ten years earlier.

*   *   *   *   *   *   *   *   *

Fig. 9.2   From Alexander Taylor, *A new map of Ireland* (Dublin and London, 1793). Based on Vallancey's military map of 1785 with added road information. An early cartographic response to the introduction of Ireland's first official mail coaches in 1789, and an implicit criticism of the road information on Beaufort's *New map of Ireland* published in the previous year. Taylor's map was reissued by James Wyld in about 1840.

Since the military survey of the 1770s and early 1780s had been confined to southern Ireland, a map of the whole country required additional research. Some field work was done in the summer of 1784, when Vallancey reported having sent three parties 'to the north'.[14]

254

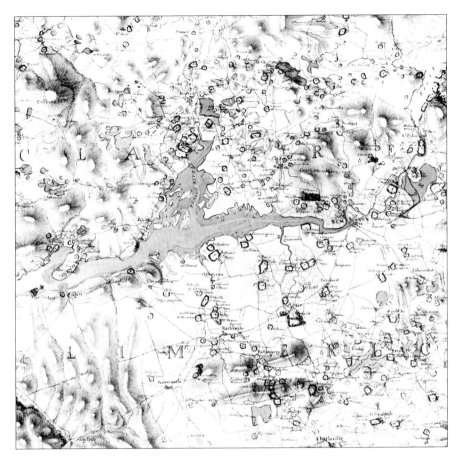

Fig. 9.3   From Charles Vallancey, 'The royal map of Ireland', 1785, Ordnance
Survey Office, Dublin. In the midlands and north Vallancey's surveys
were often much sketchier than was required by his scale of half an inch
to one Irish mile.

Perhaps each group was assigned a different province, for there is a
later reference to Taylor's 'manuscript reduction of Connaught'.[15] On
any reckoning the surveyors must have worked quickly but in the
eighteenth century speed was still an acknowledged prerequisite of the
soldier's cartographic art: Vallancey himself had made this point in a
general essay on military surveying presented to the king.[16] As we have
seen, he also admitted by implication that his northern surveys were
less than accurate and less than 'particular'. All of which makes one
wonder how far Vallancey, in the words of John Speed's famous
confession, had put his sickle into other men's corn. If he did resort to
cartographic larceny, the thefts were certainly restrained and discreet.

Although the detail on his maps can be seen on close inspection to vary in density, its general texture is satisfyingly consistent. Vallancey stayed true to his own cartographic temperament, his own subject matter, his own personal curvature (especially in the treatment of roads) and his own ways of spelling Irish names. There is no large tract of country that he can be accused of lifting bodily from any other map. Even in counties with grand jury map-coverage on a scale several times his own, he managed to find some detail that the county surveyors had missed – for instance Holyhill, Marlay and Mullglibane in Co. Dublin (not in Rocque, 1760), Collestown and Deansrath in Louth (not in Taylor and Skinner, 1778) and Barley Field, Leslie Hill and Portmore in Antrim (not in Lendrick, 1780).

For much of the north and west coasts of Ireland the only likely source in 1785 was Murdoch Mackenzie's charts published nine years earlier (Fig. 9.4).[17] Again, differences are easily found. Vallancey's Dinish Island, north of Lettermullan, is much smaller than Mackenzie's. He widens the inlets in Bertraghboy Bay and Mannin Bay, and marks an island west of Finavara where Mackenzie has a peninsula. In the same region he names Old Head and Boathaven, unidentified in the charts, and ignores many opportunities of copying his predecessor's coastal settlements. Inland the strongest temptations to plagiarism were the road maps of Taylor and Skinner which, even more recently than Mackenzie's charts, had shown exactly the kind of information that Vallancey needed. Many of his names for landed proprietors probably did come from this source – why look elsewhere? – and the road mileages introduced in 1795 certainly did so. More revealingly, both parties go similarly wrong in the outlines of lakes near Ballyjamesduff and Finnea, while their bogs and hills east of Lough Ramor are also suspiciously alike. But the road surveyors' coverage was naturally confined to narrow strips and they seldom combined these strips (in print anyway) into an extensive two-dimensional spread. In any case Vallancey often differed from them or added to them, even within the strips. Examples are his Lisodouagha (Mr Skidding) between Shrule and Headford, Myolagh (Dr Bland) near Killarney, Roxboro (Mr Pearce) near Craghwell Bridge, and Tyon Mills (Mr O'Brien) near Nenagh.

Thematically Vallancey's general maps come as close to his regional surveys as their smaller scale allows. Communications by land and water set the tone, and Ireland's developing canal system is fully recorded. Roads are narrowed to single lines, with no distinction between major and minor (postal services and turnpikes had little relevance for an army at war) but outside the towns none appears to have been altogether crowded out. The main casualties of the

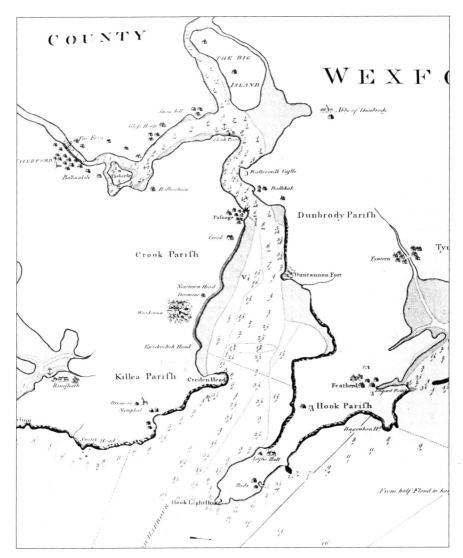

Fig. 9.4   Waterford Harbour from Murdoch Mackenzie senior, *Maritim survey of Ireland and the west of Great Britain* (London, 1776). Both outline and detail were disregarded in Charles Vallancey's military map (1785) but certain features, such as the dotted line representing submerged sand banks, appear to have been copied in Arrowsmith's *Ireland*.

reduction process were fields and small houses, though there was still just enough room for towns and villages to appear in generalised outline. A diagrammatic hedge pattern, 'improved planted country' in the key for 1785 (it was omitted in 1795), is used very sparingly in the body of the map, its main occurrences being within twenty miles of Dublin, in the lowlands of eastern and central Ulster, and in very small patches next to towns and country mansions. In its military context this symbol was evidently not meant for enclosures as such – a much larger proportion of Ireland was said to be enclosed in 1771[18] – but for terrain where the field boundaries were substantial enough to impede visibility and mobility. The effect of scale-reduction on the fieldscape was to increase the prominence of gentlemen's seats. Vallancey was the first cartographer to find room for demesnes in a general map of Ireland. He identified them by surrounding each landed proprietor's house with a narrow belt of woodland, schematic in width and continuity but except in the smallest examples approximately following the true perimeter, and altogether more effective than the scattered tree symbols put to the same purpose by Taylor and Skinner. The emphasis is strengthened by naming both house and owner, even where this meant writing 'Mr Rice' next to 'Mt Rice'.

The idea of recording gentlemen's properties on a full-size national map as an aid to economic development had already been suggested by the engineer and projector George Semple,[19] and Vallancey's work can be interpreted in the same vein as a homage to the spirit of improvement, with mountains and bogs rightly stressed as an obstacle to the improver, not yet ready for belittlement by nineteenth-century optimism. Of course there were also good military reasons for emphasising certain aspects of the landed estate. Demesne woods provided cover for soldiers, outbuildings could serve as billets or stables, and lawns could be grazed by troopers' horses, while the house itself would always be a focus of upper-class loyalty and cooperation. Vallancey disproves the theory that the gentrification of topographical maps was no more than a marketing ploy designed to flatter potential customers.

Presumably any rich man's landscape expresses a commitment to the status quo, but no cartographer can map the spirit of what used to be called the 'common people'. At half an inch to a mile one could hardly hope to map their habitations, and it was only in parts of the far north and west, which were too wild and inaccessible to attract many resident proprietors, that Vallancey provided a scattering of what look like small farmers' house clusters.

Minor settlements in Vallancey's Donegal, 1785

Mulloderry	Ballynish	Irus
Aothen	Binastocker	Burnfoot
Cloghglass	Mulroy	Crowen
Minntoy	Dunedorn	Burt
Clogh	Dunfanaghy	Morres
Maghera	Kiluff	Castle Ward
Tarmon	Machi	Masigten
Dunaff	Muff	Port Sallac
Ryefort	Tower	Ballynally
Saltpans	3 Trees	Summerhill
Kilgarve	Quigly	Moree
Arhurry	Kined	Balringy
Carkad	Binian	Fahan

One resemblance between Vallancey and Beaufort is that the conservatism of their placename policies was relieved by an occasional gesture of respect for Ireland's native language. This was less an attempt to restore genuinely Irish words than a modification of current spellings for the same reason that had made earlier English scholars insert a 'b' in 'debt' and a 'd' in 'adventure' without actually breaking all the way into Latin. Among Vallancey's innovations were several un-English-looking substitutes for 'Slieve' (their Irishness often negated by appending a redundant 'mountain') and a definite preference for 'cnoc' over 'knock'. Other orthographic oddities like 'Alt Oisin', 'Quilqua' and 'Slieve In Irin' were apparently aimed at improving pronunciation rather than approximating the Irish written forms as Beaufort had sometimes done. But both of them were happy enough with English names where these could be found. In the physiographic realm, for example, where the names on sixteenth-century maps had been mainly Gaelic, Vallancey deployed an extensively anglicised vocabulary including descriptions (White Hill), legendary allusions (Devil's Bit Mountain), proprietorial claims (Agnew Hill), and false etymologies (Bessy Bell).

But whatever his personal linguistic preferences, there is no sign that Vallancey ever himself translated Irish names into English, or vice versa, as a prelude to mapping them. Nor do his maps show much trace of the leisure-time interest in Irish history and antiquities for which he was so well known to contemporaries. This was not because such topics might offend his employers as unsoldierly: that possibility did not deter him from including flagrantly antiquarian space-fillers like 'Spenser the poet lived here' and 'There is an old English settlement by Strongbow. The inhabitants retain much of the old Saxon tongue'. It would be unfair to treat the rarity of such captions as evidence against Vallancey's personal involvement in his own survey. It is more probable that despite the example of Beauford, O'Conor and others, this historian simply did not see history as a subject for map-making.

*   *   *   *   *   *   *   *   *

In Scotland Arrowsmith had been much impressed with the military survey made by Vallancey's counterpart William Roy. He praised it for recording the sinuosities of the Scottish coastline more accurately than any other map, and rather oddly cited the notorious Highland 'clearances' (not yet matched in Ireland) in defence of its out-dated human geography. Roy's work, Arrowsmith argued, was a 'permanent memorial of the habitations formerly scattered through the highlands, before a more profitable application of the soil transferred the people to situations of more useful activity'. But even with no Scottish precedents, Arrowsmith's general debt to Vallancey in Ireland would be immediately obvious – so much so that Beaufort and Arrowsmith are best regarded as typological contemporaries despite the nearly twenty years that separate them.

Arrowsmith's precise source or sources are now beyond recovery, however. His Vallancey material, we have seen, is said to have included a large 'map' in the singular. But some of Arrowsmith's information appears only in one of Vallancey's two surviving general maps, some only in the other. He may have alternated between the two, a theory not disproved by his omission of many details common to both. As often happens in such circumstances, error eventually justified itself as a tool of historical analysis, though in this case (as also often happens) the tool is not quite sharp enough. For instance according to Vallancey Lough Mourne in Co. Donegal drained to Lough Foyle in 1785 and to Lough Erne in 1795. Arrowsmith compromised by draining it in both directions, but this does not preclude his 'synthesis' having been copied ready-made from a third Vallancey map that no longer exists.

Although Vallancey and Arrowsmith occupy the same general position on the continuum of practicable map scales, their approach to this common ground had been from opposite directions. Vallancey had begun in the field as a delineator of landscapes. His method for a map of Ireland was to miniaturise the cartographic symbolism appropriate to a bird's eye view. Arrowsmith's first publication had been a map of the world: in 1811 a quarter-inch to a mile was the largest scale he had ever attempted in print (Figs 9.5-9.7). The result, in his *Ireland*, was a

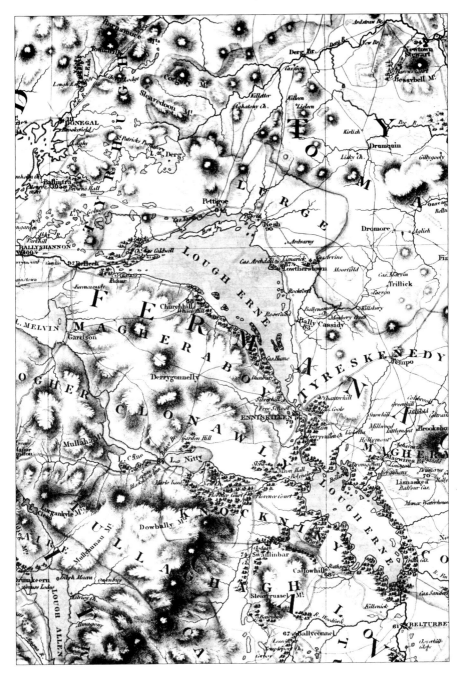

Fig. 9.5   Lower and Upper Lough Erne, from Aaron Arrowsmith, *Ireland* (London, 1811). In the lower lake Arrowsmith improves considerably on Beaufort, especially in recognising the curvature of the south coast, but the distance of Derrygonnelly from this coast is made about two statute miles too long and numerous islands are omitted.

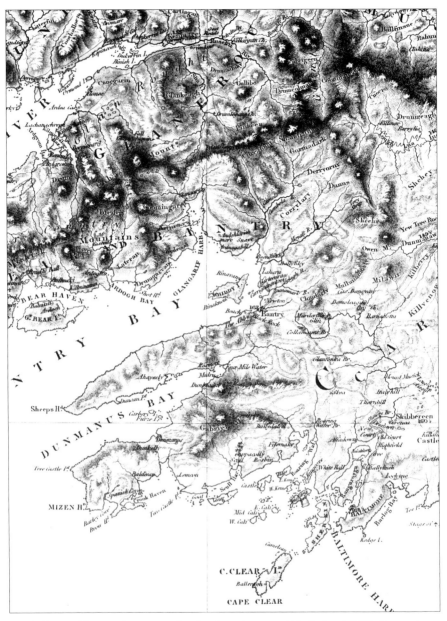

Fig. 9.6   The south-west peninsulas from Arrowsmith's *Ireland*, 1811. Mountains
and rivers are less correct than coastal 'sinuosities', and placenames (by
Ordnance Survey standards) are considerably worse. The 52nd parallel is
about nine statute miles south of its true position.

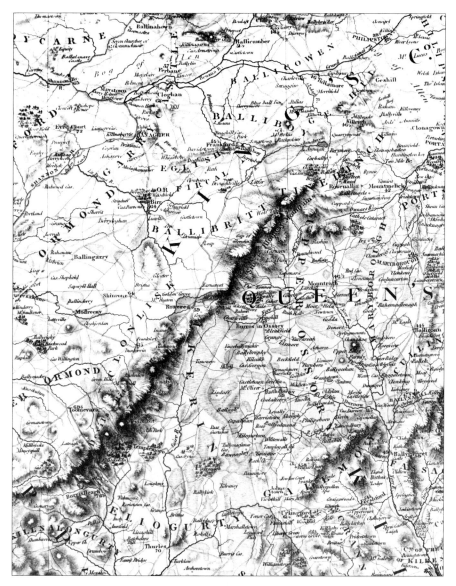

Fig. 9.7   Part of the upper Nore valley from Arrowsmith's *Ireland*, 1811. The
            hachures are most effective in areas of medium relief, including the
            esker ridge shown north of Maryborough. Toponymic oddities include
            Bleakfield, Cas. Gorgon, Rackethall, Slieve Blomer, Songstown, and the
            habit of prefixing river names by 'The'.

low priority for landscape texture. For certain subjects, it is true, he treats his model with well-deserved respect. His hachures, for example, are commendably prominent, and do as much justice to Vallancey's relief as could be expected from any engraving. In some ways manuscript and print are almost too closely related. Unintentionally Arrowsmith demonstrated that military cartography does not always lend itself to the precision of a copper plate. Pen and ink are common to field-sketcher and draughtsman; engraving evokes an indoor atmosphere of care and deliberation. Through this association of ideas, a wavy manuscript line for a stream can appear deliberately inexact and the reader makes allowance for the modesty of the author's intentions. In print the same feature will simply look like a mistake. Arrowsmith has his full share of wavy lines.[20]

In other cases he simply thought on a smaller scale than Vallancey, one might say on a scale too small for his own map. His bogs were less conspicuous, he made no attempt at 'improved planted country', and he ignored all but the largest demesne woodlands. He gave conventional signs for features which on a larger scale would have been treated planiformly with or without accompanying inscriptions, such as obelisks, lighthouses, barracks and offshore rocks. But his main importation from small-scale mapping was a diminutive unembellished open circle to locate a settlement-site, and it was here that he incurred criticism from Wakefield for marking townlands 'as villages, though they have no title whatever to that appellation'. Wakefield also implied that these townlands had been arbitrarily chosen from a total of several thousand, of which total he said that 'to insert them in a map would be impossible, and if practicable it would have been useless'.[21]

Here then is yet another Irish instance of the typical map-reader's obsession with villages. In fact Arrowsmith had identified nothing as either a village, a townland or any other kind of settlement. Wakefield's real complaint was that the absence of a key had forced him to become a mind-reader, but it should have been clear from both manuscript and printed versions of the Vallancey-Arrowsmith map that villages in an Anglo-Saxon sense were distinguished by roman as opposed to italic lower-case script. Vallancey's names in this village script were written larger or smaller – without being grouped in discrete size-categories – to suit the importance of their referent. Arrowsmith's were of uniform size, and this sometimes gave implausible results, especially for settlements that had been declining in population. His villages of Kilmain Hill, Killeen and Carnhill (Caron Hill) in Co. Meath, for example, were all exposed as negligible by William Larkin's county survey within a year of their appearance. On the other hand Arrowsmith failed to notice a number of rising settlement nucleations such as Ballymacarret in Co. Down, Clarinbridge in Co. Galway, New Inn and Enfield in Co. Meath, Ederney in Co. Fermanagh, and Binghamstown, Cahermorris and Louisburgh in Co. Mayo.

The objection to townlands on a small-scale map was stronger than Wakefield realised, but it was an objection to Petty or Pratt rather than to Arrowsmith. In fact most of Arrowsmith's point-symbols and their names denote not townlands as such but country houses, which he had injudiciously made unrecognisable by removing their peripheral tree-belts. Some of the names are too odd for anything but an individual habitation, for instance Friendly Quarters, India Villa, Liberty Green, Mount Musick, Nymph Hall, Paradise Lodge, and The West. A few could easily be mistaken for a different kind of settlement, like those embodying fashionable romantic fictions such as 'abbey' or 'fort'. Other circles represented Vallancey's small settlement-clusters with the new symbol placed more or less centrally in the area that would have been occupied by the houses if they had not been left out. Some are isolated churches, though Arrowsmith like Vallancey more often showed these by a cross; there are also a few inns with an occasional mine or well. The same symbol is used less appropriately for the hills called the Sugarloaves near Maryborough and – strangest of all – for the River Lyons near Philipstown. Sometimes Wakefield was right to interpret a circle as a genuine village, though if he had been an Irishman he would have regarded many of Arrowsmith's 'villages' as medium-sized towns: they included Ballina, Bushmills, Dromore, Ferns, Mountmellick, Newcastle West and Roscrea.

In short, the small circles were not a success. They were the price that Arrowsmith paid for eliminating the townland 'floater', or rather for trying to eliminate it, because like other cartographers with the same object he did allow a few exceptions (notably in Co. Sligo) either by mistake or under pressure from his source materials. Finally it was typical of Arrowsmith, at any rate in his dealings with Ireland, that while drastically editing these minor names and symbols he should also spare several idiosyncratic gestures more proper to manuscript cartography than to print, such as 'Very steep', 'Salmon Leap fall 13 feet', 'Caves like gothic arches' and 'Curly Grennan Hill from which the Old Head of Kinsale is seen'.

* * * * * * * * *

Memoir-writing cartographers seldom find much to admire in earlier published maps with the same subject as their own. In Scotland Arrowsmith admitted no debt to any well-known national map, and he must have given a similar impression when discussing his map of Ireland, to judge from Wakefield's description of the military survey as 'the' data for this work. This suggests a parasitic relationship like that of Boazio to Lythe. A better comparison would be with Pratt, though Arrowsmith's editorial contribution went well beyond Pratt's – in quantity if not necessarily in merit – if only because the range of accessible sources was now so much wider. One purpose of his input was to bring Vallancey's subject-matter into the mainstream of published cartography; to demilitarise him, in fact. Here the first and most difficult requirements were latitude and longitude. Arrowsmith's scale demanded more geographical exactness than Beaufort's, with marginal divisions of one minute instead of three and a graticule of thirty-minute intervals rather than whole degrees. No doubt the new map could have been adjusted on to Beaufort's graticule without intolerable difficulty. Having assembled his Scottish coordinates from over twenty different sources, Arrowsmith was more ambitious. Both he and Beaufort put Wicklow Pier at 52° 59', and Londonderry at 55°, but elsewhere their values are different, sometimes by more than a minute, and this includes most of the astronomical stations that Beaufort had adopted as controls.

The argument from silence counts against Arrowsmith's having made or organised any observations of his own in Ireland; the only recent findings known to Wakefield, for example, were those of Lieutenant T.G. Shorland, and his coordinates were different from Arrowsmith's.[22] In Scotland Arrowsmith had drawn many of his control points from marine charts, which for 'general directions and bearings' he preferred to Roy's military survey (despite the latter's success with 'sinuosities'), but in Ireland he cannot be shown to have followed any particular hydrographer. He must have made his selection from a variety of existing maps either by choosing what seemed the best single value or by striking some kind of average. The results can be judged from a table of latitudes compiled by the eminent engineer William Bald.[23] Six cartographers are represented in the table. At five places out of twenty-two Arrowsmith's latitudes are the most correct, correctness being defined by the one-inch Ordnance Survey map of 1856-62, whereas Beaufort achieved the same feat in eight cases out of twenty-two. Beaufort's mean latitude error, according to Bald's cartometry, is 2' 53"; Arrowsmith's is 4' 4". To this extent another critic, Alexander Nimmo, was right to describe Arrowsmith's Ireland as 'extremely incorrect in latitudes and longitudes'.[24]

	Beaufort	**Arrowsmith**
Shark Head	53.20.00	53.40.08
Achill Head	53.58.00	54.05.00
Erris Head	54.18.20	54.27.20
Killala	54.12.20	54.17.00
Castlebar	53.50.00	53.54.00
Clare Island	53.49.30	53.54.00
Inishtrahul	55.23.40	55.23.00
Copeland Islands	54.40.30	54.42.30
Arranmore	55.01.30	54.58.30
Fannet	55.16.40	55.15.00
Pigeon House	53.21.00	53.21.40
Arran	53.06.00	53.07.00
Wicklow Head	52.58.30	52.58.00
Loop Head	52.31.00	52.37.00
Kerry Head	52.23.00	52.29.30
Cape Clear	51.19.30	51.19.20
Kinsale	51.37.00	51.34.40
Hook	52.06.00	52.05.40
Tusker	52.13.00	52.12.30
Bengore Head	55.15.30	55.15.20
Brandon Head	52.17.00	52.22.00
Cork	51.54.00	51.53.50

The *Dictionary of national biography* praises Arrowsmith's knowledge of map projections. There is no record of how he projected Ireland, but for Scotland he wrote: 'From the middle meridian, the foundation of all projections, I measured and marked the other meridians east and west of it, according to the known length of half degrees of longitude on the several parallels of latitude included in Scotland: for these parallels no other care was necessary than to make them cross the several meridians as nearly as possible at right angles.' This passage would have won less than full marks in a nineteenth-century geography examination.[25] It looks like an attempt to describe Bonne's projection. In a map of Ireland on Arrowsmith's scale this like all other projections (excluding any deliberately chosen for their freakishness) would be indistinguishable from the available alternatives. Arrowsmith's planimetry may therefore be freely compared with Beaufort's without regard to latitude and longitude but with similar results. The RMS errors are Beaufort 0.039, Arrowsmith 0.049. This was Beaufort's reward for taking trouble with his mathematical control.

Another of Arrowsmith's non-military additions well justified by precedent was the names and boundaries of the Irish baronies, the names being emphasised by bold roman capitals, the boundaries left faint perhaps in expectation of supplementary hand colour. The names are generally spelt as in Beaufort, including several forms like 'Catherlogh', 'Downamore', 'Fassachdining', 'Rathline' and 'Tyreskenedy' which in the early nineteenth century would have been widely considered obsolete if not incorrect. The boundaries too may have been loosely translated from Beaufort, but a good deal of editorial courage would have been needed to match them with Vallancey's representation of the visible landscape, and Arrowsmith may also have consulted Petty's maps to settle points of detail. More surprising was his revival of 'country' nomenclature, familiar in Elizabethan maps but subsequently (as Jefferys had seemed to imply) driven towards the Atlantic by the anglicisation of administrative structures in central and eastern Ireland. Examples, mainly shown in large and elegant lower-case italics, were Fannet, Rosquil, Dunmore, The Rosses, Lettermacward, Glen Leighan, the Mullet, Coraan, Joyce's Country and Connemara.

A more conservative and indeed anachronistic gesture was to capitalise the names of parliamentary boroughs. Many of these – including Ardfert, Clonmines, Randalstown and St Johnstown – had been disenfranchised following the act of union, as was clear from a map of Irish parliamentary representation published as recently as 1806 by Robert Wilkinson. But at least Arrowsmith had weeded out the rottenest of all the rotten boroughs at Bannow and Harristown, while the generalised street-plans that he drew for urban settlements effectively conveyed the relative unimportance of the others. Another post-Vallancey distinction was between single- and double-line roads. The difference, like everything else on Arrowsmith's map, is unexplained. His main roads (Fig. 9.8) do not match those chosen by Taylor and Skinner, who were evidently the source for Arrowsmith's distances from Dublin, shown in Irish miles beside the principal towns.[26] Harder to understand are the discrepancies between the principal roads allegedly existing in 1811 and the roads on William Larkin's *Map of the post roads of Ireland* published in 1805. In Ulster, for instance, Arrowsmith but not Larkin shows main roads serving Ballaghy, Brookborough, Broughshane, Clogh, Clogher, Glenavy, Frederickston (a settlement hard to find on any map later than Arrowsmith's), Newtown Hamilton and Portrush. On the other hand it is Larkin and not Arrowsmith who runs main roads from Armagh to Caledon, Bangor to Newtownards, Castleblayney to Cootehill, and Glenarm to Newtown Glens. Worse still, some of Larkin's post towns – Miltownmalbay, Moville, Mount Nugent – are totally ignored by Arrowsmith. Finally we may notice Arrowsmith's habit of imparting a very slight curvature to certain Irish roads which both earlier and later

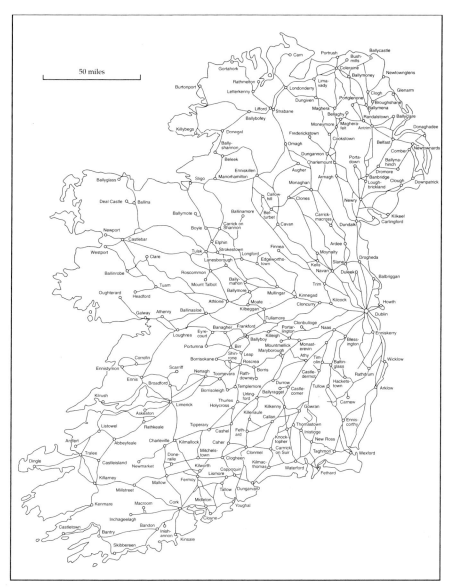

Fig. 9.8   Roads shown by double lines in Aaron Arrowsmith's *Ireland*, 1811. Arrowsmith does not explain his criterion for distinguishing these routes from the much more numerous minor roads represented on his map by single lines.

cartographers agreed in rendering as perfectly straight. Roman survivals apart, such straightness was a rarity in both Scotland and England; it had also fallen out of fashion among contemporary Irish civil engineers. Like many map-readers (some would say all map-readers) Arrowsmith was seeing what he wanted to see.

Arrowsmith's views on Scottish placenames had been fair if somewhat cynical. His preliminary drafts, like those of many cartographers, were criticised more for their placenames than anything else. But since the critics' opinions cancelled each other out (another common experience) he had no alternative but to take his own orthographic decisions. Clearly no London publisher could afford to travel the roads of Scotland hearing local pronunciations of local names as John O'Donovan was later to travel through much of Ireland at government expense. No doubt it was for this reason that Arrowsmith rejected a purely phonetic policy as impracticable. So should the conscientious mapmaker follow 'the etymology of names' or 'the customary orthography'? His answer betrayed the nervousness that was to become a national characteristic of English cartographers turned loose in the world of Celtic toponymy. Custom, he wrote, 'is universally allowed the preference in England but in Scotland, where Gaelic names have not yet attained to a fixed orthography, some licence perhaps must be allowed'. The same might equally well have been said of Ireland. If modern Irish readers balk at Arrowsmith's allowing only 'some' licence to etymology, that is because they have forgotten (under the influence of their own Ordnance Survey department) how closely the average cartographer prefers to follow the herd in this respect. In Scotland the herd was boldly interpreted to mean Roy's military survey, the only higher authority acknowledged by Arrowsmith being the census of population, which included relatively few names. In Ireland no official census had yet been taken, so Roy's Irish counterpart could take precedence over other national sources.

*　*　*　*　*　*　*　*　*

In Scotland Arrowsmith drew on various estate surveys while professing scepticism about the value of previously-published county maps. In Ireland it seems to have been the other way round. There is no evidence that he copied any local surveys (though admittedly such evidence would be hard to find), whereas county maps were a source that he 'had the benefit of', as Alexander Nimmo phrased it. Ten Irish counties were now in print at scales of one inch to one statute mile or larger. Arrowsmith's treatment of these maps was not quite uniform. In south Donegal, for example, he remained perversely loyal to the military survey, despite Vallancey's manifest inferiority to the grand jury's cartographer William McCrea. Perhaps the only copy of McCrea's map available to him was incomplete for some reason. But in general the counties with previously published maps stand out in Arrowsmith as islands of exceptionally well-patterned terrain. Most of this effect is due to more articulated hachuring together with closer stream and road networks, though Arrowsmith showed commendable vigilance in leaving no loose ends at county boundaries. Only rarely were tell-tale fragments of unwanted detail imported from the larger scales, a stretch of demesne boundary at Newbery, Co. Kildare, for example, and an unexplained deerpark at Davidstown near Kilcullen in the same county. With more ruthless pruning Arrowsmith could have achieved a more even texture; perhaps like Petty he was simply being honest about his sources.

Manuscript county maps presented a different problem, as Wakefield was evidently given to understand. He wrote that Arrowsmith had 'received many assurances with several of the county maps constructed for the use of the grand juries of Ireland, but he complains that, except in the case of a very young nobleman, the earl of Desart, the performance of most of these offers have been forgotten'.[27] Wakefield's use of 'except' to qualify 'most' is muddling. It does not of course imply as a matter of logic that the earl's offer extended to more than one county, but the confusion might have been more likely to arise if that were actually the case. Lord Desart's seat was in Co. Kilkenny, and here Arrowsmith certainly records a number of features not shown by Vallancey, among them the earl's spelling 'Desart' as opposed to Vallancey's 'Dysert'. The same is true of the neighbouring Co. Tipperary, which like Kilkenny had been mapped around the turn of the century by the estate surveyor Neville Bath. Manuscript county surveys of varying dates may also have existed for Armagh, Derry, Kerry, Meath, and Tyrone. From Wakefield's account it seems unlikely that any of them had become available to outsiders, but this was hardly Arrowsmith's fault.

There must have been other 'antecedent maps of which he might have availed himself',[28] to quote John Leslie Foster's criticism of Arrowsmith, but future researchers will have some difficulty in saying what they were. One of them, easy enough to identify in the present context, was Daniel Beaufort's. Among the features of this map that Arrowsmith on his larger scale had ample space for, but chose to leave out, are Mula Rock in Mayo, Inishgun in Lough Corrib, Screeb, Carrickmachin, Annachuan and Knockduagh in Connemara, and Ballydavid Head and Cahirconree Mountain in the Dingle Peninsula, all of them later to be verified by the Ordnance Survey, though not always with Beaufort's spelling.

But in considering antecedent maps there is a broad historical distinction to be drawn between Arrowsmith and Speed, and correspondingly between Vallancey and Lythe. In an earlier chapter certain features in the work of other cartographers were attributed to Lythe without having been found in his extant holographs, simply because these later maps can in most other respects be matched with his. Vallancey resembles Lythe in that some of his recorded maps are available and some are not, but in his case the analogical argument is less convincing, for three reasons. First, his maps can be seen to vary more among themselves than Lythe's, which makes the content of any lost Vallancey map correspondingly hard to infer. Secondly, there were more non-Vallancey maps in the nineteenth century than there were non-Lythe maps in the sixteenth century. Thirdly, and another mark of evolutionary progress, cartographers like Arrowsmith are known from documentary evidence to have taken more trouble in assembling diverse sources than had been customary among Speed's contemporaries.

On the subject of Arrowsmith's sources it can at least be said that no cartographer of 1811 is likely to have used the new mail coach and bog surveys mentioned earlier, because hardly any of them had yet been finished. Yet it was not difficult to catch the occasional cartographic ripple from the wave of Irish civil engineering projects that had been gathering strength since Vallancey's time. Arrowsmith mapped the Grand Canal and several of its branches complete to Athy (reached in 1791), Edenderry (1802) and Shannon Harbour (1804); the Royal Canal to Coolnahay near Mullingar, which remained its head of navigation from 1809 to 1814; and the military road through the Wicklow Mountains, built between 1800 and 1809. Sometimes he was too up-to-date, marking canals that never materialised to Dungannon and to Goresbridge for example. On the other hand he omitted the Strabane Canal (1791-6), the new bridges at Londonderry (1789-92), Waterford (1794), New Ross (1795) and Wexford (1795), and the new lighthouses at Arranmore (begun in 1798), Clare Island (1806) and Cape Clear (1810). In another sphere he missed some of the earliest stages in a rationalisation of Ireland's administrative geography when baronies were divided at Banagh and Boylagh, Co. Donegal (1791), Slane, Co. Meath (1791) and Idrone, Co. Carlow (1799).

The last count against Arrowsmith is that some of his editing was surprisingly poor, worse than Petty's, far worse than Speed's or Pratt's. Mistake after mistake falls unbidden into the critic's lap. A lake is invented at Stonebrook, Co. Kildare; another is left without water at Lough Mourne, Co. Donegal; an imaginary basin of inland drainage is recorded north of Skibbereen in Co. Cork. Many placenames differ so widely from their pronunciations that no linguist, however eccentric, could conceivably approve of them – Ardeath for Ardcath, Ballynamutt for Ballynamult, Vallyvaghan for Ballyvaghan, Brures for Bruree, Kilnessan for Kilmessan, and perhaps worst of all, Clontrachnoir for the famous early monastic city of Clonmacnoise. These were serious blunders in an increasingly error-conscious age,[29] but they were not necessarily committed by Arrowsmith himself. Up to eight assistants had worked on his map of Scotland and some similar arrangement may well have been made for Ireland, in which case he can still be held responsible for letting his organisation exceed its optimum size. It was not until the Ordnance Survey came to Ireland that accuracy was reconciled with economy in the employment of a large cartographic labour force.

Arrowsmith's *Ireland* went through two or three more editions. One, in 1821, allowed him to appear as hydrographer to the king (George IV) instead of the prince of Wales, but just missed the chance of introducing the new name 'Kingstown' at Dun Leary and indeed made very few changes of any kind. Another edition was published by G.F. Cruchley of Fleet Street, London, in 1840 and reissued with additions in 1846, doubtless as a response to the Irish railway mania.[30] On the whole, as Wakefield, Foster and Nimmo have already been seen to testify, the map's reception in Ireland was lukewarm. Retailers' stocks were modest, to judge from the experience of a would-be Dublin purchaser in 1814 who had to ask an acquaintance in London to buy him a copy.[31] One Irish shop that did stock the map advertised it as large and 'most complete' without claiming either accuracy or up-to-dateness.[32] Some criticisms of it were unfair, presumably in reaction to the author's Englishness. The Galway historian James Hardiman regretted that Arrowsmith had made no use of the Irish maps in Trinity College, Dublin, though having catalogued those maps himself Hardiman must have known that they were too old to be relevant.[33]

Other complaints had more foundation. The hardest test applicable to any cartographer is the plotting of somebody else's ground measurements on his map, and it is no surprise that much of the sternest criticism of nineteenth-century topographical maps should have come from field geologists engaged in just this task. Arrowsmith suffered two geologically-inspired attacks, from John MacCulloch in Scotland[34] and from Richard Griffith in Ireland. For Griffith in 1818, the Londoner's map was the least of several evils:

Unfortunately there is no map of Ireland, at least none deserving the name. Arrowsmith's which is the last is by much the most incorrect and Taylor's and Beaufort's are on too small a scale. I have made an attempt to colour Arrowsmith's map but the positions it gives to many of the towns is so different from the true ones, and the general incorrectness both in the courses of rivers and the situation and extent of mountains renders it impossible to lay down any one geological district in its true form and position.

As late as 1835 Griffith felt obliged to make Arrowsmith the base for a geological map of Ireland submitted to the British Association for the Advancement of Science, but he refused to publish the result on a scale larger than ten miles to the inch.[35] As we shall see, his definitive map of 1839 took its scale from Arrowsmith but everything else from more recent sources, and particularly from the Ordnance Survey. Thenceforward most other maps of Ireland followed suit.[36]

Altogether Arrowsmith's Irish contemporaries would have been bewildered by the praise he has won from modern map historians.[37] His main difficulty in Ireland was simple ignorance. Despite the union, up-to-date materials on the country's geography were physically located in Dublin rather than London and knowledge of these materials, like knowledge of most things Irish at most periods of history, was to be gained more by word of mouth than by reading catalogues and reference books. Arrowsmith was one of many eminent cartographers who never visited Ireland or established an adequate network of useful contacts there. In that case why not rest content with mapping other countries? Perhaps he felt a political imperative for all parts of the United Kingdom to be treated in the same way. Or, discounting imperialist motives, it may have seemed more helpful, more respectful, more comradely even, for Ireland to be mapped inaccurately than not to be mapped at all. Griffith's reluctant acceptance of Arrowsmith as a base-map certainly went some way towards justifying this victory for pragmatism over perfectionism. Some people might also have concluded from Griffith's experience that the mapping of Ireland was too important to be left to Irishmen. This was not a question of cartographic talent, with which Ireland had been plentifully endowed at least since the mid eighteenth century. The country's own mapmakers were simply either not ambitious enough, being still wedded to the outmoded ideal of the county atlas, or else – like Griffith and his fellow engineers – too ambitious to be satisfied with an attainable objective. For some time to come, progress in Irish mapping would continue to depend on Englishmen, but no longer on Englishmen resident in London.

References

1. 45 Geo. III, c. 43; National Library of Ireland, Irish road maps, 15.A.3-15.
2. J.H. Andrews, 'Charles Vallancey and the map of Ireland', *Geographical Journal*, cxxxii (1966), pp 48-61.
3. R.V. Tooley, 'Aaron Arrowsmith', *The Map Collector*, ix (1979), pp 19-22.
4. *Memoir relative to the construction of the map of Scotland published by Aaron Arrowsmith in the year 1807* (London and Edinburgh, 1809).
5. Public Record Office of Northern Ireland, D.207/36/44.

6. Edward Wakefield, *An account of Ireland, statistical and political*, i (Dublin, 1812), p. 3.

7. Edward Ledwich, 12 May 1789, Trinity College, Dublin, miscellaneous autographs, 334.

8. Vallancey's scientific notebooks, Royal Irish Academy, Dublin, MSS 12.K.34, 35.

9. National Archives, Dublin, official papers 526/165/17.

10. Public Record Office, London, SP 63/480/154, 171, 173; HO 100/1/172; 100/5/156.

11. Public Record Office, London, SP 63/480/154.

12. Public Record Office, London, HO 100/5/158.

13. The royal map is now at the Ordnance Survey office, Phoenix Park, Dublin, the 1795 map at the Institution of Royal Engineers, Chatham. For other possible copies see J.H. Andrews, 'Charles Vallancey's maps of Ireland, a new reference', *Geographical Journal*, cxlvi (1980), p. 150.

14. Public Record Office, London, HO 100/5/189-90; 100/11/142.

15. *Report from the select committee on the survey and valuation of Ireland*, House of commons sessional papers, H.C. 1824 (445), viii, p. 78.

16. D.W. Marshall, 'Instructions for a military survey in 1779', *Cartographica*, xviii (1981), pp 1-12.

17. A.H.W. Robinson, *Marine cartography in Britain, a history of the sea chart to 1855* (Leicester, 1962), ch. 3.

18. One-third, according to *Hints for improving the kingdom of Ireland, in a letter to his excellency, George Lord Viscount Townshend, lord lieutenant of Ireland* (Dublin, 1771), p. 16.

19. George Semple, *Hibernia's free trade* (London, 1780), pp 163, 186.

20. In the 1770s Thomas Harrington had recommended that small rivers on maps should be 'described by a single, crooked, waving line' (*A new introduction to the knowledge and use of maps* (4th ed., London, 1775), pp 19, 102).

21. Wakefield, *Ireland*, i, p. 3.

22. Wakefield, *Ireland*, i, pp 3-4.

23. *Report on survey and valuation*, p. 70.

24. *Report on survey and valuation*, p. 78.

25. The difficulty in this passage is that the drawing of latitude-parallels is treated as the last stage of the construction, later than the measuring of distances east and west from the central meridian. However, measurements to east and west could not be taken unless the shape of the parallels had already been determined. Perhaps by 'east' and 'west' Arrowsmith meant perpendicular to the central meridian.

26. Taylor and Skinner's mileage figures were soon to be criticised for having been made 'egregiously erroneous' by the realignment of many roads since the 1770s (Review of *The traveller's guide through Ireland* in *Cox's Irish Magazine*, viii (1815), p. 426). But Arrowsmith was not the only authority of his generation to depend on Taylor and Skinner. The same distances reappeared in William Beauford's Irish county atlas (another work of eighteenth-century origin, admittedly) and as late as 1828 they were acknowledged in a government report as the most accurate available (list of Irish post towns in *19th report of the commissioners of inquiry into the collection and management of the revenue arising in Ireland and Great Britain [Post office revenue, Ireland]*, p. 370, H.C. 1829 (353), xii). No doubt Arrowsmith had decided that the best way to avoid self-contradiction was to take all his mileages from a single source.

27. Wakefield, *Ireland*, i, p. 3.

28. *Report on survey and valuation*, p. 32.

29. A scientific attitude to placenames had recently been shown in a new edition of James Enouy's *New map of Ireland, compiled from actual surveys* (London, 1808), where a marginal note in the manner of Hondius and Boazio gave more or less correct meanings for the elements 'ard', 'ath', 'bally', 'clon', 'dun' or 'rath', 'ennis' or 'innis', 'kill', 'knock', 'lis', 'lough', 'magh' and 'sliebh' or 'slieb'.

30. Eighty-eight railways, operative, in progress and projected, were shown on a large (*c.* four miles to an inch) skeleton map of Ireland published by John Arrowsmith and J. Basire on 20 April 1846. Aaron Arrowsmith had died in 1833. The revisions to his *Ireland* in 1840-46 were some of the most extensive ever made to a pre-Ordnance Survey map of the country. Many new physical and habitation names were added, others were made more specific by the addition of 'Ho', 'Ch' etc. New roads were inserted and minor roads upgraded. Some villages were reclassified as smaller settlements. Some features were completely renamed (for example Cualoc Bay, Co. Kerry, as Quoilagh Bay).

31. G.L. Herries Davies, *Sheets of many colours: the mapping of Ireland's rocks 1750-1890* (Dublin, 1983), p. 39.

32. *Cork Mercantile Chronicle*, 16 September 1812.

33. James Hardiman, 'A catalogue of maps, charts and plans relating to Ireland, present amongst the manuscripts in the library of Trinity College, Dublin, with preliminary observations', *Transactions of the Royal Irish Academy*, Antiquities, xiv (1824), p. 60.

34. R.C. Boud, 'Aaron Arrowsmith's topographical map of Scotland and John MacCulloch's geological survey', *The Canadian Cartographer*, xi (1974), pp 24-34; R.C. Boud, 'The Highland and Agricultural Society of Scotland and the Ordnance Survey of Scotland, 1837-1875', *The Cartographic Journal*, xxiii (1986), p. 4.

35. Davies, *Sheets of many colours*, pp 60-61. No copy of Griffith's quarter-inch Arrowsmith-based map is known to survive.

36. The revival of Arrowsmith in the 1890s as a base for G.W. Bacon's cycling map of Ireland was perhaps due to fear of infringing government copyright by a publisher with some unfortunate experience of this problem. For Bacon's use of equally obsolete base maps in England see Eugene Burden, 'John Cary and G.W. Bacon', *The Map Collector*, liii (1990), p. 52.

37. See for instance Alexander McGechaen and Coolie Verner, *Maps in the parliamentary papers by the Arrowsmiths*, part 1, Map Collectors' Series, lxxxviii (1973), p. 1; Tony Campbell, 'Saleroom survey', *Geographical Magazine*, xlv (1972), p. 160 and xlvi (1974), p. 223.

Chapter 10

The shape of maps to come: Thomas Larcom, 1839

The union began a new age of government commissions and committees in Ireland. Their proposals were usually followed by new laws, and the new laws by executive action. Such progressions soon seemed part of the natural order, but before 1800 there had been less formality. The early history of the Ordnance Survey provides an obvious case in point. Draughtsmen employed by the English board of ordnance were already drawing maps before the end of the seventeenth century. In 1784 an ordnance officer, William Roy, began directing certain geodetic operations in south-east England on behalf of the Royal Society. In 1791 two other officers were instructed by the master-general of the ordnance to continue Roy's 'trigonometrical survey'. Four years later the same officers, assisted by an ordnance draughtsman, had begun to assume responsibility for topographical mapping within the framework of the trigonometrical survey, and in the first year of the new century a county map was issued by a private publisher on the basis of these activities. Later this and other ordnance county maps became a single national map. Somewhere along the way a mighty official department had sidled into existence.[1]

These tasks were so absorbing that for many years no one asked whether the union would require a similar map to be made in Ireland, and the only short-term effect of the new constitutional arrangements on Irish official cartography was the discontinuance of Vallancey's military survey. By this time it was not much of a loss. The director was well over seventy, the principal assistant in his middle fifties – too old for either of them to start integrating military and scientific cartographic traditions with the reforming zeal of a William Roy. Instead Vallancey went into semi-retirement and Alexander Taylor found a supervisory role in the new post office surveys of Irish mail-coach roads.

Seen in retrospect, Ireland now contained a large Ordnance-Survey-shaped void. The first attempt to fill the gap was by a commission appointed in 1809 to investigate the country's bogs (Fig. 10.1). It was fitting that the chair should be taken by Vallancey, even in old age, for his military map had been the best depiction of the bogs since Petty's

Fig. 10.1   Bogs near the Mayo-Sligo border, with surveyor's levelled lines and
proposed drainage channels, William Bald, 1813, from *Third report of the
commissioners appointed to enquire into the nature and extent of the
several bogs of Ireland, and the practicability of draining and cultivating
them*, House of Commons sessional papers, H.C. 1813-14 (130), vi.

time; and it was equally appropriate that he should be succeeded by John Leslie Foster, already encountered in an earlier chapter as a critic of the map that Aaron Arrowsmith had based on Vallancey's surveys. The commission began work at a time of hope for Irish agriculture. Imports of grain had been much reduced by Napoleon's blockade; farm prices and land values had risen correspondingly; even the larger peat bogs suddenly looked worth bringing under cultivation. As a first step it was decided to have them mapped with appropriate lines of levelling at four inches to one Irish mile. With an eye to current events in Britain, the commissioners hoped also to lay the trigonometrical foundations for a future map of all Ireland, but this aim soon proved impracticable: the bog surveys covered less than a tenth of the country and were far from evenly distributed, there being very few extensive peat deposits in south Leinster or east Munster.[2]

The real value of the bogs commission was its legacy of map-making talent. Several of its engineers went on to dominate the nation's cartography for twenty years or more. Besides their technical and administrative gifts, these men were public spirited, highly articulate and inexhaustibly energetic. Their contributions to civil engineering and regional mapping could fill a book. Yet they have no place in this one, because none of them drew a map of all Ireland. The reasons for the omission are easily understood. Compiling in the manner of Beaufort or Arrowsmith was out of style. So were latitude and longitude as control points for a country of modest size. The new vogue was for accurate triangulation as practised by the British Ordnance Survey, and such an operation was to prove beyond the powers of any one individual. The only member of the bogs generation who cannot be omitted from the ensuing narrative is Richard Griffith, a native of Dublin who studied various practical and theoretical sciences in Scotland before becoming both the director of the government's Irish valuation service and the father of Irish geology.[3]

Griffith's valuation of Ireland was the brain-child of another parliamentary committee. By the 1820s the socio-economic optimism of the immediate post-union period had almost disappeared. The wars were over, prices had fallen, population growth was out of control, and many regions were troubled by agrarian unrest. Several leading Irish engineers were employed to supervise public works in relief of distress. A more comprehensive basis for improvement would be to equalise the notoriously irregular burden of local taxation in Ireland, and this was the task assigned in 1824 to the select committee on survey and valuation. The committee proposed a new central govern-ment valuation of land and buildings in every Irish townland, the county authorities being left to divide the townland total among its individual taxpayers. Such a valuation would need a much larger-scale base-map than the Ordnance Survey had embarked upon in Britain, but the Survey was rightly judged capable of making it.[4] Its current director, Major Thomas Colby, agreed to survey all thirty-two counties at six inches to one statute mile, as well as performing all the other cartographic duties in Ireland that he had been given in England. A new Ordnance Survey headquarters was accordingly established at Mountjoy House in Phoenix Park, Dublin. Meanwhile the committee had also recommended that except for hydrographic surveys all major cartographic operations in Ireland, whether by private enterprise or local government authorities, should cease. Colby had nothing to do with the process of valuing, however. That was left to Griffith.

Decision-making on Irish map-scales in the 1820s reflected a different balance of foreign and domestic danger from that of Vallancey's early days. The national military survey (one-inch) could now be postponed indefinitely, but the survey for local tax relief (six-inch) appeared urgent to a degree beyond all previous Ordnance Survey experience. It was therefore arranged that the Irish detail parties would follow on the heels of the Survey's trigonometrical department, filling up each triangle as soon as it had been observed. But the detail survey quickly ran into difficulties, and nine years after the select committee's rousing send-off not a single six-inch sheet had been published. Rumours of mismanagement were circulating widely outside the Survey and many civil practitioners looked forward to redoing all the work themselves after the military had been forced to admit defeat. By contrast Colby's Irish trigonometrical survey had been an almost complete success and in 1832 it was virtually finished: only a few more observations would be needed to eliminate minor anomalies before the definitive mathematical adjustment.

In the short run the triangulation of Ireland did little to help the general public. The Survey's British trigonometrical observations were separately published in numerical form between 1799 and 1811 and several private individuals based their own maps on them, including the well-known county cartographer Christopher Greenwood.[5] By the time the department got to Ireland it was already regretting its earlier permissiveness.[6] The new policy was for triangulation data to remain unpublished in official custody until all the six-inch maps were safely on sale, and when an independent surveyor sought access to the Irish figures in 1833 he was curtly refused.[7] So anyone hoping to benefit from the new survey of Ireland would have to wait for the government to print it. This was not a happy situation. A publisher harbouring old and inferior maps would be tempted to make the most of them while the going was good (perhaps Grierson's motive for reissuing his county

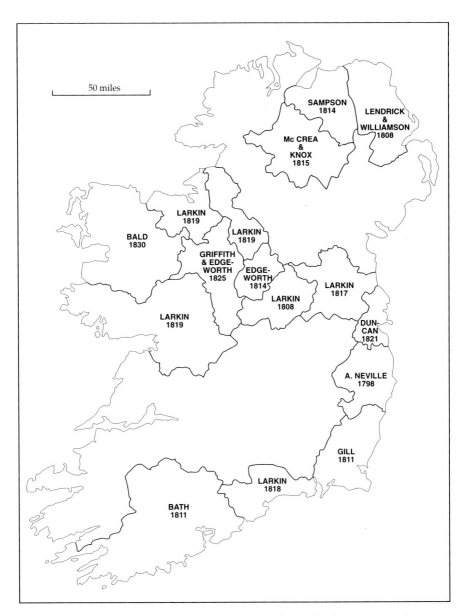

Fig. 10.2   County surveys, 1792-1824. Dates are those of publication, which was sometimes considerably later than the date of survey. For further details see J.H. Andrews, *Plantation acres: an historical study of the Irish land surveyor and his maps* (Belfast, 1985), p. 350.

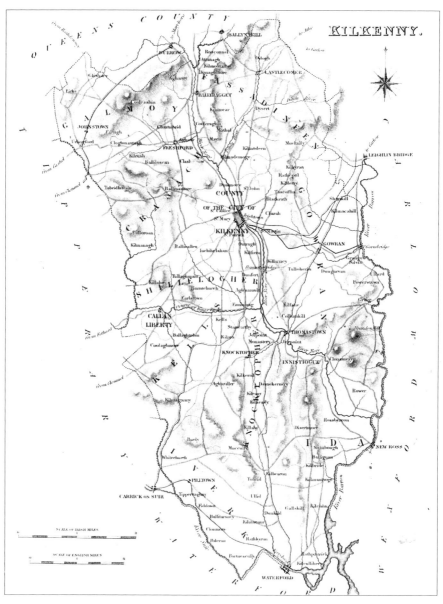

Fig. 10.3   County Kilkenny, from Samuel Lewis, *Atlas comprising the counties of Ireland* (London, 1837). In the south of Ireland Lewis's maps were original productions in the sense of being not obviously derived from any one previous national or county map. The 'floating' parish names provide a useful index to his dictionary, but there are not enough named settlements to elucidate the close network of roads and rivers and the representation of relief is weak.

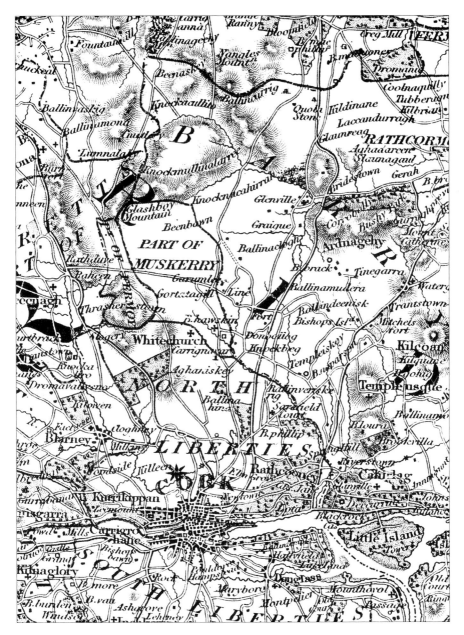

Fig. 10.4   Part of Co. Cork from James Wyld, *Ireland* (London, 1839), scale four
statute miles to an inch. Castles are shown by squares, non-parochial
churches by circles. Wyld gave more detail than any previously
published national map of Ireland, with 44 settlement names in the
Liberties of Cork, for example, compared with 19 in the Larcom-Griffith
'railway map' at the same scale. County Cork is largely based on Neville
Bath's grand jury map published in 1811, but Bath does not show the
boundaries of demesnes, or the road running through the 'l' of Quola.

atlas in *c.*1825)[8] while cartographers with new ideas were more likely to be deterred by a form of what later came to known as 'planning blight'.[9] But such inhibitions naturally grew weaker with the passing years. By 1832 many would-be customers must have been wondering whether they would live to buy an Irish ordnance map. At any rate it was at this time that the next major private map of Ireland began its gestation.

*   *   *   *   *   *   *   *   *

The new initiative came appropriately enough from London's leading commercial map publisher, James Wyld of Charing Cross. Wyld's father had been one of Thomas Jefferys's successors as geographer to the sovereign, and had acquired his business from Jefferys's one-time partner William Faden. Wyld died in 1836 – from overwork according to the *Dictionary of national biography* – and was succeeded by a son (also called James) still in his twenties. Wyld junior announced his intentions in the course of belittling a competitor's map of Ireland that was said to have cost twelve hundred pounds. Such a sum, he pointed out, must soon be spent in journeying and sketching. Then he dropped his bombshell: 'Hobson's map of Ireland, which I shall shortly publish, has occupied six years in its construction, and consumed £8000.'[10] The reference was to William Colling Hobson, of whom hardly anything seems to be recorded; even at the end of his career he was credited only with county maps of Yorkshire and Durham and contributions to a not very ambitious atlas designed for the fox-hunting market. But evidently Hobson had more affinity with Pratt and Beaufort than with Jefferys or Arrowsmith. Wyld had made it clear enough that this was a journeyer and sketcher as well as a compiler.

Certainly Hobson's map deserves the close attention of both the cartographic and the landscape historian. For one thing, it includes many features not to be found in Taylor and Skinner, Beaufort, Vallancey, Arrowsmith or even the Ordnance Survey. In some counties it drew on grand jury maps too recent to have been used by previous cartographers (Fig. 10.2). But even in counties where no such maps are known, such as Tipperary and King's County, Hobson collected a number of placenames that seem to have been new to Irish cartography: among them are physical features (The Rocks), vegetation-units (Wood of Inch), rivers (Consall River, the Ordnance Survey's Black River), parishes (Primult, the Ordnance Survey's Ballyburley), gentlemen's seats (Foxboro, Gamblesderry, Honoraville, Stubbsgrove, Waterville), and even what appear to be ordinary townland names like Coolyboy, Derrynay, Gurrane, Kilcolagh and Makin.

Hobson thus represents a new and more active phase in the private cartography of Ireland. Its origins are not far to seek. A railway from Dublin to Kingstown had been opened in 1834 and several other lines came under consideration in the course of the next two years. Though almost insignificant by the standards of the current British railway mania, this expression of interest was enough to strengthen the demand for maps. Another influence may have been the county atlas published in 1837 as part of Samuel Lewis's *Topographical dictionary of Ireland* (Fig. 10.3). This was not so much a reaction to developments in Ireland as a counterpart to similar dictionaries published by Lewis for England and Wales, but it seems to have acted as a spur to criticism and competition.[11] In March of the following year a new map of Ireland was engraved by John and Charles Walker for the Society for the Diffusion of Useful Knowledge. Three months later a rival map was published by Edward Holt.

The most impressive member of this new generation was the map published by Wyld in six sheets at four miles to the inch (Fig. 10.4). Unfortunately its history is obscure.[12] Hobson seems to have got into difficulties and been forced to change sides. His name was pointedly omitted from Wyld's map but turned up unexpectedly on Holt's, which declared itself to have been bought from Hobson's assignees. Wyld also set another puzzle for historians by claiming to have used the Ordnance Survey triangulation of Ireland on payment of a suitable fee – a statement supported on the map by latitudes and longitudes closer to those of the Survey than anyone else had yet achieved. The Survey with obvious sincerity denied this allegation and made ready to bring a prosecution, only to draw back when the crown lawyers despaired of finding a jury who understood the law of copyright.[13] Here is a major problem for future research.[14] A son could easily misunderstand arrangements made by his late father but how could unprinted Ordnance Survey data reach the public domain without the department's knowledge? At any rate Wyld stood his ground. In later editions he stated roundly and conspicuously that 'the copyright of this map was purchased from government'. Since most of the map was of non-Ordnance Survey origin he was now adding the insult of 'personation' to the injury of copyright-theft.

No doubt this dispute helped to sour the notoriously bad relations between the disputants.[15] But there is no sign that the queen's geographer lost any esteem in other quarters. Reviews of Wyld's map in the Irish press were abundant and favourable, in some cases almost ecstatic. There was only one discordant note, and that was quickly resolved. The *Freeman's Journal* found the map 'rather confused, in consequence of the proximity of the names but this, which at first sight might be considered as a defect, is its greatest perfection, as it shows a degree of minuteness which in itself constitutes the great superiority of the work over all others with which we are acquainted'.[16] The map is indeed uncomfortably overcrowded, but by the rules of the present study this fault must be dismissed as irrelevant unless it can be shown to have affected sales and circulation. Here the only evidence is favourable – a new edition of 1842 and another of c.1851. What finally disqualifies Wyld was the fame, not least among map historians, of another map on the same scale. He himself came near to admitting defeat by quickly bringing out a smaller map of Ireland avowedly based on his rivals' work.[17]

*   *   *   *   *   *   *   *   *

The rivals were Thomas Larcom of the Ordnance Survey and Richard Griffith of the Irish general valuation office. In some respects there was nothing new about their achievement. Once again map history and transport history could be seen interacting; once again better communications were the cure prescribed for Ireland's ills; once again the story begins with a government commission. In 1836 Ireland had six miles of railway, Britain 1500 miles. The difference confirmed a belief, widespread in both countries since the union, that Ireland was too poor to help itself and too unattractive to be helped by British or foreign investors; its economic progress must therefore depend on government measures not considered necessary among mainland entrepreneurs. In any case railways engaged the government's interest by occupying their own place between the extremes of public and private jurisdiction. Even in Britain the current 'mania' for them was exposing the hazards of an uncoordinated free-for-all.

So, against the whole trend of abstract political theory in contemporary London and Manchester, official commissioners were appointed in October 1836 to 'consider and recommend a general system of railways' for Ireland.[18] The importance of their task was acknowledged by selecting as chairman the under-secretary of Ireland, Thomas Drummond, a royal engineer officer of rare mathematical talent and high integrity whose public spirit was to be epitomised for future quotation-collectors in the saying that 'property has its duties as well as its rights'. He was also a distinguished ex-member of the Ordnance Survey and inventor of the limelight used in its triangulation of Ireland. His most senior colleague on the commission was another royal engineer, Sir John Burgoyne, current chairman of the Irish board of works. Burgoyne was consulted about the choice of the other members. He rejected Thomas Colby presumably because Colby was already burdened with running the Ordnance Survey[19] but did not hesitate to recommend Richard Griffith, who as head of the Irish valuation department ought to have been just as busy. It was thanks to Griffith that the commissioners' inquiries were so much dominated by the science of geology. Three of them could thus claim direct or indirect links with the cartographic profession. The fourth, Professor Peter Barlow of the Royal Military Academy, Woolwich, was a specialist in the mechanics of railway locomotion.

Eventually Drummond and his team commissioned numerous special large-scale surveys of individual railway routes.[20] To start with, however, they were free from territorial constraints – unlike the earlier mail coach road surveyors and bogs commissioners – because in theory a railway might be built anywhere in Ireland regardless of physical or human geography. They therefore needed maps of uniform quality and comprehensive coverage. One of their first acts was to acquire copies of Beaufort and Arrowsmith, without apparently considering any alternative cartographic source for Ireland apart from expendable base-maps on which to sketch their proposals. To an outsider Arrowsmith might have seemed just minimally adequate as a groundwork for planning new surveys. The commissioners took a less indulgent view. 'At the commencement of our inquiry', said their first report, presented in March 1837, 'the want of a map of Ireland on which lines might be laid down with some degree of accuracy offered a very serious impediment to our progress. There did not exist any on which the relative positions of our leading towns, still less of inferior objects, were marked with the precision which our purpose required and as to the features of the country, the delimitation was, for the most part, extremely incorrect, often purely fanciful.' They must have hoped to measure the lines under consideration with unheard-of accuracy, and of course the distances along pre-existing carriage roads on earlier maps, even if correct, would be irrelevant to a low-gradient medium that had to blaze its own trail. At first sight the criticism of 'features' looks comprehensively damning, but this term almost certainly referred to the depiction of relief by hachuring, an art in which all earlier maps were undeniably deficient by the standards of the Ordnance Survey, though where precise gradients were wanted nothing short of contour lines would meet the case, as was soon to be generally understood.

Thus Drummond and his colleagues were forced into the business of cartographic compilation, moribund among Irish mapmakers for several decades and not yet resuscitated by Hobson and Wyld. They would make their own map of Ireland at four statute miles to an inch. By coincidence the problems of designing just such a map were currently under review at the British Ordnance Survey office. 'It appears to me', wrote Colby in this context on 12 May 1837, 'that the insertion of the hills is a very difficult question, because if they are not engraved very light, the geological features will be unintelligible, and if many slopes are to be shown, light engraving is out of the question. Next, the towns and villages, if we put in every parish church with a [cross], it will not confuse the map, and they will serve as points for reference, but if we put in streets and houses, it will take much engraving and confuse the map I fear. . . . Roads being lines, will interfere with the streams and geological lines on the map – therefore perhaps they may be either wholly omitted or confined to turnpikes.'[21] As always with Colby, these comments were thoroughly reasonable. He might have added that some design problems can be solved only by dividing the cartographer's information between two maps instead of trying to put it all on one. The railway commissioners must have been familiar with this principle because they now made a point of throwing it into reverse. Their initial programme allowed for two four-mile maps, one showing geology and the other relief. Instead they produced a single map that showed both.

Despite Colby's implicit reservations (and despite Drummond's personal dislike of him), there was no one better qualified to produce the Irish 'railway map'. His response however was predictably unenthusiastic, although this time the objections had more to do with content than with style. The Ordnance Survey had been ordered in the autumn of 1836 to give the commission as much help as possible, but no one could expect Colby to finish his own hugely burdensome assignment in Ireland fast enough to meet Drummond's deadline. At best the new 'railway map' would have to mix ordnance and non-ordnance materials, and this is where Colby drew the line. Many British map-users of many periods have seen the Ordnance Survey as inhabiting a different universe from ordinary cartographic mortals, and its maps have been accepted nearly everywhere as a standard of perfection – not really maps at all, it almost seemed, but miniature duplicates of the real world and therefore self-evidently accurate. Colby was happy to leave this gulf unbridged. In May 1837 he protested against adding the Survey's imprint to a cartographic hybrid intended 'only for temporary expediency'. He added: 'I cannot consent to the permanent character of the Ordnance Survey office being staked on its validity. The unpropitious circumstances under which it was executed, will soon be forgotten, but the map itself will remain. I trust therefore the commissioners will do me the favour to expunge those words that connect the map permanently with my department.'[22]

* * * * * * * *

The words that offended Colby were duly expunged.[23] The publishers of the railway map were named on its surface with considerable prominence as Hodges and Smith of Dublin and James Gardner of London. (The former were also nominal publishers of the Ordnance Survey's regular six-inch maps of Ireland, though on those their name was relegated to the smallest possible size of script.) At the same time the map's 'temporary expediency' was emphasised in its main title by the words 'to accompany the report of the railway commission' and by adding: 'This map was constructed by order of the government for the specific purpose of the railway commission . . . . It must not be considered as aiming at minuteness or accuracy of detail.' This looked like protesting too much, an over-reaction against ad-man's licence more familiar in academic circles than among ordinary publishers. To print more than two hundred words of commentary *in situ* was itself a repudiation of the Ordnance Survey, which throughout its history had flouted eighteenth-century tradition by keeping quiet about its non-trigonometrical activities. The words in question showed a touch of prolixity attributable to Lieutenant Thomas Larcom, whose name appears in printed autograph facsimile immediately below them and who was formally acknowledged by the railway commissioners as the author of the map.[24] Such facsimile signatures were and are unusual. As Colby's Dublin deputy Larcom's status was unassailable, but the simulated handwriting makes his name look more like a personal afterthought than a considered official statement.

Griffith's name was similarly treated in the geological explanation of the map, and in his case the autograph was no doubt intended to dissociate the Survey from private scientific opinions, all the more necessary when geology was a subject that Colby had long hoped to bring within his own department's ambit. In the same spirit, of the thirteen individuals named on the map only one apart from Larcom was employed by the Ordnance Survey, and this man, as we shall see, was probably regarded as contributing in a private capacity. Taken as a whole the map thus broke Colby's rule of publicly naming the principal staff-members responsible for each Ordnance Survey sheet.

All this makes it hard to assess the Survey's precise responsibility for the railway map. Documentary sources are almost equally unhelpful. The commissioners acquired various maps in the winter of 1836-7 but these were probably for general study purposes rather than sources that they intended to process for themselves. They may have employed a few draughtsmen but they can hardly have had access to a fully equipped drawing office. On the Survey side, the departmental records are uncommunicative; so too are the personal papers of Thomas Larcom, despite his undoubted role as driving force behind the whole enterprise.[25] One not very helpful snippet of information is that on 13 December Colby was told about the maps and information required from his office. More revealing, ten days later, was Larcom's query as to whether the projected railways should be marked on 'the map now constructing', a question he would hardly have put (having no official concern with the railways himself) unless the map was being made by his own staff. The commission replied in the negative: perhaps it was Larcom who subsequently persuaded them to show the projected lines after all. Certainly contemporaries attributed the non-geological content of the map to Larcom, and certainly the finished product bore all the marks of Mountjoy design and execution: fineness of detail; perfect balance between writing, outline and ornament; avoidance of overcrowding; a wide range of well-matched lettering styles and sizes each with its own meaning; a relatively small reliance on point symbols needing explanation in the key; and an absence of decoration except as a way of emphasising the principal word in the map's title. The Survey had plenty to teach James Wyld under most of these heads (Fig. 10.5) – but then Wyld unlike Larcom had no parallel large-scale series on which to off-load burdensome information.

As Larcom's note on the map points out, its various components were all related to a single trigonometrical framework supplied by the Ordnance Survey. By this time it was customary for large territories to be triangulated in two stages, primary and secondary, the former being calculated independently of the latter. The angles and distances of Ireland's primary triangulation had now been determined and rendered self-consistent by the head of the Survey's Irish trigonometrical department, Captain J.E. Portlock. This network was later readjusted and fully published in mathematical form as part of the triangulation of the British Isles (Fig. 10.6). The secondary triangulation, never separately published, was still incomplete in 1836; its progress may be partly gauged by the spot heights on the railway map, for these were obtained not by spirit levelling but by vertical angles observed with a theodolite.

The Survey's own six-inch coverage was being published as a series of thirty-two independent county maps, twenty-six of them with origins chosen from the secondary rather than the primary triangulation. Each origin had its own azimuth governing the six-inch sheet lines for that county, and in the thirties these had not yet been harmonised for the benefit of the forthcoming national one-inch map. Nor were there any latitudes or longitudes on the Irish six-inch sheets. It was presumably Portlock who calculated provisional values for the trigonometrical points used in the railway map. Dublin observatory had probably been incorporated into the triangulation by this time, and other coordinates

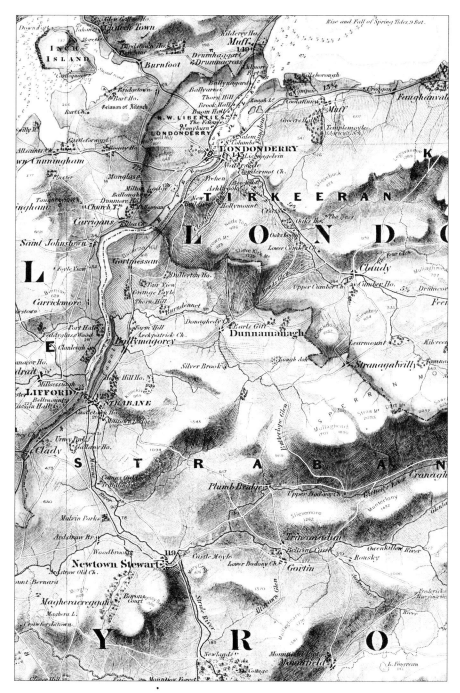

Fig. 10.5   Part of Co. Londonderry and adjoining areas from Thomas A. Larcom and Richard Griffith, *Map of Ireland to accompany the report of the railway commissioners* (London, 1839). The most elaborate hachuring attempted in print for Ireland at this scale, with north-west-facing slopes illuminated.

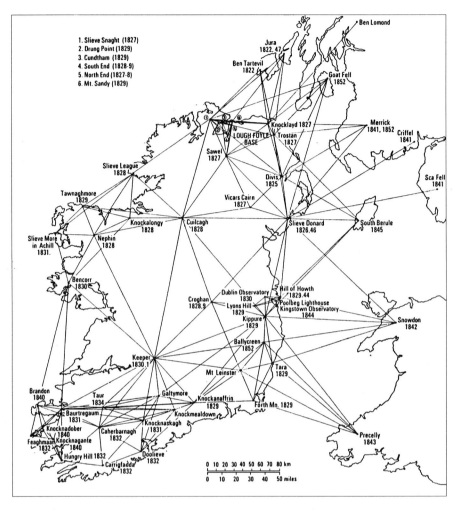

1. Slieve Snaght (1827)
2. Drung Point (1829)
3. Cundtham (1829)
4. South End (1828-9)
5. North End (1827-8)
6. Mt. Sandy (1829)

Ben Lomond

Jura
1822, 47

Ben Tartevil
1822

Goat Fell
1852

Knocklayd 1827

Merrick
1841, 1852

Criffel
1841

LOUGH FOYLE
BASE

Trostan
1827

Sawel
1827

Slieve League
1828

Divis
1825

Sca Fell
1841

Tawnaghmore
1829

Vicars Cairn
1827

Knockalongy
1828

Cuilcagh
1828

Slieve Donard
1826,46

South Berule
1845

Slieve More
in Achill
1831.

Nephin
1828

Bencorr
1830

Hill of Howth
1829,44

Dublin Observatory
1830

Croghan
1828,9

Lyons Hill
1829

Poolbeg Lighthouse
Kingstown Observatory
1844

Kippure
1829

Snowdon
1842

Ballycreen
1852

Keeper
1830,1

Mt Leinster

Tara
1829

Brandon
1840

Taur
1834

Galtymore

Knockanaffrin
1829

Forth Mn. 1829

Baurtregaum
1831

Knockmealdown

Knocknaskagh

Knocknadober
1840

Caherbarnagh
1832

Knocknagante
1840

Precelly
1843

Feaghmaan
1832

Hungry Hill 1832

Doolieve
1832

Carrigfadda
1832

0 10 20 30 40 50 60 70 80 km

0   10   20   30   40   50 miles

Fig. 10.6   Ordnance Survey triangulation of Ireland, 1826-52, from J.H. Andrews,
A paper landscape: the Ordnance Survey in nineteenth-century Ireland
(Oxford, 1975), Fig. 1.

were doubtless obtained from current admiralty charts.[26] The results
were very close to those of the regular one-inch map of Ireland as
published in the 1850s. Portlock must also have chosen the projection
for the railway map. Larcom's printed note, despite its length and
scope, did not say what that projection was: on this subject centuries of
obscurantism prevailed (and still prevail) against his own belief in frank
disclosure. The natural choice would have been the Cassini projection
used in the British one-inch and Irish six-inch maps of this period, and

no doubt with the same central meridian of eight degrees west that was chosen for the later one-inch map.

* * * * * * * * *

Larcom is unlikely to have proceeded by first listing all the facts that a railway planner might wish to know. That is not how maps were made in the nineteenth century. Like the Ordnance Survey's previous output the railway map was the product of all-round cartographic experience and instinct – in this case the experience acquired by British and Irish topographical surveyors over more than a century, adapted with unfailing judgement to an unusually small scale. The sources were the six-inch ordnance maps 'in the northern counties' and, further south, 'county maps and other materials'. With no further help the northern counties are difficult to define. They obviously included all those whose ordnance maps were in print before the commission started work, namely Londonderry (published in 1833), Antrim (1834), Tyrone (1834), Down (1835), Fermanagh (1835), Armagh (1836), Monaghan (1836) and Louth (1836). Counties published while the commission was deliberating were Donegal (1836), Cavan (1837), Meath (1837), Leitrim (1837), Longford (1838), Sligo (1838), Roscommon (1838) and Westmeath (1838). Here, to judge from the selection and spelling of placenames, the Survey's findings became available in time for the railway map, if not as published maps then as either manuscript documents or proofs.[27]

In theory the position of each Ordnance Survey triangulation station or six-inch sheet corner could have been recalculated in relation to a single central meridian before being inserted on the railway map, and the detail then redrawn to fit the new positions. In practice Portlock probably found it easier to transfer the county origin and meridian to the new scale and then reduce the whole county as a block. It is not clear what happened to counties where the Survey had got no further than its manuscript parish plans. Parishes as such were not wanted on the railway map, but with the help of the secondary triangulation their boundaries could have been pieced together on the quarter-inch scale and then erased after the necessary landscape detail had been properly connected.

Pre-ordnance maps of nine counties were acquired by the railway commissioners and mentioned in their minutes, though without naming authors. Those of Clare, Cork, Meath, Queen's County and Wicklow had been printed. Those of Kerry, Kilkenny, Limerick and possibly Carlow were still in manuscript, but like the Anglo-Irish Daniel Beaufort (and unlike the English Thomas Jefferys and Aaron

Arrowsmith) the commissioners had no difficulty in gaining access to such unpublished materials. Apart from these minuted examples, the Ordnance Survey office may have had direct access to certain county maps without reference to the commission: Galway, Kildare, Mayo, Roscommon, Westmeath and Wexford were available in print, and Tipperary probably in manuscript. In the absence of recorded dates and authors for any of the commission's sources, it is possible that some of the older printed maps had been replaced by later and better manuscripts of which there is no record and that the compilers of 1837 made use of these. Some well-authenticated county manuscript maps were subsequently lost. In Kerry and Tipperary, for example, the railway map and perhaps Wyld's map may be our only clue to the contents of these missing sources (Figs 10.7, 10.8).

The only regional non-county map mentioned in the commission's minutes is John Brownrigg's survey of the Grand Canal. This had been published as long ago as 1788 and is unlikely to have told them anything they could not have found elsewhere. But they managed to update the county maps with other evidence, though it is not always clear what form this took. Sometimes it was doubtless no more than a commonsense knowledge of current events in Ireland. Information was also probably drawn from a new class of Irish local government officer, the county surveyors, first appointed in 1833.[28] No county surveyor is known to have produced a new county map from an original survey of his own – that would have been unnecessary when the Ordnance Survey detail parties were expected within a few years – but they were all capable of revising or augmenting their local grand jury map or any base-map that might have been supplied by Larcom. The commission did ask some of them to add landlords' demesnes to their county maps so that these could be transferred to the railway map, and the same may well have been done with roads – as is known to have happened later when the one-inch map of Ireland was being prepared from the six-inch maps. This is the most likely reason why Co. Clare, for example, not surveyed at the six-inch scale until 1840, has many more roads on the railway map than on Henry Pelham's published grand jury map of 1787.

*　*　*　*　*　*　*　*　*

In compiling from various sources, Larcom avoided discontinuities with an apparent ease that many earlier cartographers would have envied. His uniform texture was achieved by accepting a rather low common thematic denominator composed of coasts, rivers, towns, villages, hamlets, country houses, roads, county and barony boundaries (not yet

Fig. 10.7   Dublin and district from Larcom and Griffith's map of Ireland, 1839.
Probably the greatest density of detail, terrestrial and hydrographic, that
the quarter-inch scale could comfortably admit, including martello
towers, 'military antiquities' (shown by a gothic letter 'M'), three
categories of railway actual and proposed, and an inn called the
Shoulder of Mutton.

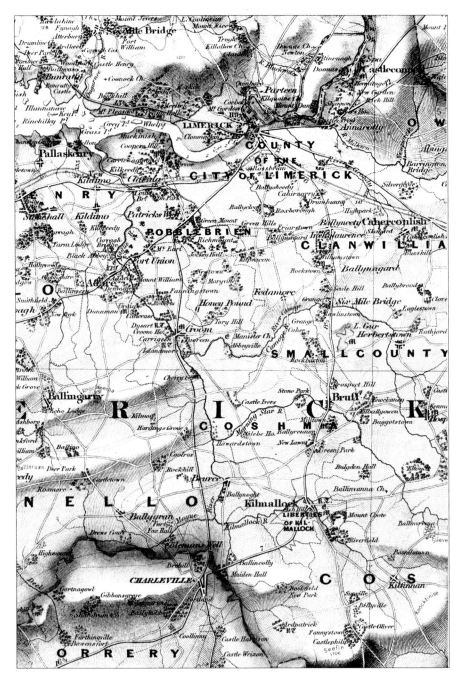

Fig. 10.8   From Larcom and Griffith's map of Ireland, 1839. Generalisation hides
              most of the differences in planimetric accuracy between districts already
              surveyed by the Ordnance Survey and those that were still awaiting
              survey, like this area near Limerick. The spelling of placenames in this
              region was drastically revised on later ordnance maps.

affected by a series of reforms that began in November 1839)[29] and a miscellany of objects that can be grouped together as landmarks. He was evidently determined to avoid floating townland names. Occasionally, as in Co. Cork, his sources left him no other way of achieving a consistent density, but in most places he was completely successful – more so than the Ordnance Survey itself in maps designed after Larcom had left the department. His success had two principal foundations. One was that the railway map's hachured relief features took up much of the space that might otherwise have seemed to call for script; and an identifiable hill, it could be argued, did more to guide the traveller than a floating name, because he could see it for himself without having to ask the inhabitants where he was.

Another advantage was Larcom's skill in anchoring each potential floater to some definite object. Many of these were gentlemen's houses and demesnes. Such a choice can of course be put down to social attitudes predictable in a member of the officer-class. Less interestingly, it can be explained as a matter of scale. Demesnes as such had been omitted from the earliest six-inch ordnance sheets and, as we have seen, from some grand jury surveys. These larger maps had ample room for country mansions, ordinary farmhouses and clusters of cabins. At Larcom's scale of four miles to an inch space was more limited – as Wyld's descent into visual near-chaos would soon show. Here it was a clear choice between big houses and small, and whatever the map-reader's social status a large house with its park had the simple merit of being identifiable from a longer distance. Avoiding a misjudgement of Arrowsmith's, Larcom gave parklands their correct shape as far as his scale would allow. Some appeared with an outer boundary line, others were defined simply by tree-symbols, but the Survey should not be accused of inconsistency on this point without asking whether (as in some contemporary estate maps) the single-line boundary was meant to distinguish a stone wall from a bank or hedge. But however successful with demesnes, the railway map ignored the growth of small-farm population that had now become Ireland's most desperate social problem.

Wyld caused confusion by making all his parish names look like village names. Larcom did not attempt to show parishes or even to identify parish centres as a matter of principle but the hand of the anglican establishment lay heavily on his map. Glebes and rectories abounded, and churches were shown by plain crosses with their parish names wherever they were sufficiently isolated to act as landmarks. This policy also justified the inclusion of graveyards devoid of buildings and of numerous 'old churches', the latter being easily distinguishable in the landscape from the many new Protestant churches that had been built with tall square towers since about 1810. But this was also the era of Catholic emancipation, and new cartographic ground was broken by the inclusion of a few 'chapels' (as Roman Catholic churches were called throughout nineteenth-century Ireland) as well as the occasional nonconformist meeting house.

'A few remarkable antiquities have been inserted', said Larcom's note rather apologetically. Antiquities could help to tie down minor placenames, but their use on the railway map went well beyond this, as was shown by its use of initial letters to distinguish the three categories of round towers, other ecclesiastical antiquities, and military antiquities. Initialisation was contrary to normal Ordnance Survey practice. It was justified here by the fact that the names of many famous sites had been pre-empted to denote nearby modern settle-ments; an alphabetical symbol could also exploit the now well-established convention of identifying archaeological detail by gothic script. At pagan sites, where there was usually no modern settlement to confuse the nomenclature, the whole name could be gothic.[30] The 1830s were rather early for archaeological tourism to be seen as a motive for railway travel. A more probable reason for emphasising antiquities was to sustain the morale of George Petrie, the Ordnance Survey's Irish historical specialist.[31] On this occasion Petrie's data could reasonably be classified as private, and Larcom was therefore free to mention his name on the map. No doubt both men were glad to match Beaufort's coverage of round towers, which had recently been given renewed publicity by Edward Holt.[32]

At four miles to an inch the sizes and shapes of nucleated settlements could be left to speak for themselves, so it is pedantic to criticise the scripts of Larcom's town names. He used roman capitals for county towns, italic capitals for other principal towns, bold roman lower case for market towns, and lower-case italic (reviving one of Henry Pratt's usages after more than a century) for 'villages, gentlemen's seats etc.' The definition of 'other principal' towns is hard to deduce from the map. In the new era of census-taking, population would have seemed as good a criterion as any, but Larcom's principal towns included Dungannon and Letterkenny, both with fewer than 4000 people in 1831, while Tipperary and Tuam, with populations of more than 6000, were placed in a lower category. On the whole principal towns are surprisingly few whereas nucleated rural settlements are surprisingly numerous, perhaps because miniature central places were rather too freely passed off as villages in order to take up space that might otherwise have been invaded by floating names.

* * * * * * * * *

Larcom's draughtsmen thus offered the image of a rural Ireland that knew its place, with an official church, a settled class of landed gentry and a well-ordered administrative hierarchy. By implication it was also an Ireland mainly dedicated to agriculture, or at least to primary production. Mines were marked in some profusion – this was after all a geological as well as a topographical map – but their influence on the settlement pattern was evidently slight. And Ireland seemed devoid of manufacturing enterprises except for the Arigna ironworks in the hills of Co. Roscommon. In reality, for every twenty Irish workers in primary production, the 1841 census recorded eleven in 'industry'. Admittedly much of the industry was domestic, no more capable of being mapped at this scale than were the small farms in which it was carried on; and much of it was in towns, where lack of map-space made even large buildings impossible to distinguish. But still there was a scattering of rural manufacturing sites on the ground – flour mills, bleach works, cotton and flax factories – that would have been as easy to show as Petrie's antiquities.

Another mark of rural stability in any country is the persistence of regional nomenclature. Most popular names of this kind in Ireland were also the names of baronies and appeared on the railway map as a matter of course in bold roman capitals. The map was unusual, however, in collecting a number of non-barony names, printed smaller and finer to show their lack of administrative significance. The same fine script was used for bogs. In most earlier maps of Ireland it was only the Bog of Allen in north-west Kildare that received a name. The railway map was more explicit. The bogs themselves were shown by clusters of reed-like vegetation; since few of them had been recently drained, their outlines in the south of Ireland could safely be copied from the famous government reports of 1810-14. The symbol was so lightly drawn and inconspicuous that to name the bogs as well did a useful service in attracting attention to them, even though the word 'bog' was omitted except where it was needed to avoid confusion ('Bog of Mounds' would obviously work better than 'Mounds')[33] or to make a very short name more noticeable. The names were a selection from those conferred by the bogs commission's engineers and had mainly been derived from nearby settlements.

Perhaps the most interesting regions, though, were neither administrative entities nor single physical features. Some of their names, like Joyce's Country, recalled the possessive forms familiar in the sixteenth century. Others meant nothing to English ears, just as 'Weald', 'Arden' and 'Wirral' are without connotations in modern England. Once such names get on to maps they tend to stay there; at the time the main reason for including them was that they should not interfere with other script. Non-interference was in fact a cardinal principle of the whole map, and one of the reasons for its success, just as flouting the same rule was one of the reasons for Wyld's failure. Similar considerations justified the omission of the four historic provinces. Larcom's reason, that the provinces now served no practical purpose, was unconvincing; his pagan antiquities served no practical purpose either.

For the spelling of placenames the Ordnance Survey already had its own policy, which was to collect existing versions of each name from a wide range of authorities and to select whichever of these spellings came closest to the presumed original Irish form. This principle was modified by standardising those recurrent placename elements – such as 'caher', 'slieve' etc. – that always had the same meaning and the same pronunciation. The intensive research entailed by this system was impracticable except as part of the complete six-inch survey which in many parts of the country had not yet taken place. But a beginning could at least be made with the supplementary principle of standardisation just mentioned, and even in the south of Ireland the compilers of the railway map would often choose to differ in spelling from their sources for this reason.

Like other Irish Ordnance Survey publications the railway map made no reference to the turnpike system.[34] No doubt many observers expected the turnpikes to lose what was left of their utility when long-distance traffic began to go by rail – though in fact the last remaining Irish turnpike trusts were not dissolved until 1857. The only distinction on the map was between roads for which distances were worth stating and less important roads, the former apparently being those followed by the public coach services.[35] Trunk roads from Dublin were also distinguished by thickening one of their edges. The distances were given to the nearest quarter-mile in statute measure, which had officially replaced Irish measure in Ireland under legislation of 1824 and 1826. Some of them appeared mid-way between successive towns. Others, placed as near as possible to built-up areas, were reckoned from Dublin, which despite the recent growth of Belfast was generally expected to form the hub of any Irish railway system. These figures owed nothing to Taylor and Skinner or any other earlier source, being calculated either from the new six-inch maps or from the railway map itself.

By another, less obvious, distinction dead ends and minor lanes were omitted as irrelevant to the business of railway planning. Their exclusion is betrayed by a tendency (seen for instance in Bandon, Co. Cork) for minor town streets to stop short without penetrating the adjacent countryside. For heavy traffic such as grain, still a major Irish export in the 1830s, the main rivals to the railway would be the canals: these accordingly were shown in full – not forgetting their locks, which facilitated the map-reader by helping to differentiate waterways from roads. In the same way gradients, altitudes, and transversely written distances from Dublin distinguished possible railway routes from existing lines of communication. Avoiding confusion among so many different linear features was not the least of Larcom's achievements. Only once did his designers have recourse to a pecked line in this context – for railways not surveyed but authorised by act of parliament.

*   *   *   *   *   *   *   *   *

The most spectacular qualities of the railway map remain to be considered. These, as its title made a point of emphasising, were 'the principal physical features and geological structure of the country'. The main physical feature was relief, said to have been 'taken from various sources combined and corrected as far as time and means were allowed'. This like some of Larcom's other marginal notes was designed to exonerate the Ordnance Survey, but one of the 'various sources' was the Survey's own hill sketches done for the benefit of its future one-inch map. The sketchers had been supervised by Lieutenant R.K. Dawson, son of the department's famous hill artist Robert Dawson. They had covered about half the country and their drawings were available for reduction to the quarter-inch scale.[36] Dawson himself, now on secondment to the English tithe commissioners, took charge of the relief on the new map. Two Ordnance Survey sketchers were employed in 1836-7 for 147 man-days, either to fill in the rest of the quarter-inch outline, or to correct the recent county maps (most of which had shown relief by hachures) or more probably to combine these two procedures.[37] Dawson's hills were ready for the commission by April 1837. He must have worked on a preliminary manuscript of the quarter-inch map, which continued to receive new topographical information for some time afterwards. His hachures followed the 'oblique' principle in which an imaginary bright light threw all south-east-facing slopes into shadow. In other contexts this effect would have been over-dramatic: here it suited the small-scale representation of data that were inevitably much simplified.

Dawson's hachures deal effectively with peaks, summits, ridges, valleys and bold gradients. In gentler terrain they show the existence of appreciable local relief by broad notional slopes without distinguishing minor landforms such as drumlins. This last technique was both interesting and unusual: in the past the generalisation of relief had often meant inserting imaginary minor landforms as well as sup-

301

pressing real ones. To supplement the hachuring there was a wealth of hill names in sans-serif lower-case roman script, usually written non-horizontally to show the trend of the relief or perhaps just to make hill names more recognisable. The origins of this rich nomenclature deserve investigation. Even in the north, much of it came from non-Ordnance-Survey sources. On the other hand the Survey had a near-monopoly of spot heights for summits, lake surfaces and other key points, William Bald in Mayo being the only independent cartographer to have featured these extensively. In the northern counties they were taken from the six-inch maps, and included positions on low-lying roads as well as on hill tops. In the south they were calculated from the vertical angles of the triangulation. The southern values were more numerous than might have been expected and some of the horizontal distances needed to calculate them may have been measured on grand jury or other independent maps: this would give extra point to Larcom's warning that the heights in the south should be considered as approximations.

Physical features also account for much of the map's abundant hydrographic information. Certain coastal placenames can perhaps be included in this category.[38] Then there are numerous offshore depths in fathoms (also shown for several estuaries and lakes, among them the small but famous Lough Derg in Co. Donegal), shoals and reefs with their names, anchorages marked by an anchor symbol, lighthouses and lightships with their distinctive signals, sea-marks guiding vessels into port, the directions, speeds and times of tidal streams, tidal ranges in a number of bays and harbours, the character of the seabed in selected areas, and the location of coastguard stations. The subtext is that Ireland, an easy country to enter and to leave, deserves to benefit from international relations in an era of free trade. A more specific function of the map might be to suggest which harbours deserved a railway link and whether a trans-insular railway could create a major Atlantic outport for the whole United Kingdom.

Cartographically the desire for completeness had produced an impressive blend of map and chart. Professionally it was a goodwill gesture towards the Ordnance Survey's comrades in the admiralty: relations between the two departments had always been friendly and there were interesting parallels in their histories, with Colby's dynamism matched by his opposite number Francis Beaufort. Larcom's nautical information from Dublin northwards to Bloody Foreland in Donegal was credited to the admiralty charts of the late Commander William Mudge. Acknowledgements were also made to a survey of Lower Lough Erne by Lieutenant [James] Wolfe, completed in March 1836, to Lieutenant [Thomas] Graves for Lough Neagh, and to Mr

[Thomas] Rhodes for the Shannon above Limerick, surveyed in the summer of 1832.[39] Like the Ordnance Survey, the admiralty had still not finished Ireland when the railway map went to press, and the rest of the coast was taken from Alexander Nimmo's chart for the Dublin Ballast Office.[40]

The geology of the railway map has been fully described by geologists.[41] All that need be said at present is how little it detracted from the map's effectiveness as a topographical portrait. The geological formations are bounded by very fine pecked lines. Other geological data such as known mineral occurrences were too localised to cause much trouble. But there was an element of cheating here. The formations themselves were unidentifiable until the map had been hand-coloured, and a purchaser could get his map finished only by copying from an impression that had been coloured by some one else. In the official Geological Survey maps of Ireland, published from the 1850s onwards, this problem was solved by printing a distinctive mark within each outcrop and repeating the same mark in the key. On the railway map such marks would probably have toppled the whole design into an abyss of confusion. Without them it was massively if precariously comprehensible, a triumph of brinkmanship. It may even have set a fashion for the inclusion of geology in general maps.[42]

* * * * * * * * *

Authority for engraving the railway map at the Ordnance Survey's Dublin office was received in April 1837 and in September Larcom was hoping to finish it by the end of the year. In the manner of Ordnance Survey operations it was too meticulous to meet its deadline, and the printed version was incorrect in claiming to 'accompany' the commissioners' text: their second and last report bore the date 14 July 1838, but new geological information was being added to the plates throughout the following winter and the date of Griffith's printed signature in the margin was 28 March 1839.[43] By this time the treasury had authorised the separate publication of the map at a price of one pound: Wyld was asking three guineas for a map on the same scale and had hoped to charge four. It was fair competition considering that the reducing, drawing and engraving of Larcom's map had cost only about a thousand pounds.[44] His explanation of the decision to publish – 'in the hope it may prove of some general utility' – strikes the same modest and almost defensive note as his other marginal statements. Two thousand copies were initially printed, of which (if other parliamentary publications are a guide) 1500 were intended for their original purpose of illustrating the report and the remainder to be put on sale.[45] As an influence on transport history the whole enterprise was a poor advertisement for 'the power of maps'. The Drummond recommendations were ignored, first by the government and then by private enterprise: more railways were built in Ireland than the commissioners would have considered prudent, mostly in places that they had not recommended. But by the end of 1846 the number of railway maps in circulation had reached 5406.[46] It was a publishing triumph.

In due course the railway map was rather sheepishly embraced by its one-time detractors and admitted to their official catalogue under 'Various maps etc. published by the Ordnance Survey department' *(sic)*. It was still being advertised in 1933. The Survey adopted the quarter-inch scale for Britain in 1859, but such was the durability of Larcom's achievement that the preparation of a similar map of Ireland entirely from Ordnance Survey sources was allowed to drag on for nearly thirty more years. By this time the railway map had generated several important derivatives. Two of these, in 1852 and 1855, were new editions mainly intended to accommodate Griffith's extensive geological revisions together with a degree of topographic and toponymic change that can be reasonably described as minimal.[47] Another, prepared at Larcom's initiative, was a relief map formed by adding approximate contour lines in manuscript to a railway-map base. Though never published, this did something to help popularise a method of relief representation that eventually took the place of hachuring. It also encouraged economic optimism by showing that nearly half the country lay within 250 feet of sea level.[48] Very different in spirit but equally interesting from a map-historical standpoint was the administrative version of the railway map published in 1847 at the height of the great Irish famine. Here steam-age optimism gave way to a gloomier prognosis, for the new 'electoral divisions' shown on this map were entirely concerned with the management of workhouses for the destitute poor. But at least it was a happy occasion in the technical sense, being the first complete map of Ireland produced by the new process of electrotyping in which thematic detail (in this case the new territorial units) could be added to duplicate copper plates without preventing the subsequent re-use of the unmodified originals.[49]

All this added up to a respectable progeny but, as often happens, the most numerous derivatives of the Griffith-Larcom quarter-inch map were drawn at smaller scales than the original – that is if a derivative can be earlier than its prototype. The railway commissioners' atlas had included five maps of Ireland at ten miles to the inch, one topographical and the others thematic. The latter became much better known – they are Griffith's geological map and three pioneering statistical maps by Henry D. Harness[50] – but the topographical map seems to have provided the base for the whole series. It was engraved under Larcom's superintendence at Phoenix Park and although this operation had been completed by May 1837 its outline must surely have been reduced from a draft of the quarter-inch. Later descendants of the ten-mile map, including a layered contour version, appeared in a number of parliamentary reports until the 1860s, when it was superseded by a new Ordnance Survey ten-mile map based entirely on the department's own materials.[51]

So Colby could have felt proud of the railway map after all. Perhaps in the end he did feel proud. All the same his first reaction had been right. To blend the Ordnance Survey's topography with that of any independent map-maker was an experiment that none of his nineteenth-century or early twentieth-century successors cared to repeat.

References
1. W.A. Seymour (ed.), *A history of the Ordnance Survey* (Folkestone, 1980), ch. 1.
2. *Reports of the commissioners appointed to enquire into the nature and extent of the several bogs of Ireland, and the practicability of draining and cultivating them*, House of commons sessional papers, H.C. 1810 (365), x; 1810-11 (96), vi; 1813-14 (130, 131), vi.
3. G.L. Herries Davies and R.C. Mollan (eds), *Richard Griffith 1784-1878*, Royal Dublin Society Historical Studies in Irish Science and Technology, i (Dublin, 1980).
4. *Report from the select committee on the survey and valuation of Ireland*, H.C. 1824 (445), viii.
5. J.B. Harley, *Christopher Greenwood, county map-maker, and his map of Worcestershire, 1822* (Worcester, 1962), pp 28-9.
6. In 1817 the master-general and the board of ordnance cautioned map sellers against 'copying, reducing or incorporating into other works, and publishing all or any part of the . . . "Trigonometrical Survey" or of the ordnance maps which have been or may be engraven therefrom' (Seymour, *History of the Ordnance Survey*, p. 76). 'Trigonometrical survey' here meant the numerical record of the British triangulation published between 1799 and 1811.
7. National Archives, Dublin, Ordnance Survey letter register 4354, application of John Phillips, land surveyor, 5 February 1833.
8. See above, ch. 8, n.18. The date *c*.1825 is derived from the evidence of watermarks.
9. One sufferer from this experience was the map of Ireland prepared by the Society for the Diffusion of Useful Knowledge as part of its world-wide coverage in the 1830s. The society's cartographic expert was Captain Francis Beaufort, son of the illustrious Daniel Augustus. But in trying to base itself upon the Ordnance Survey the map of Beaufort's homeland – poor neglected, ill-used unfortunate Ireland, as a would-be purchaser called it – became one of the slowest and most expensive in the whole series. See Mead T. Cain, 'The maps of the Society for the Diffusion of Useful Knowledge: a publishing history', *Imago Mundi*, xlvi

(1994), pp 151-67. Francis Beaufort's contribution to this 'very nice and accurate map' was acknowledged by Lord Monteagle in *Report from the select committee . . . [on] . . . the present state of the Ordnance Survey in Ireland*, p. 29, H.C. 1846 (664), xv.

10. *The Times*, 27 August 1838. For Wyld's career in general see David Smith, 'The Wyld family firm', *The Map Collector*, lv (1991), pp 32-8.

11. For example in *Dublin Evening Mail*, 16 March 1838.

12. This is the completed version of the proof map that the present writer wrongly described as 'abandoned' (and also wrongly described as being in four sheets) in J.H. Andrews, *A paper landscape: the Ordnance Survey in nineteenth century Ireland* (Oxford, 1975), p. 34.

13. National Archives, Dublin, Ordnance Survey letter register 8792 (23 September 1839 to 20 July 1840); CS ORP 1839/62 9975 (29 November 1839). The ordnance solicitor's opinion is more fully reported in Public Record Office, London, WO.47/1867, pp 8891-3, a reference kindly supplied by Dr Richard Oliver.

14. It may be relevant that Wyld senior had previously used the Ordnance Survey's triangulation of Britain as the basis for a map of England and Wales published in 1826, though here no question of illegality had arisen as the figures were already available in print. Another difference was that the English map included an explanatory note, which may be worth quoting as a source of conjecture about the methods used in Ireland: 'Principles on which this map was constructed. The extent of the most external points ascertained, the projection was made to the dimensions required. A scale was formed from the number of feet contained in the middle degree of latitude, and admitted as an average data [sic] for all the distances: from that scale, the position of the principal and many of the secondary stations were laid down by 3, 4 and sometimes 5 intersections, and every one proved by the distance from the appropriate meridian and the perpendicular. In fact the same operations that had been made on the surface of the country were performed on the projection, and the whole diagram was closed at the Souldrope station. The county surveys were made subservient by corresponding latitudes and longitudes, and the map was drawn from them. The general post office admeasurements were used and assisted in placing the intermediate towns on the roads to their respective distances.' No accurate post office road distances are known to have been published in Ireland.

15. For Wyld's relations with the Ordnance Survey see Ralph Hyde, *Printed maps of Victorian London, 1851-1900* (Folkestone, 1975), pp 3-5.

16. Laudatory reviews from seven Dublin newspapers, including the *Freeman's Journal*, were reprinted in a long advertisement in the *Westmeath Guardian*, 17 October 1839.

17. To avoid confusion the title of Wyld's small map is given in full: *To her most gracious majesty Queen Victoria this map of Ireland, compiled from the surveys of the board of ordnance and other approved documents of the railway commissioners is with her majesty's gracious permission respectfully dedicated by her majesty's devoted servant, James Wyld. To Thomas Larcom Esq, R.E., Richard Griffith, Esq., and to Messrs Vignolles and MacNeill, the publisher begs to return his acknowledgements for the information afforded him by their maps, plans and sections. Published by James Wyld, Geographer to the Queen, Charing Cross East 1839*. It was apparently this and not the six-sheet map that was criticised under the name of Wyld's in *A walking tour round Ireland* (London, 1867), pp 42, 51, 57.

18. The unpublished minutes and correspondence of the railway commission are in

National Archives, Dublin, OPW 1/10/l, 1/10/2/1 and 2. Its main report is printed in H.C. 1837-8, xxxv.

19.   National Library of Ireland, MS 13382 (3).

20.   The routes were surveyed by Charles Vignoles and John MacNeill. Their plans and sections occupied 114 sheets and were produced at a cost of £8575 (*Railways (Ireland). A return . . . of the expenditure of the commission in Ireland*, H.C. 1839 (88), xlvi). See also National Archives, Dublin: OPW 1/10/3 (letter book of Charles Vignoles), OPW 1/10/4 (reports of surveys by John MacNeill).

21.   Colby to Henry de la Beche, 12 May 1837, National Museum of Wales, Cardiff, De la Beche papers.

22.   Colby to Col. H.D. Jones, secretary, Irish railway commission, National Library of Ireland, Larcom papers, MS 7459.

23.   The wording of the map's title as far as the publishers' credit was *A general map of Ireland to accompany the report of the railway commissioners shewing the principal physical features and geological structure of the country. Constructed in 1836 and engraved in 1837-8.*

24.   *Second report of the commissioners appointed to consider and recommend a general system of railways for Ireland*, H.C. 1837-8, xxxv, p. 1. Larcom appears in this citation as a lieutenant of the Royal Engineers. His connection with the Ordnance Survey is not mentioned. 'Captain Larcom's map' was an acceptable form of reference in the 1840s (*Report on Ordnance Survey in Ireland*, 1846, p. 28, Lord Monteagle's evidence).

25.   Larcom's records of this episode may conceivably survive in some unidentified repository, but have not been found in the main body of his papers, which was left to the Statistical and Social Inquiry Society of Ireland and later acquired by the National Library of Ireland. The 136 volumes of this collection were arranged in an orderly fashion by Larcom himself, but they have never been indexed or adequately calendared.

26.   An undated MS volume entitled 'Principal altitude book: Ireland', formerly in the Ordnance Survey office, Dublin, gives latitudes of several stations in eastern Ireland, apparently based on direct observations to the celestial pole, and the longitude of Armagh observatory supplied by Francis Beaufort in his capacity as hydrographer of the navy. These may be records of Portlock's work on the railway map.

27.   The differences between the railway and six-inch maps in this north-midland zone may reflect either simple copying errors (unavoidable in a task of great urgency) or incomplete revision of pre-Ordnance-Survey data. Examples are the railway map's Straid (Longford), Quiganalahy (Sligo) and Lough Lane (Westmeath) where the six-inch maps show Sraid, Quignalahy and Lough Lene.

28.   J.H. Andrews, *Plantation acres: an historical study of the Irish land surveyor and his maps* (Belfast, 1985), p. 255.

29.   These were itemised in successive editions of the *Dublin Gazette*. Their most important effect was to absorb detached portions of counties into the counties surrounding them.

30.   The pagan antiquities are Duhela, Dun Aillinne, Dun Conor, Dun Angus, Emania, Grianan of Aileach, New Grange, Rathcroghan, Staig Fort, Tara, Tailtean, Tlachtga, Ushnagh and Worm Ditch.

31.   William Stokes, *The life and labours in art and architecture of George Petrie* (London and Dublin, 1868).

32.   Holt's map of 1838 included an acknowledgement to Captain Francis Beaufort, for information about round towers. The towers also appeared on Wyld's small

map of 1839. The fashion for tabulating them on maps was long-lived: a late example is the four-sheet map of Ireland in Letts's *Popular atlas* (London, 1884).

33. On the bogs commission map of 1810 (by Richard Griffith) this had been 'Bog of Mouds'.

34. This was in contrast with the Survey's English one-inch map, on which turnpike roads were engraved with thicker and more widely spaced lines than other roads (*Report on survey and valuation*, p. 15, Colby's evidence).

35. Roads with mileages on the railway map compare well with the coach routes listed in Pettigrew and Oulton's *Dublin almanac and general register of Ireland* for the years 1837-9, less well with *Sketch of a map of the circulation of letters in Ireland corrected to January 1838* in *First report of the select committee on postage*, H.C. 1837-8 (278), xx (i). The latter map distinguishes mail coaches, mail cars, horse posts and foot posts. All the mail coach routes but only some of the mail car routes appear as main roads on the railway map.

36. Andrews, *Paper landscape*, pp 113-14.

37. Railway commission minutes, 30 March 1837, National Archives, Dublin, OPW 1/10/1.

38. An example is the name Tranarossan Bay in Co. Donegal, which had been omitted from the six-inch Ordnance Survey map.

39. L.S. Dawson, *Memoirs of hydrography* (London, 1969, reprinted from edition of 1885), i, pp 123-4; ii, pp 20, 58. Charts by Mudge and Wolfe are listed in *Return of the hydrographical survey of the coasts of the United Kingdom, showing the extent of survey completed or in progress, by whom made, when received at the admiralty, when published, and if not published, the reason why*, H.C. 1852-3 (235), lx, p. 465.

40. This chart was probably a by-product of surveys made by Nimmo for the commissioners of Irish fisheries from 1820 to 1824 (*Sixth report of the commissioners of the Irish fisheries*, p. 4, H.C. 1825 (385), xv). The archivist of the Dublin Port Board, Mr Gerry Daly, kindly confirms that no copy of it now survives among the Board's records.

41. G.L. Herries Davies, *Sheets of many colours: the mapping of Ireland's rocks, 1750-1890* (Dublin, 1983), ch. 3.

42. Eighteen geological categories were included in *Fraser's travelling map of Ireland* published by James McGlashan of Dublin in 1853.

43. *Second report, railway commission*, pp 1-2. The commission blamed the delay on the engravers (usual scapegoats on such occasions) and on the additional hill sketching required especially for this map.

44. *Report on the Ordnance Survey in Ireland*, 1846, p. 11 (Larcom's evidence).

45. *Railways (Ireland): a return of the expenditure of the commission*, H.C. 1839 (88), xlvi.

46. The numbers disposed of annually were 1839, 2412; 1840, 546; 1841, 576; 1842, 180; 1843, 240; 1844, 360; 1845, 894; 1846, 198 (*Trigonometrical surveys*, H.C. 1847 (171), xxxvi).

47. G.L. Herries Davies, 'Notes on the various issues of Sir Richard Griffith's quarter-inch geological map of Ireland, 1839-1855', *Imago Mundi*, xxix (1977), pp 35-44. The revision of 1854 is documented in National Archives, Dublin, Ordnance Survey letters, OSL 871 (1854). The main non-geological changes were the addition of railways and of certain placenames necessary to the location of mineral occurrences. Otherwise 'Cove' was replaced by 'Queenstown' (a name adopted in 1849 to mark the visit of Queen Victoria) and 'Ballydahob' corrected to 'Ballydehob', but many pre-Ordnance Survey spellings were retained (e.g.

Ballyhigh for Ballyheige, Castletownroach for Castletownroche, and Feathard for Fethard) and there was no revision of built-up areas.

48. National Library of Ireland, MS 7545 (Larcom to T.R. Robinson, 20 May 1844), MS 7574 (Larcom's autobiography).

49. For other derivatives see Andrews, *Paper landscape*, pp 184-5. Not mentioned there (and brought to the author's attention by Andrew Bonar Law) is a version of the map with greatly simplified relief features published in Philadelphia by Thomas Doran, Denis Behen and Thomas H. Maher in 1860.

50. A.H. Robinson, 'The 1837 maps of Henry Harness', *Geographical Journal*, cxxi (1955), pp 440-50.

51. Roger Hellyer, *The 'ten-mile' maps of the Ordnance Surveys* (London, 1992), pp 54-6, 59-62, including a list of every known edition and state.

Chapter 11

Conclusion

It was natural in the 1830s to view any mixture of Ordnance Survey and non-Ordnance-Survey mapping as a temporary aberration. The government had brought more resources to the cartography of Ireland than had ever been applied before, and when Colby disclaimed responsibility for the Larcom-Griffith railway map he had about 1500 employees scattered across the island and was spending about £50,000 a year with no obligation to show a profit. A survey so generously funded would surely soon be complete and then it went without saying that all future maps of Ireland would be based on its results (Fig. 11.1). In practice the outcome was not so simple. From a national standpoint Colby's maps had two serious disadvantages. One was their omission of latitude and longitude. Another was their unmanageably large scale of six inches to one statute mile, requiring for each county a number of sheets that ranged from 25 in Louth to 153 in Cork. It was not much consolation that the county index maps showing the six-inch sheet lines could themselves each be accommodated in one sheet, especially as this was only at the cost of varying their scale.

From the beginning of the six-inch survey it was expected that Charles Vallancey's military map would eventually give way to an appropriate Ordnance Survey replacement, but as the Napoleonic wars receded this intention began to seem less urgent. It is true that the national triangulation required by such a map was pushed forward with great enthusiasm, but the main motives for doing so were scientific rather than strategic. Not until the 1850s were the counties brought into mathematical harmony and a single outline of Ireland produced at one inch to one mile with a graticule of the highest attainable accuracy. In scale, style and method of printing the new map followed British precedents, but to make up for lost time it was published in quarter-sheets, of which 205 were needed to cover the whole country, and in the first instance without hachures. This so-called outline edition appeared between 1856 and 1862. Like its six-inch source-maps it used few conventions and relied heavily on explanatory script (Fig. 11.2). Water, woods, uncultivated land, roads

310

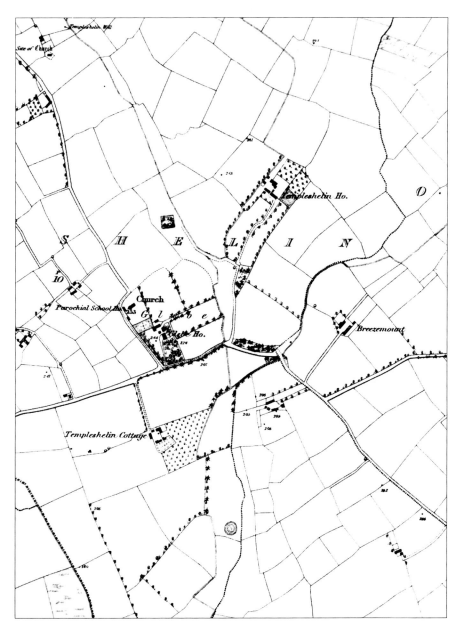

Fig. 11.1   From Ordnance Survey, six-inch map of Co. Wexford, first edition,
             sheet 30 (1841).

311

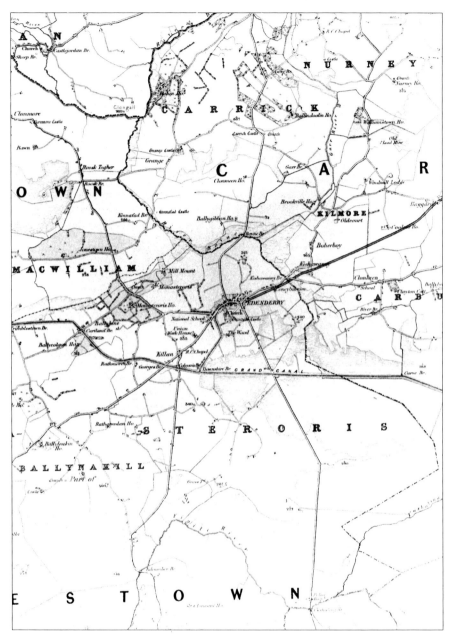

Fig. 11.2   Parts of Co. Kildare and King's County, from Ordnance Survey, one-inch
map of Ireland, first (outline) edition, sheet 110 (1858).

and most buildings were shown but not fields. There was no attempt to match the thematic versatility of the railway commissioners, both geological and marine cartography now being left to the appropriate government departments.[1] Defying military necessity, a much older Irish cartographic tradition was acknowledged by the prominence given to baronies and parishes in the new one-inch map: at first it was even hoped to show the boundaries and names of townlands.

The hachured one-inch (Fig. 11.3) took much longer, partly because of the time spent in sketching, drawing and engraving the hills but also, perhaps, because of the Survey's half-conscious recognition that black hachures were gradually losing their hold on public taste.[2] This meant that the railway map was not finally superseded until 1895 – only three years before the abolition of nearly all its administrative divisions under the Irish local government act. At any time during this long gestation a literal-minded reader might have argued that no map is really a map until its parts have been put together, but the Survey probably never foresaw that all 205 one-inch sheets would be assembled into a mosaic 24 feet long and 19.5 feet wide. (Otherwise there would presumably have been a title sheet covering a suitably-placed patch of ocean.) Silencing the literal-minded reader was a task that fell upon T.W. Conway of the Irish education department. Conway's three-dimensional one-inch relief map of Ireland was to adorn the grounds of the national model schools in Dublin for several years, in due course appearing as a small rectangle on the Ordnance Survey's city plan.[3] Sadly this masterpiece – in one sense the first definitive map of Ireland – no longer exists, another illustration of the rule that large maps are easier to lose than small ones.

At the time, the last one-inch sheet might well have seemed to mark the end of national Ordnance Survey mapping, at least in the rather narrow sense of 'national' used above. In the Survey's early years, maps on smaller scales had been left to private enterprise. But the department's fifth director, Henry James, was not content with this division of labour. Aspiring to the lordship of a duplicate cartographic universe, James hoped to meet the needs of every map-user not just in the British Isles or the British Empire but in the rest of the world as well. Among the steps he took to achieve this ambition were a single-sheet ten-mile map of Ireland (1868) and a posthumously-published quarter-inch map in four sheets (1887).[4] Like the one-inch these were black and white engravings, originally published without any representation of hills.

All the above-mentioned Ordnance Survey maps were eventually revised, or replaced by new maps on roughly comparable scales. Nevertheless, delays between editions sometimes seemed intolerably

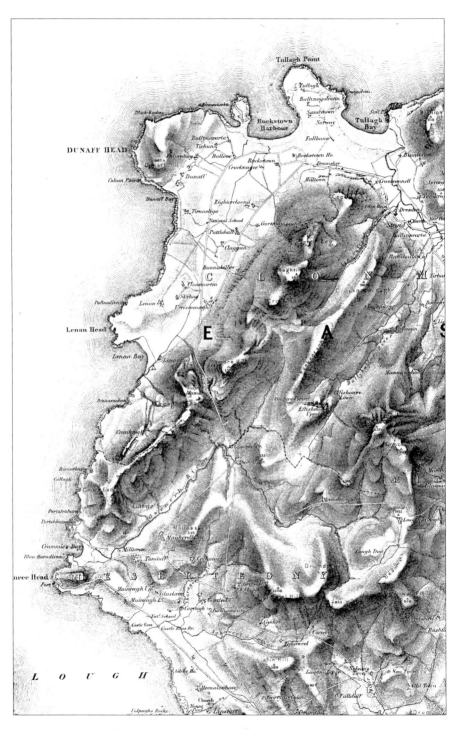

Fig. 11.3   Part of Inishowen, Co. Donegal, from Ordnance Survey, one-inch map
of Ireland, first (hill) edition, sheet 5 (1862).

long, even in a slowly changing country like Ireland. Nor was this the Survey's only handicap in its new capacity as all-round cartographic entertainer. Its maps were badly publicised and badly packaged. Its style was too austere for many modern readers, and so too was its conception of relevance, despite the thoroughness of the original six-inch survey. Mention has already been made of the well-known cartographic principle that not all small-scale maps can be entirely derived from pre-existing large-scale maps of the same areas. In the compiling of the one-inch map, for example, not only the forms of the hills but in many cases their names were absent from the six-inch maps and had to be specially surveyed. Another principle is that although small scales may be created out of larger scales, they are usually easier to revise. The simplest kind of revision for a one-inch or quarter-inch map was to insert new detail such as railways, roads and important buildings. It was more difficult to decide which whole categories of information, if any, should be added to or subtracted from a long-familiar map to bring it up to date. Most difficult of all, perhaps, at least in a psychological sense, was to impose a new classification on existing detail – by distinguishing different grades of road, for instance, or by reconsidering whether any given settlement deserved an individual name. The Ordnance Survey confronted these problems with mixed success.

*   *   *   *   *   *   *   *   *

For nineteenth-century commercial map publishers, state intervention brought both bad and good news. Certain kinds of original private cartography were manifestly unfitted to resist the Ordnance Survey onslaught: large free-standing county maps disappeared almost at once, and estate maps went into a slow decline. Unusual formats, as with road strip maps or pocket atlases, stood a better chance of survival,[5] and the remarkable growth of thematic cartography was totally unaffected. Single-sheet mainstream maps of Ireland continued to flourish because they cost so little. The crucial case was that of topographical maps depicting the whole country in the spirit of Pratt or Arrowsmith. In this *genre* the first consideration was to facilitate the road traveller, but the mapping of minor territorial divisions remained an important secondary desideratum, notably among expatriate Irishmen with an interest in family history.[6] The topographical market also posed one question of cartographic economics that had never troubled mapmakers in the public sector. What was the largest scale at which a map could be profitably sold? The answer was a function of both population density (permanent or temporary) and per capita purchasing-power in the country represented. To judge by the actual course of events, the economic threshold was half an inch to a mile in Britain and a quarter of an inch in Ireland.

No independent publisher would wish to change the Ordnance Survey's graticules or its outline of large quasi-permanent features. Such information was easily reduced and copied by draughtsmen or photographers and in any case a commercial firm could hardly afford to test its accuracy. The legality of copying from the Survey was therefore an important issue. In theory this right had been firmly denied by government lawyers before the Irish survey began.[7] In practice the relationship between public and private domains was governed by gentlemen's agreements. In England, for example, at some time before 1850, at least two publishers promised the Ordnance Survey not to produce maps on larger scales than five miles to an inch.[8] By the end of the century this unofficial upper limit seems to have been generously raised from 1:316,800 to 1:63,360. At any rate there was considerable reluctance to prosecute the medium-scale copyists even when they pre-empted the very name 'ordnance'. Private firms had thus gained a strong foothold in the topographical market before the copyright question was more or less laid to rest in the opening years of the new century.[9]

The alternative to copyright prosecutions was commercial competition, and by the 1890s the Ordnance Survey was increasingly disposed to fight its rivals on their own ground. In Ireland two new influences were now at work. One was a revival of military preoccupations to match the growth of late-Victorian imperialism. The other was an increase in tourism as the country gradually recovered from the great famine of the 1840s. A first step was to re-design the one-inch in a more military style, omitting all administrative boundaries except the counties. Less successfully, settlement was now to be emphasised by adding more non-administrative and non-physical nomenclature, though as any map-historian could have predicted this turned out to consist mainly of townland names with no identifiable small-scale referent.[10] Then there was the advent of printed colour. Here the Survey was so far behind the times that it had to seek advice from a competitor, John Bartholomew of Edinburgh,[11] but colour was duly introduced for a new edition of the one-inch map, a new quarter-inch map of Ireland and a new ten-mile map, all begun between 1902 and 1905. The most vulnerable of the coloured maps was the hill-shaded quarter-inch, which came nowhere near to defeating Bartholomew, mainly because Bartholomew's sheets were larger (seven covered Ireland instead of the Survey's sixteen) without being more expensive.[12]

The twentieth century also brought with it a brand new Ordnance Survey scale, the half-inch. Its choice for a regular series is usually attributed to British military experience in the wider landscapes of South Africa during the Boer War. Again there was a brief but humiliating period when the army had to buy its half-inch sheets from Bartholomew,[15] but the new ordnance map was rapidly pushed ahead for the whole United Kingdom until Ireland's turn for publication came in 1911. The country was now covered by twenty-five half-inch sheets, each published with contours in both a layer-coloured and a brown-hachured edition. The former, with an improved road classification and a new national grid, was later to become the Irish Republic's leading topographical map, equally acceptable for walking and motoring, while the one-inch was allowed to stagnate.

*   *   *   *   *   *   *   *

Indeed on a broad view the whole of Irish cartography was now to remain stagnant for half a century, beginning with the outbreak of the first world war, continuing with the separation of the Irish Free State (later Republic) and Northern Ireland in 1922, and ending in 1964 with an official investigation of the Republic's mapping requirements.[14] Seen in retrospect the main achievement of this interregnum was a primary re-triangulation of Ireland to serve as the basis for a reference grid covering both north and south. When the progress of 'hard-copy' mapping recovered its momentum in the 1970s the theoretical priorities were no different from those of late Victorian times: to popularise, to diversify, to accelerate. Practical implications for the published map were rather different. The late twentieth-century cartographer's subject-matter was increasingly affected by two contrasting kinds of land cover – housing estates and forestry plantations – extensive enough to appear conspicuously at scales as small as a quarter-inch to a mile. Meanwhile a larger proportion of his customers were motorists and especially holiday-makers – with hill-walkers and archaeology-enthusiasts forming very small but surprisingly influential minorities. At the same time air survey, satellite technology and computerisation were setting the scene for scales, sheet-lines and styles that owed nothing to Ordnance Survey precedent. It was also becoming possible for private firms to escape the Survey's influence by publishing on their own account from purely satellite-based sources, though so far the main products of this facility have been small-scale photomaps with little to offer but novelty-value. On the whole the Ordnance Surveys of both Dublin and Belfast have confronted shifting circumstances with more success than some of their critics would have thought possible.

With further technical progress, the impetus for radical change has been carried downwards through the pyramid of official scales. Near the top of the pyramid the first of the new maps actually preceded the technological revolution. There were single-sheet maps of Ireland at 1:500,000 and 1:575,000 and a not very successful map in five sheets at 1:250,000.[15] Next, following British and European examples but in an Irish context spectacularly new, came a map of the whole island at 1:50,000 in 89 sheets. In different styles for north and south but with a common system of sheet lines and sheet numbers, this was completed for Northern Ireland between 1978 and 1982 and started for the Republic in 1988.[16] Unlike the one-inch, it is based on independent surveys which are said to be accurate enough for plotting at 1:10,000.

The development of the larger scales has inevitably been slower. For centuries map-making at 1:10,000 or more formed an independent strand of Irish cartographic history. Early plantation and estate maps, for example, might conceivably have supplied some of the data for a national map, without themselves constituting such a map, but in practice it was only in exceptional circumstances that they actually did so. For many decades a similar fault-line ran through the Ordnance Survey. Despite the existence of a national triangulation, there were not one but thirty-two six-inch Irish ordnance maps, one for each county, each projected on its own central meridian. The same arrangement held good when a 1:2500 'cadastral' scale was introduced for all except uncultivated areas in 1887; in most of the Republic it holds good today, not yet affected by the government's adoption of a national grid system a generation ago. But according to present policies the historic county system is destined to be swept away. A single nation-wide resurvey at 1:2500 should be finished early in the twenty-first century, weaving a 'seamless web' from which sheets of any size and shape can be cut at will. With the completion of this great enterprise there will be one all-embracing map of Ireland – conceivably the ultimate map – which will doubtless be brought up to date from time to time but which it is hard to imagine being replaced.

*   *   *   *   *   *   *   *

It remains finally to consider some of the supra-national issues raised by the foregoing essays. In recent decades the principles of map-historical scholarship have come under such close scrutiny (in the writings of J.B. Harley, Denis Wood and others),[17] that it now seems almost obligatory for any writer on this subject to put some philosophical cards on the table. At the same time no book on maps outside the realm of 'vanity publishing' can be more than a compromise between practical and theoretical interests. The present work is just as ambivalent in this respect as any other. Its underlying principles, as far as it has any, may be summarised as follows.

Nearly all map catalogues are almost unreadable as literature because they give the appearance of reducing every item to the same level of *prima facie* importance and therefore fail to satisfy the human desire for generality. But that desire is by no means all-consuming, and a map-history without names or dates would attract few readers apart from academic theoreticians. The trick must be to provide such details in just the right quantity, and this itself entails an act of prior generalisation, because what gives a map its special interest is to contradict some general principle. From the innumerable early maps of Ireland that survive, this book has chosen exceptions to two rules. One rule states that most maps are not very good, the other that most maps have very little effect on mankind at large. This is another way of defining our two entrance qualifications as merit and influence.

The word 'merit' here carries its narrowest possible geographical sense. It means the veracity with which the earth's surface is represented. The questions it raises are: Does the map show distances and bearings correctly, apart from errors rooted in the rules of projection and scale or in the demands of symbolism? Is its subject-matter properly classified, with woods shown as woods and not as lakes? And how comprehensively is that subject-matter recorded? In this last respect merit can have no absolute meaning: the fuller the record, the better the map. Of course no map can ever be complete, but a cartographer can at least ensure that what he includes is more worthy of note than what he omits. Noteworthiness is admittedly a subjective concept, but different subjectivities do sometimes coincide, and a map-maker's choice of detail should follow rules acceptable to his clientele even if there is no way of proving that these rules are the best.

Most modern readers, though happy enough with the foregoing tests of cartographic merit, would probably wish to add a few others – legibility, for instance, or aesthetic appeal. In choosing examples for discussion such design features have been ignored (though this restriction does not apply to the analysis of the maps once they are chosen) and as a matter of definition no derivative map has been judged better than the map on which its geographical content is based. Since most maps are copies of other maps this rule has greatly simplified the author's task. In the present case it may also help to justify confining attention to works of English authorship, admittedly using 'English' in a broader sense than some Irish readers might approve. There may well be more original French, Spanish and other continental maps of Ireland than any English-speaking historian has realised, but few of them are likely to embody as much first-hand knowledge as those discussed in this book.

Any supposedly absolute standard of cartographic value is in danger of confining an author to his own era. To the historian merit must be a relative notion, each map qualifying as good or bad against its own background of expectations, resources and techniques. Thus Gerard Mercator's map of Ireland in 1564 deserves either praise or censure depending on which of his other maps, earlier or later, we choose to treat as a standard. John Speed's map of 1610 was better than any of Mercator's, but inferior to William Petty's outline of 1685. Such comparative judgements and counter-judgements can be carried at least as far as the mid-nineteenth century.

Some critics may wish to see this principle of relativity extended. An early cartographer, they will point out, was not necessarily disposed to meet the conditions laid down in the foregoing paragraphs. His concern may have been less for planimetric accuracy than for aptness of religious or metaphysical symbolism or for the expression of socio-political preferences. But however carefully we may reconstruct the map-philosophies of the past, it is impossible and undesirable to ignore the interests of our own contemporaries. History itself teaches that every period judges earlier periods by its own lights: why should we be different? Perhaps the only way to avoid self-deception in this matter is by consciously switching viewpoints, adopting the values of yesterday and today – obsolete and modern, historical and scientific, sympathetic and impartial – in rapid alternation and with equal enthusiasm. In contributing to current map-historical literature, however, the choice of emphasis need not be even-handed, and prevailing fashions may legitimately be complemented rather than reinforced. One influential recent fashion has been to judge an early mapmaker as he seems likely to have judged himself. In this book, as a modest attempt to redress the balance, the standards have been those of the present day, with maps considered as specimens of cartography and not of iconography, propaganda or imaginative art.

Our second test of importance may go some way to meet the relativist case. It is that to be worth prolonged consideration a map must have some influence on people other than later historians. Within the narrow confines of the cartographic fraternity such influence presents few historiographical difficulties, for it is usually possible to show whether one early map has been copied from another or at least whether both are descended from a common archetype. A study of derivations may also help with our first criterion by revealing contem-porary assessments of merit, for the model a cartographer chooses to copy is likely to be the one he considers best. But influence must embrace users as well as makers. Outside the cartographer's workroom the most consequential maps are those that shape great events, causing expeditions to be mounted, battles to be won, or armadas to be sunk; the only problem here is that unfortunately men of action seldom tell posterity what maps they have been looking at. On a less glamorous level, the strongest influences occur within distinct occupational groups, as when military maps are used on army manoeuvres, charts as guides to navigation, property maps for estate management, statistical maps in modern geography teaching and so on. These specialist cartographies need their own specialist historians. For the general reader, influence must be judged by breadth rather than depth, and thematic or single-subject maps must be left for separate consideration. This is one reason for not taking more notice of hydrography in the present study. Sea charts were made, sold and used in different ways and by different groups of people from land maps, and for long periods there was little contact between terrestrial and maritime streams of cartographic development.

Influence is harder to recognise in general maps than in thematic maps. In principle a map may qualify for special attention if people have its image before their eyes or carry that image in their minds, but these again are experiences difficult to identify in the historical record. Maps may be widely circulated without anyone ever scrutinising them, especially if they form part of a large atlas. Sometimes cartographic history yields its own evidence on this point – the correction or non-correction of obvious errors on a long-lived printing plate, for example – but the map student will often have to risk mistaking the illusion of influence for the reality. All the same, it seems at least probable that since the sixteenth century printed maps have been better known among the general public than manuscripts. For this reason Baptista Boazio's derivative printed map of Ireland (1599) has been regretfully preferred in the foregoing chapters to the original hand-drawn surveys by Robert Lythe on which it was based. By the same token Aaron Arrowsmith (1811) must take precedence over the author of his principal manuscript source, Charles Vallancey.

Having excluded the historian as a recipient of map influence for reasons of principle we may now admit him, at least in a subordinate capacity, as a matter of practical convenience. Maps like those of Lythe and Vallancey, rescued by scholars from oblivion centuries after becoming out of date, have indeed forgone their right to a separate chapter, but historical and historiographical effectiveness may be allowed to reinforce each other by giving some weight to the views of modern collectors, librarians, printsellers and facsimile-publishers. This may seem an excessively theoretical issue, because on the whole the famous maps of today are those that were famous in their own time, but there are some cartographers, Boazio among them, who owe most of their posthumous celebrity to attractive and well-publicised twentieth-century facsimiles. This concession cannot be carried too far, however: not many maps have become widely known through black-and-white illustrations in journals or monographs.

Within the cartographic profession, if nowhere else, merit and influence have for several centuries been closely linked, which seems another way of saying that maps have 'evolved', so long as evolution in this context is a metaphor and not a biological theory. Lacking a reproductive instinct, maps have no inherent disposition to start a family. Several first-class examples have lain for centuries on the shelf, almost unknown except among historians, a notable Irish case being John Browne's excellent map of Connacht in 1591. At the same time good content can easily be nullified by bad design – thus restoring under the title of influence a quality previously rejected as a separate criterion of merit. On the other hand many unworthy models have become familiar through repeated copying. In general, however, the most glaring discrepancies between merit and influence are concentrated in the earlier phases of map history – in Ireland, before the 1590s – and this asymmetry itself chimes well with evolutionary doctrine. Even in the mid-sixteenth century, the word 'new' was habitually included in map titles as a term of praise. Later, the best new maps were indeed usually better than the best old ones, as witness the sweeping and impressively quick victories won by three maps of Ireland with different formats – those of John Speed (in an atlas of the British Isles, 1611, and later of the world), William Petty (a county atlas of Ireland, 1685), and Henry Pratt (separate sheets, 1708). Such triumphs justify expressions like 'typologically old' for maps that appear on evolutionary grounds to be derived from sources much earlier than themselves.

How do maps evolve? More specifically, how does merit declare itself? Those who transmit cartographic influence – copyists, editors, publishers and the like – are not usually themselves field observers, and few of them would personally inspect a region, let alone a whole kingdom, to prove that one model is better than another. Their approval may sometimes depend on reputations already won: it was this advantage that gave currency to Thomas Jefferys's map of Ireland for several decades after its first appearance in 1759, its own merits, though substantial, being not quite sufficient to lift it out of the ruck. In other cases a cartographer's methods of work may become known and approved among his successors. This kind of knowledge cannot be taken for granted without good documentary evidence, however, and such evidence is unhappily by no means common; Daniel Beaufort's published explanation of his own map (1792) is almost the only Irish example.

When two or more maps compete for approval among non-experts the only distinguishing feature visible at a glance may be their size. Hence the almost universal inclination to take quantity as a sign of quality, with new geographical detail attributed to direct observation in the field simply because there is nowhere else for it to come from. This argument, despite the shakiness of its premise that all cartographers tell the truth as they see it, has apparently been found convincing by most indoor map-users, with the result that small maps have generally been superseded by large ones. Large does not always mean good. New maps can make new mistakes; they can also revive errors that other cartographers have already corrected. But if a map is put to the test of experience such mutations must sooner or later become extinct. As J.B. Harley puts it, 'in the mapping of large areas . . . the less realistic maps, with many instances of regression, were gradually ousted by more realistic maps.'[18]

The final stage of the foregoing argument is to postulate a series of key or foundation maps,[19] each incorporating new material or new combinations of material, and each widely accepted and repeatedly copied until rising standards, or changes in external reality, elicit something more comprehensive and more correct. An advantage of this approach is to make more room for the principle of causation in map history: the key map is a cause, the derivative map an effect. It is not a principle of universal application, however. One of its prerequisites is a free market in cartographic information. If each map had no more than one reader, and if no two mapmakers knew of each other's existence, there could be no such thing as a key map. Medieval European cartography came dangerously close to this anarchic state. It did so partly because mapmaking had not yet become an organised profession, but perhaps also for another reason. Most maps of that era were based not on ground measurement, or on any programme of systematic field observation, but on records or memories of journeys undertaken mainly if not wholly for non-cartographic reasons. Even in its own time a map known or suspected to have been made by such imperfect means would carry less authority than a genuine survey. Rival cartographers might well prefer to start afresh and apply the same techniques to their own experiences, which would probably differ from those of other authors but which at least they knew to be genuine. When this free-for-all comes to an end, as happened in late sixteenth-century Ireland, we can expect a 'take-off' in which map accuracy begins to trace an upward curve. The key-map model may still be difficult to apply, however. Its 'keys' do not necessarily give access to equal-sized metaphorical rooms all independently opening off the same metaphorical corridor. When maps are partly original and partly copied from other maps, the 'rooms' are better conceived as nesting together, so that in Ireland Jefferys's space is part of Pratt's space – a cupboard in Pratt's room, to pursue the metaphor – and Pratt's in turn is part of Petty's. In these circumstances key-map status like so many other cartographic properties becomes a matter of degree.

Eventually, in any case, the accumulation of geographical data must put the key-map concept under a different kind of strain. If there is more new information than one author can digest, the evolutionary flow may divide instead of converging, and one powerful family may be challenged by another of the same generation, as in the early nineteenth century Beaufort's map of Ireland was challenged by Arrowsmith's. The solution is then to treat both contenders as key maps, but as progress accelerates this remedy inevitably grows less effective. If every map is a key map the distinction loses its point and history relapses into catalogue.

Another problem posed by the march of progress is the difference between whole and part. A cartographer may command so much information that, at the scale needed to accommodate it, his study-area can no longer fit into one sheet or one practicable mosaic of sheets. Before the twentieth century the largest scale convenient for mapping Ireland on a single piece of paper was something like ten statute miles to an inch (1:633,600) and the largest scale suitable for a block of sheets mounted together was about four miles to an inch (1:253,440). As information piles up, the accuracy attainable at these scales begins to level off: maps become as correct as paper and ink will allow – or, for that matter, as their users desire. There may even be a decline in quality as publishers learn how much simplification they can get away with. The customer for his part can now find more precision on the larger-scale map-series that progress has called into existence, which in nineteenth-century Ireland were the thirty-two county maps published by the Ordnance Survey at six inches to a mile (1:10,560). On small scales, improvement lies henceforth in selectiveness rather than completeness. Competing national maps will now be differentiated by such non-geographical considerations as colour schemes and decoration, or by marginal text-matter, or by specialised thematic material aimed at a minority of readers. In Ireland such changes gradually become observable from the late eighteenth century onwards and more rapidly from about 1810. In this country, then, the key-map concept is appropriate to a time-span of about two and a half centuries. Even within that period it must be seen as a way of introducing the reader to traditional map history and not as a contrivance for avoiding the real thing.

References

1. The responsibility of the British Geological Survey was extended to Ireland in 1845 (G.L. Herries Davies, *Sheets of many colours: the mapping of Ireland's rocks, 1750-1890* (Dublin, 1983), ch. 5). A number of charts of Irish waters are listed in *Return of the hydrographical survey of the coasts of the United Kingdom, showing the extent of survey completed or in progress, by whom made, when received at the admiralty, when published, and if not published, the reason why*, House of commons sessional papers, H.C. 1852-3 (235), lx, p. 465, but there is no history of official hydrography for late nineteenth- and early twentieth-century Ireland. Since 1922 no history is needed, at any rate for the Republic, because no official charts have been made (Kevin Mooney and Frank Prendergast, *Surveying and mapping in the Republic of Ireland*, Department of Surveying and Building Technology, Dublin Institute of Technology, 1991, pp 27-9).

2. For a rare contemporary comment on the diminishing appeal of hachures at this period see P.H. McHaffie, 'The public cartographic labor process in the United States: rationalization then and now', *Cartographica*, xxx, 1 (1993), p. 57.

3. J.C., *Journal of the Royal Historical and Archaeological Society of Ireland*, 4th series, ix (1889), p. 326. For the location of the model see sheet XVIII.47 of the 1:1056 Ordnance Survey plan of Dublin (1891).

4. John Cruickshank, 'The four mile map before the first war', *Sheetlines*, xiv (1985), pp 2-10; Richard Oliver, 'The origins of Ordnance Survey quarter-inch mapping in Great Britain, 1837-72', *Sheetlines*, xv (1986), pp 9-14; Roger Hellyer, *The 'ten-mile' maps of the Ordnance Surveys* (London, 1992), pp 56-8.

5. Philip's *Handy atlas of the counties of Ireland* was first published in 1876 (George Philip, *The story of the last hundred years* (London, 1934), p. 103). Later editions were numerous but there appears to be no comprehensive list of them (George Philip & Son Ltd, personal communication, 8 October 1980). The maps were compiled by John Bartholomew and in later editions revised by the well-known Irish-language scholar P.W. Joyce. For a non-bibliographical notice see J.D. Blackwell and L.C.C. Stanley Blackwell (eds), *Philips' 19th century county atlas of Ireland* (Kingston, Ontario, 1984), pp ix-xii. Bartholomew's *Pocket atlas of Ireland* was published by John Walker of London in 1887.

6. A notable expression of this trend was *Memorial atlas of Ireland showing provinces, counties, baronies, parishes etc. . . . compiled and drawn from reliable official data and the latest information* (Philadelphia, 1901). Advertisements (for example in *The Gael*, xx (1901), p. 397) described this work as 'compiled from the latest revised ordnance surveys of the government'.

7. W.A. Seymour (ed.), *A history of the Ordnance Survey* (Folkestone, 1980), p. 75.

8. National Archives, Dublin, Ordnance Survey letters, OSL 566 (1849).

9. The copyright issue is inadequately dealt with in printed sources. There is much useful information in a departmental paper of *c.*1931 entitled 'History of copyright of Ordnance Survey publications' (Public Record Office, London, OS1/233: CR 7772) but this is entirely concerned with the period after 1855.

10. J.H. Andrews, *A paper landscape: the Ordnance Survey in nineteenth century Ireland* (Oxford, 1975), p. 293.

11. Richard Oliver, 'New light on the New Series', *Sheetlines*, xii (1985), p. [8].

12. National Archives, Dublin, OSL 10338 (1906), 10639 (1906), 15278 (1913).

13. Report of symposium on half-inch Ordnance Survey maps, *Sheetlines*, ix (1984), p. 15.

14. The report of the investigating committee was never published in full: a summary appeared in P.G. Madden, 'Proposed mapping policy for the Republic of Ireland',

Proceedings of the commonwealth survey officers' conference (London, 1967), pp 480-86. See also J.H. Andrews, 'Ireland in maps' in G.L. Herries Davies (ed.), *Irish Geography: the Geographical Society of Ireland golden jubilee 1934-1984* (Dublin, 1984), pp 281-2. The achievements (generally more impressive) of the Ordnance Survey of Northern Ireland must be omitted from this brief review: our subject is maps of the whole island, and in this field as in any dual enterprise progress has depended on the speed of the slower partner.

15. *Irish Geography*, iv (1960), p. 142; iv (1961), p. 217; v (1964), pp 103-4. This Dublin-produced map was published for the whole of Ireland between 1959 and 1962 (the Ordnance Survey of Northern Ireland issued a quarter-inch map of its own province) but is ignored in the most recent official history of the department (*An illustrated record of Ordnance Survey in Ireland* (Dublin and Belfast, 1991)), where the 1:250,000 is made to begin in 1980 with a four-sheet 'holiday map' (p. 84). A sheet of the holiday map was reviewed by E. Buckmaster in *Irish Geography*, xv (1982), pp 142-3. A precursor of this map, for Northern Ireland, had appeared in 1970 (review by J.A.K. Grahame, *Irish Geography*, xii (1979), p. 129).

16. Review of the first Northern Ireland 1:50,000 sheet by J.E. Killen, *Irish Geography*, xii (1979), pp 142-3; reviews of Republic sheets by Arnold Horner, *Irish Geography*, xxiii (1990), p. 66; xxiv (1991), pp 52-4. See also Arnold Horner, 'New medium-scale mapping for Ireland', *Geographical Viewpoint*, xix (1990-91), pp 5-17.

17. For a list of Harley's writings on this theme see J.H. Andrews, *Meaning, knowledge and power in the map philosophy of J.B. Harley*, Trinity Papers in Geography, vi (Trinity College, Dublin, 1994), pp 15-17. A similar bibliography is under preparation for Denis Wood.

18. J.B. Harley, 'The map and the development of the history of cartography' in J.B. Harley and David Woodward (eds), *The history of cartography*, i (Chicago and London, 1987), p. 10, n. 67.

19. An alternative expression, used in this sense more than a century ago, is 'mother map' (Mark Monmonier and George A. Schnell, *Map appreciation* (Englewood Cliffs, 1988), p. 75, citing Henry Gannett, 'The mother maps of the United States', *National Geographic Magazine*, iv (1892), pp 101-16; see also *Proceedings of the Royal Geographical Society*, xiv (1892), pp 459-61). A more modern but less vivid epithet is 'basic as opposed to non-basic' (J.B. Harley, 'Deconstructing the map',*Cartographica*, xxvi (1989), p. 118, n. 59). Perhaps the best of these terms is Denis Wood's 'standard map' *(The genesis of geographic knowledge: a real time developmental study of adolescent images of novel environments (London, Rome and Paris)*, Ph. D. dissertation, Clark University, Worcester, Mass., 1973, pp 22-4).

Appendix

The measurement of planimetric accuracy

MATTHEW STOUT with HELEN MacMAHON

In 1965 a method of assessing map accuracy was developed by Waldo R. Tobler which sought to compare the margin of error between early and modern map points after first adjusting the scale and orientation of the early map. To achieve this, a computer programme was devised which minimised the average distance between all the points by performing what is essentially a least squares regression analysis carried out on two two-dimensional point coverages. The mean centres of both point coverages are calculated and superimposed, then the early coverage is adjusted to the modern by performing a change of scale for the entire coverage and a rotation.[1] This methodology assessed map accuracy and permitted an objective quantitative comparison between two or more maps mainly through the bidimensional statistic r^2 (the coefficient of determination). The methodology described in Tobler's paper has been used by researchers on a variety of maps; for example Murphy assessed the relative accuracy of sixteenth- and early seventeenth-century maps of Ulster,[2] and Waterman and Gordon used Tobler's method to compare the accuracy of 'mental maps' of Israel drawn by school students, undergraduates and university teachers.[3] The latter paper, however, did not use r^2 as a means of comparing maps.

The increasingly widespread use of geographical information systems (GIS) has made this transformation technology more accessible. It is now possible to perform adjustments to map point coverages (in a manner similar to Tobler's method) using commercially available programmes which produce a statement of error and perform the transformation on the early map to a modern Ordnance Survey base allowing direct comparison between early surveys and modern maps.[4] Like Tobler's method, the TRANSFORM function of the widely used GIS programme Arc/Info achieves this best fit by performing four functions: (1) a change of scale for the entire coverage, (2) a rotation, (3) a shift along the x axis and (4) a shift along the y axis. When the transformation is complete, this function in Arc/Info then calculates a residual root mean square (RMS) error

$$rms = \sqrt{\frac{e_1^2 + e_2^2 + e_3^2}{n}}$$

which is in essence the average of all the differences between (in this analysis) the early map points after transformation and the accurate Ordnance Survey grid references. A perfect transformation produces an RMS error of zero. Unfortunately, Arc/Info does not calculate the r^2 statistic.

In this study a large number of identifiable points, as evenly distributed as possible, were measured from a point near the south-west corner of each of the early maps (to the nearest millimetre on the map) and the corresponding national grid reference was calculated to eight figures (bringing the estimate to within 100 metres on the ground). Correlation analysis established the strong linear relationship between early and Ordnance Survey x and y coordinates and showed where, in a few cases, points had been incorrectly entered. In addition, r^2 (the coefficient of determination is used here in the more conventional bivariate sense rather than the bidimensional statistic generated in Tobler's method) provides a crude index of map accuracy and a rough index of what to expect from the transformation process. It was found that a ranking of RMS errors provided for each map in modern map units (i.e. metres) bore no relationship to the expected ranking indicated by the correlation analysis. This was due to the variation in area covered by the range of maps. The provincial maps, for example, with proportionately greater distortions have smaller RMS errors than more recent all-Ireland maps. Waterman and Gordon attempted to overcome this problem by determining a 'distortion index' by dividing the RMS error by the maximum possible error which in their view would result if all points on the inaccurate map coincide. It is not clear why these researchers did not use the bidimensional r^2 generated in Tobler's method.[5] To overcome this problem in the present study and permit the comparison of RMS errors for maps of differing sizes, areas and numbers of sample points in both the early-map and Ordnance Survey point coverages were standardised; that is, the numbers were converted in such a way that the new data sets had a mean of 0 (half the entries are negative) and a standard deviation of 1 (68 per cent of entries fall between 1 and −1). RMS errors calculated in this way correspond to expected results based on the correlation analysis making possible the construction of a 'league table' of map accuracy as follows: Beaufort 0.039, Arrowsmith 0.049, Petty Ulster 0.049, Petty Munster 0.056, Petty Leinster 0.063, Petty Connacht 0.077, Speed Munster 0.134, Speed Ulster 0.172, Speed Leinster 0.175, Speed

Ireland 0.196, Boazio 0.239, Mercator 0.259, Speed Connacht 0.364. The use of Tobler's bidimensional r^2 statistic would provide a more straightforward means of overcoming the problem created by differences in map size and subject matter (i.e. scale), but as this is not possible using Arc/Info and as Arc/Info has become one of the most widely used GIS programmes, standardised data is suggested as a means by which future cartographic analysis might be rendered comparable.

References
1. W.R. Tobler, 'Computation of the correspondence of geographical patterns', *Papers and Proceedings of the Regional Science Association*, xv (1965), pp 131-9.
2. Joan Murphy, *Quantitative methods of map accuracy assessment with reference to some early maps of Ulster*, unpublished B.A. Mod. dissertation, department of geography, Trinity College, Dublin, 1977; Joan Murphy, 'Measures of map accuracy assessment and some early Ulster maps', *Irish Geography*, xi (1978), pp 88-101.
3. S. Waterman and D. Gordon, 'A quantitative-comparative approach to analysis of distortion in mental maps', *Professional Geographer*, xxxvi (1984), pp 326-7.
4. Such an analysis is described by Matthew Stout in J.H. Andrews with K.M. Davies, *Irish Historic Towns Atlas*, no. 5, *Mullingar*, Royal Irish Academy (Dublin, 1992), p. 4.
5. Waterman and Gordon, 'Analysis of distortion in mental maps', p. 328.

Index

Lizard Point, Cornwall, 23
Lluyd, Humphrey, 40
Loghill, 78
London: as prime meridian, 2, 176, 192; as publishing centre, 137, 153, 185, 190, 226, 249-50, 274, 284, 289
Londonderry, city, 113, 147, 171, 232, 266, 272
Londonderry, County: 113; in maps, 271, 293
Longfield, Dr, 230
Longford, 142
Longford, County, maps of, 118, 293
longitudes, 7, 27, 41, 115, 135, 222; *see also* latitudes
Loop Head, 225, 229, 267, Fig. 3.4
Loughrea, 115
Loughros Bay, 111
Louth, County: 49, 103, 167; in maps, 256, 293, 310, Fig. 8.6
Low Countries, 168; *see also* Flanders, Holland
Luttrel, Mrs, 177
Lyons River, 265
Lythe, Robert: 16, 61, 104, 132, 157, 271-2; cartographic activities, 61-71, 81, 103, 105, 119, Figs 3.3, 3.4, 3.5; importance, 71-5, 141; influence: on Boazio, 60, 71, 75-7, 78-9, 82, 266, 321; on Speed, 94, 97, 98-102, 105

McCool, David, 232
McCrea, William, 231, 233, 270
MacCulloch, John, 273
Mackenzie, Murdoch, 217, 226, 230, 232, 246-7, 256, Fig. 9.4
McMahond, Caloe McBrun, 83
MacNeill, John, 306, 307
McSwyne Bay, 83
McTaggart's Cross, 174
Maghera, 105
Magheralin, 195
Maguire, family, 17, 111
Maigue, River, 70
Main, River, 70
Maine, River, 70
Makenton Bay, 145
Malahide, 37
Malin Bay, 200
Malin Head, 111
Mallow, 168, 201, 207

Malynes, Gerard, 179
Manchester, 286
Mangerton, 196
Mannin Bay, 256
Manor Cunningham, 173
Manor Hamilton, 171
mappaemundi, 26
market towns, 162, 171, 175, 195, 298, Fig. 6.8
martello towers, 295
Martines, Joan, 56
Mary I, Queen, 40
Maryborough, 45, 80, 142, 263
Mask, Lough, 50
Mason, Mr, 230
Maxwell, John, 178
Maynooth, 115, 142
Mayo, County: 101, 103, 167, 201; in maps, 58, 103, 138, 159, 223, 278, 294, 302
Meade, Bradock, 185; *see also* John Green
Meath, County: 49, 228; in maps, 204, 232, 265, 272, 293
Meath, province, 91, 93
meeting houses, 242, 298
mensurator or measuring wheel, 165, 251
Mercator, Gerard: 26, 27, 29, 207; *Nova descriptio*: analysis, 38, 40, 42, 44-50, 61, 62, 67, 69, 70, 71, 109, 155, 171, 320, Fig. 2.8; influence, 50-53; *Atlas*: analysis, 73, 75, 78, 80, 96, 109, 139, Fig. 3.8; influence, 94, 97, 98, 101, 103, 109, 111, 112
Mercator, Michael, 73, 75
Mercator, Rumold, 73
meridians, central, 3, 85, 97, 176, 267, 293, 318
meridians, prime, 2, 224
Midleton, 147
miles: English and Irish, 24, 105, 164, 176, 192, 300; length, 40, 64, 139; toponymic references, 22, 174
milestones, 22, 174
Milltown Pass, 174
Miltownmalbay, 268
Mine Head, 206
mines and minerals, 174, 235, 299, 303
Mizen Head, 27, 206
Mohaliffe, 207
Moland, Thomas, 160, 175, 178